Comparative Politics

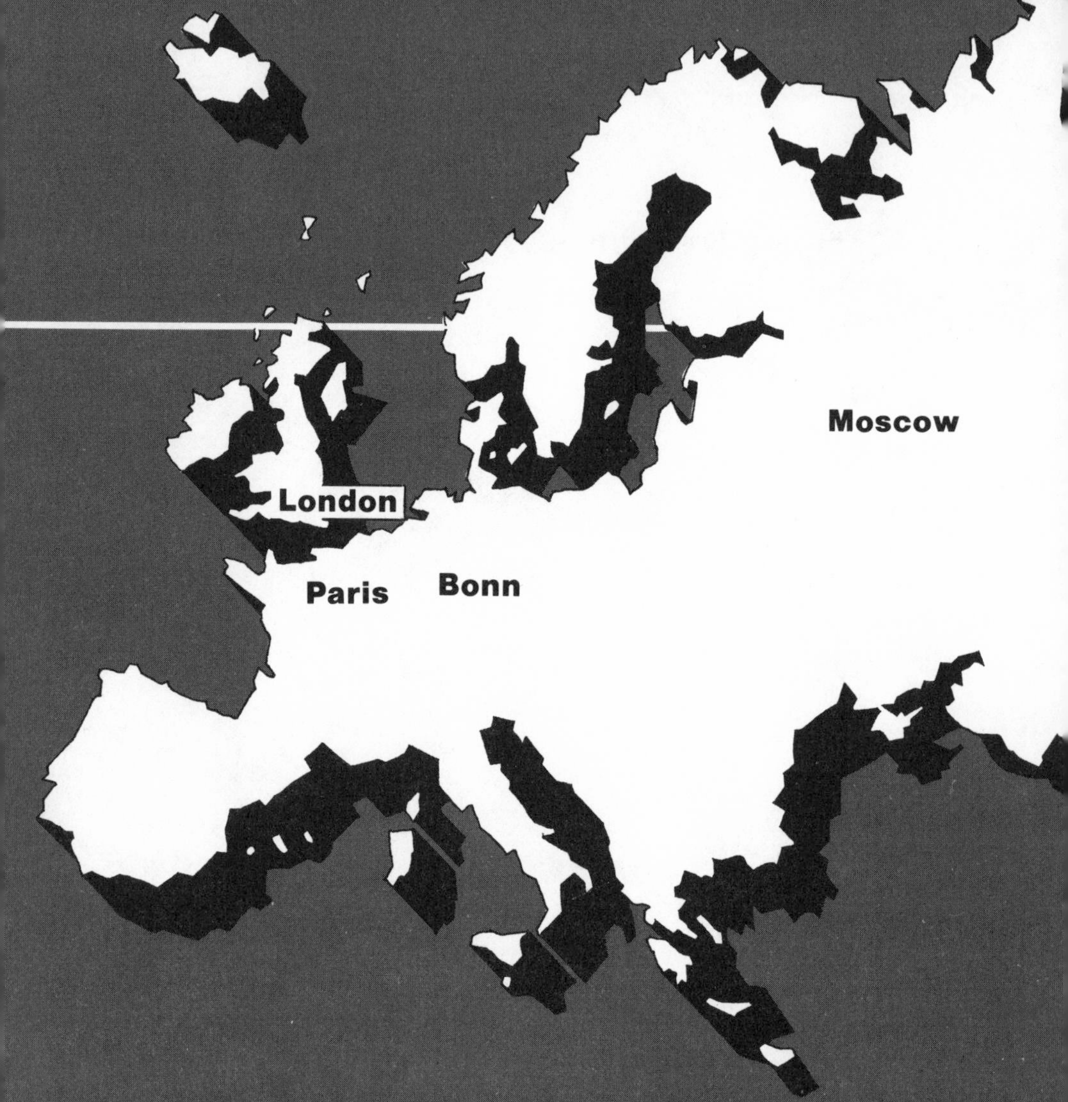
Moscow
London
Paris
Bonn

Comparative Politics

An Introduction to the Politics
of the United Kingdom, France,
Germany, and the Soviet Union

Dan N. Jacobs
Miami University, Oxford, Ohio

David P. Conradt
University of Florida, Gainesville

B. Guy Peters
Tulane University, New Orleans

William Safran
University of Colorado, Boulder

Chatham House Publishers, Inc.
Chatham, New Jersey

COMPARATIVE POLITICS
An Introduction to the Politics of the United
Kingdom, France, Germany, and the Soviet Union

CHATHAM HOUSE PUBLISHERS, INC.
Post Office Box One
Chatham, New Jersey 07928

PUBLISHER: Edward Artinian
INTERIOR DESIGN: Quentin Fiore
COVER DESIGN: Lawrence Ratzkin
COMPOSITION: Chatham Composer
PRINTING AND BINDING: Hamilton Printing Company

LIBRARY OF CONGRESS CATALOGING IN PUBLICATION DATA
Main entry under title:

Comparative politics.

   Bibliography: p.
   Includes index.
   1. Comparative government. 2. Great Britain--
Politics and government. 3. France--Politics and
government. 4. Germany--Politics and government.
5. Soviet Union--Politics and government. I. Jacobs,
Dan N. (Dan Norman), 1925-
JF51.C615   1983   320.3'094   83-1913
ISBN 0-934540-05-5

Manufactured in the United States of America
10 9 8 7 6 5 4 3 2 1

Contents

List of Figures

Introduction

One of the great coming-of-age experiences is the sudden realization that there is a world beyond the immediate environment and that it is not only knowable but worth knowing about. In many countries, especially relatively small ones in close proximity to neighbors with different languages and customs, this realization has come early. In others, entire generations have passed through the life cycle with little awareness or concern about life beyond their own frontiers. For the great majority of Americans up to the 1930s, what took place beyond the great oceans was not important; it was almost within the category of the trivial.

World War II forced the United States into the world. At war's end the United States was the mightiest country in the world. It was Number One, and it began doing things number-one countries do, such as developing first-class foreign policy establishments, staffed by knowledgeable diplomats and councillors aware of the history and traditions of the nations of the world.

In part, "fate" pushed the United States into the world; in part, vanity did; but in part there was also a perceived need to protect the "free world." The year 1946 saw the beginning of the cold war. A world but recently relieved of World War II was widely regarded as the battleground of the rival ideologies of democracy and communism, represented by the United States and the USSR.

In earlier times, Britain, France, or even Germany might have led the struggle in defense of Western democratic values. But Britain was exhausted, France demoralized, and Germany discredited and defeated. The United States had to pick up the reins or allow the contest to go by default.

Programs were generated in universities to prepare Americans for the leadership role thrust on them. Training was offered in Russian and Chinese, in Polish, Bulgarian, Hungarian, and other languages labeled "exotic." Institutes were organized for the study of the geography, history, economics, literature, and politics of the USSR, Asia, Africa, and Latin America. A cadre of experts was developed that was larger and more knowledgeable than any the world had previously seen. America had good reason to be proud of its intellectual and governmental institutions.

Although Americans had more contact with the outside world, and greater opportunities to become informed about it, this did not betoken a widespread and committed acceptance of that world. Most Americans, forced into contact with the world beyond their frontiers, felt less than comfortable. The world outside was distant, different, and corrupt. Americans continued to regard what happened in Europe, Asia, and Africa as something remote from their daily interests, more matters of curiosity than concern. The cold war, the threat of nuclear attack, the Korean conflict, and the launching of Sputnik made it difficult to maintain such attitudes; but they survived and were waiting when American policies failed in Vietnam.

Vietnam was interpreted differently in various circles. To some it indicated a failure of will: we lacked the determination to do what was necessary to achieve victory. To others, it meant that the United States had overestimated its resources. To still others, it signified just punishment meted out to an aggressor America. Whatever the reason, there developed in the United States the widespread wish to withdraw from the world. How had foreign involvement benefited the United States? We had become ensnared. There were more than enough problems in America without attempting to solve the problems of the rest of the world.

In the post-Vietnam period, American support for international programs weakened. Many academic institutes founded after World War II curtailed or closed their programs. The study of languages in American universities declined. Linguists, particularly those proficient in the exotic languages, found no demand for their skills. When students at some schools protested against the foreign language requirement, claiming it to be irrelevant, administrators dropped the requirement. Generally speaking, the international studies field, peopled with faculty in the 1950s and '60s, and short of students by the middle '70s, became a dry hole.

In the late 1970s, the United States began to recover from Vietnam. Once again there was a dawning recognition that the United States could not hide behind its own walls, that no matter how badly it preferred to stay at home, its welfare would not permit that luxury. Nevertheless, a negative attitude toward the non-American world persisted.

It is ironic that precisely at that time when the interdependence of the world, and more specifically, American dependence on the rest of the world, became dramatically apparent, the United States turned away from the world. The oil crises that followed the Yom Kippur war in 1973 signified the vulnerability of the United States. We were clearly dependent on others. American factories relied on raw materials not available in this country. Given that Americans could not or would not curtail their oil-guzzling habit, they were faced with the cruel need to pay huge sums to foreign petroleum producers to keep the country running. To secure those sums, the United States for the first time was required to produce for export. It was imperative that the United States sell to others. But in the struggle to increase exports, American industry had lost its competitive edge. What U.S. factories produced no longer had the qualitative nor often the technological edge that had typified American products in the past. Although it remained the leading industrial nation in the world, if the United States was going to compete with the world, it was more important than ever that it know as much as possible about the competition.

In other ways as well, the possibility of America's remaining oblivious to the outside world diminished. Not only could the United States not withdraw from the world for economic reasons; it was increasingly threatened by the world politically and militarily. The weakening of the American military potential in the second half of the 1970s heightened the danger of nuclear confrontation because, if threatened, the United States would be ill prepared for any other reaction. The increased utilization of terrorism by individuals, movements, and states rendered the United States still more vulnerable. As a consequence of such developments, previously unaligned countries, such as Afghanistan, were taken over by the Russians—and there was nothing the United States could do about it. American ambassadors were shot, as in Lebanon—and there was nothing the United States could do about it. American citizens were taken hostage, as in Iran—and there was nothing the United States could do about it.

Still, the United States cannot pick up its marbles and go home. It has to remain in the world. To cope with the world effectively, the United States has to know as much as possible about it.

As essential as knowledge of the world is to American survival, there are additional reasons for learning about other societies. There is the simple pleasure of knowing for its own sake. There are fascinating, dissimilar societies out there. Their people are born and live and die according to the inexorability that determines us all—but they do it to a different rhythm.

They have different habits and traditions. They have theories and practices of education and government and work that are at great variance to our own.

In this learning about those who are different from ourselves is the opportunity to learn more about ourselves. The realization that others do things one way, while we do them other ways, serves to provide us with insights into our own behavior that are the mark of educated men and women, and gives us a more profound understanding of our institutions and values.

Why the United Kingdom, France, Germany, and the USSR? First, each of the authors possesses a particular expertise about the country on which he has written. Second, these are the four countries covered in most courses. (Who wants to write a book no one will use?)

Going beyond practical considerations, the choice of the four countries is eminently justifiable. Collectively, the four countries are, in addition to the United States, generally regarded as the four major world powers. Individually, each embodies experiences and institutions that are standards and models for the world. Great Britain is where modern democracy was born and nourished. Where democracy exists today, outside of Western Europe, it is almost without exception where Great Britain planted it a century and more ago. Though Great Britain may no longer hold the strings of empire, its governmental institutions nevertheless remain the yardstick by which other parliamentary regimes are measured.

France, also a much diminished power as a result of the loss of empire, is a prime example of a parliamentary regime forced to mediate among various persistent and antithetical political traditions—revolutionary, democratic, monarchical, and clerical. France has developed its political institutions out of centuries of turmoil.

The Federal Republic of Germany is a modern state with tremendous industrial capacity and an authoritarian and totalitarian background that has had democratic institutions, drawn up by alien commissions, forced on it from outside. One of the great unanswered questions of modern politics is whether German democracy, protected from crises during the past four decades, first by the occupying powers and then by industrial might, will survive political and economic crises when they come.

The Union of Soviet Socialist Republics is one of the two superpowers and has been the political and developmental model for over a dozen communist states, scores of communist parties aspiring to power, and like numbers of Third World nations. While most states and parties have generated institutions and attitudes that vary from the Soviet model, and the Third World has lost some of its enthusiasm for the Soviet system, that model nevertheless remains the point of departure for grasping what transpires in a significant sector of the international scene.

Certainly there are other major countries beyond the four considered here. The United States, Japan, China, and many other nations, both developed and developing, are interesting and instructive. Justifications for covering or not covering each can be found, but the chief reason they are excluded here is that of space. The authors seek to provide a concise book, and they are aware from their own experiences that it is difficult to cover four countries effectively in an academic term. Suffice to say, the four countries present examples of varying political and institutional developments that are representative of the developed polity, and knowledge of them is indispensable for a sophisticated comprehension of the politics of most systems operating today.

The emphasis in this volume is obviously on individual nations and perforce the differences among them, the mind finding it easier to note and retain differences than similarities. Certainly it would be a mistake not to note those circumstances, attitudes, and qualities that separate the French from the British from the Germans from the Russians. For in spite of abundant forecasts to the contrary, nationalism, with its emphasis on what is uniquely French, British, German, or Russian, has become more, not less, a fact of international life. It would be an equally egregious error not to indicate those circumstances that have drawn nations together. All the countries and people discussed here, and all who aspire to modernization, are subject to the influences of industrialization and urbanization. All are subject to the rigors of the factory, the need to develop habits of punctuality, the problems of leaving the countryside and adjusting to city life.

People have been brought closer together not only because of shared developmental experiences but also because of a growing awareness of international dependency. It is not merely, or principally, the United States that has become more dependent on other countries. The world requires Saudi Arabia's oil, Canada's asbestos, Malaysia's tin, Russia's antimony, and Algeria's natural gas. There is, moreover, the widespread dependence on foreign markets to buy the raw materials and manufactured goods produced at home. If the nations of the world cannot sell abroad, they have no way of obtaining the funds necessary to buy abroad.

The existence of a commonality of interests and the need for cooperation on a world scale has been recognized by the establishment of the League of Nations after World War I and the United Nations after World War II. The second still exists, but it has not succeeded in establishing the priority of international over national interests. And in the past quarter century two organizations have arisen that have made some progress in that regard on a regional basis: the European Economic Community (EEC) and its East European counterpart, the Council for Mutual Economic Assistance (CMEA), popularly called Comecon. The EEC in particular plays a vital role in the economics of its constituent states. While the futures of all three organizations seem clouded, and in recent years all have at best marked time and at worst fallen back, there is a possibility that at least the EEC will become an active economic factor and perhaps a significant political factor in the future.

The objective of the authors in writing this volume has been to produce a book that would provide undergraduates with concise up-to-date information on the four major developed countries in which the writers have expertise, to provide examples of political analyses, and at the same time to introduce the student to the possibility of making meaningful comparison among the political processes of these and other countries.

We have interspersed comparative data, collected by B. Guy Peters and graphically presented by Robert Sabol, at random throughout the text. These contain basic information about the four countries under consideration, as well as the United States. Having this information allows students to make direct comparisons of these countries, with the United States included to provide a familiar point of reference. Some instructors may choose to orient their courses toward the comparative data we present; others may prefer a country-by-country analysis in the text. We have taken care to ensure comparability across countries by using recent sources such as publications of the Organization for Economic Cooperation and Development, the International Monetary Fund, and the Stockholm International Peace Research Institute. However, the Soviet Union presents difficulties as it is not included in some of these sources, and the only information available for some variables, such as unemployment and inflation, are the official figures influenced by ideological considerations.

Seeking to provide a focus for the study of the four countries, the authors have concentrated on five basic questions clustered around the power essence of each system: What is the context of power? In what institution is it to be found? Who has it and how was it acquired? How is power used? With what results? In attempting to answer these questions, the authors are descriptive and analytical. They are concerned with how things *seem* to work, but more important, with how things *do* work: how the systems attempt to solve their problems. The chapters discuss formal arrangements, but only as a prelude to introducing informal ones. The aim is to present a cogent analysis that will inform and interest the student.

The emphasis is on students. They are the concern of the effort. The authors are not seeking to offer new theoretical departures for our colleagues nor specifically to locate their effort among the responses that have been forthcoming during the past decades to the Almond and Easton theory building. This does not indicate that the volume is a throwback to prebehavioral traditionalism. Far from it. In its categorizations, in the questions it seeks to answer, in its analyses, and in its basic attitudes, the book reflects a sensitivity to what has been happening in comparative studies and the world in recent years. Despite their individual analytical interests, it is perhaps unique in that its four authors have attempted to adhere to a common analytical framework.

It is likely that in the years immediately ahead, the United Kingdom, France, Germany, and the USSR are going to find themselves under increasing pressure internally and externally. There are going to be demands to do things that have never been done before and that the regimes don't want to do. Socialist regimes are going to be compelled to consider solutions that violate their sense of fair play. Regimes that consider military power unacceptable as a means to secure their ends are going to consider such means. All these things will be done to satisfy the demands of their people and the times; to stay alive.

The decades ahead are going to threaten the governments considered here, in concert with most of the countries of the world, in a variety of ways. They are confronted by serious economic crises; at the same time they are facing demands from the underprivileged, or those who consider themselves such—demands for greater equality, for more opportunities, for additional services. But to the extent that the regimes spend their capital on services, they take away from the resources to continue industrial development. All are hearing the call for greater expenditures on weapons. To the extent that they answer, they are reducing the funds with which to continue development. All are aware of demands for greater conservation, but to the extent that they limit their capacity to produce resources, they reduce their ability to continue development. All, though some more than others, take heed of the finite amount of oil available in the world. To the extent that they expend their capital on fuel that becomes increasingly dear, they are limited in furthering development. And without development, they will be incapable of satisfying the rising material demands of their people and of providing what is regarded as a satisfactorily modern and adequate force to oppose the enemy.

The demands placed on regimes are not only economic. They are political and national as well. Each of the countries faces a rising tide of minority ethnic opposition that resents the leading role played by what is seen as the chief national group. The demands of ethnic minorities all over the world have become increasingly vocal since World War II. They have broken up the European empires in Asia and Africa, bringing into existence a hundred new countries — and now they threaten the "homelands" as well.

These are among the problems that our four countries, along with the other nations of the world, are going to have to resolve. In the pages of this book, it is our objective that students begin to acquire the information that will help them to understand the problems in their particular contexts and make it possible for them to develop the solutions their generation will be called on to provide.

DAN N. JACOBS

Comparative Politics

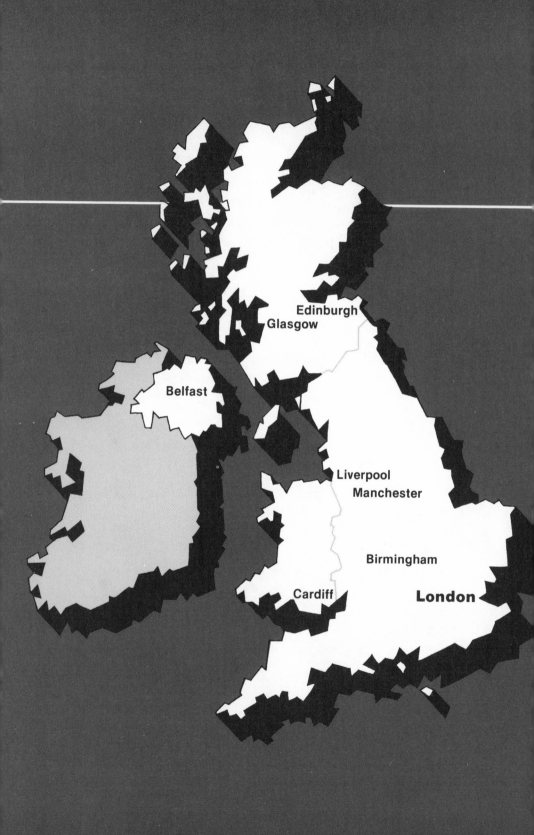

Part One

The United Kingdom

B. Guy Peters

1

The Context of British Politics

British society and British politics are usually discussed in terms of homogeneity and integration. Authors have spoken of the lack of significant social cleavages other than social class and of the presence of a uniform set of political and social values. Consensus is said to exist on the nature of the political system and the general policies of government. The impression commonly given is of homogeneity, stability, and indeed of a rather boring locale in which to study politics.

In reality, the social and political systems of the United Kingdom are substantially more diverse than they are frequently portrayed, and many of the same factors that divide Americans politically divide the citizens of the United Kingdom. Not only is there diversity, but the setting of British politics has a number of seemingly contradictory elements that make the management of government much more of a balancing act than might be thought at first glance. In fact, the genius of British politics in maintaining a stable political system over several centuries is not the good fortune of operating in a homogeneous society but the development of a set of institutions, values, and customs that allow the pragmatic acceptance of diversity and accommodation to gradual change. In this chapter we explore some of the contradictory elements in the environment of British politics and their relationship to the functioning of the political system.

A United Kingdom of Four Nations

Perhaps the fundamental point of diversity in British politics is that the United Kingdom is a single country composed of four nations. To begin, therefore, let us introduce some nomenclature that has real political importance. The proper name of the country usually referred to as Great

Britain is the United Kingdom of Great Britain and Northern Ireland. Great Britain, in turn, is composed of England, Wales, and Scotland. These four countries are all constituent parts of the United Kingdom, albeit rather unequal partners in terms of population and economic production. Over 83 percent of the total population of the United Kingdom lives in England; over 9 percent lives in Scotland, 5 percent in Wales, and 2 percent in Northern Ireland. Almost 89 percent of total wages and salaries are paid in England, with only 1 percent going to residents of Northern Ireland.

The three non-English components of the United Kingdom — or the Celtic Fringe, as it is sometimes called — joined with England at a number of times and in a number of ways.[1] Wales was added first, by conquest, in 1301. The English and Scottish crowns were united in 1603 when the Scottish James I became the first Stuart King of England, and the Parliaments of the two countries were joined in the Act of Union of 1707. This did not, however, terminate the conflict between the northern and southern portions of Great Britain. Scottish uprisings in 1715 and again in 1745 resulted in English (or British) occupation of Scotland and the outlawing of a number of Scottish customs such as the kilt and bagpipes. These restrictions were removed, at least informally, in 1822, and manifestations of Scottish nationalism have been less violent since that time.

The involvement of the British government in Ireland has had a long and tortuous history. British armies began invading Ireland in 1170; the island was finally conquered in 1603, and was joined with Great Britain to form the United Kingdom in 1800. The unity was more legal than actual, and Irish Home Rule was a persistent political issue during the second half of the nineteenth century. Political arguments were joined by increasing violence and then by armed uprisings against British rule. Following a long period of negotiation, the 26 southern counties of Ireland were granted independence in 1922 as Eire, while six of the northern counties in Ulster remained a part of the United Kingdom. This partition did not solve the "Irish Question." Continuing violence between Catholics seeking to establish a unified Ireland by joining with Eire and Protestants desiring to maintain their unity with the United Kingdom is a constant problem for any British government.

The unity of the United Kingdom does not prevent the expression of a number of differences among the constituent parts, and to some degree those differences are enshrined in law and the political structure. The three non-English components of the United Kingdom each have a Cabinet department that is responsible for their affairs. Laws are commonly passed in Parliament with separate acts for England and Wales, for Scotland, and for Northern Ireland; and Scottish and Welsh legislation is treated somewhat differently in Parliament. Also, prior to the imposition of direct rule in Northern Ireland in 1972, Stormont, which is the Parliament of Northern Ireland, had a major role in policy making for that province.

Law, language, and religion also differ in the four parts of the United Kingdom. Scottish law is derivative of French and Roman law rather than common law, and a variety of legal procedures and offices differ between Scottish and English practice. Language is different in different parts of the United Kingdom; Welsh is accepted as a second language for Wales, although only about 20 percent of the population can speak that language, and only about 1 percent of the population speak Welsh as their only language. Also, some people in Scotland and Northern Ireland speak forms of the Gaelic language, although it has not been accorded formal legal status, perhaps because just over 1 percent of the population speak Gaelic. Finally, the established religions of the parts of the country are also different, with the Church of England (Anglican) established in England and the Church of Scotland (Presbyterian) established in Scotland; Wales and Northern Ireland do not have established churches because of their religious diversity. The diversity in Wales between Anglicans and various "chapel religions" (Methodism in particular) has not had the serious consequences of the differences between Catholics and Protestants in Northern Ireland.

Finally, the four components of the United Kingdom differ economically. This is true less of their economic structures than their economic success. Differences in the proportion of the working population employed in manual jobs, or even in the proportion employed in agriculture, are relatively slight between England and the Celtic Fringe. Perhaps the major differences in patterns of employment are much higher rates of public employment in the Celtic Fringe. Measures of economic success do differ, with levels of unemployment much higher in the non-English parts of the country than in England as a whole (although rates in some regions of England are higher than in Scotland). Average personal income in all three parts of the Celtic Fringe is also lower than in England, and by a large margin in the case of Northern Ireland. These economic differences have political importance, for they create a sense of deprivation among these national groups within the United Kingdom.

The differences among the four nations of the United Kingdom are manifested politically, although fortunately infrequently with the violence of Ulster politics. Scottish nationalism never really died following the Act of Union, but it has experienced a number of cyclical declines. Votes for the Scottish National party had an upsurge in the period from the 1959 to the 1979 elections. The SNP at least doubled its vote in every election from 1959 to 1974, and received more than 30 percent of the Scottish vote in the October 1974 election. Welsh nationalism has been less successful as a political force, but Plaid Cymru, the Welsh National party, won over 13 percent of the Welsh vote in the October 1974 election. Party politics in Northern Ireland, which are based on cleavages of the seventeenth rather than the twentieth century, bear little resemblance to those of the rest of the United Kingdom.

The first thing, therefore, that we must understand about the United Kingdom is that it is a united country composed of separate parts. Unlike the states of the United States, these elements of the Union have no reserved political powers, but only receive delegated powers from the central government. The political system remains unitary while still allowing a certain degree of latitude for the Scottish, Welsh, and Northern Ireland Offices in the administration of policies. Only rarely has the unity of the United Kingdom been questioned by its constituent parts, at least since the suppression of the Scottish uprising of 1745. One such challenge was at least partially successful, however, and parts of Ireland did receive their independence. The failure of referenda on the devolution of additional powers to Scotland and Wales in 1979 appears to make the unity of the country even more secure, but this is but one more act in a long history of regional and national politics with the United Kingdom.

Stability and Change

A second feature of the context of contemporary politics in the United Kingdom is the continuity of social and political institutions combined with a significant degree of change. If a subject of Queen Victoria were to return during the reign of Elizabeth II, he or she would find very little changed—at least on the surface. Most of the same political institutions would be operational, including the monarchy, which would have vanished in a number of other European countries. Laws would still be made by the House of Commons and the House of Lords, and there would still be a Prime Minister linking Crown and Parliament. There would be a new political party commanding one of the more important positions in partisan politics — the Labour party — but party politics would still be primarily *two*-party politics. Finally, the majority of the subjects of the Queen would be loyal and supportive of the basic structures and policies of the government.

At the same time that there has been this great continuity, there has also been great change. The political system has been greatly democratized since Victorian times. When that Queen came to the throne, only about 3 percent of the adult population were eligible to vote; this despite the "Great Reform Act" of 1832. In the reign of Elizabeth II, almost all adults are entitled to vote. Prior to 1911, the House of Lords was almost an equal partner in making legislation, while after 1911 the Lords became a minor influence over policy. Victorian Prime Ministers were definitely *primus inter pares* (first among equals), while changes in the twentieth century have changed collegial patterns of decision making and created something approaching a presidential role for the Prime Minister. And the monarchy, which in Victorian times still had substantial influence over policy, has today been constitutionally reduced to a point of virtual impotence. Finally, but not least in importance, Britain has changed from perhaps the strongest nation on earth and the imperial master of a far-flung empire to a second-class power in a nuclear age.

Social and economic trends have paralleled political trends. Just as the monarchy has been preserved, so too has a relatively stratified social system with hereditary (as well as life) peerages. On the other hand, the growth of working-class organizations such as trade unions has tended to lessen the domination of the upper classes and to generate some democratization of the society as well as the political system. The economic structure of the United Kingdom is still primarily one of free enterprise, but now government ownership and regulation have a heavy impact. Also, compared with other industrialized nations, the economy is no longer the great engine of production it once was. The relative poverty of the United Kingdom when compared with its European and North American counterparts has placed severe restrictions on the policy choices that can be made by government, but has not yet threatened the political stability of the nation.

The evolutionary change so characteristic of British political life has been facilitated by the absence of a written constitution. It would be more accurate to say the absence of a single written document serving as a constitution, for a number of documents (e.g., Magna Carta, the Bill of Rights, the Petition of Right, and the Statute of Westminster) have constitutional status. In addition, the Parliament of the day, expressing the political will of the British people, is competent to do virtually anything it deems necessary, without the possibility of judicial review as in the United States. Such powers without formal constitutional limitation have the potential for great tyranny, as governments are restrained only by other politicians, the threat of elections, and their own good sense.

The same political system has persisted for a number of years in the United Kingdom, except that it is greatly changed. British constitutional principles, as with American ones, are undergoing constant change and adjustment in the face of changing conditions. Perhaps the major difference is that formal change is less necessary in the United Kingdom as change in practice is sufficient to produce a change in principle.

Traditional and Modern: The Political Culture of the United Kingdom

Much of the accommodation to political change while maintaining older political institutions in Britain may be explained by the political culture of the United Kingdom. That is to say, it may be explained by the values and beliefs that citizens have about politics and government. One way of describing this culture has been "traditionally modern." A number of traditional views are combined with a number of modern elements to produce a blend that, if apparently internally contradictory, appears to function well and produce effective government.

The traditional elements of the political culture are best known, with deference, trust, and pragmatism the most important for an understanding of how the British political system functions. As with any statement about national cultures or patterns of values, these statements may appear to be a stereotype, but taken with a grain of salt, these observations on political culture can help us understand not only how British politicians and citizens function but also how they think about politics.

In the first place, the British population is generally said to be deferential to authority, both in general and in terms of a more particular deference to the "authority" of the upper classes. Authority implies the lack of opposition by citizens to the actions of their government, or perhaps even the positive acceptance of those activities. The British government has, by all accounts, a large reservoir of authority, for few citizens question the correctness of the current political arrangements or the right of the government to make and enforce laws. The diffuse support the population gives the political system, and the willingness to obey laws and accept the authoritative decrees of government, combine to make the United Kingdom a much easier country to govern than most.

Perhaps the only major challenge to the authority of the elected government of the day—aside from the peculiar politics of Ulster—that has occurred in recent years is the trade-unions' use of their economic strength to bring down a Conservative government and its economic and industrial policies. By striking and throwing the economy of the country into chaos, the unions (particularly the miners) were able to bring about political change through nonpolitical means. For one of the few times since the formation of the United Kingdom, the question "Who rules Britain?" was raised, and the answer was not necessarily "Her Majesty's Government."

A special case of deference is deference to the upper social classes. Even in a modern, secularized political system a number of citizens still feel obliged to defer to their "betters" and accept the upper classes as the only appropriate rulers of the society. In political terms, this gives the Conservative party an immense advantage and prevents it from being the permanent minority it would be if people voted only on class lines. This traditional attitude is being transformed, however, as many "working-class Tories" have adopted a more pragmatic conception of the upper classes as being better educated and trained to govern, as opposed to a deferential attitude.

Associated with deference toward authority and political leaders is a high degree of trust in the political system as a whole and in the leadership; higher than in almost any other political system. Survey evidence indicates an extremely high level of trust in the fairness and general benevolence of government.[2] This high level of trust permits a form of political democracy to flourish in the United Kingdom that would be out of place in almost any other industrial society. It is a form of democracy in which the decision-making process is closed to scrutiny or participation by citizens, or even by politicians who are not members of the Cabinet. The United Kingdom is a democracy, but a system of democracy "by consent and not by delegation, of government of the people, for the people, with, but not by, the people."[3] Citizens expect to participate in politics at election times; most are then content to settle back, watch the government work, and pass judgments at the next election. Recent breaks in official secrecy have given citizens and academics a better view of the internal work-ings of government, but much of this still remains hidden to outsiders.[4] To run a government on such a basis requires an extraordinary level of trust on the part of citizens.

The other side of the trust of the public is the responsibility of elected leaders. Government has generally been responsible and benevolent and has not violated existing political norms. Even when those norms have been violated, as when elections were suspended during the two world wars, this has been by broad agreement among the political parties. Re-sponsibility has also meant that parties and governments are expected to deliver more of what they promised in the campaign than would be true for American parties. While there is continuing agitation for increased openness in government, the responsibility of the great majority of British politicians has helped prevent these demands from gaining wide popular acceptance.

The acceptance of a rather secretive government in exchange for re-sponsible performance — assuming these two traits are connected — em-

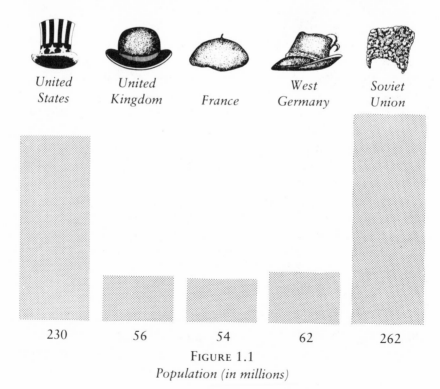

United States

United Kingdom

France

West Germany

Soviet Union

230   56   54   62   262

FIGURE 1.1
Population (in millions)

phasizes another feature of the political culture of the United Kingdom: its pragmatism. British politics is extremely pragmatic in practice, although ideologies are frequently spouted during campaigns or in speeches delivered for mass consumption. An empirical, pragmatic mode of political thought has dominated British political life to the point that justifications for the preservation of traditional political institutions such as the monarchy are not that they are right and just, but only that they have worked. Rather obviously, such a political epistemology would be associated with gradual change and a constant adjustment to changing environmental conditions, a factor that has assisted the system in changing in all but its essential features to accommodate a modern world.

The traditional values of deference, trust, and pragmatism exist in the context of a modern, or even postindustrial, political system. The policies pursued, the presence of mass democracy and mass political parties, a very large level of public revenue and expenditure, and neocorporatist linkages between state and society are evidence of the modernity of the political system. Yet political leaders are allowed the latitude to discuss and decide political issues without direct involvement of the public or press. This is a modern democracy, but a democracy permitting an elite to govern and exercising latent democratic power only at agreed upon times.

Class Politics, but . . .

The characteristic used most commonly when describing politics and political conflicts in the United Kingdom is social class. The principal basis of social differentiation and political mobilization is social class, meaning primarily levels and sources of income. The major partisan alignments in politics are along class lines, with the Labour party representing the interests of the working classes and the Conservative party (and to a lesser extent the Liberal party) reflecting the interests of the middle and upper classes. We have already seen that the correspondence between class and party is less than perfect, but the generalization remains a useful one.

Social class is an objective and a subjective phenomenon. The United Kingdom does have significant inequalities of income — even after the redistributional effects of taxes and expenditures are taken into account. Given the dominance of class politics in Britain, however, the levels of inequality are in general less than in similar countries. The bottom one-tenth of income earners in the United Kingdom earn 2.1 percent of the total income in the country, while in the United States the same proportion of income earners receive only 1.2 percent of total income.[5] The highest decile in the United Kingdom earns 24.7 percent of total income, compared with 28.4 percent in the United States and 31.3 percent in Germany. Britain is more class based, however, in that the majority of income earners in Britain are still employed in industrial working-class occupations, meaning primarily manual labor, whereas the largest single category of employment in most North American and European countries is now service jobs.

Access to other goods and services is also affected by class considerations, although again perhaps not to the extent of other European countries. In particular education is class related, both in the small elite private sector and in the larger state sector that until very recently tracked or streamed all children at an early age. Access to secondary and tertiary education has a pronounced upper-class bias, although again less than in many European countries. And, in part because of the class basis of education, social mobility is rather low in Britain—but still higher than in much of continental Europe.[6]

As much as an objective phenomenon, social class is also a subjective phenomenon. People in the United Kingdom are generally more willing to identify themselves as members of different social classes than are Americans, who overwhelmingly identify themselves as members of the middle class. Also, issues of all kinds may become polarized on a class basis. Any policy that preserves or extends the privileges and power of the more affluent is immediately suspect to the Labour party and the unions, even when (as with pay beds in National Health Service hospitals) the policy may have a number of positive side benefits for working-class families and the government.

Several caveats must be raised about a simple class model of British politics. The first is that there has been some change and the "embourgeoisment" of the working classes, so obvious in many European countries, is also occurring to some degree in Britain. Manual labor is a declining share of the labor force, even though it remains a large share in the United Kingdom. Also, the wages paid to manual workers now often approach or even surpass wages and salaries paid to many nonmanual workers. Changes are occurring within the occupational and economic structure, then, that may mitigate the impact of class on politics.

A number of other issues also mitigate the dominance of class. We have already mentioned the existence of ethnic and regional cleavages based on the constituent elements of the United Kingdom. Scottish and Welsh nationalism has tended to cut broadly across class lines, and to be concerned with national as opposed to class consciousness. A "new ethnicity" has entered British politics, as the formation of the anti-immigrant National Front would indicate. In 1977 it was estimated that there were 1.8 million people of "New Commonwealth and Pakistani" origin (i.e., "coloured") in Great Britain, or 3.4 percent of the population. These ethnic minorities now dominate many older industrial towns, and in some inner-city schools English is taught as a second language. As these groups are also multiplying more rapidly than white Britons, the specter of non-white domination and loss of jobs are powerful weapons for some political groups.

Religion is also a factor in British politics. The monarch is required to be a Protestant, which in practice has meant a member of the Church of England. This Anglican monarch (Presbyterian while in Scotland) rules a population that is only approximately three-quarters Anglican and that contains a significant Roman Catholic minority. This issue has surfaced most obviously in Northern Ireland, but cities such as Liverpool and Glasgow also have large and politically relevant Roman Catholic populations.

Politics in Britain is not entirely about class, but it is very much about class. The importance of other cleavages varies with the region of the country, with the Celtic Fringe being the most influenced by nonclass cleavages, and by the time and circumstances of the controversy. Nevertheless, to attempt to understand British politics through only class divisions is to miss a good deal of the complexity of politics and the political system.

Conservatively Liberal Policy Ideas

Another apparent paradox about British political life is the conservatively liberal nature of many of the policies and policy ideas of the country. Members of the Labour party regularly speak of socialism, and they sing the "Internationale" at their party congresses. Members of the Conservative party regularly speak about the restoration of laissez-faire economics and dismantling a good deal of the welfare state. In practice, however, most of the policies adopted by most governments bear a remarkable resemblance. The Labour party accepts that most of the British economy is, and will continue to be, privately owned, and at the same time presses nationalization of certain industries and the extension of social services to the disadvantaged. The Conservative party while in office tends to accept the virtual entirety of the welfare state, as well as government ownership of many industries such as coal, steel, and the railways. The major deviation from this pattern in recent years has been Margaret Thatcher's Conservative government. This government has begun to sell off government stock in nationalized industries such as British Airways, as well as to encourage local authorities to sell off their council (public) housing to tenants. There has been talk of ending the Post Office's monopoly over the delivery of mail. It is not known just how far these changes in the public sector will go, but they represent something more of an ideological style of policy making than has been true for most recent governments.

Despite the intrusions of ideology, there does appear to be a belief in a mixed-economy welfare state. All major parties favor the major programs of the welfare state such as pensions, other social insurance programs such as unemployment, and the National Health Service. At the same time the majority of the population accept private ownership and management as the major form of economic organization, despite the presence of a number of nationalized industries. What the parties and politicians do appear to disagree about is just what is the proper mix of the mixed economy, and just how much welfare there should be in the welfare state.

Isolated but European

One of the standard points made about British history is that its insular position relative to the European continent has isolated it from a number of influences and has allowed Britain to develop its own particular political institutions and political culture. The mental separation from Europe was to some degree greater than the geographical separation, so that Britain may have looked European from North America, but Britons did not always feel European on their islands.

The separation of Britain from the Continent and from the world can be overstated. Britain has not been successfully invaded from 1066 to the present, but has been deeply involved in European politics and warfare. Also, Britain was by no means insular when dealing with the rest of the world and managed a far-flung empire, and even more far-flung trade routes, from its little islands. And, unlike that other great island nation,

Japan, Britain was never isolationist but was always involved in world politics and trade.

One of the major changes in the political environment of the United Kingdom has been its entry into the European Communities (EEC, or Common Market). After two denials of admittance, largely at the instigation of France, Britain joined the EEC in 1973, followed by the first advisory referendum in its history. This obviously has brought Britain closer to its continental counterparts, but has had important internal effects as well. Joining the EEC introduced a whole new level of government to the United Kingdom, and means that some of the rights of Parliament to legislate for British subjects now actually reside in Brussels.

Joining the EEC has also required something of a retreat from long-standing British commitment to its Commonwealth countries, whose special economic privileges are gradually being phased out as Britain slowly aligns its policies to European policies. The political commitment remains, and the Queen and Prime Minister both make a point of attending Commonwealth meetings and attending to Commonwealth business, including attempting to mediate in the affairs of Commonwealth, or former Commonwealth, nations such as Zimbabwe.

The environment of British politics is not a neatly ordered picture of class politics among an otherwise homogeneous population isolated from the currents of European politics. The environment is actually rather turbulent in the early 1980s. Britain is not homogeneous, and four separate nations exist within the confines of the United Kingdom, not to mention millions of immigrants who have flocked there. Class politics are certainly important, and even dominant, but a variety of other issues also influence British politics. In addition, the consensus that is sometimes said to exist on the policies of government is less universal than it once was, and the economic problems of the nation may encourage more drastic actions by both Labour and Conservative governments.

Just as the environment of politics is not uniform, so too the institutions that make policy in Britain are a mixture of traditional and modern elements. They frequently represent compromises between what Walter Bagehot, a nineteenth-century commentator on the British Constitution, called the "dignified" and the "efficient" parts of government. We now turn to a description of those institutions as institutions, and will return somewhat later to look at them in action as they make policy.

Notes

1. Richard Rose, *The Territorial Dimension in Government: Understanding the United Kingdom* (Chatham, N.J.: Chatham House, 1982).
2. Gabriel A. Almond and Sidney Verba, *The Civic Culture* (Princeton: Princeton University Press, 1963), pp. 142-43.
3. L.S. Amery, *Thoughts on the Constitution* (London: Oxford University Press, 1947), p. 20.
4. Richard Crossman, *The Diaries of a Cabinet Minister,* vols. 1-3 (London: Jonathan Cape and Hamish Hamilton, 1975-1977); "Killing a Commitment: Cabinet Against the Children," *New Society,* 17 June 1976, pp. 630-32.
5. Organization for Economic Cooperation and Development, *Public Expenditure on Income Maintenance Programs* (Paris: OECD, 1976), p. 108.
6. Richard Bourne, "The Snakes and Ladders of the British Class System," *New Society,* 8 February 1979, pp. 291-93.

2

Where Is the Power?

The fundamental difference in the constitutional and institutional composition of American and British government is the relationship between the executive and legislative branches of government. In the United States we have become accustomed to a presidential form of government with a separation of powers between the legislature (Congress) and the executive (the President). Each is legitimated by election, and each can claim equally to represent the people. Also, each institution has powers that can be, and are, used to block actions by the other branch. Such a system was designed to limit executive power, and indeed to limit the power of government in general.

Parliamentary government, on the other hand, links executive powers directly to legislative powers. The executive of a parliamentary government such as that of the United Kingdom is not elected directly and independently of the legislature, but depends upon election by the legislature. With modern political parties voters know that when they vote for a certain political party, if they are in the majority, they will have a certain person as the next executive (Prime Minister in the case of the United Kingdom), but becoming Prime Minister still requires the action of Parliament. So, Margaret Thatcher did not become Prime Minister in 1979 because the British people voted for her to be Prime Minister, but because they voted for a majority of Conservative party members of Parliament, who in turn voted to have the party leader as Prime Minster. If at any time the majority of the members of Parliaments decide they no longer want the current government to continue in office, they can vote that government out by a vote of no confidence, or by defeating a major government legislative proposal. As there are at present a majority of Conservatives in Parliament, this would require the defection of some members of Mrs. Thatcher's own party — an uncommon but not unheard of occurrence. Remaining the "Queen's First Minister" requires the continual support of Parliament, and if that support is lost, the Prime Minister and the other ministers must by convention either reorganize themselves or go to the people for a new election.[1] And it would not be just the Prime Minister who would be gone. The doctrine of collective responsibility makes the government as a whole responsible for actions and in turn requires that the government as a whole resign.

Both presidential and parliamentary forms of government have their advantages and disadvantages. Presidential government is commonly valued because checks and balances restrain a single individual or group, and the system also provides a focus for national political leadership. Also, having a President in office for a fixed term provides a predictability to policies that is not necessarily found in parliamentary regimes, which may have frequent changes in executives. Such instability has not plagued British government, but the possibility is there, especially as the established two-party system threatens to dissolve.

The parliamentary form of government allows an executive, once in office, to govern. While presidential governments frequently have conflicts among the two branches of government over which should control a policy issue, this rarely occurs so overtly in a parliamentary regime. If the political executive cannot command the acquiescence of the legislature, then they will soon cease to be the executive. On the one hand the parliamentary system allows voters to make more clearly defined policy choices, but on the other hand the greater policy stability of presidential regimes may make citizens feel more secure.

British Parliamentary Government

While a number of political systems practice parliamentary government, each practices it differently. Several features of parliamentary government as practiced in the United Kingdom should be understood before going on to a brief description of each of the major institutions. The first is the principle of government and opposition. Bipartisanship has little place in this form of parliamentary government, and it is the job of the Opposition to oppose the government. Even if the Opposition should agree with the basic tenets of the government's policy, it is still their job to present constructive alternatives to that policy. It is assumed that through this adversarial process better policies will emerge, and the voters of the country will be given two alternative conceptions of government from which to choose at the next election.

British parliamentary government is also party government. While there are certainly barriers to the effective implementation of party government, the idea that political parties are a major instrument for governing pervades the system. Parliament is conceived of to some degree not as an institution in itself but a place in which political parties clash. Parties are expected to be responsible, to stand for certain policies and programs, and to attempt to carry out those programs if elected.

Finally, British parliamentary government is sovereign. There are, strictly speaking, no legal limitations on the powers of Parliament. There are no means by which a citizen can challenge an act of Parliament as unconstitutional. There are, of course, very real political limitations on the activities of a Parliament, but its actions, once taken, are law.

With these considerations in mind, let us now proceed to a brief description and discussion of the six major institutions of British national government: the monarch, the Prime Minister, the Cabinet and government, Parliament, the courts, and the civil service. Each is worthy of several books, but we will attempt to describe the most salient features for an understanding of the manner in which the British system converts proposals into law.

The Monarch

The United Kingdom is a constitutional monarchy, and although there is some grumbling about the cost of maintaining the royal household and about the wealth of the Queen and the royal family, there is little serious question as to the continuation of the monarchy. The powers of the monarchy, however, are very circumscribed; although many acts are performed by the Queen or in her name, the actual decisions are made by the Prime Minister or the Cabinet. Declarations of war, making treaties, granting peerages, and granting clemency to prisoners are all royal prerogatives, but all are exercised only on the advice of the Prime Minister and other ministers. Likewise, the royal assent is necessary for legislation to become law, but this has not been refused since Queen Anne in 1703.

One major point at which the monarch could possibly influence policy and politics substantively is in the selection of the Prime Minister. There is little or no possibility for the exercise of independent judgment if one major party wins a clear majority. The British party system tends to fragment, however, and the possibility of a clear majority appears to be lessening. If there were no clear winner, the monarch might be able to exercise some independent judgment, albeit with the advice of the outgoing Prime Minister.

The monarch must also dissolve a sitting Parliament, and this judgment could be made independently if the government did not abide by a vote of no confidence, or if it lost on a major issue. As governments in the 1970s seemed unwilling to resign in the face of defeats, this power of the monarch to force a government to go to the people may become important in making policy choices. It would, however, be exercised at some peril for the monarch, as such a direct intervention might threaten the legitimacy of the institution of the monarchy.

Bagehot described the monarchy as a real part of the policy-making system in Britain, hiding behind a cloak of mere dignity and ceremony. Much of the impact of a monarch on policy and politics remains hidden and is very subtle. It is exercised through frequent meetings and consultations, and requires that the monarch be as well briefed as her ministers. The power of the monarch, then, may be as personal as the power of any other political actor, or even more so. It would be easy for a monarch not to have influence, given the dominant partisan mold of the policy-making system. For the monarch to be effective, she must not only exercise the extensive ceremonial functions of the office but also be a real politician in her own right. The most important function of the monarch, however, is to be a symbol of the nation as a whole, and to be above politics. She must be a unifying force when much else in the political system tends to be centrifugal and adversarial.

The Prime Minister

The monarch is head of state; that is, she is the representative of the nation as a whole. The Prime Minister is head of government and the chief executive officer of the government. Of course, in the United States, the two roles are merged, and the President is both head of state and head of government.

The office of Prime Minister has evolved slowly since the beginning of the eighteenth century. The Prime Minister is at once just another minister of the Crown and above the other ministers. There is increasing discussion of the role of the Prime Minister becoming presidential. This alleged "presidentialization" of the Prime Minister derives from several factors. The first is that parliamentary campaigns have become increasingly directed toward electing a particular Prime Minister rather than toward the selection of a political party to govern. Also, the staff of the Prime Minister has begun to evolve in much the same way as the Executive Office of the President, although on a much smaller scale. And there has been a tendency for the Prime Minister, both through control of the Cabinet Office and through the hiring of personal assistants, to attempt to gain greater personal involvement in policy. Mrs. Thatcher's placement of several special assistants in departments, especially the Treasury, indicates the extent to which the Prime Minister may be seeking a role expanded beyond *primus inter pares.*

Certain characteristics, powers, and limitations on the Prime Minister are important for understanding the office. First, the Prime Minister is the leader of the majority party in the House of Commons. Until 1902, Prime Ministers frequently came from the House of Lords, but by convention now, the Prime Minister is a member of Commons. For example, Sir Alec Douglas Home renounced his hereditary title in order to sit in the House of Commons and eventually become Prime Minister. Also important is that the first selection of a potential Prime Minister is made by the political party, and he or she who would be Prime Minister must first be able to win an election by the political party. This is but one of many ways in which the customs and conventions of the British political system serve to reinforce the strength and integration of political parties. And this also requires that the Prime Minister, as well as commanding the apparatus of government, must be able to command the apparatus of a political party.

In addition to being the leader of a political party, the Prime Minister must be the leader of the House of Commons. Becoming Prime Minister indeed may say more about one's abilities in Parliament than about the skills necessary to run a government. The Prime Minister is expected to lead parliamentary debates, and the ability to win in verbal jousts in the House of Commons frequently seems to be more important to performance than winning policy and administrative battles. Thus, the skills usually associated with the rise to office of Prime Minister are by no means those we might identify as being crucial to running the government of a large industrialized nation.

Although technically only *primus inter pares,* the powers of the Prime Minister are actually more substantial. First, the Prime Minister is the formal link between the Crown and the rest of government. The Queen invites a prospective Prime Minister to form a new government, and relationships between the monarch and Parliament are channeled through the Prime Minister. Likewise, the Prime Minister serves as chief political adviser to the Queen, especially on major issues such as the dissolution of Parliament. The Prime Minister also dispenses office. Once the Queen has invited a prospective Prime Minister to form a government, it is the Prime Minister who assembles a team. Certainly members of that team will have political followings of their own, and may have to be included to placate segments of the party, but the office held by each Cabinet member will be a decision of the Prime Minister. The power to dispense office also extends to a number of other offices, including life peerages, which are nominally appointed by the Crown but in actuality are in the gift of the Prime Minister.

Once in office, the Prime Minister has considerable personal power over policy and the activities of the Cabinet. We have already mentioned the growth of the staff of the Prime Minister and the presidentialization of the office. Also, the Prime Minister as the organizer, leader, and summarizer of the business of the Cabinet is in a position to enforce views over

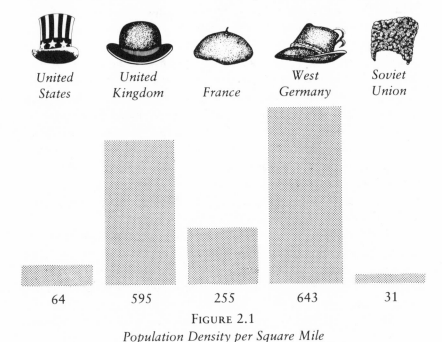

FIGURE 2.1
Population Density per Square Mile

her nominal equals. As the head of the government, the Prime Minister has substantial visibility and influence. Finally, in time of emergency, the powers of a Prime Minister are not limited by a constitution, as are those of an American President.

We should also mention the role of the leader of the Opposition who, as leader of the largest minority party in the House of Commons, would probably be Prime Minister if the sitting government were defeated in an election. Although lacking the official powers of office, the role of the leader of the Opposition is not dissimilar to that of the Prime Minister. He is expected to be both the leader of a political party and a leader in Parliament, as well as the leader of a Cabinet, albeit one out of office (the "Shadow Cabinet"). The adversarial style of British politics places the leader of the Opposition in the role of opposing the program of the government and proposing "searching alternatives" to all government programs, in preparation for the day when the Opposition becomes the government and must make its own policy proposals.

Cabinet and Government

Working beneath, or with, the Prime Minister is the Cabinet and the government. Although these terms are often used synonomously, they actually imply different things. The Cabinet is composed of those individuals — in the first Thatcher government the twenty-one men — who meet with the Prime Minister as a collectivity called the Cabinet. The term "government" is a more embracing term, including all ministers regardless of their seniority or degree of responsibility. The Cabinet is technically a committee of the government selected by the Prime Minister to provide advice in private meetings and share in the responsibility for policy. Although the Prime Minister is certainly primarily responsible for government policies, the Cabinet is also collectively responsible, and all Cabinet members tend to rise and fall as a unit rather than as individuals.

There are several varieties of ministers: secretaries of state, ministers, and junior ministers; to some degree, parliamentary private secretaries are also ministers. The distinction between secretaries of state and ministers is rather vague. Each tends to head a department of government (e.g., the Department of Health and Social Security or the Department of the Environment), although secretaries of state tend to head larger or more prestigious departments. Some may carry titles other than minister (e.g., chancellor of the exchequer or attorney general). Also included in the government, and in some instances the Cabinet, are a number of posts without departmental responsibilities, either ministers without portfolio or holders of such titles as Lord Privy Seal, included in the government as general or political advisers. Junior ministers are attached to a department minister to provide political and policy assistance in the management of the department, and these positions serve as steppingstones for those on the way up in government. Ministers of state are in a position somewhere between junior ministers and ministers, and are commonly members of the House of Lords. Finally, parliamentary private secretaries are unpaid (aside from their normal salaries as MPs) assistants to ministers, responsible primarily for liaison with Parliament. There are, then, in any government, some seventy to eighty positions to be filled in the political executive, most coming from the House of Commons.

The job of a minister is a demanding one. Unlike American political executives, a British minister remains a member of the legislature and an active legislator for a constituency, and consequently must fulfill a number of positions and responsibilities simultaneously. The first of these multiple tasks is to run the department. The minister must be able to run the department in two ways. First, he is responsible for the day-to-day management of the large, bureaucratic organization of which he is the head. As few politicians have experience with the management of such large organizations, they are at some disadvantage at making the department run effectively. Also, the minister must manage department policies. That is, he must develop policies appropriate to the area of responsibility of the department, and which correspond to the overall priorities of the government. In this the minister is generally hindered by his own lack of expertise. Few ministers are chosen for their expertise in a policy area; more often, it is for their general political skill and following. It is estimated that only 5 of 51 ministerial appointments in the Wilson government of 1964-70 had any prior experience in their departmental responsibilities.[2] This lack of expertise is exacerbated by the tendency to shift ministers from one department to another, even during the lifetime of a government. Also, the minister is faced with experienced and relatively expert civil servants in the department who tend to have views of their own on the proper policies for the department. A minister then must fight very hard just to manage his own department.

The minister may also be a member of that collectivity of the Cabinet, and if so, will have additional time demands. The Cabinet meets on average five to six hours per week, and preparation for those meetings requires even more time. Membership in the Cabinet requires that each minister be at least briefed on all current political issues. And there are the Cabinet committees necessary to coordinate policies and deal with issues requiring consideration prior to determination by the Cabinet. A minister cannot afford to take Cabinet work lightly, even though he may be only a part of a collectivity dominated by the Prime Minister, for it is in Cabinet as well as Commons where political reputations are made, and where the interests of one's department must be protected.

The minister remains an active member of Parliament. As such he is required to be in Parliament for a substantial amount of time, especially when the government has a small majority. The minister must also be prepared to speak in Parliament on the policies of his department or the government as a whole. Also, he must be prepared to respond to questions in the four question hours per week, and may have to spend hours being briefed and coached on the answers to questions.

The minister, as a member of Parliament, also retains constituents in the constituency from which he was elected, and these must be served. This involves spending weekends in the "surgery" in the constituency, and receiving delegations from local organizations. And, since there is no fixed term for a Parliament (other than that an election must occur within five years), even more than American politicians, British politicians always must be preparing for the next election.

Finally, the minister must be just a general politician and representative of the government. This may involve a number of honorific functions as well as a number of more demanding appearances. As one former minister put it, a minister is at the beck and call of every Tom, Dick, and Harry. The combination of all these duties amounts to a very demanding task for any individual, and is even more demanding given that ministers lack the personal staff American political executives enjoy. These demands on the time and energy of ministers also limit the ability of a political party coming to office from rapidly or effectively placing their stamp on the public policies of the United Kingdom. The resistance within any political system to change, combined with the limitations of ministers, means that policy changes resulting from changes in governments will, on average, be slow.

Despite the rigors of office described above, any number of people seek to become ministers. Most of these are in the so-called Shadow Cabinet, which is the leadership of the Opposition party. Just as the leader of the Opposition is the alternative Prime Minister, so too does every member of the government have a shadow minister in office who is prepared to be the Opposition's spokesman on that policy area.

The Cabinet does not work entirely alone, and one of the important developments in British politics in recent years has been the development of the Cabinet Office and the Central Policy Review Staff (CPRS). The Cabinet Office, or Secretariat, grew out of the Committee of Imperial Defence in World War I. Currently, a very senior civil servant, along with a few associates, serves the Cabinet. The secretary to the Cabinet is himself influential in shaping Cabinet decisions, although not by obvious means. The Cabinet agenda is set by the secretary, and he distributes Cabinet papers to the appropriate individuals. By so doing, he determines which ministers will be heard quickly and which will have to wait for their day in Cabinet. Also, although the Prime Minister summarizes Cabinet meetings orally, the secretary to the Cabinet drafts the written communications to the departments for action as a result of the meetings, as well as drafting the written records of the meetings. These are not subject to change, even by the Prime Minister. While there is little or no evidence of these powers being abused, the secretary to the Cabinet is in an extremely influential position.

There is also a small Cabinet Office of political and personal advisers. This is far from approaching the magnitude of the White House staff in the United States, but it has been growing and is seen as one more bit of evidence of the concentration of policy-making powers in the Cabinet rather than in Parliament as a whole. Also, there is the Central Policy Review Staff, a creation of the Heath government, which is an attempt to provide a research staff for the Cabinet. It primarily conducts research at the request of ministers, but at times is allowed to provide its own directions; several of its reports have become controversial. This body provides the Cabinet with an ongoing research capability almost unique in British government.

Parliament

The government of the United Kingdom has already been described as parliamentary, implying a significant role of Parliament in government. Despite the nominally strong position of Parliament in the constitutional arrangements of the United Kingdom, there are serious questions as to the effective powers of Parliament. With the growing strength of the political executive, and the discipline of political parties, Parliament as an institution is less capable of exercising control over policies than it once was. Parliament has been attempting to reassert its position in the political process, but the evidence is not yet in on how successful those efforts will be.

Members of Parliament

The first thing to understand about a legislative body such as Parliament is the nature of the individuals involved and the incentives offered to them to participate. Parliament has 640 members, elected from a like number of constituencies, meaning that the average member of Parliament (MP) represents less than 70,000 people, compared with approximately 500,000 represented by a member of the U.S. House of Representatives. Compared with other legislative bodies, MPs have few advantages. Their pay, even with recent raises, is only £9,450 ($15,000 at current rates of exchange), compared with $69,800 for U.S. congressmen. MPs also receive a limited travel allowance for parliamentary business, which is commonly used to cover travel back to the constituency on weekends when Parliament is in session. Some MPs may have sponsoring organizations that will either help with their expenses or provide some direct remuneration. For Labour politicians these are commonly unions, while for Conservatives and some Liberals they are generally industrial groups or large corporations.

In return for these modest benefits, MPs receive long hours and relatively few staff supports. While American legislators are accustomed to having several dozen staff members working for them, the average MP has funding only for a part-time assistant or secretary, unless he or she is personally paying for the help or is receiving assistance from a sponsor. MPs often lack even a private office, and unless they are in the government or the Shadow Cabinet, they may share a small office with other MPs in the Palace of Westminster (the Houses of Parliament).

Organization

Parliament is composed of the House of Commons and the House of Lords. As the House of Lords has become relatively unimportant in the policy-making process, let us first describe it briefly and then proceed to a more extended discussion of the House of Commons.

The House of Lords is composed of hereditary and life peers. The hereditary peers attain their right to sit in the House of Lords on the basis of inherited titles, while life lords are appointed by the Queen (on the advice of the government) only for their lifetime. The development of the concept of life peerages (in 1958) was in part to rectify the partisan and ideological balance in Lords against the Labour party. As there are currently only about 300 life peers out of a total body of 1,000, and the majority of the hereditary peers are Conservative, there remains a strong majority against Labour in Lords.

The major impetus for removing the powers of the House of Lords was Lloyd George's "people's budget" of 1909. This budget introduced a progressive income tax (the first since the Napoleonic wars) and a rudimentary public health insurance program. The Conservative Lords balked at this Liberal proposal and refused to pass the budget. Parliament was then dissolved, but when the Liberals were returned with a (reduced) majority, the House of Lords accepted the budget. And after a second election in 1910 in which the Liberals were again successful, the House of Lords accepted the Parliament Bill of 1911, which greatly limited its powers.

Lords now cannot delay money bills longer than one month—and cannot vote them down—and any legislation passed by two successive sessions of Parliament, provided one calendar year has passed, goes into effect without approval by Lords. Lords does still occasionally delay legislation; mainly, however, it serves as a debating society, and as a locus at which the government can accept amendments to its proposals that it would be less willing to accept in the more politicized House of Commons. The House of Lords does actually serve a useful function in British policy making despite its diminished role, as many useful modifications to legislation result from the attention of the Lords.

The structure and functions of the House of Commons have evolved over centuries, and to some degree still reflect their medieval roots. Much of the ceremony and procedure derives from the past, but despite complaints about the vestigial aspects of the procedures these do not seem to inhibit the functioning of a modern legislative body. To the extent that the House is seriously overshadowed by other institutions of British government, the fault rests more with other characteristics of British government than with the trappings of power within the House of Commons.

British politics is conducted in an adversarial style, and the design of the House of Commons emphasizes that fact. Most legislatures sit in semicircles, and the individual members sit at desks and go to a central rostrum to address the body. The House of Commons is arranged as two opposing sets of benches, placed very close together in a small chamber. Speakers generally face their political opponents, and although the form of address is to the Speaker, the words are clearly intended for the opponents. The front benches on the two sides of the aisle are populated by leaders of the government and the Opposition. From these two front-row trenches the two major warring camps conduct the verbal warfare that is parliamentary debate. Behind the front benches are arrayed the foot soldiers of the "back benches," ready to vote to their party's call, and perhaps to do little else. The style of debate in the House of Commons, as well as being contentious and rather witty, is very informal, and there are few protections against heckling for the MP addressing the House.

As well as being a partisan body, the House of Commons is a national institution. Ideas of Cabinet government and collective responsibility are closely allied to ideas of party government, and there is a strong sense that political parties should present clear and consistent positions on policy issues either in or out of government. They can then be judged by the electorate at the next election on the basis of those policies. In addition to responsibility for policy, the dependence of the executive on the ability to command a majority of the House requires that parties vote together. Political parties are organized in order to deliver votes when required. Not only do members know that voting against their party on an important issue is tantamount to political suicide, but each party has Whips whose job it is to be sure that the needed votes are present. The British system of government does not allow much latitude for individual MPs to have policy ideas of their own, although the parties allow their members free votes on issues of a moral nature such as abortion or capital punishment.

Following from the partisan nature of the House is that it is a national body. The U.S. House of Representative is usually conceptualized as a set of ambassadors from the constituencies. British thinking is generally that the MP is more responsible to the party and its national goals and priorities than he or she is to the individual interests of the constituency. This is emphasized by the fact that MPs are not required to live in their constituencies, and many do not. Of course, the MP tries to satisfy the constituency whenever possible, but it is generally assumed that the member owes the office to the party and the national policies advanced in the election campaign rather than to the narrow geographical interests of the constituency. Nevertheless, as with free votes on moral issues, MPs are often allowed to abstain from voting for party proposals when these would clearly be inimical to the interests of their constituency.

Amid this adversarial and partisan politics, the Speaker of the House is an impartial figure. The Speaker is seated between the two front benches, on his "throne," and is dressed in the style of the eighteenth century. The otherworldliness of his dress is perhaps to accentuate the complete impartiality assumed to reside in the office. Although an MP and elected from the House, the Speaker is selected for not having been a vociferous partisan; the aim is to find someone who can be elected unanimously rather than as a result of a partisan confrontation. Once elected, the conventions are that a Speaker may remain in the office as long as he wishes, with his seat rarely if ever contested (only four times since 1714). Although still an MP, his constituency duties are discharged by another member, and the Speaker will vote only in case of a tie. Then, by convention, the Speaker's vote is cast to preserve the status quo. As an impartial figure, the Speaker can discharge his role as moderator and, to some degree, be the embodiment of the dignity of the House. The Speaker is not without real influence over decisions, however; for example, his use of the "kangaroo" decides which amendments to legislation will be debated and which not, and his acceptance of a motion of closure ends debate.

To an American student of legislatures, the first question to be answered concerning the House of Commons would be the nature of the committee system. The answer would be that while the House of Commons does have committees, these are by no means as central to the legislative process as the committees in the U.S. Congress or the German Bundestag. There are 8 standing committees, composed of from 16 to 50 members, in the House of Commons. Unlike American committees, only the chairman of the committee is permanent; other members are added to the committee depending on the nature of the bill being considered. Any one committee may consider a variety of bills during a session of Parliament, with the composition of the committee changing to match the nature of the bills. The composition of the committees, as well as reflecting the expertise of its members, also reflects the partisan composition of the House as a whole, and a small majority in the House may result in a more substantial majority in committee. Also unlike American committees, the standing committees of the House of Commons are not really independent of the whole House but tend to reflect the whole House. Their role is not expert, as is that of U.S. committees; rather, they are miniature legislatures where bills may be discussed and improved and places where the government can accept amendments without jeopardizing its political stance in Commons. As an indication of this more limited capacity, the committee stage for legislation in the United Kingdom is *after* the principal political debate on the bill, rather than before its primary consideration. As such, the major battles over the legislation have already transpired before the committee sees the legislation. Their purpose is to refine and amend the bill, rather than significantly influence its basic nature.

The preceding description of the committee system in the House of Commons holds true for legislation in England and to some extent Wales. As most legislation is passed with a separate Scottish bill, in part the result of special features of Scots law, there is a separate committee system for Scottish bills. If a bill is meant primarily for Scotland, a special standing committee will be composed of approximately 30 MPs for Scottish seats and 20 others chosen for their interest in the legislation and to provide a proper partisan balance. Also, for Scottish affairs there is the Scottish Grand Committee, composed of all 71 MPs for Scottish seats along with such other MPs as are necessary to provide a partisan balance. The Scottish Grand Committee has rather broad responsibility for legislation intended for Scotland, reviews expenditures for Scottish concerns, and any general matters of concern of Scotland. There is an analogous set of Welsh committees, but these generally have not been so influential as the Scottish committees. This is in part because much Welsh legislation is joined with English and in part because of the significantly fewer (36) Welsh MPs.

In addition to the standing committees, there are also several select committees in the House of Commons. The most important of these are the Statutory Instruments Committee and the Public Accounts Committee. The first of these committees monitors the issuing of statutory instruments, or delegated legislation, by government departments. Like all governments of industrialized societies, the workload of British government has increased to the point that Parliament cannot make all of the needed laws. Instead, it delegates the authority to decide many legislative matters to the executive with the provision that this delegated legislation be subject to review by the Statutory Instruments Committee and potentially by the entire House of Commons. On the other hand, the Public Accounts Committee is a modern manifestation of the traditional parliamentary function of oversight of expenditures, and monitors the government's ex-

penditure plans from inception to auditing of the final expenditures. While not as effective as might be wished by some, this committee provides a place to ventilate views on expenditures and serves as a review of the massive volume of government expenditure.

One of the most interesting developments in the committee structure of Parliament has been the creation of twelve select committees to follow the activities of government departments. This is an as yet untried attempt to establish the legislative oversight by committee so familiar to American political executives, although a similar suggestion was made by Richard Crossman in 1963.[3] As indicated by the activities of the select committees, one of the important functions of Parliament is the scrutiny of the political executive and its policies. Perhaps the most famous mechanism through which this takes place is the question hour. On four out of five sitting days during the week the House of Commons opens its legislative day with an hour of questions for the government from members of the House. These questions have been submitted at least forty-eight hours previously in writing, so that a minister has some opportunity to prepare an answer. In recent years, however, the practice has been to ask a very vague question in writing and then follow it with more probing supplemental questions orally. Thus, a seemingly innocuous question as to whether the Prime Minister intends to visit Finland during the year may be an introduction to more important questions about foreign policy. All members of the government may be subjected to the question hour, and the Prime Minister answers questions on two of the four days. The question hour places an additional burden on already overburdened ministers, but in a political system where secrecy is the norm, this institution serves as one mechanism for the Parliament, and the people as a whole, to find out what is happening in government and exercise some control through the ventilation of possible malfeasance.

As an institution, Parliament is threatened. It has had difficulty maintaining its independent powers in the face of the growing powers of the Cabinet. Most of the important weapons in this struggle are in the hands of the executive. These include information, access to staff, and more important, party discipline. Parliament now rarely exercises free and thorough scrutiny of the activities of a government; votes are known in advance, and it is the rare politician who will threaten his political career on the basis of a principle. Parliamentary government has in effect become Cabinet or party government. Even these venerable institutions are threatened by the power of the next actor in the political process: the civil service.

The Civil Service

The domination of the policy process by the British civil servants, or the "mandarins," as they are sometimes known, is one of the great mysteries of British government, at least on the surface. On the face of it, the British civil service is unprepared to perform the expert role it now performs in policy making. The recruitment of civil servants is less on the basis of expert knowledge in a substantive policy area than on the basis of general intellectual abilities. Also, for a large proportion of their careers, civil servants are moved from job to job and from department to department, only gaining a permanent appointment rather late in their careers. The cult of the "talented amateur" and the generalist dominates thinking about selection and training of civil servants, despite attempts at reform following the Fulton Commission, which expressed concern for expertise in the selection of civil servants.[4]

How can civil servants who themselves are hardly expert in the policy areas they administer have the influence over policy described by commentators and participants in policy making? Several factors seem to be related to this influence. The first is that, although it may lack formal training in a policy area, the senior civil service is a talented group of individuals, and thus has the intellectual ability to grasp readily the subject matter it must administer. Second, despite their relative lack of specialized training compared with civil servants in other countries, compared with their political masters, British civil servants are generally knowledgeable about the relevant subject matter of departmental policy. Finally, civil servants have a much longer time perspective than politicians and so are able to wait out and delay any particular minister with whom they disagree.

The relationship between civil servants and their political masters is important for defining and understanding the role of the civil service in policy making. The prevailing ethos of the civil service is that it can serve any political master it may be called upon to serve. However, this "service" may be an attempt to impose the "departmental view," or the particular set of policy ideas of the department, on the minister.[5] Any number of reasons can be advanced to explain why the ideas of the minister are not feasible, and why only the proposals made by the department itself will ever work. It requires the exceptional minister to be able to counter such views.

The difficulties of the minister in countering a departmental view are exaggerated because the department may appear to speak with one voice.

American executive departments tend to be fragmented, with a number of independent bureaus advancing their policy ideas. Executive departments in Britain lack these independent organizations, and the ideas of the department are channeled upward through a hierarchical structure, with the major point of contact between the political and the administrative actors being the relationship between the minister and the permanent secretary. The permanent secretary is the senior civil servant in a department (although several departments have two or more civil servants of this rank), who serves as the personal adviser to the minister. As the minister lacks a personal staff, he must rely heavily on the permanent secretary both for policy advice and management of the department. This in turn gives the civil service, through the permanent secretary, a significant influence over policy. We would not argue that the civil service abuses this position, and in general the evidence is that it is responsible and scrupulous in the exercise of its office. Nevertheless, the structural position in which it is placed as the repository of information and of a departmental perspective, and the lack of alternative views from most ministers, places it in an extremely powerful position.

The Judiciary

By this time, the American student of politics would have wondered what has happened to the court systems. There are courts in the United Kingdom, but they are by no means as central to the political process as courts in the United States. In large part this is the result of the doctrine of parliamentary supremacy and the consequent inability of the courts to exercise judicial review of legislation. There is simply no way that British courts can declare an act of Parliament unconstitutional. As Dicey put it: "If Parliament decided that all blue-eyed babies should be murdered, the preservation of blue-eyed babies would be illegal."[6]

The courts do have some role to play in the policy-making system. Although they lack the ability to declare actions unconstitutional, the courts can issue a number of writs including *ultra vires* (literally, "beyond the powers") inquiring as to the statutory authority of specific actions; and *habeas corpus*, requesting to know under what authority a citizen is detained by the authorities. Each case is each case, however; the courts cannot make sweeping statements about the legality of actions, and even the issuing of these writs may be suspended, as in Northern Ireland.

Over the last several years, the courts have become more aggressive in declaring the actions of a government to be *ultra vires*. This is in part a function of Britain's joining the European Communities and the necessity of monitoring government implementation of Community law and in part because of the relative parliamentary weakness of several recent governments. The courts do follow the election returns, however, and there are serious questions by some as to the extent to which there can truly be a government of laws when there is little independent ability to adjudicate the laws. This difficulty is further exacerbated by the attorney general's being a political official who in several instances in the late 1970s was charged with allowing his political affiliations to interfere with his legal duties.

The Rest of Government

This final section on government institutions is obviously a catchall for the remaining activities and structures of government and is composed primarily of two parts: local government and public corporations. British government is unitary, but local governments have a substantial impact on the ultimate shape of public policies in the United Kingdom. In like manner, many public activities are carried out through public corporations rather than directly by a government department. This choice has consequences for the ability of government to control these functions.

First, local government is not an independent set of institutions with its own constitutional base of authority; rather, it is the creation of central government. Local government is divided into a two-tier system. The larger tier, the region, covers a large population and/or a large land area. For example, the Greater London Council governs a population of over 7 million, while the Highlands Region of Scotland has an area of over 6 million acres. Beneath the regional level are districts, corresponding to cities or territories roughly equivalent to American counties. The numerous functions of subnational governments are divided among these two tiers of local government in a manner roughly related to the size of the necessary catchment area for efficient service. In fact, the local government reorganization that created the current system of local government has been the subject of a number of criticisms, both on the efficiency of the arrangements created and the loss of political influence in such large units as the regions.

Unlike American state and local governments, local governments in the United Kingdom are closely supervised by the central government. In England the Department of the Environment supervises local governments; the Scottish, Welsh, and Northern Ireland Offices supervise local governments in their respective portions of the United Kingdom. Also, a much larger proportion of the expenditures of local governments in the United Kingdom are funded through grants from the central government than is true in the United States (49 as opposed to 18 percent in 1976), making British local authorities more dependent on the center. These factors do not preclude conflict between central government and local authorities, especially where the two happen to be governed by different political parties. The conflicts between Conservative central governments and Labour local councillors in Clay Cross (1974) and Lambeth (1979-80) are indicative of such conflicts.

Public corporations are an equally important part of the total governmental sector in the United Kingdom, although they are, at least in theory, distinct from the government itself. The central government has the right to appoint members to the boards of the nationalized industries and makes broad policy decisions—including which corporations will become or will remain nationalized—but the day-to-day decisions of these industries are made independently. This independence is constrained by their reliance on government funds both to cover operating deficits and provide capital for new ventures. Also, decisions by a nationalized industry may produce political discontent with a government, as when the decision by the National Coal Board in 1979 to close several less productive Welsh pits prompted a strong outcry.

The nationalized industries constitute a significant share of economic activity in the United Kingdom, including such industries as coal, steel, shipbuilding, railroads, electricity, gas, road transportation, and most automobile manufacturing. Such a large share of industry in public hands obviously gives government a great, albeit indirect, influence over the economy. This is especially true in a period of high inflation when wage settlements in the nationalized industries are frequently used as guidelines for settlements in the private sector, and when consequent pressures to keep wage settlements down may produce labor unrest.

The preceding has been a discussion of the major institutions of British government. While the functions performed by these institutions are almost certainly familiar to the American student of politics, the manner in which they are performed almost certainly are not. Perhaps even more important, the assumptions underlying the activities are frequently quite different. Most fundamental here is the lack of a formal limitation on the powers of a government and a Parliament. In addition, the familiar American doctrine of the separation of powers has no place in British politics, and an executive (Prime Minister) must have the support of the legislature (Parliament) in order to govern. Although it is at times popular to speak of "Anglo-American democracies," and although the United States and the United Kingdom share many common political precepts, there may be as much separating the two systems as uniting them.

Notes

1. Ivor Jennings, *Cabinet Government* (3rd ed.; Cambridge: Cambridge University Press, 1969), pp. 277-89.
2. Bruce Headey, *British Cabinet Ministers* (London: George Allen and Unwin, 1975).
3. See the introduction to Walter Bagehot, *The English Constitution* (London: Fontana, 1963), p. 44.
4. *The Civil Service: Report of the Committee* (Fulton Report), Cmnd. 3638 (London: HMSO, 1968), 1:78-79.
5. Peter Kellner and Lord Crowther-Hunt, *The Civil Servants: An Inquiry into Britain's Ruling Class* (London: Macdonald, 1980), pp. 209-19.
6. A. V. Dicey, *Introduction to the Study of the Law of the Constitution* (10th ed.; New York: St. Martin's, 1959), p. 74.

3

Who Has the Power and How Did They Get It?

A democratic political system requires a means for the public to influence the decisions of political leaders. This influence may be exercised only intermittently, as during elections, but in most democratic systems it is exercised almost constantly through mechanisms such as political parties and, of increasing importance, interest groups. The government of the United Kingdom is no different. While some have said that the United Kingdom is a democracy only once every five years (the statutory maximum length of a sitting Parliament), in fact the day-to-day decisions of British government are influenced by popular demands and pressures. The popular pressures are in part transmitted through partisan institutions, but the influence of pressure groups and the growing "corporatist" nature of modern British government also requires careful scrutiny. This chapter is an investigation of the impact of popular demands on British government and the linkage of organizations such as political parties and interest groups with decision-making institutions.

Political Parties

To an American reader accustomed to political parties that are little more than electoral aggregations that mean little or nothing in organizational or policy terms, British political parties may come as a surprise. British political parties have discernible policy stances, even if these are nothing more than to oppose the policies of the other party. On the other hand, British parties are primarily "catchall" parties and include a relatively wide range of opinion within any one party. Perhaps the major differences between British and American parties is that the parliamentary system in Britain requires greater party responsibility and the absence of federalism allows the parties to act as national organizations. Thus, although a single British party may contain a variety of opinions on issues, it is expected that once the party as a party has spoken, the members of the party will attempt to implement those ideas if in office or will continue to espouse them if out of office. Further, the party is expected to say about the same thing in the north of Scotland as it says in the south of England.

The Party System

The British party system has been described variously as a two-party system and as a two-and-one-half-party system. But election results during the 1970s and party realignments in the early 1980s indicate that a more complex multiparty system may be evolving.

The two major parties in the United Kingdom are the Labour party and the Conservative (Tory) party. These are national parties in every sense of the word and almost always run candidates in every parliamentary constituency in Great Britain. The "half party" that has sometimes been mentioned is the Liberal party, once one of the two major parties but surpassed by the Labour party when the franchise was opened to virtually all adults after the end of World War I. The Liberal party ran candidates in 576 constituencies (out of 635) in the 1979 election and won seats scattered from the Shetlands to Cornwall.

Two other political parties regularly win parliamentary seats in Great Britain. These are the Scottish National party in Scotland and Plaid Cymru, the Welsh National party, in Wales. There was a marked decline in the electoral fortunes of the two nationalist parties in the 1979 election, apparently related to the defeat of the devolution proposals in a referendum in 1978. Together, however, the two parties captured 2 percent of the total vote in the United Kingdom and 4 parliamentary seats. Their vote as a percentage of the vote in their regions also declined, but was still 17 percent for the SNP in Scotland and 8 percent for Plaid Cymru in Wales.

Finally, the partisan politics of Northern Ireland reflect the troubled history of that province and the religious and nationalist cleavages that divide the population. In 1979 four political parties each received over 10 percent of the vote in Northern Ireland. Two of these—the Official Unionist and the Democratic-Unionist—are Protestant and dedicated to the union of Northern Ireland with the United Kingdom. These two parties differ primarily in the intensity of their commitment with the Democratic

Unionist, led by the Reverend Ian Paisley, leading that race. The Social Democratic Labour party is overwhelmingly Catholic and is committed to the union of Northern Ireland with the Republic. The party would make both the northern and southern parts of Ireland socialist societies, and despite its appeal to Catholics, it is a secular organization. Finally, the Alliance party could perhaps be best described as an attempt at a "catchall" party in Northern Ireland. This party cuts across religious lines, although it advocates continuing allegiance to the British Crown. It also attempts to provide a program that would cut across class lines.

TABLE 3.1

Changes in Percentages of Partisan Voting, 1959-79

| | | | | Election Year | | | |
Party	1959	1964	1966	1970	Feb. 1974	Oct. 1974	1979
Labour	43.8	44.1	47.9	43.0	37.2	39.3	36.9
Conservative	49.4	43.3	41.9	46.4	38.2	35.8	43.9
Liberal	6.0	11.2	8.5	7.5	19.3	18.3	13.8
Scottish National	0.1	0.2	0.5	1.1	2.0	2.9	1.6
Plaid Cymru	0.3	0.2	0.2	0.6	0.5	0.6	0.4
Other	0.4	0.1	1.0	1.4	2.8	3.1	3.4
	100.0	100.0	100.0	100.0	100.0	100.0	100.0
Two-party	93.2	87.4	89.8	89.4	75.4	75.1	80.8

As noted, the two-party nature of British politics seems to be changing. As shown in table 3.1, the two-party share of the vote has declined rather steadily since the late 1950s and increased again in 1979. This is in part a function of the strength of the smaller parties mentioned above—especially the resurgence of the Liberals in the 1970s—but it also reflects the growing strength of minority parties such as the Communist party and the relatively new National Front, a political party advocating restricted immigration into the United Kingdom. The two major parties have continued to hold the vast majority of parliamentary seats, in large part because of the nature of the British electoral system (described below). Nevertheless, the two major parties have not been able to retain the loyalty of voters, and at their nadir one voter in four chose a party other than Labour or Conservative. The party nature of the British electoral system was somewhat restored during the 1979 election, with the two major parties receiving just over 80 percent of the vote.

In the early 1980s there is a new and perhaps more significant challenge to the two-party nature of British politics. When the left wing succeeded in altering the constitution of the British Labour party to allow a greater influence by constituency parties in the selection of the leadership and in the writing of the party manifesto, several former leaders of the party broke away to form the Social Democratic party. These leaders — Shirley Williams, Roy Jenkins, and David Owens — were among the most popular of the party's leadership, and they appealed to a significant moderate faction within the party and its electorate. A number of other Labour members of Parliament joined the group, as did left-wing Tories who were disgruntled with Mrs. Thatcher's severe economic policies. Practically overnight, the Social Democratic party became the third largest party in Parliament, with twelve seats. Some polls showed that if an election had been held in March 1981, a coalition of the new Social Democrats and Liberals might have gotten as much as 43 percent of the vote. But, to be successful, the new Social Democratic party must do several things. First, it must develop a workable party organization. Second, and perhaps more important, it must work out an accommodation with the Liberal party so that the two parties do not split votes. Finally, it must decide how it can differentiate itself from the other parties and make a distinctive appeal to voters.

Before going any farther, we should add several notes on the British electoral system. The system is a single-member district, plurality system. Each constituency elects a single representative (member of Parliament), and all that is required is a plurality (i.e., the individual with the most votes wins whether receiving a majority or not). Such a system has the advantage of producing majorities for Parliament, and although Britain has not recently had majority victories in terms of votes, there have been parliamentary majorities. As a consequence, the smaller parties are severely disadvantaged; the Liberal party and the Social Democrats have advocated proportional representation as a more equitable means of selecting members of Parliament.

One aspect of the British electoral system unlike that of the United States is that the legal principle of "one-person, one vote, one value" is not honored. Scotland and Wales are overrepresented, while Northern Ireland was significantly underrepresented until 1980 (see table 3.2 on page 44). The reason behind this maldistribution of seats is that Scotland and

TABLE 3.2
Citizens per Parliamentary Seat

	England	Wales	Scotland	Northern Ireland
Seats	516	36	71	12
Citizens per seat	89,800	76,900	72,900	128,300

Wales, because of their national identity and history, were deemed to have special interests requiring greater representation. On the other hand, Northern Ireland was underrepresented because until 1974 Northern Ireland had substantially greater self-government than did other parts of the United Kingdom so that an equal share of parliamentary seats may have been inequitable to other parts of the country. With the imposition of direct rule from Westminster, this justification is no longer valid.

Another feature of the British electoral system that differentiates it from the American is the importance of by-elections. If a seat becomes vacant during the life of a Parliament, an interim election (by-election) is held to fill the seat. As well as ensuring full membership of the House of Commons, by-elections serve as something of an ongoing vote of confidence by the people and can be quite embarrassing for a government. For example, a by-election in early 1980 that the Conservatives won by only a small majority in a normally safe Conservative constituency was read as a sign of significant discontent with Mrs. Thatcher's austerity program. And, if a government has only a small majority, by-elections may actually help force elections, as they did in 1979.

The Two Major Parties

Although many voters may choose other parties, only two parties—Labour and Conservative—can be expected to form a government. These governments may depend on the explicit or implicit support of smaller parties, as did the Labour government from 1974 to 1979. During this period, the Labour party had a narrow majority from the beginning of the session and frequently depended on Liberal votes, as well as the tacit support of the Scottish National party and portions of the Northern Ireland delegation, to prevent a significant defeat in Parliament. There was not a formal coalition government, however, and the Liberals had no positions in Cabinet.

There is a great deal that divides the two major parties in Britain, but in many ways they are similar. They are both "elite" or "caucus" parties, having a relatively small mass membership compared to their electoral strength. The parties are also aggregative, with both covering a range of social and political opinion and consequently having internal ideological divisions as well as disagreements with the other party. Also, both are relatively centralized and disciplined parties compared with decentralized American parties. Finally, both are national parties, drawing strength from all parts of the country, and they are generally the two top vote getters in each constituency.

The Conservative Party

The Conservative, or Tory, party has its roots in the political conflicts of the nineteenth century, and to some degree those roots produce conflicts within the Conservative party today. At present, the majority of adherents of the Conservative party would feel akin to Conservative parties in Europe and North America, resisting encroachments into the affairs of individuals by government. Traditionally, however, the Conservative party has advocated strong central government, in part because of the perception that the poor and less educated cannot be counted on to make decisions on their own and need the guidance of their "betters." Thus, "old Tories" want a significant degree of control over the private sector by government, albeit in the direction of preserving the interests of the upper classes. "New Tories" tend to advocate greater freedom for private-sector action and consequently a diminished role for government in economic and social life. The programs of Margaret Thatcher's first year in office would clearly correspond to the newer conception of Conservatives.

The Conservative party is an elite party in terms of the socioeconomic characteristics of its adherents and in terms of the relationship between party members and the voting strength of the party. The voting strength of the Conservative party is at least four times greater than its membership, and although the party has over 3 million members, it remains a relatively small organization compared to its ability to organize voters and campaigns.

The Conservative party outside Parliament has two major components. The first is a mass organization, headed by an organization entitled the National Union of Conservative and Unionist Associations in England and Wales, with similar bodies in Scotland and Northern Ireland. The governing body of the National Union is its Central Council, composed of representatives from the constituencies, Conservative members of Parliament and prospective candidates for that position, representatives of the Conservative Central Office, and other leaders of the party. The total membership is some 3,000 individuals. In practice, however, the National Union is run by a president and an Executive Committee of some 150 members elected by the Central Council. Power further tends to concentrate in a General Purpose Subcommittee of the Executive Committee, composed of only 50 members.

The territorial organization of the Conservative party is similar to the national organization. There are twelve provincial Area Councils; within each council the party is organized by constituencies, each with a leadership structure similar to that of the national party. The constituencies are also served by agents responsible for the administrative functions of the party. The constituency parties are important because it is at this level that most funds are raised and the majority of campaigning is managed. Also, the constituency must decide to accept candidates offered to them by the national party or develop candidates of their own who will be acceptable to the national party. Thus, although the Conservative party is centralized for many functions, such as the manufacture of the party platform (manifesto), in many important ways the party is decentralized.

Assisting the local and national officers is the second major arm of the Conservative party outside Parliament: the Central Office. This office is directed by the chairman of the party organization and contains a number of professional workers and the Conservative Research Department. The major officials in the Central Office are appointed by the party leader, and it is from this direct connection with party leadership that the Central Office derives most of its authority.

The latter points to the overriding fact that the Conservative party is largely a party based on Parliament. Certainly the annual conference of the party is much more assertive than it once was, and a leader must pay attention to the mass members of the party, but the real control over a leader comes from the party in Parliament rather than from the mass membership.

The basis of Conservative party organization in the House of Commons is the 1922 Committee, composed of all Conservative members of the House of Commons other than ministers when the party is in government. The 1922 Committee has exercised considerable power over Conservative leaders, and that power seems to be increasing. The leader of the Conservative party does not have to stand for annual election, but five of the ten leaders of the party since 1902 have been forced out of the leadership by backbenchers, either by direct vote or by an obvious disapproval of the leader by the led.

In addition to exercising control over the leadership of the party, another function of the party in Parliament is to maintain the voting discipline of the party members. The Conservative party has not "denied the Whip" (expelled) any of its members since 1945, although a number of members have refused the Whip during that period. In general, the Conservative party has not been beset with the deep internal splits that have plagued the Labour party and therefore the Conservatives have found it less necessary to employ available sanctions. Also important for conflict management within the party are certain genteel traditions such as not taking votes in the 1922 Committee but instead reading the "sense of the meeting" and the withdrawal of minority candidates for leader of the party after the first vote.

The selection of party leader is left almost entirely to the parliamentary party, although there are provisions for constituency parties and other concerned groups to make their views known. To select a leader, a ballot is held of all Conservative MPs. In order for a candidate to be elected, he or she must receive not only a simple majority on the first ballot but at least 15 percent more votes than the nearest competitor. If there is no successful candidate on the first ballot, a second ballot is held with only a simple majority required for election. If the second ballot fails to produce a winning candidate, a third ballot is held among the three top contenders with MPs indicating their second choices. If no candidate receives a majority of first-place votes, the second choices of those voting for the weakest candidate are distributed and a new leader is elected. As noted, however, it is now conventional for less successful candidates to resign after the first ballot to prevent divisions in the party.

The Conservative party in the 1980s offers a clear choice, a choice made even clearer by the first two years of Mrs. Thatcher's rule. Although purporting to accept many tenets of the welfare state, the Conservative government has moved vigorously to reduce government expenditure and the role of government in industry and society. The party, to some surprisingly, actually did what it said it would do in its election campaign. The question remains whether the voters would have supported the party if they had expected such sincerity.

The Labour Party

The roots of the British Labour party are in the Industrial Revolution. The Labour party is the principal representative of the "working class" in British politics, although its support is broader than industrial labor. The Labour party professes socialism as a major portion of its program, but at the same time is an aggregative party that includes a variety of definitions of socialism and many who do not accept socialism as the goal of the party or society. Ideological cleavages within the Labour party are both more pronounced and more intense than those found in the Conservative party. As the party moves into the 1980s, cleavages between the left wing, led by Anthony Wedgewood Benn, and the right wing, led by the former leader of the party, James Callaghan, and Denis Healey, promise to become even more intense. The apparent victory of the left on several issues dividing the party led to some of the members splitting to form the Council for Social Democracy in early 1981.

To comprehend the organization of the Labour party outside Parliament, one must first understand the role that the labor unions play in the party. The British Labour party originally was an alliance of unions and socialist organizations, with the unions the dominant element in that coalition. Currently, both the majority of the party membership (5 million of 6 million members) and the majority of the party's financial base comes from the labor movement. Thus, when one speaks of the membership of the Labour party, one is really speaking of the unions, although members through socialist organizations and constituency parties have influence that is much greater than their numerical strength. This power was increased by a change in the party's constitution, electing the leader of the party through an electoral college that will probably have a disproportionate share of constituency party members.

As with the Conservative party, the Labour party has a National Executive Committee (NEC) that supervises party operations outside Parliament and, to an increasing extent, manages the whole party. Twelve of the twenty-eight members of this committee are direct representatives of the labor unions, while only seven are representatives of constituency parties. The remaining members are the leader and deputy leader of the party (from the House of Commons), five women members, and a treasurer elected by the annual conference of the party. Major voices in the NEC and the annual conference make the membership less predictable and manageable than that of the Conservative Party Executive Committee.

This is especially true when the Labour party is the opposition party and the leader lacks the power of office.

The bureaucratic arm of the party—equivalent to the Conservative Central Office—is the Labour party secretary and his staff. As noted, party bureaucracy is rather closely controlled by the National Executive Committee. This control extends to having subcommittees of the NEC supervise various sections of the organization such as research, press and publicity, and finance.

As with the Conservative party, the Labour party has regional organizations, but these organizations do not have the degree of importance of their equivalents in the Conservative party. Also, there are constituency parties that, until the 1980 changes in the party's structure, lacked even the autonomy granted to their equivalents in the Conservative party. These constituency parties now have the right to reselect their candidates before each election, removing that power from the central party.

The power of the unions in the Labour party is especially evident at the Labour party's annual conference. Of the approximately 4,000 participants in these autumnal affairs, there will be more representatives of constituency parties than unions. Voting is not based on the number of delegates present, however, but on the number of party members represented by those present. Unions therefore hold the balance of power, with approximately five-sixths of all votes. In fact, the votes of the six largest unions constitute a majority.

The relationship between the Labour party's annual conference and the party in Parliament is not so clearly defined as in the Conservative party, and at times the annual conference has attempted to force its views on the parliamentary Labour party (PLP). Formal statements of the party do in fact indicate that the annual conference has the right to make binding policy decisions for the PLP, but party leaders from the inception of the party have been unwilling to be guided by policy pronouncements of those out of office, especially when there is a Labour government. The tension arises from the fact that "Labour began as a movement which created a Parliamentary party to serve its interests," so that there is a greater tradition of mass party control than in the Conservative party, which began as a faction in Parliament.

Some tensions between the segments of the Labour party—both institutional and ideological—have been illustrated by the conflict over the Commission of Inquiry mandated by the 1979 annual conference. This commission was charged with investigating the structure and constitution of the Labour party, especially questions of the authorship of the party manifesto, the reselection of parliamentary candidates in each constituency prior to each general election, and the election of the party leader by a more broadly constituted body than the PLP. All these issues pitted the ideological left of the party, based in constituency organizations, against the ideological right in the PLP, especially the leadership of the PLP (e.g., James Callaghan and Denis Healey). These issues came to a head after the annual conference accepted the report of the commission favoring the stand of the left, whereupon Callaghan resigned as party leader. The provisions of the new constitutional arrangement for electing a party leader were not finally decided, and Michael Foot—a representative of the left, although a less divisive one than most—was elected leader. These changes in the Labour party led to the previously mentioned split within the party, and although they have not been fully implemented, seem to be pushing the Labour party farther left than has been true in the past.

The parliamentary Labour party (PLP) is composed of all Labour MPs, including ministers or shadow ministers. As this group is not strictly a backbench group (such as the 1922 Committee), there is a greater emphasis on its role in liaison committee to keep the leadership informed of the opinion in the party; and when in Opposition, the annual election of a Parliamentary Committee serves as a mechanism for linking the average Labour MP with his or her leadership.

The leader of the party is elected annually in an election of the PLP. To be elected requires a majority vote. If this cannot be obtained on the first ballot, the candidate having the fewest votes is eliminated and another ballot is held a week later. This continues until someone receives a majority. While this is potentially a cumbersome procedure, in practice no more than two votes have ever been required. More important, annual election places a great deal of pressure on the leader of the Labour party, especially when in Opposition, pressure that does not exist for the leader of the Conservative party. When a system of electing the party leader through an electoral college is implemented, it will weaken the PLP and the party leader even more.

When there is a conflict, it is clear that the PLP is the dominant element in decision making for the party. This may change, however. It is also clear that there are already more opportunities for the mass membership to challenge the leadership than exist for members of the Conservative party. And the PLP itself is frequently not united, with a left-wing Tribune Group of some seventy members frequently opposing the more conservative leadership and a right-wing Manifesto Group tending to support the leadership of the party but also pressing for even more conservative policies.

Voting and Elections

Elections are a crucial driving force for democratic politics. Or are they? Certainly all conventional analyses of British politics assume that the policies of government are decided by the clash of political parties over issues. In like manner, voters are assumed to be both interested in politics and to make their choices among parties on the basis of issues. These may be assumptions largely unsubstantiated by evidence. Let us look at the evidence about the turnout of voters and reasons for their voting choices and then ask a few pertinent questions about the role of elections in policy choice.

Before we do that, however, we should point to several salient features of British elections. British elections are national elections, but they are national elections conducted in constituencies. Although it is clear who will be Prime Minister should one party or the other win, only two constituencies actually vote for prospective Prime Ministers (or, in an unlikely case, only one). Also, these constituencies are quite small compared with electoral districts in most Western countries. The average English MP represents 90,000 people, and the average Scottish MP 73,000 people. By way of contrast, the average member of the National Assembly in France represents over 100,000 people and the average congressman in the United States over 500,000 people. Also, the expenses of campaigning in Britain are tightly regulated so that a candidate cannot spend more than £1,750, plus 1½ pence (about 3 cents) per voter in urban districts and 2 pence per voter in rural districts. This combined with the short campaign period (six weeks or less) and the difficulty of purchasing media time other than for specified "party political broadcasts" makes British campaigns very different from the extended electronic contests familiar to Americans.

Also, the parties control the selection of candidates more centrally than do American parties. The concept of a primary is unheard of, although the constituency parties do have an active voice in the initial selection of their candidates. A prospective candidate must be accepted by the constituency party, with the central office exercising a tutelary role. This holds true for the acceptance of a new candidate, although candidates already sitting for a seat in Parliament, or having stood for a seat in the constituency in the previous election, do not have to be reselected in the Conservative party but now do in the Labour party.

Turnout

British citizens tend to vote more readily than do American citizens, although not so readily as citizens in other Western democracies. Turnout is also relatively evenly distributed across the country. As is true for most other countries, the abstainers are concentrated in the working class, a factor that goes a long way to explain the ability of the Conservative party to win as many elections as it does, given that approximately 65 percent of the population are generally classified as working class, and perhaps even a higher percentage identify themselves as working class. The British gov-

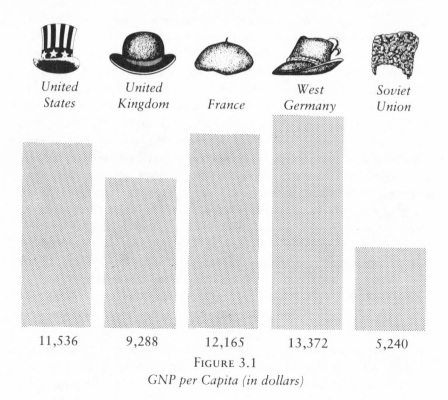

United States	United Kingdom	France	West Germany	Soviet Union
11,536	9,288	12,165	13,372	5,240

FIGURE 3.1
GNP per Capita (in dollars)

ernment is active in registering citizens to vote with the local government having a positive obligation every October to bring the electoral rolls up to date and to register all possible electors.

Partisan Choice by Voters

As well as deciding whether to vote, a voter must decide for whom to vote. There has been a great deal of research on the determinants of the partisan choices of voters. Three major factors are usually discussed as the principal determinants of partisan choice in Britain: social class, region of the country, and issues. The three factors obviously interact. Members of social classes are not evenly spread across the country, with more working-class voters living in Scotland, Wales, and the industrial Midlands of England and more middle- and upper-class voters living in the southeast or southwest of England. The issues to which citizens are assumed to respond also have different impacts on members of different social classes and residents of different regions. Consequently it is difficult to disaggregate the effects of these different influences, but let us at least describe some apparent effects.

Social Class. Social class is generally considered to be the dominant factor in explaining voting in Britain. As noted, much of British politics has been conceptualized in class terms. While there is strong evidence that class is an important factor in the voting decision, there is also some evidence that it is not so overwhelming as often believed. For example, in 1979, 40 percent of the electorate voted for the party (between the two major parties) not usually associated with its class interests.* This statement may be taken to say either that over half the voters seem to vote along class lines or that almost half do not, and over one-third cross class lines rather explicitly when voting.[1]

Several factors reinforce class voting among citizens, especially members of the working class. Three factors of importance are membership in certain organizations, patterns of residence, and patterns of communication. In general, members of labor unions are substantially more likely to vote Labour than are members of the working class as a whole. For exam-

*The additional 10 percent gave answers for parties whose class benefit could not be readily identified (e.g., the Scottish National party).

ple, in 1970, 60 percent of union members voted Labour while 44 percent of working-class voters who were not members of unions voted Labour. This was true even though many of those not voting for Labour were in objectively worse socioeconomic conditions than the union members.

Membership in religious organizations also tends to affect the class dimension of voting. On the one hand, adherents of the Church of England tend to vote Conservative more than do members of other churches. The characterization of the Church of England as the "Tory party at prayers" may be somewhat overstated, but there is an influence of church membership. On the other hand, Catholic members of the working class tend to vote Labour more consistently than do workers as a whole. Even leaving aside the influence of Northern Irish politics on voting, Catholic immigrants into cities such as Glasgow and Liverpool are among the most consistent Labour supporters.

Finally, certain "life-style" characteristics are important in explaining why members of the working or middle classes tend to vote for or against the nominal interests of their class. Working-class voters living in council (public) housing are much more likely to vote Labour than members of the working class living in other accommodations. Similarly, members of the middle class who enjoy such middle-class amenities as automobiles and telephones (neither so widely distributed as in the United States) are more likely to vote Conservative than their more deprived colleagues. Some have argued that these life-style factors have become more important in explaining patterns of voting behavior than simple membership in a social class.[2]

Patterns of Residence. Where people live seems to affect their voting behavior. First, living in the Celtic Fringe may affect voting. Leaving aside opportunities and motivations to vote for third-party candidates, the division of votes between the two major parties also differs in different parts of the country. Wales is the most heavily Labour portion of the United Kingdom, followed closely by Scotland. On the other hand, were it not for Wales and Scotland, the Conservatives would have a perpetual majority in the House of Commons because of their strength in England.

Second, rural voters tend to vote Conservative in greater proportions than urban voters do. This is in part a function of the concentration of workers in urban industrial areas, but there also appears to be some direct effect of residence. This may be due to the traditional deference of rural residents to the local squire, and the consequent unwillingness to offend him by voting Labour. Finally, the constituency in which a voter lives influences voting. This is especially true of prospective Labour voters who vote Labour in much greater proportions in safe Labour seats than in competitive, or safe Conservative, seats. This is a function of the reinforcing effects of interactions with other Labour voters and of union efforts to mobilize the vote.

Issues. Voters are assumed to respond to candidates on the basis of the issues. British parties are at once centrifugal and centripetal. They express class differences more clearly than do American parties, but they are also sufficiently centrist to try to disguise some of their potential differences in order to gain votes. Although some issues divide voters, the majority of voters of both parties tended to be on the same side of most major issues in British politics in 1979. Labour and Conservative majorities were on the same side of seven of ten issues in 1979, with the issues on which they were more divided having to do primarily with the powers of labor unions.[3] Also, it should be noted that there was substantial disagreement within the parties on the issues, especially within Labour, and that the level of agreement *within* parties was not always higher than the level of agreement *across* parties.

In addition, there is evidence that the parties are increasingly perceived by British voters as "much of a muchness," rather than parties that present distinct policy alternatives. During the 1950s, at least two-thirds of the citizens polled perceived important differences between the two major parties, while by 1979 only slightly over half recognized any important differences. And in the nonelection year of 1977, only one-third of the voters reported any significant differences between the parties.[4]

These findings indicate that political parties are not the repositories of ideas they are often presumed to be, or that if the parties are, the differences may be more over style than content of issues. That is, voters may be interested in how the government will run rather than in the actual content of policies the government is to pursue. On the latter, there appears to be a broad consensus across the political spectrum in Britain.

There is no neat means of summarizing voting behavior in Britain. The class model does not seem to fit the complexity of the situation as well as is often assumed. Yet no other model can adequately describe the complexity of the situation either. As important as elections and parties are for the choice of governments in the United Kingdom, a number of interacting factors enter into party choice.

More important, there is some question whether elections and the choice of parties really have much consequence for the policies of government. Richard Rose has done a detailed analysis of whether parties in Britain make a difference in policy terms, with the conclusion that such differences as do result are more matters of emphasis and the timing of policies than absolute differences in the content of policies. Clearly parties do make a difference, but the differences are subtle and not much based on a simple class model of politics.

Part of the reason for the consensual nature of the policies between the two major parties is the nature of the individuals recruited by the two parties to their leadership. If we look at the social and educational origins of Conservative and Labour politicians, we find more similarity than difference. The Labour party began as a party of the workingman, with the majority of the leadership coming from the ranks of manual workers. The party in 1980 had few in leadership positions with this background—the majority were Oxford or Cambridge graduates, many with private school secondary education. And some leaders of the Conservative party (e.g., Margaret Thatcher and Edward Heath) come from less elegant social backgrounds than the usual caricature of the Tory party.

British politics is built on an adversarial model, but in recent years much of the controversy generated seems to be over rather minor points of doctrine rather than the great issues of policy and the direction of government. The two major parties do have different basic goals, but the means by which they seek to attain those goals often look remarkably similar.

Pressure Groups and Corporatism

One factor that has pushed toward the homogenization of policies between the two parties is the growing influence of interest groups in British politics. As with most industrialized countries, there has been a movement toward "corporatism" in British politics, with interest groups granted something approaching an official status as generators of demands and implementers of policies once adopted.[5] The role of groups is rarely acknowledged officially—the doctrine of parliamentary supremacy is still invoked—but in practice much public policy is influenced or even determined by interest groups. So, no matter which party is in office, there are pressures for continuity of policies rather than change from one government to the next. Also, the policies made in conjunction with pressure groups tend to be made through stable patterns of interaction between civil servants and pressure-group leaders so that changes in government would have little opportunity to affect the basic content of the policies.

Major Groups

A number of different groups affect policy. These range from small "attitude" groups with narrow and largely noneconomic concerns (e.g., ecological groups) to large, influential "interest" groups that seek to have their economic interests magnified through the policy process. The most notable example of the latter are labor unions.

Labor Unions. The largest and most influential of the interest groups are the unions, with a total membership of 11.5 million workers, or about 45 percent of the total labor force. These unions are organized into one national federation, the Trades Union Congress (TUC). As noted, the TUC is directly linked to the Labour party and has gained a reputation as one of the world's most vociferous labor movements because of the large number of strikes called annually.

The unions are a major counterpoise to the power of government, and British elections have been fought over whether the unions or the government actually ran the country, with ambiguous results. The political power of the unions, combined with the threat of industrial action by their members, makes them a formidable political influence indeed. This influence is perhaps best exercised when Labour is out of government, for the close ties between the Labour party and the unions tend to restrain their political activities; restrain, but by no means stifle.

Management. While there is a single large labor movement, management groups are more divided into several groups. The Confederation of British Industries (CBI) is the major management organization, but a number of other general and specialized industrial groups also speak for management. The tie between management groups and the Conservative party is not so close as that between unions and the Labour party, although it certainly does exist. The CBI and its affiliates sponsor many Conservative MPs and donate significant sums to the party. They have relatively less direct influence on party policies and programs than the unions do in Labour.

Agriculture. Relatively few workers are employed in agriculture in the United Kingdom, but farmers and their associates in fishing are well organized. The most important organization is the National Farmers Union (NFU), but commodity groups ranging from beekeepers to dairymen are actively engaged in political activity. Agricultural groups have traditionally been successful in obtaining subsidies for their crops and have been especially advantaged by Britain's entry into the Common Market and the access to the subsidies of the Common Agricultural Policy of the EEC.

Professional Organizations. A large number of professional organizations exist in the United Kingdom, such as the British Medical Association, the Royal College of Nursing, and the British Association of Social Workers. These groups tend to be politically unaffiliated and as much concerned with the maintenance of professional standards of practice as the protection of the economic interests of their members. In the former role, professional groups frequently serve in a public capacity as the source and implementers of standards and as accrediting agencies for practitioners.

The major education associations in the United Kingdom are at once professional associations and unions. The National Union of Teachers and the Association of University Teachers are both affiliated with the TUC, and both have struck or threatened striking. They are also vitally concerned with professional issues such as academic freedom.

Patterns of Influence

As in virtually all democratic systems, there are a number of means through which pressure groups in the United Kingdom can attempt to influence the policies of government. The four major methods in the United Kingdom are lobbying, direct sponsorship of MPs, direct representation on government bodies, and consultation with ministries.

Lobbying. Lobbying is perhaps less common in the United Kingdom than in the United States, in part because party discipline makes it less likely to influence an MP's vote. Lobbying does occur, with the purpose being to get a voice in Parliament more than a vote. MPs receive delegations from their constituencies or from nationally based organizations.

Such delegations are particularly influential when a constituency has a single major economic interest, as with automobile manufacturing in Coventry or coal mining in many Welsh constituencies. Some pressure groups are sufficiently well organized to hire "parliamentary agents" or "correspondents" to maintain contact with MPs, attempting to influence the few potential cross-over MPs and feeding friendly MPs ideas and information. In turn they receive attention for their interests at those opportunities that even backbench MPs have to introduce business (e.g., the question hour or adjournment debates).

Direct Sponsorship of MPs. In the United Kingdom it is permissible for interest groups to "sponsor" prospective MPs, that is, to pay the majority of their electoral and other expenses. A group may even keep an MP on a retainer as long as that is registered. This has been especially common in the Labour party as a means of permitting manual laborers to go to Parliament. Naturally, sponsorship involves some degree of control by the sponsor, although in cases such as those of unions and working-class MPs, it is unlikely that the sponsor would ask the MP to do anything he or she would not otherwise have done.

Direct Representation. Interest groups have direct and official links with government in several ways. In some instances interest groups are directly represented in advisory committees attached to ministries. In other cases, pressure groups may actually compose the majority of public organizations, such as the National Economic Development Council ("Neddy"), established to promote economic growth through the cooperation of business, labor, and government. Finally, interest groups may actually administer programs for government, as the Law Society does with Legal Aid. In all these cases, it is clear, first, that governments cannot readily ignore interest groups so closely tied to the public sector, and second, that many of the traditional ideas about the separation of state and society in Western democracies make relatively little sense in the light of the increasing use of private organizations for public purposes.

Consultation. Less formally, government organizations frequently consult with interest groups. Interest groups have expert knowledge of their particular areas, and they are able to predict the reactions of their members to proposed policy changes. A government agency can gain not only in the technical quality of its proposals but also in their legitimacy by full consultation prior to the enactment. In an era in which delegated legislation is increasingly important, this means that a substantial amount of policy will be determined by consultations between civil servants and interest-group members. And interest groups are having an increasing impact on policies of all kinds, with a consequent decline in the relative influence of political parties and elective politicians.

This chapter has sought to outline the basic features of the party and pressure-group universe in the United Kingdom. In so doing it has also raised some questions about the way in which policy is made, and the impact of elections on policy. The purpose was not to put the efficacy of elections and mass democracy in doubt, but rather to point to the immense difficulties of making mass democracy an effective influence on policy in contemporary political systems such as that of the United Kingdom. The next chapter proceeds to a more detailed discussion of how the institutions of government arrive at decisions, and how they put those decisions into effect.

Notes

1. David Butler and Dennis Kavanaugh, *The British General Election of 1979* (London: Macmillan, 1980), p. 350.
2. Richard Rose, "Britain: Simple Abstractions and Complex Realities," in Rose, ed., *Electoral Behavior* (New York: Free Press, 1974).
3. Richard Rose, *Do Parties Make a Difference?* (Chatham, N.J.: Chatham House, 1980), p. 39.
4. Ibid., p. 43.
5. J.J. Richardson and A.G. Jordan, *Governing Under Pressure* (London: Martin Robertson, 1979).

4

How Is Power Used?

To this point we have described a number of institutions of British government, but in rather a static fashion. This chapter attempts to bring these structures to life and show how actors and institutions produce policies. We also show how the distinctive character of British governmental institutions affects the policies produced so that they may be different from those emanating from other political systems, even those faced with similar problems.

It is helpful in this discussion to think of two kinds of policy making that must go on in any government. The first is making *new* policies, as when the institutions of government decide to engage in new activities or in current activities in different ways. This is typically a legislative process, although administrative actors are certainly involved in the initiation of new policy ideas and in implementation. Also, the making of new policies tends to be more politicized, with parties and interest groups directly involved in the process.

The second major form of policy making is simply maintaining the existing policies and programs of government. This is frequently less political in a partisan sense; instead, it involves the bargaining of existing program managers with their financial overseers (in Britain, the Treasury) and overt or covert competition between existing programs. Thus the majority of this kind of policy making is not legislative but involves executive and administrative actors. We now look at the British political system as it processes both kinds of policy decisions.

The Parliamentary Process and New Policies

To understand how new policies are made and then put into operation, it is convenient to follow a "typical" piece of legislation through the process of lawmaking from getting the issue on the agenda for consideration through implementation. Of course, no bill is typical; some bills are passed in a matter of days the first time they are proposed, while others drag on for years before being passed. And some policy ideas never are made into law, or they have their meanings almost totally altered through implementation. Despite these differences, an underlying process is common to all.

Agenda Setting and Policy Formulation

The first thing that must be done if a piece of legislation is to be adopted is to place it on the policy-making agenda. This is true in an informal sense in that the policy must be considered important for the government to act on, and is true in the more formal sense of being placed before Parliament for consideration and possible adoption.

In the formal sense, the easiest way for an issue to come before Parliament is to be a part of the government's legislative program. Parliament's time is limited, and the government must select those issues and bills it believes are most important. This requires difficult choices because relatively few government bills are introduced in any year. In the nine years from 1970 to 1979 governments introduced an average of forty-seven bills per session. Since several of these involved budget and finance, and a large number of others involved consolidation of existing legislation, few significant policy bills were introduced at each parliamentary session.[1]

Bills and issues may also come before Parliament without acceptance by the government. Backbenchers can introduce legislation, although it has little chance of being passed. First, a backbencher must win a lottery to have the opportunity to introduce a bill and then there are generally only twenty Fridays—the day on which private members' bills are debated—during a session. Bills may also be introduced under the ten-minute rule, which allows for ten minutes of debate, pro and con, and is followed immediately by the vote. Both kinds of legislation allow for a consideration of issues the government may as soon forget, or issues of a moral nature on which the government does not wish to take a stance. Backbenchers cannot introduce legislation involving the expenditure of public funds.

It is easier to get issues discussed than to pass legislation. The question hour is an obvious example. Adjournment debates and motions by private members also allow individual MPs to air grievances. On average, backbenchers receive approximately 15 percent of parliamentary time, an allocation made by the government, and much of that time is spent discussing constituency grievances, thus allowing for little impact on major policy issues.[2] The Opposition is also given a substantial amount of parliamentary time to present alternatives to the government program, the major times being the debate on the Queen's Speech (actually written for her by the government), which opens each session of Parliament, and the twenty-six supply days scattered throughout the session.

In addition to controlling the agenda and timetable, the government must be heavily involved in formulating legislation. This is generally done by Cabinet prior to the legislation's being proposed to Parliament. Much of the impetus for policy formulation comes from the party's election manifesto. Nevertheless, parties are not the only source of policy intentions and policy formulation, and many policy ideas come up from the departments themselves. And, as with many industrialized democracies, the balance of power between elective and nonelective officials may have swung in favor of the unelected. In any case, the process of formulating policy is complex, involving the interaction of ministers with their civil servants and in turn consultation with the affected interests in society. And in Cabinet, legislation is typically considered by a Cabinet committee composed of interested ministers with some Treasury representation before consideration by the entire Cabinet.

Policy Legitimation

Once the Cabinet has agreed upon a policy it is then introduced into Parliament, with all politically controversial legislation by convention first going to the House of Commons. For a bill to become law, it must pass the House of Commons, pass the House of Lords (unless it is passed by three successive Houses of Commons), and gain royal assent.

When a bill is introduced into the House of Commons, it is given a formal first reading and then printed for distribution. After two or three weeks, there is the second reading, which is the major political debate on the principles of the legislation. For noncontroversial legislation, however, the second reading may occur in committee. After the second reading, a bill typically goes to committee for detailed consideration and possible amendment. Note that this occurs *after* Commons has agreed to the legislation in principle. The government is much more willing to accept amendments in committee than on the floor of the House where this might be seen as an admission of defeat. Finally, the bill is reported out with any amendments, a third reading is given, and the legislation is passed. The bill then goes to the House of Lords for consideration and possible amendment. Any amendments made in Lords must be considered by Commons. And although deadlocks are possible, they are infrequent. After agreement is reached, the bill is given to the Queen for royal assent, which is virtually automatic.

Of course, legislation does not necessarily move so easily through the policy-making system, and so there must be some means of regulating the flow and particularly of preventing the delay of important legislation. At the report stage, a number of amendments may be reported out of committee, and the Speaker is given the power to decide which should be debated and which would be repetitious of debates in committee. The government can also impose closure and the "guillotine" (allocation of time order). Closure is a motion to end debate made by a hundred or more MPs, but it will be accepted only if the Speaker believes all relevant positions have been heard. When there are a number of points of dissent, closure may be ineffective and then the guillotine is employed. An allocation of time order is voted by the House of Commons, and the government makes a determination of how much time will be spent on each portion of the bill. Once that time is exhausted, the Speaker must move the section to a vote. The use of the guillotine is often cited as opposed to the interests of the House as a deliberative body, especially when it is imposed on major constitutional issues, such as the devolution debates during the Callaghan government.

With party discipline, much of the activity of Parliament seems foreordained, but it is still important. First, legal procedures exist for the passage of legislation. Second, amendments must be accepted and legislation approved, both in the committee stage in Commons and in Lords. Finally, some legislation that seems perfectly reasonable to the majority of the Cabinet may not seem so reasonable to backbenchers in the party, and the legislation may never be passed. An average of 10 percent of all government bills introduced from 1974 to 1977 did not become law; thus, although the presence of disciplined majorities is certainly important, legislative action is not certain.

British democracy has long been representative democracy, but there were several interesting occurrences of direct democracy as a means of le-

gitimating policies during the 1970s. In particular, there were two significant referenda on policy issues—on whether Britain should have entered
the Common Market in 1975, and on the devolution proposals in Scotland
and Wales in 1979. The latter proposal was voted on only in Scotland and
Wales, but the principle was the same: The government and Parliament to
some degree abdicated their decision-making powers to the people in an
election. Although these referenda were not legally binding, they were declared binding by the major parties. Referenda represent a major departure from the traditional means of decision making in British government
and have potential importance for major policy decisions.

Policy Implementation

After a bill is passed by Parliament, perhaps the most difficult portion of
the process of changing society through government action occurs: the
implementation process. This is the process of taking the bare bones of
parliamentary legislation and putting some meat on them. This meat consists of both substantive policy declarations and organizational structures
to carry out the intent of Parliament, or at times, to thwart those intentions.

Implementation may be carried out in a number of ways. One is
through the departments of the central government. Most legislation
coming from Parliament is a broad mandate of power, with the ministry
then having the power and the task of making the necessary regulations
and activities for the intent of the legislation to come into being. A principal means of doing this is through statutory instruments developed pursu-
ant to acts of Parliament. Statutory instruments contain more detailed
regulations than the acts, and allow the executive to have a major impact
on the nature of the policy implemented. Parliament exercises scrutiny
over these instruments but cannot hope to fully master the volume or technical content of all such regulations. Even when the issuance of a statutory instrument is not required, the departments are heavily involved in
shaping the meaning of policy and making it work. The departments may
also be barriers to effective implementation, especially when the policy enacted by Parliament seems to run counter to their usual practices. In like
manner, the existence of regional and local offices of the ministry is frequently associated with varying patterns of implementation and, at times,
great variations from the original intentions.[3]

Policies of the central government are also implemented through local authorities. Unlike a federal system, the local authorities in Britain are the creatures of the central government, and there is less differentiation between national and local policy than in the United States. While the major policy decisions in areas such as education, health, social services, and the police are made by the central government, these services are actually delivered by local authorities. These services are not delivered uniformly; local authorities provide different quantities and qualities of service, albeit within centrally decided parameters and subject to inspection and control by the center. This relationship between central policy making and local administration does not work without friction, especially when local and central governments are controlled by different parties. Recent examples of conflicts include Conservative local authorities delaying implementation of Labour policies for comprehensive education, and Labour local authorities refusing to implement Conservative cash limits on expenditures for health care. Thus, while it may at times be impossible to do so, the central government needs to "bring along" the local authorities when it is considering a new policy if it hopes to have that policy implemented effectively.

In return for the administration of national policies, the local authorities receive the majority of their revenue from the central government. Some of the grants to local authorities are tied to the provision of specific services (e.g., the police), while the largest single grant—the rate support grant—is a general grant.* If a local authority *wishes* to do things not supported by the rate support grant or other categorical grants from central government, then it must be willing to raise funds from local revenue, generally "the rates" (property tax).

Finally, policies may be implemented by private organizations. Interest groups are usually regarded as barriers to effective implementation, but such groups may have an important positive role to play in implementation. Minimally, the interest group can serve as a watchdog on the implementation of a policy, substituting for the army of inspectors that might otherwise be required. Environmental groups have been particularly active in this monitoring role. A more important involvement of groups in implementation has the group actually implementing a policy for government. This occurs frequently in agriculture when the National Farm-

*The formula for computing the rate support grant does, however, include weightings for the levels of service provided by a local authority.

er's Union applies general laws to individual cases, for example, in compensation for crop or livestock damage. These activities would otherwise require huge amounts of time and public money. Further, at times government subsidizes an organization to provide a service that government supports as a matter of policy and that would have to be provided at public expense if the private organization were not willing to provide it.

Policy Evaluation

The last stage of making a policy occurs some time after the policy has been adopted. This is the evaluation of the policy. Here we are discussing the formal evaluation of the policy, whereas informal evaluation begins almost at the time of passage. This topic is also related to policy making for continuing policy, which is our next major topic, for the annual decisions to continue policies and programs made in the budgetary process to some degree involve evaluation of policy.

Parliament is assumed to conduct ongoing scrutiny of the policies of government, and there are a number of instruments for policy evaluation housed within the government itself (e.g., the Central Policy Review Staff attached to the Prime Minister's Office). Also, the now defunct Programme

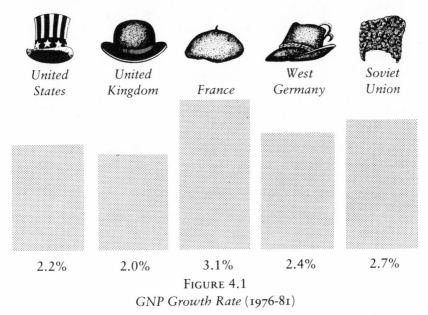

United States	United Kingdom	France	West Germany	Soviet Union
2.2%	2.0%	3.1%	2.4%	2.7%

FIGURE 4.1
GNP Growth Rate (1976-81)

Analysis and Review (PAR) and the Public Expenditure Survey Committee linked program evaluation to financial management. Also, through the parliamentary commissioner, or "ombudsman," Parliament maintains some evaluative control over the administration of policy.[4]

A number of mechanisms for policy evaluation exist independent of the government. One of the most commonly used devices is the appointment of parliamentary or royal commissions to investigate particular policy concerns that are more fundamental than any government may want to become involved in without advice. These commissions and their reports often constitute milestones in the evolution of policy and program management, as with the Fulton Report on the civil service, the Plowden on public expenditure control, and the Kilbrandon on devolution. The commissions have no formal powers, however, and even excellent reports often go unheeded.

Finally, there are a number of less official mechanisms for policy evaluation. The press is one, although it is severely hampered by the Official Secrets Act and the lack of access to important information. A number of policy "think tanks" also exist; some represent clearly defined ideological positions, while others strive toward greater objectivity. Finally, research units of political parties and pressure groups also produce evaluations of existing policies. A great deal of official and unofficial policy evaluation occurs, although tight control by the government over the parliamentary agenda makes consideration of many policy changes unlikely.

Policy Continuation: Budgeting

Most policy making is not making new policies; it is reaffirming old policies or making marginal adjustments in those policies. In many ways this form of policy making is politically more sensitive than making new policies, for existing programs have existing clients and organizations, while new policies have no inertia pushing existing commitments forward. The most important decisions for continuing policies are made in the budgetary process in which the huge number of existing policy commitments are financed each year and their relative priorities determined in pounds and pence.*

---

*Here we are speaking of the budget in an American sense, whereas in Britain the term refers to the government's revenue, not expenditure, proposals. More on revenue later.

The control of the public purse has been central to the powers of Parliament historically, but the existence of disciplined partisan majorities has transformed substantially the locus of effective budgetary powers. Budgeting can be best thought of as taking place in two stages. One is an administrative stage during which the spending ministries negotiate with the Treasury and with the Cabinet over expenditures. The second stage is the parliamentary stage during which these decisions are legitimated and occasionally changed.

The Executive Stage

The Treasury is the central actor at the executive stage of budgeting. The Treasury is charged not only with making recommendations on macroeconomic policy but also with formulating expenditure plans within those economic constraints. The Treasury has traditionally been the most prestigious appointment for a civil servant, and those in the Treasury have held a "Treasury view" about the proper amount of spending and who should spend the money. This view does not always prevail, but must always be considered.

The first round of bargaining over expenditures is typically at the level of civil servants. This bargaining takes place with the knowledge of the relevant ministers, but can be conducted more easily by officials who both know each other and the facts of the programs. Both elements are important. Interpersonal trust and respect are important components of the success of any bargainer, especially when the spending departments must have their requests reviewed annually.[5] Also, civil servants tend to understand the technical aspects of their programs better than ministers do. In addition to their annual (or at times more frequent) bargaining for expenditures, departments must also bargain for deviations from expenditure plans during the year, allowing the Treasury a number of opportunities to monitor and intervene in departmental policies.

The second stage of executive bargaining occurs among the spending ministers, the Treasury, and the Cabinet as a whole. Budget decisions are manifestly political, and if nothing else, they reflect the relative political powers and skills of the ministers involved. The task of the spending ministers is to fight for their programs and try to get as much as they can. The Treasury ministers (the chancellor of the exchequer and the chief secretary of the Treasury) are the guardians of the public purse and play the role of skeptic. The Prime Minister must moderate this conflict, but knows that she can rarely go against her Treasury ministers if the government is to function smoothly. Also, in the more conservative period of the early 1980s, there is some political advantage to opposing expenditure increases. The fight over the budget occurs on a one-to-one basis between spending and Treasury ministers, in Cabinet committees, and finally in the Cabinet meeting. The Treasury is in a strong position politically and in terms of having the right to make the first presentation of expenditure figures in the Cabinet, but there is a tendency for the spending ministers to gang up against the Treasury. As this is a political process, a coalition can usually be formed to increase expenditures that enables all spending ministers to make their constituents happy, and to make themselves look good in the eyes of their departments.

British government has made a great deal of effort to control the costs of government through analytic programs such as PESC (Public Expenditure Survey Committee) and PAR (Programme Analysis and Review). The major input of PESC into the decision process is a projection of the expenditure implications of existing programs, showing what the level of expenditure would be if things were left to themselves. PAR was intended as a comprehensive evaluation of specific programs, with the intention of making those programs more efficient or perhaps eliminating them. PAR obviously ran counter to the established norms of government and budgeting, and has been quietly phased out of existence.

The Parliamentary Phase

After the civil servants and the Cabinet prepare their expenditure plans (estimates), these are presented to Parliament for adoption. Although the emphasis on control and on techniques for budgeting such as PESC have produced significant modernization, much of the terminology and procedure used by Parliament when considering public expenditure dates from earlier periods in which the monarch and Parliament were engaged in more intense conflicts over power. The major debates on expenditures occur during the twenty-six supply days each session, although the topics selected by the Opposition for these days range far beyond expenditures. The civil estimates are introduced into Parliament by the chief secretary of the Treasury in February, with the minister of defence introducing the defence estimates. Parliament then has until July or early August to pass the Consolidated Fund (Appropriations) Bill authorizing the expenditure of funds. Given the difficulties in forecasting expenditures, especially in uncertain economic circumstances, the government must also introduce supplemental estimates in December and March.

The budget is an important locus for parliamentary control over the executive. By standing order, Parliament cannot increase expenditures on its own; any increases must be recommended by a minister. Parliament can, however, recommend decreases. One means of expressing displeasure with the management of a ministry is to move the reduction of the salary of the minister, frequently by a trivial amount such as £100. This signals a debate not so much on the £100 as on the policy of the ministry.

Parliament as a whole is perhaps too large and disorganized to effectively scrutinize expenditure programs, and so it has developed a pair of committees to more closely examine the government estimates. One is the Expenditure Committee, the successor to the Estimates Committee. The Expenditure Committee does its work in subcommittees, but unlike the Appropriations Committee in the U.S. Congress, it does not presume to cover the range of public expenditures each year. Rather, each subcommittee focuses on a particular topic for a detailed analysis. Given the ability of the government to get what it desires passed by Parliament, the Expenditure Committee has been unable to alter much policy directly, although it has played an important role in ventilating ideas and opinions about the expenditure of funds. The committee is also important in restoring some parliamentary control over expenditures.

The second important parliamentary committee for controlling public expenditure is the Public Accounts Committee (PAC). Unlike most committees in Parliament, PAC is headed by a member of the Opposition; it has the task of monitoring expenditures after they have been spent and after they have been audited. Out of the mass of public expenditures, PAC selects certain topics for consideration and has the power to call civil servants before it to account for their actions. Other than calling attention to mismanagement or outright deception, however, PAC has few powers to improve the expenditure of funds.

In addition to the two principal committees examining expenditures, the appointment of the new select committees monitoring the activities of ministers may be a useful device for parliamentary control of expenditure. It remains to be seen just how successful these committees will be, both in attracting the interest of MPs and in effectively keeping track of the huge volume of work produced by the ministers.

Revenue

To this point we have been discussing the expenditure side of budgeting. On the revenue side, there is the same balance of power in favor of the Cabinet and the Treasury. If anything, the balance of power is more in the hands of the executive, as Parliament has yet to develop a committee structure for monitoring revenue. And, within the executive, the balance appears to favor the officials, as there are no ministers pushing for increased taxation as they do for increased expenditures. This is not to say that there are no political influences on taxation, as the shift from direct taxation (income taxes) to indirect taxation (VAT) in the first Thatcher budget indicates.

Revenue recommendations are introduced around the first of April each year in the chancellor's budget message. Immediately, Commons will pass the budget resolutions, allowing for the immediate collection of some portions of the tax proposals. There follows a period of debate and the formal introduction of the Finance Bill to be passed some time before Parliament takes its summer recess in August.

One of the common criticisms about the British budgetary process, which is also true of the budgets of many other nations, is that there is no integration of revenue and expenditure decisions. Citizens and politicians both tend to like expenditures and loathe taxation, and this commonly results in a failure to collect adequate revenue to meet expenditures and the creation of a deficit budget. Changes would involve change in many historic procedures but might well produce an improvement in the management of public-sector finance.

Policy making in Britain involves the interactions of Cabinet, Parliament, and the civil service — to mention only the primary actors. In this interaction the formal location of power and the actual location of decision may be markedly different. The formal powers of decision reside in Parliament, but the effect of strong party discipline has been to make the Cabinet the primary decision-making institution. Given a government majority, once the Cabinet decides on a policy the dutiful members of the party will almost certainly ratify it on the floor of the House of Commons. There are, of course, instances in which the backbenchers overtly or covertly oppose government policy, and the Cabinet rarely tries to run roughshod over its own party members, but the Cabinet does have the ability to get most of what they choose passed into law.

The powers of the Cabinet are restrained in other ways. The ministers must contend with skillful and permanent civil servants. Especially in the budgetary process, the Treasury and its "mandarins" dominate the decision making. Even in nonfinancial decisions, the expert knowledge of the civil servants, compared with the expertise of their nominal political masters, places them in a crucial postion to influence policy.

Finally, a number of interests and organizations other than these three major actors influence policy decisions. Interest groups not only attempt to influence policy as it is being formulated but also may directly implement policies for the government. Local governments administer and implement a significant share of the programs of central government, and the central government must try to coopt and encourage local governments to implement the policy as it was intended.

Making policy in Britain, as elsewhere, is difficult and complicated. Many good intentions are rendered ineffective by the need to gain agreement from a number of actors. British policy making is especially complicated by the many vestigial procedures and offices, although to abandon these may threaten the legitimacy of the system of government.

Notes

1. Derived from Ivor Burton and Gavin Drewry, "Public Legislation," *Parliamentary Affairs,* various years.
2. See Peter G. Richards, *The Backbenchers* (London: Faber and Faber, 1972), pp. 89-113.
3. This is perhaps especially pronounced for programs that are administered through the Scottish Office, the Welsh Office, and the Northern Ireland Office.
4. Frank Stacey, *The British Ombudsman* (Oxford: Clarendon Press, 1971); also, *The Ombudsman Compared* (Oxford: Clarendon Press, 1979).
5. Hugh Heclo and Aaron Wildavsky, *The Private Government of Public Money* (Berkeley: University of California Press, 1974), pp. 76-128.

5

What Is the Future of British Politics?

Governments constantly face challenges. Even in the most prosperous and well-managed political system there are crises and decisions. As Britain is not the most prosperous and well-managed country on earth, it faces a number of challenges to its political and economic systems.

Slow Growth

Perhaps the overriding problem of any British government is the state of the British economy. Even with the bonanza of North Sea oil, the British economy is weak and slow-growing compared with that of its European neighbors. This poor economic performance may be beyond the realm of political control, but government may be blamed for the poor performance and the resulting unemployment and inflation. This is especially true because the effects of poor performance are concentrated in Scotland, Wales, and the north of England.

The two governing parties have approached the problem of slow growth differently, but apparently with equal success or lack of it. The Labour party has been more interventionist and stimulative in its approach, seeking to affect the growth of the economy by public expenditure and affect inflation by voluntary or mandatory wage and price controls. The Conservative party has been more reluctant to become involved in the economy and has sought to encourage growth by allowing more latitude and profit for the private sector. Severe economic situations have, however, prompted direct intervention by the Tories. The underlying economic philosophy of many in the Conservative party is indicated by the approach of Margaret Thatcher in reducing industrial subsidies and denationalizing some previously nationalized industries (e.g., British Airways). Mrs. Thatcher and two of her aides, Sir Geoffrey Howe (chancellor of the exchequer) and Sir Keith Joseph (minister of industry), have sought to restore British industry to the "chill wind of free enterprise," but the report is not in on the success of their efforts.

The Public Sector

Associated with the slow growth of the economy is the rapid growth of the public sector. Tax revenues in the late 1970s averaged almost 35 percent of gross national product, and when borrowing is included, that figure climbs to over 40 percent of GNP. We have discussed some of the sophisticated machinery Britain has developed for analyzing public expenditures, but these devices seem to have been ineffective when faced with the political pressures to spend more.

The size of the public sector is a problem to Britain in several ways. One is that a large public sector may slow the rate of economic growth. People employed by the public sector produce valuable goods and services: education, transportation, and in Britain health care and steel. But many "products" of the public sector are services that employ large numbers of personnel and grow slowly in terms of output.[1] Any service industry—whether publicly or privately owned—tends to grow more slowly than manufacturing industries do; thus, public-sector growth depresses the overall rate of economic growth.

The size of the public sector is also important to the taxpayer. While much of the total tax bill is returned to the citizen as cash benefits (pensions) or benefits in kind (roads or the health service), these benefits must all be paid for from taxes. As taxes rise, so does resistance to taxation; and with this resistance there is potentially a decreased legitimacy of government.[2]

Who Rules Britain?

We have mentioned the power of interest groups, especially unions, in Britain several times. One prospective difficulty is maintaining the locus of authority in the political institutions of the country rather than in other segments of society, be they unions or the CBI. Unions present the major challenge to government, possessing as they do a large number of members, the potential to curtail essential services, and direct ties to a political party.

The style by which unions attempt to influence government policies varies relative to which major party is in office. When the Labour party is in office, unions have direct access to government, although there were numerous instances during the last Wilson government and the Callaghan government when the government was clear in asserting its mandate to rule against the unions over economic policy. When the Conservatives are in office, the style is more confrontational, as indicated by the miners' strike during the Heath government and the (unsuccessful) attempt at a one-day general strike in the late spring of 1980.

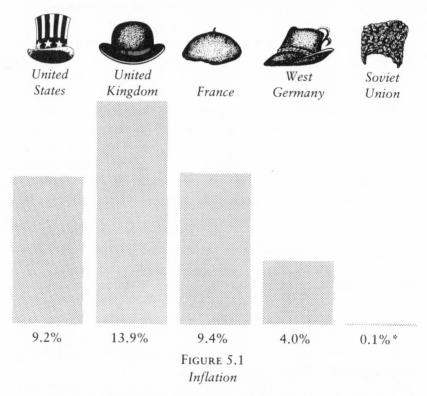

United States	*United Kingdom*	*France*	*West Germany*	*Soviet Union*
9.2%	13.9%	9.4%	4.0%	0.1% *

FIGURE 5.1
Inflation

NOTE: Average annual change in consumer prices, 1976-81; official figure for the USSR almost certainly understates real price increase.

* In most basics the system has maintained prices at the post-World War II level or nearly so. But in the case of many nonessential consumer items the prices have been increased many fold, by withdrawing "old" models from the market and replacing them with scarcely altered "new" models at much higher prices.

Any group in a liberal democratic regime has the right to try to influence public policy. The question that arises is: To what extent may that influence be extended before the nature of the democratic regime is fundamentally altered?

Who Rules in Government?

Even if we could say with certainty that the government ran Britain, we would still need to know which institution(s) were most influential. The problem here is also one of democratic governance. Voters in the United Kingdom go to the polls every few years and make choices about the party they wish to govern them for a period of up to five years. And the Parliament to which the members of that party are elected nominally has the power to govern. As we have been emphasizing, however, the Cabinet within partisan institutions of government and the civil service within government as a whole are increasingly important in policy making. This means that the voting choices of millions of citizens may be negated, or perhaps only ignored, in the policy-making process. This is a serious problem for all democratic political systems, as citizens believe that the institutions of government are no longer responsive to their wishes and are overly bureaucratic and technocratic, rather than democratic. This alienation is apparently less evident in Britain than in several other industrialized countries, but it is still an important threat to the legitimacy of the system of government.

Devolution, Breakup, or What?

Will there continue to be a United Kingdom? Indications are that this question can be answered in the affirmative, at least for the time being. The referendum of Scottish and Welsh devolution in 1979 indicated that there is certainly substantial support for a more independent Scotland (less so for Wales) but that this support is not overwhelming. In the country as a whole, it is certain that there is relatively little sympathy for devolution or other substantial changes from the current constitutional arrangements. Still, the demand for the accommodation of long-standing cultural, social, and economic interests for the nation is unlikely to disappear.

Related to the question of Scotland and Wales, although certainly more serious, is the problem of Northern Ireland. The country continues to be an open sore in the side of the United Kingdom, with little or no hope for quick resolution. A number of attempts have been made to find institutional mechanisms for accommodating the interests of both religious groups, but all have ultimately failed and the violence continues. This is an intractable problem that will continue to plague British policy makers and threaten the legitimacy of the system of government. This threat is direct in that forces in Northern Ireland renounce the rule of London; and it is indirect in that the use of extreme measures in Northern Ireland to suppress terrorism may place the benevolence of the government, and the rights of citizens, in question.

British policy makers are much like other policy makers, although they have their particular problems and potential. The conduct of modern government requires them to balance traditional norms and procedures that legitimate decisions with the more modern techniques for analysis and control. Older institutions for policy making are challenged by more technically sophisticated and professionally qualified officials. And the underlying social divisions in society refuse to be homogenized despite the pressures of mass media, industrialization, and urbanization. Whether in the United Kingdom or elsewhere, modern government is a balancing act between the new and the old; those things that unite and those that divide.

Notes

1. Robert Bacon and Walter Eltis, *Britain's Economic Problem: Too Few Producers* (London: Macmillan, 1978).
2. Richard Rose and B. Guy Peters, *Can Government Go Bankrupt?* (New York: Basic Books, 1978).

For Further Reading

ASHFORD, DOUGLAS E. *Policy and Politics in Britain: The Limits of Consensus.* Philadelphia: Temple University Press, 1981.

BOGDANER, VERNON. *Devolution.* London: Oxford University Press, 1979.

BUTLER, DAVID, and KAVANAGH, DENNIS. *The British General Election of 1979.* London: Macmillan, 1980. This is the latest of an ongoing series of analyses of British elections commonly referred to as the Nuffield series.

_____, and STOKES, DONALD E. *Political Change in Britain.* 2nd ed. London: Macmillan, 1975.

CROSSMAN, RICHARD. *The Diaries of a Cabinet Minister.* 3 vols. London: Hamish Hamilton and Jonathan Cape, 1974-77.

HEADEY, BRUCE. *British Cabinet Ministers.* London: Macmillan, 1976.

HECLO, HUGH, and WILDAVSKY, AARON. *The Private Government of Public Money.* Berkeley: University of California Press, 1974.

JOHNSON, NEVIL. *In Search of the Constitution.* Oxford: Pergamon, 1979.

KAVANAGH, DENNIS, and ROSE, RICHARD. *New Trends in British Politics: Issues for Research.* London: Sage, 1977.

KELLAS, JAMES. *The Scottish Political System.* 2nd. ed. Cambridge: Cambridge University Press, 1975.

KELLNER, PETER, and CROWTHER-HUNT, LORD. *The Civil Servants: An Inquiry into Britain's Ruling Class.* London: Macdonald, 1980.

MACKINTOSH, JOHN. *The British Cabinet.* 3rd ed. London: Stevens, 1977.

MILLER, WILLIAM E. *Electoral Dynamics.* London: Macmillan, 1977.

PUNNETT, MALCOLM. *Front Bench Opposition.* London: Heineman, 1973.

ROSE, RICHARD. *Governing Without Consensus.* London: Faber, 1971.

_____. *The Problem of Party Government.* London: Macmillan, 1974.

WALKLAND, S., and RYLE, MARTIN. *The Commons in the 70's.* London: Fontana, 1977.

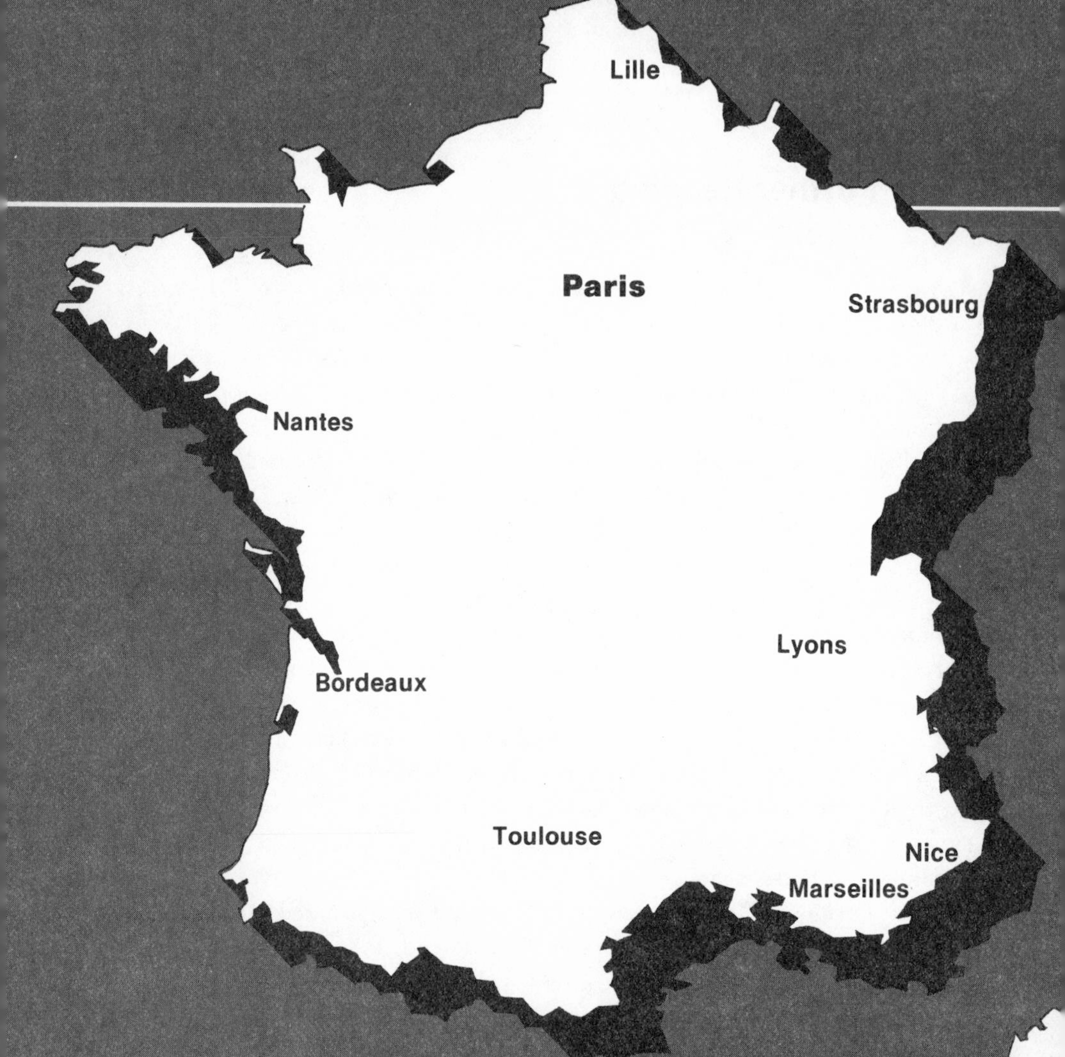

Lille

Paris

Strasbourg

Nantes

Lyons

Bordeaux

Toulouse

Nice

Marseilles

Part Two

France

William Safran

6

The Context of French Politics

France has been one of the important countries in the world. Its culture, architecture, and cuisine have been much admired and copied; its language has served as the chief medium of diplomacy; its political philosophies and institutional patterns have exerted influences far beyond the country's borders. Until the end of World War II, France was the second greatest colonial empire, with possessions in Southeast Asia, the Caribbean, and North and West Africa.

The second largest country in Europe (after the Soviet Union), France is more than twice the size of Britain or West Germany and somewhat smaller than Texas. Except in the north and northeast, France has natural frontiers: the Atlantic Ocean on the west, the Pyrenees in the south, and the Alps and Jura mountains in the east. Wide variations in landscape — the northern flatlands of Flanders, the forests of Normandy, the mountainous east and center, the beaches of the Vendée in the west, and the subtropical Riviera coast in the south — are accompanied by regional trends in cuisine, dress, speech, and attitude.

It cannot be said that the French are of a single stock; the mixture of Celts, Latins, Germanic elements, and the descendants of more recent Slavic, North African, and other immigrants have made the population of the country truly multiethnic. As one of the first large European countries to have its boundaries more or less permanently fixed, France has a highly developed sense of national identity. At the same time, it should be pointed out that the Alsatians, Bretons, Corsicans, and other minority ethnic groups — and more recently the Jewish community — have not been content with being merely French and have demanded that their cultural uniqueness be recognized.

Ever since the country's early efforts at unification under centralized auspices, Paris has been the locus of national political power. Unchallenged by other cities, the political capital is also France's cultural and economic center. Paris contains the biggest university complex, three-fourths of the nation's theaters, and the majority of its museums and art galleries; and it is the hub from which most of the railroad lines radiate. The Paris region comprises about 2 percent of the nation's land area, but by the early 1980s it included 20 percent of its total population, boasted its largest factories, and accounted for a third of its industrial production.

The impression, widespread among foreigners as well as natives, that, apart from Paris, France is essentially a peasant country, can be traced to a number of factors. The Industrial Revolution did not proceed so early and so thoroughly in France as it did in Britain and Germany: by the end of World War II, an estimated one-third of the French labor force was still employed in agriculture. Most of the farms were—and are—small; the consolidation of landholdings was impeded by the traditional division of a family's acreage among several descendants, and industrialization was long delayed by the lack of private investment capital and the limited need for industrial manpower in the cities. In the past twenty-five years, however, there has been impressive progress in agricultural modernization. Thus, whereas in 1946 the labor of 10 farmers fed 55 persons, in 1975 it fed 260. Whereas in 1946 more than 30 percent of the active population was in agriculture, in 1975 it was less than 10 percent. In 1946, 21.5 out of 40.5 million people lived in cities; in 1980, nearly 40 million out of 53 million did.

Despite this urbanization, many French men and women continue to share the view that life in the country is more satisfying than an urban existence. For many years, a "peasant romanticism" was fortified by the patterns of family loyalty, parsimony, and conservative moral values carefully nurtured by the Catholic church; today this romanticism has been rediscovered as an ideal by those disenchanted with the economic insecurities, overcrowding, unemployment, and growing social disorganization and crime in the cities. There is no doubt that urbanization has contributed to a rapid increase in criminality. In 1977 the crime rate (with over 2 million crimes) was 39.2 per thousand, compared with 32.3 in 1972 and 13.6 in 1963.

Religion and Social Class

For a long time, Roman Catholicism embraced most of the population;

France was considered the "most Catholic" of countries. To be sure, the Reformation spread to France; in the sixteenth century, the country was riven by bitter struggles between Catholics, who were supported by the ruling elite, and Protestant Huguenots (mainly Calvinists), many of whom were massacred. After a period of toleration, the privileges of the Protestants (e.g., the right to live in certain fortified towns) were revoked in the seventeenth century, and many Protestants left the country. With the consolidation of absolute rule under the Bourbon kings, the position of Catholicism as the state religion was firmly established. Dissatisfaction with monarchism meant a questioning of the church and its privileges, and revolutionary sentiments were accompanied by anticlerical attitudes.

The hold of Catholicism gradually weakened as a consequence of industrialization; the rise of a new working class; the development, in the nineteenth century, of a unified school system; and finally, demographic and social changes. In the first decade of the twentieth century the Catholic church was formally "disestablished," and France became, like the United States, a secular country, at least in constitutional terms. (The one exception is the province of Alsace where, for historic reasons, the clergy is supported by public funds.) Today more than 90 percent of the population is Roman Catholic, but little more than a third of it is "practicing"; a large proportion of inhabitants of the larger cities, and the great majority of industrial workers, are "de-Christianized" except in the most formal sense.

Yet Catholicism cannot be divorced from French culture and political consciousness. The cathedral remains the heart of small towns, most legal holidays are Catholic ones, and many political movements and interest groups are largely influenced by Catholic teachings. Furthermore, public policy attitudes have often been inspired by Catholic social doctrine: aid to large families, the notion of class collaboration and the "association" of employers and workers in factories, the long-held opposition to the legalization of birth control and abortion, and the legal dominance — until well into the 1960s — of the male head of the family. Today, between 15 and 20 percent of parents opt to send their children to Catholic parochial schools, which benefit from governmental financial support.

There are about a million French Protestants, many of them prominent in business, the free professions, and, more recently, politics and administration. In addition there are some 700,000 Jews, whose presence in France predates the Middle Ages. During the Dreyfus Affair in the 1890s, antirepublican feelings were accompanied by a campaign to vilify Jews and eliminate them from public life. With the Nazi occupation of France (1940-44), and the resulting persecutions and deportations, the Jewish community was decimated; with respect to these events, Catholic Frenchmen maintained an ambivalent attitude. Since the early 1960s, the number of Jews was augmented by repatriates from North Africa. Jews, much like Protestants, have tended to support republican regimes and have shown a decided preference for left-of-center parties identified with anticlericalism. Since the mid-1960s there has also been a significant influx of Moslems, primarily from North Africa, many of whom belong to the category of "guestworkers" and perform the most menial work in the industrial cities.

Superficially, the French social system is typical of that found in other European countries. The old feudal divisions of society into nobility, clergy, townsmen, and peasants gradually gave way to a more complex social structure. The traditional, land-based aristocracy declined as a result of the use of the guillotine and the diminishing economic value of agriculture, and today the aristocracy has a certain vestigial importance only in the military officer corps and the diplomatic service.

The modern upper class, or *haute bourgeoisie* — a status derived from graduation from a prestigious national university, the inheritance of wealth, or both — comprises the higher echelons of the civil service, the directors of large business firms, and bankers. The next social group is the *grande bourgeoisie,* which includes university professors, high school teachers, engineers, members of the free professions, middle-echelon government functionaries, and the proprietors of medium-sized family firms. The middle and lower middle class — today the largest social category — comprises elementary school teachers, white-collar employees, petty shopkeepers, and lower-echelon civil servants. The lower classes *(classes populaires)* include most of the industrial workers, small farmers, and possibly artisans. These class divisions have been important insofar as they have tended to influence a person's political ideology, general expectations from the system, life style, habitat, and choice of political party. Thus — as will be seen below — a free professional has tended to adhere to a liberal party, a businessman to a conservative (or moderate) one, and an industrial worker to a socialist party. It should, however, be kept in mind that the class system is constantly changing, that there is no precise correlation between class membership and adherence to a specific political party, and that there has been in recent years a growing underclass of uprooted farmers and artisans and an army of foreign workers who cannot be properly categorized and whose relationship to the political system is often marginal. Moreover, distinctions between classes have been partially obscured by the redistributive impact of a highly developed system of social legislation and the progressive democratization of the educational system. Table 6.1 gives an idea of some of the changes that have taken place in the past generation.

TABLE 6.1

France: Some Changes in Thirty Years

	1946	1975
Total population (in millions)	40.5	52.6
Number of adolescents over 14 enrolled in schools (in thousands)	650	4,000
Average annual duration of full-time work (hours)	2,100	1,875
Infant mortality per 1,000 live births	84.4	13.8
Standard of living (growth of net per capita income: 1938 = 100)	87	320
Number of private cars in circulation (in thousands)	1,000	15,300
Longevity of males	61.9	69.1
Longevity of females	67.4	77.0

Based on Jean Fourastié, *Les Trente Glorieuses ou la révolution invisible* (Paris: Fayard, 1979), p. 36.

Education

Since the last century, a centralized national school system has existed, based on uniform curricula stressing national, secular, and republican values and theoretically creating opportunities of upward mobility on the basis of talent, not wealth. The Ministry of Education has controlled village elementary schools as well as major universities. In practice the system (at least until the late 1950s) only fortified existing social inequalities because most children of the working and peasant classes were not steered toward the lycées—the academic secondary schools whose diplomas were required for admission to university—and thus were condemned to perpetual lower-class status. Since the early 1960s there has been a spate of reform legislation aimed at the "comprehensivization" of schooling, at least up to the age of sixteen. Curriculum design has been handed over, in part, to local authorities; the content of education has been made more practical, more technological, and less classical-humanistic; and laws have been passed permitting university structures to become more flexible and less hierarchical and allowing students to participate in decision making. Many of the reforms have remained on paper and have not been fully implemented owing to insufficient funds and the resistance of the academic elite as well as many students. In recent years there has been a veritable explosion of university enrollments—they reached 850,000 in 1979; but the inability of many university graduates to find jobs has acted as a brake against further significant increases. A large proportion of students drop out after one or two years at a university; many others, coming from families in straitened circumstances, complain that state scholarship aid is insufficient.

The attitudes of the French toward politics have been shaped by their education and by their social condition. Scholars have suggested that the French are more critical of their regime than are Americans or Englishmen. French citizens have frequently participated in uprisings and revolutions; they have exhibited "anticivic" behavior patterns such as tax evasion, alcoholism, and draft-dodging. They have often shown contempt for law (and the police), and large segments of the lower classes in particular have been convinced that the legal-penal system favors the "established" classes. Finally, a large segment has adhered to political ideologies and political parties oriented to the *replacement* of the existing political order.

The insufficient acceptance of the existing regime—a phenomenon called "crisis of legitimacy"—has in the past been produced by, and in turn reflected in, the apparent inability of the French to create a political formula that would resolve, in a satisfactory fashion, the conflict between state and individual, centralism and localism, the executive and the legislature, or representative and "direct" democracy. Since the abolition of the Old Regime of royal absolutism there has been a dizzying succession of governments—republics, monarchies, empires, and republics again— most of them embodying drastically different conceptions of the proper division of governmental authorities (see table 6.2).

Revolutions, Regime Changes, and Legitimacy Crises

Many regimes created institutional solutions that were too extreme and therefore could not last. The Revolution of 1789 led to the abdication of

TABLE 6.2

Political Cycles and Regimes

Moderate Monarchy	*Liberalization*	*Conservative Reaction*
Constitutional monarchy of 1791	Republic of 1792	Dictatorial government of 1795
Restoration of 1815	"July Monarchy" of 1830	Second Empire of 1852
Early Third Republic (1870-79)	Later Third Republic (since 1879)	Vichy regime (1940-44)
	Fourth Republic (1946-58)	Fifth Republic (since 1958)

Based on Dorothy Pickles, *The Fifth French Republic* (3rd ed.; New York: Praeger, 1965), pp. 3-5.

King Louis XVI in 1792 and was followed by a series of experiments that, collectively, has been termed the First Republic. It was characterized by the abolition of the old provinces and the restructuring of administrative divisions; the reduction of the power of the church and the inauguration of a "rule of reason"; the proclamation of universal human rights; and the passing of power from the landed aristocracy to the bourgeoisie. It was also marked by assassinations and mass executions (the "Reign of Terror"), which were ended when order was established under Napoleon Bonaparte. At first leader of a dictatorial Consulate (1799), then President (1802) of what was still, formally, a "republic," he had himself proclaimed Emperor in 1804. Napoleon's Empire collapsed after ten years, but the Emperor left behind a great heritage of reforms: the abolition of feudal tax obligations, a body of codified laws, the notion of a merit-based professional bureaucracy—much of it trained in specialized national schools —and a system of relationships (or rather, a theory about such relationships) under which the chief executive derived his legitimacy directly from the people (through popular elections or referendums) and whose rule was unimpeded by a strong parliament, subnational government units, or other "intermediary" institutions or groups. At once heroic and popular, the "Bonapartist" approach to politics had a strong impact on segments of the French nation; much of what came to characterize Gaullism was heavily influenced by that approach.

The power of the clergy and nobility was revived in 1814 when the Bourbon monarchy was restored, but that was to be a constitutional regime patterned on the English model and guaranteeing certain individual liberties and a (limited) participation of parliament. In 1830 the Bourbon dynasty, having become arbitrary and corrupt, was in turn replaced by another rule, that of Louis Philippe of the House of Orleans. In 1848 the French rebelled once more, and inaugurated what came to be known as the Second Republic. They elected Louis Napoleon (a nephew of Napoleon I) President for a ten-year term, but he soon (in 1852) proclaimed himself Emperor. It was a "republican" empire insofar as a weak legislative chamber continued to exist and—more important—because Louis Napoleon derived his power from the people rather than from God.

The Second Empire was noted for many achievements: industrial progress, a stable currency, and the rebuilding and modernization of Paris. But popular disenchantment with what had become a dictatorial regime, boredom, and France's military defeat at the hands of the Prussians in 1870 brought it down.

The Third Republic, the regime that followed, was inaugurated in bloodshed: the Paris Commune of 1871, in which thousands of "proletarians" rebelled and were brutally suppressed by bourgeois leaders. Most of these leaders did not, in fact, want a republic. The assembly elected to

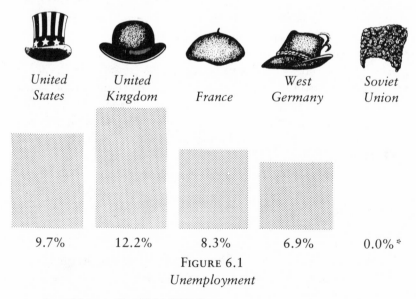

United States	United Kingdom	France	West Germany	Soviet Union
9.7%	12.2%	8.3%	6.9%	0.0% *

FIGURE 6.1
Unemployment

NOTE: Annual figure, 1982; official USSR figure.

 * While there is a manpower shortage in many areas of Soviet industrial life, there are many able-bodied and trained people who do not choose to work at jobs that the system finds politically acceptable.

make peace with the Prussians was dominated by monarchists, but the latter disagreed on which of the competing pretenders—Bourbon, Orleans, or Bonapartist—should be given the throne. Consequently, the assembly adopted a skeleton constitution that provided, on a temporary basis, for an executive and legislative branch and outlined the relationship between them. This constitution, which contained no bill of rights, was to last nearly seventy years and set the pattern for subsequent republican regimes. In the beginning, the President (elected by parliament for seven years) tried to govern while ignoring parliament, and to dissolve the Assembly, whose political composition he did not like.

In 1877, parliament rebelled and forced the President to resign. Henceforth, Presidents became figureheads, and Prime Ministers and their Cabinets were transformed into obedient tools of powerful parliaments and were replaced or reshuffled about once every eight months. This instability was viewed by many as endemic to republican systems as such, and encouraged romantic monarchists in attempts to subvert the republic. Yet this republic had many achievements to its credit, not the least of which was that it emerged victorious and intact from World War I, and might have lasted even longer had France not been invaded and occupied by the Germans in 1940.

The Fourth Republic, which was instituted two years after Liberation, essentially followed the pattern established during the Third. Although its constitution was highly detailed and democratic, and included an impressive bill of rights, it made for a system even less stable than that of the Third Republic. There were twenty governments (and seventeen Prime Ministers) in a twelve-year period; the Assembly, though theoretically supreme, could not provide effective leadership. Ambitious deputies, seeking a chance to assume ministerial office, easily managed to topple Cabinets, and a large proportion of the legislators—notably the Communists on the left and the Gaullists on the right—were not interested in the maintenance of the regime.

The Fourth Republic was not without accomplishments. It inaugurated a system of long-term capitalist planning under which France rebuilt and modernized its industrial and transport structures. It put in place an extensive network of welfare state provisions including comprehensive statutory medical insurance. It took the first steps in the direction of decolonization—relinquishing control of Indochina, Morocco, and Tunisia —and paved the way for intra-European collaboration in the context of the Coal and Steel Community and, later, the Common Market. Some of its failures — for example, its inability to institute meaningful local democracy and its foot-dragging on tax reform — were to be failures, equally, of the political system that replaced it.

It is likely that the Fourth Republic would have continued if it were not for the problem of Algeria and the convenient presence of a war hero, General Charles de Gaulle. Algeria could not be easily decolonized, or granted independence, because more than 2 million French men and women — many of them tracing their presence in that territory several generations back — considered it their home and regarded it as an integral component of France. Fourth Republic politicians lacked the will or the stature to impose a solution of the problem; the war that had broken out in the mid-1950s in Algeria threatened to spill over into mainland France and helped discredit the regime.

Under the pressure of the Algerian events (and the threat of a military coup), the Fourth Republic leadership decided, in mid-1958, to call upon de Gaulle. General de Gaulle had been a professional soldier, a member of the general staff, and, several months after the outbreak of World War II, deputy minister of war. After France capitulated in June 1940 and entrusted its fate to the aged Marshal Pétain, a hero of World War I, de Gaulle refused to accept the permanence of surrender and the legitimacy of Pétain's rule over the unoccupied southern half of France, which was becoming a puppet of Nazi Germany. Instead, de Gaulle fled to London; there he established a "government in exile" and the "Free French" forces that were joined by numerous Frenchmen who had escaped in time from the Continent. In 1944 de Gaulle became the provisional civilian leader of liberated France, presiding over a government coalition composed of Communists, Socialists, and Christian Democrats. In 1946 he retired from the political scene, having failed to prevent the ratification of the Fourth Republic constitution (a document he opposed because it granted excessive powers to parliament). In retirement de Gaulle continued to be a political force: more precisely, a force of inspiration to a political movement (the RPF, i.e., the original "Gaullists") that wanted to replace the Fourth Republic with a new regime that would be led by a strong executive.

The Fifth Republic, which was set up in 1958, provided for an institutional mixture in which the President is very powerful and the legislature is weak. The institutional relationships will be discussed below; for the moment it is useful to make some remarks about French "political culture" (i.e., political attitudes that are widely held and behavior patterns that cut across specific social classes and party ideologies).

Aspects of French Political Culture

Most French people—except for parts of the industrial working class—
share the universal ambitions of French civilization and do not seem to
consider the (often exaggerated) chauvinism of their intellectual elite to be
inconsistent with such ambitions. They take pride in France's international prestige, cultural patrimony, and intellectual accomplishments, although these may bear little relationship to objective reality, may not benefit all citizens equally, and may not compensate for the more immediate
economic needs of the underprivileged. The French have a tendency to
hero worship that has led them, on several occasions, to accept "men on
horseback": the two Napoleons, Marshal MacMahon (in the 1870s),
Marshal Pétain, and General de Gaulle. There is an equal tendency to re-
belliousness and, more specifically, to opting for leftist or revolutionary
ideologies and politicians; at the same time, such leftist thinking and
speaking may be a meaningless exercise because there is little expectation
that it will (or ought to) translate itself into leftist governmental policies.
Public opinion polls conducted from the 1950s to the 1970s have shown,
typically, that the proportion of French voters preferring Socialist party
candidates has been consistently larger than the proportion of those who
favor the nationalization of enterprises or the equalization of incomes—
both traditional components of Socialist ideology.

Frenchmen have often held their politicians in contempt, but have allowed them greater leeway than do Americans with respect to tax evasion,
collusion with business, or (personal) behavioral departures from bourgeois moral norms. The French may be sharply critical of the regime, but
they have a highly developed sense of belonging to a nation, and great expectations from the "state" in terms of what it should do for them. There
is a widely disseminated desire to enter the public service, and much prestige attached to it. The individualism and antigovernment attitudes for
which the French have been famous may occasionally be reflected in selected laisser-faire (or "neo-liberal") policies—as they were during the Presidency of Valéry Giscard d'Estaing; yet no French President can easily
abandon the tradition of state intervention in economic affairs that dates
back to the Old Regime and to which most Frenchmen have become accustomed.

7

Where Is the Power?

The President and the Government

The Fifth Republic constitution was drawn up several weeks after de Gaulle was invested as the (last) Prime Minister of the Fourth Republic. The new constitution, which was adopted by an 80 percent affirmative vote in a popular referendum (September 1958), was tailor-made for de Gaulle. It contains many features found in previous French republics: President, Prime Minister, and a parliament composed of two chambers—a National Assembly and a Senate. However, institutional relationships were rearranged so as to reflect the political ideas that the famous General and his advisers had often articulated, that is, the ideology of Gaullism.

De Gaulle and his advisers—foremost among them Michel Debré, the principal draftsman of the constitution who was to become the Fifth Republic's first Prime Minister—wanted to have a strong government. It would be capable of making decisions and conducting an assertive foreign policy without having to worry about excessive parliamentary interference or premature ouster.

The President is clearly the central feature of the Fifth Republic system. He is elected independently of parliament: the constitution had originally provided for his election by an electoral college composed of some 80,000 national, regional, and local legislators; but since the approval, by referendum, of a constitutional amendment in 1962, Presidents have been elected by popular vote for seven-year terms.

The President is invested with nearly monarchical powers, and these have been expanded even further through interpretation by three of the four incumbents of the office so far: Charles de Gaulle (1958-69); Georges Pompidou (1969-74); and Valéry Giscard d'Estaing (1974-81). According to the constitution, the President appoints the Prime Minister, who thereupon supposedly selects the rest of the Cabinet. But de Gaulle and Pompidou took an interest in many of these appointments, and Giscard decided the composition of the entire Cabinet on a rather personal basis. Indications are that the Cabinet headed by Prime Minister Pierre Mauroy — both after the presidential elections of May 1981 and after the parliamentary elections a month later — was wholly constructed on the basis of the political calculations of newly elected President François Mitterrand.

The President has certain other appointive powers: over military officers, political advisers, and some of the members of several judicial organs (on the advice, to be sure, of the Prime Minister). In addition, he retains the powers traditionally associated with chiefs of state: the appointment of ambassadors and other high civilian personnel, the receiving of foreign dignitaries, the signing of bills and the promulgation of laws and decrees, the issuing of pardons, and the right to preside over Cabinet sessions and send messages to parliament. The President cannot veto bills; however, he may ask parliament to reexamine all or part of a bill he does not like. Furthermore, the President has the right to dissolve the Assembly before the expiration of its maximum term of five years and thus to call for new elections. The only two constraints are rather mild: the requirement that he "consult" with the Prime Minister (whom he appointed) and the Speakers of the two chambers; and that the Assembly not be dissolved less than a year after its election.

In addition, the President may submit to the Constitutional Council (see below) an act of parliament or a treaty that is of doubtful constitutionality; and he may submit to a popular referendum any organic bill (i.e., one relating to the organization of public powers) or any treaty requiring ratification. The constitution stipulates that he may resort to a referendum only on the proposal of the government (while parliament is in session) or following a joint motion by the two parliamentary chambers; but President de Gaulle ignored this stipulation when he called for a referendum in 1962. Since the establishment of the Fifth Republic there have been five referenda: in January 1961, on self-determination for Algeria; in April 1962, to approve the Evian agreement on independence for Algeria; in October 1962, on the method of electing the President; in April 1969, on the reform of the Senate; in April 1972, to approve Britain's entry into the Common Market.

It is the President who "directs" the nation's diplomacy. He negotiates and signs (or "ratifies") treaties, and he must be kept informed of the progress of all international negotiations conducted in the name of France.

One of the most interesting—and awesome—provisions relating to presidential power is Article 16, which reads (in part) as follows:

> When the institutions of the Republic, the independence of the nation, the integrity of its territory or the fulfillment of its international commitments are threatened in a grave and immediate manner and when the regular functioning of the constitutional governmental authorities is interrupted, the president of the Republic shall take the measures commanded by these circumstances, after official consultation with the prime minister, the presidents of the assemblies and the Constitutional Council.

Such emergency powers, which can be found in a number of Western democracies, are intended for use during civil wars, general strikes, and similar public disorders that presumably cannot be dealt with through normal, and often time-consuming, parliamentary deliberative processes. De Gaulle invoked the provision once, during an abortive plot organized in 1961 by generals who opposed his Algerian policy. Although Article 16 is not likely to be used again in the near future, and though there is a stipulation that parliament must be in session during the exercise of this emergency power, its very existence has been a source of disquiet to many who fear that a future President might use it for dictatorial purposes. There are others who view Article 16 more liberally, i.e., one of the weapons of the President in his role as constitutional watchdog, mediator, and "arbiter."

The constitution makes a clear distinction in its wording between the chief of state and the government. Thus it is the Prime Minister, not the President, who "directs the action of the government," who "insures the execution of the laws," who "exercises regulatory powers," and who "proposes constitutional amendments to the president." There is, unfortunately, some doubt whether the Prime Minister and the government can be functionally separated from any President who wishes to be more than a figurehead. Indeed, the constitutional text is not without ambiguity. Thus, while one article provides that the Prime Minister is in charge of national defense, another makes the President commander-in-chief of the armed forces; similarly, the Prime Minister's power to "determine the policy of the nation" may conflict with, and be subordinated to, the President's responsibility for "guaranteeing national independence."

In fact, Prime Ministers have had little independence and little discretion vis-à-vis the President in all areas in which the latter has taken a personal interest. Furthermore, the Prime Minister may be dismissed not only by parliament but also (though the constitution does not stipulate this) by the President. Thus far, six of the seven Prime Ministers who preceded the incumbent were replaced while still enjoying the confidence of the Assembly. Prime Ministers have come and gone for a variety of reasons. Their appointment does not need to be officially approved by parliament; they do not, in principle, have to reflect the party composition of the Assembly; and they do not, in fact, have to belong to any party at all.

Michel Debré (1958-62) had been a loyal Gaullist even during the Fourth Republic; but he was eventually replaced by Pompidou (1962-68), who had been a lycee professor and banker (and not a party politician) but had once worked intimately with the General and had been the leader of his presidential staff. Pompidou was in turn replaced by Maurice Couve de Murville (1968-69), a professional diplomat, because blame for the mishandling of problems that had given rise to the mass rebellions of May-June 1968 had to be deflected from the President. Jacques Chaban-Delmas (1969-72), a former Radical-Socialist and hero of the wartime Resistance, was chosen by Pompidou on the election of the latter to the Presidency because of the President's desire to cultivate a more progressive image and thus entice centrist parties to join the government majority forces in parliament. Subsequently, Chaban-Delmas was ousted in part because his popularity threatened to eclipse the President's own, and he was replaced by Pierre Messmer, a Gaullist (1972-74). Jacques Chirac (1974-76) was chosen Prime Minister of the first government under Giscard's Presidency, as a reward for having bolted the Gaullist party — temporarily, as it turned out — and having supported Giscard's presidential candidacy; but he was later (1976) replaced by Raymond Barre (a "nonpolitical" professor of economics) because of disagreements over economic policy. Pierre Mauroy, the first Socialist Prime Minister since the establishment of the Fifth Republic, was chosen by Mitterrand (in May 1981) because of his nearly ideal background: originating in a working-class family, and trained as a teacher, he served as the mayor of a large industrial city. He had been prominent in the old Socialist party of the Fourth Republic, managed to get along well with the leaders of the party factions, and was seen as a moderate.

Cabinet stability has been much greater under the Fifth Republic than under the Fourth — with only eight Prime Ministers in a twenty-three-year period (1958-81). But there have been sixteen important Cabinet reshuffles during that time. Such "rearrangements" have been made for a variety of reasons: deaths, voluntary resignations, or changes in domestic or foreign policy orientations.

The President, in selecting members of his government, is not required to allocate ministerial posts according to the political composition of parliament. Indeed, all three predecessors of the present chief of state appointed a fairly substantial number of "nonpolitical" technicians as ministers. Nevertheless, Presidents have found it advisable to pay some heed to postelection changes in the relative strengths of parties within the Assembly so as not to jeopardize the deputies' support for governmental legislative proposals (see table 7.1).

The constitution provides that the chief of state preside over Cabinet sessions. Similar provisions had existed in previous regimes, but (especially in the Third and Fourth republics) had meant little, since *working* sessions of the Cabinet were in effect led by the Prime Minister. In the Fifth Republic, the President not only determines the size of the Cabinet (which has ranged from 24 to 44 "full" and "junior" ministers) but also leads almost all Cabinet meetings and determines their agenda. That does not mean that the Prime Minister's role is negligible: most Prime Ministers have been political personalities in their own right and have accepted the prime ministership for reasons of ambition, primarily viewing their position as a steppingstone to the Presidency. The Prime Ministers' leadership of the government has meant that they have presided over some interministerial committees, counseled the President on policy, and promoted and defended legislation in parliament. Such an association between President and Prime Minister is far from constituting a policy-making partnership; in fact, all Presidents thus far have clearly rejected the notion that there is a "bicephalous" or "dyarchical" executive, and have affirmed presidential supremacy.

The Parliament

In terms of its bicameral structure and internal organization, the Fifth Republic's legislature bears a clear resemblance to that of earlier republics. The National Assembly is composed of 491 deputies — 474 from metropolitan France and 17 from overseas departments and territories. They are elected for a five-year term by direct popular vote on a single-member constituency basis. Members of the Senate are chosen for nine-year terms by an electoral college composed of National Assembly deputies, department councillors, and delegates of municipal councils. One-third of the membership is renewed every three years. In 1979 the Senate contained 295

TABLE 7.1
Political Composition of Selected Fifth Republic Cabinets

President:	de Gaulle				Pompidou		Giscard d'Estaing			Mitterrand	
Prime Minister:	Debré	Pompidou	Pompidou	Couve de Murville	Chaban-Delmas	Messmer	Chirac	Barre	Barre	Mauroy	Mauroy
	January 1959	April 1962	April 1967	July 1968	June 1969	July 1972	June 1974	August 1976	July 1979	May 1981	June 1981
Political party:											
Gaullists	6	9	21	26	29	22	12	9	12	—	—
Republicans	—	3	3	4	7	5	8	10	11[g]	—	—
Centrists	3[a]	5[a]	—	—	3[b]	3[b]	2	2[c]	4[c]	—	—
Radicals	1	1	—	—	—	—	6[d]	5	1[h]	—	—
Left Radicals	—	—	—	—	—	—	—	—	—	3	2
Socialists	—	—	—	—	—	—	—	—	—	39	37
Communists	—	—	—	—	—	—	—	—	—	—	4
Miscellaneous	7[e]	—	—	—	—	—	—	—	3[i]	1[j]	1[j]
Nonparty	10	11	5	1	—	—	8	10[f]	10[f]	—	—
Totals include Prime Minister	27	29	29	31	39	30	36	36	41	43	44

LEGEND:
a MRP
b Center for Democracy and Progress (CDP)
c Center of Social Democrats (CDS)
d Reformers
e Includes 5 Independents
f Collectively designated as "presidential majority"
g Known until 1977 as Independent Republicans
h "Democratic Left"
i Includes one "Social-Democrat," one member of CNIP, and the Prime Minister, attached to the UDF
j Movement of Democrats, an ex-Gaullist group supporting Mitterrand in the presidential elections of 1981

members and in 1981, 305. This number is to be increased to 316 by 1983. Theoretically, both chambers have equal powers, with the following exceptions: budget bills must always be submitted to the Assembly first, and only the Assembly may oust the government on a vote of censure (see below).

The organization of parliament follows traditional patterns. Each chamber is chaired by a president (Speaker)—elected in the Assembly for five years, and in the Senate for three—who is assisted by vice-presidents (or Deputy Speakers): six in the Assembly and four in the Senate, reflecting roughly the number of major party groupings in each chamber. These officers collectively constitute the "conference of presidents" that determines, in a formal sense, the allocation of committee seats and the organization of parliamentary debates.

While in the Fourth Republic 14 deputies sufficed for a parliamentary group, the required number under the Fifth Republic is 30. This change has the effect of forcing small contingents of deputies to align (*s'apparenter*) with larger ones, thus contributing to a reduction of parties in the legislature.

The decision-making role of parliament is limited, particularly in comparison with earlier French republics and with other Western European democracies. The maximum duration of ordinary sessions of parliament is five and a half months per year: 80 days in the fall (from October 2) and 90 days in the spring (from April 2). Special sessions may be convened at the request of the Prime Minister or a majority of the deputies, but such sessions must have a clearly defined agenda and cannot last longer than 12 days. There have been few such special sessions—the most recent were convoked in the summer of 1979 to examine the problem of unemployment and in early 1980 to deal with agricultural policy.

The areas in which parliament may pass legislation are clearly enumerated in the constitution (Article 34). They include, notably, budget and tax matters; civil liberties; penal and personal-status laws; the organization of judicial bodies; education; social security; the jurisdiction of local communities; the establishment of public institutions, including nationalized industries; and rules governing elections (where not spelled out in the constitutional text). Matters not stipulated fall in the domain of ordinances, decrees, or regulations, which are promulgated by the government directly. The distinction between "laws" and "decrees" is not a clear-cut one. In some areas—for example, local government, education, or labor and social policy—the parliament often does little more than establish "general principles" and leaves it to the government to fill in the details by decree. In addition, the parliament may be asked (under Article 38) to delegate to the government the power to make decrees in areas normally under parliamentary jurisdiction—a procedure resorted to on several occasions under de Gaulle's Presidency.

As is the custom in all parliamentary democracies, a distinction is made between a government bill (*projet de loi*) and a private member's bill (*proposition de loi*). The former has priority; in fact, since the founding of the Fifth Republic less than 15 percent of all bills passed by parliament originated with private members (or "backbenchers"), and most of these passed because the government raised no objections or because it encouraged such bills. Finance bills can be introduced only by the government, and backbenchers' amendments to such bills are permissible only if these

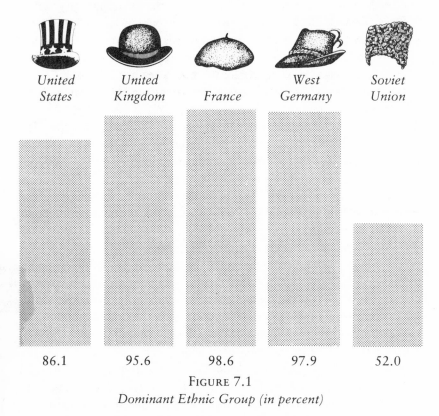

United States	United Kingdom	France	West Germany	Soviet Union
86.1	95.6	98.6	97.9	52.0

FIGURE 7.1

Dominant Ethnic Group (in percent)

NOTE: In the United States, white; United Kingdom, white; France, non-foreign; Germany, non-foreign; USSR, Great Russian.

do not reduce revenues or increase expenditures. Furthermore, if parliament fails to vote on (in practice, to approve) a budget bill within a period of seventy days after submission, the government may enact the budget by decree.

The government has a deciding voice on what bills are to be discussed and how much time shall be allocated to debate on parts of a bill. It can also make amendments to a bill virtually impossible by resorting to the "blocked-vote" procedure (i.e., requesting that the text of the bill as a whole be voted on). Thus far, this procedure has been used well over 130 times in the Assembly, with more than 90 percent of such bills passing. In the Senate, about a third of the bills introduced in the blocked-vote fashion have been rejected.

Enactment of a bill requires passage in the Assembly and the Senate. Should there be disagreement between the two chambers, a variety of procedures may be used. The bill in question may be shuttled back and forth between the chambers until a common text is agreed upon, the government may call for the appointment of a conference committee, or the government may ask each chamber for a "second reading." If disagreement persists, the Assembly may be asked to pronounce itself definitively by simple majority vote.

Constitutional amendments are subject to a special procedure. The initiative belongs both to the President (after he consults with the Prime Minister) and to parliament. An amendment bill, having passed in both chambers in identical form, is then submitted to the people for ratification. However, a referendum may be avoided if the amendment is ratified by parliament in joint session—convoked for this purpose by the President—by a three-fifths majority.

Although the constitution grants the legislature jurisdiction in areas broad enough to embrace, in principle, the most important domestic policy matters, the Fifth Republic parliament is in a poor position to exercise this power. In the Fourth Republic, more than two dozen Assembly standing committees contributed much legislative input. These committees, because of the expertise of their members, became quasi-independent centers of power. Though they produced high-quality legislative proposals, they sometimes offered "counterproposals" to government bills, designed to embarrass the government and bring it down. In contrast, in the Fifth Republic only six standing committees are provided for; they consist of 61 to 121 deputies each and do their work within carefully limited time periods and are forbidden to produce "counter bills."

In theory, the parliament can do much more than just register and ratify what has been proposed to it by the government. To begin with, there are the weekly question periods, during which questions (in written or oral form) are addressed to individual ministers. Answers to questions are not immediately forthcoming, and they may be provided by a minister or by a person deputized by him, such as a higher civil servant. Such question-and-answer sessions may be followed by a debate of very limited duration or no debate. Furthermore, they may not be followed by a vote of censure, which would cause the resignation of the government.

Motions of censure must be introduced separately in the Assembly. They require the signatures of at least one-tenth of all the deputies — who may co-sponsor only one such motion during each parliament — and can be voted on only after a "cooling-off" period of forty-eight hours; and the motion carries only if an absolute majority of the entire membership of the Assembly supports the censure. The government may also "dare" or provoke the Assembly into a motion of censure, simply by making a specific bill or a general policy declaration a matter of confidence. If no successful censure motion is forthcoming, the bill in question is considered to have passed — and the government, of course, remains in place. In twenty-three years, more than thirty motions of censure have been introduced, but only one (in October 1962) obtained the requisite majority vote. In this particular instance, President de Gaulle was required to accept the parliamentary dismissal of his Prime Minister (then Pompidou). But de Gaulle nullified the effect of the no-confidence vote by dissolving parliament and, after the new elections, simply reappointing Pompidou to head a "new" government.

Another weapon that can be used by parliament against the executive is the Constitutional Council. This body consists of nine members — one-third each chosen by the President, the Speaker of the Assembly, and the Speaker of the Senate — appointed for nine-year terms (with a one-third renewal every three years). Its function was originally viewed as largely consultative: it must be consulted on the constitutionality of an organic bill before it becomes law, and of treaties before they are considered as "ratified." It also pronounces on the legality of parliamentary regulations and the propriety of referendum procedures; it watches over presidential elections and confirms the results; and it is, of course, consulted when the President invokes the emergency clause (Article 16) of the constitution. In addition, any bills may, before they become law, be submitted for a judgment by the President, the Prime Minister, the Speaker of either chamber, and (since a constitutional amendment of October 1974) by sixty deputies or sixty senators.

Under the Fourth Republic, deputies were often too willing to unseat a government in the hope that there would be a portfolio for them in a succeeding Cabinet; and if they should in turn be ousted from the Cabinet, they would still retain their parliamentary seats. But the Fifth Republic constitution purposely changed all that. Under Article 23, a position in the Cabinet is "incompatible" with simultaneous occupancy of a seat in parliament. Consequently, any deputy (or senator) who ascends to the Cabinet must resign his parliamentary seat — which is immediately filled, without special election, by his "alternate" (*suppléant*), whose name was listed on the ballot alongside that of the deputy during the preceding Assembly elections. (If the alternate, too, resigns, there must be a by-election.)

The spirit of the incompatibility clause has been violated repeatedly. Cabinet ministers have run for parliamentary seats they do not intend to occupy; Presidents have encouraged that practice because in this way popular support for the government can be tested; and constituents have voted for such candidates because it is much better, for securing "pork-barrel" appropriations, for local voters to have their representative sit in Cabinet rather than parliament. Furthermore, deputies may be appointed by the government for special tasks (as *chargés de mission*); they are allowed to retain their parliamentary seats if the appointment is for less than six months.

The incompatibility rule has not affected what has been called the "accumulation of mandates"; most deputies are, concurrently, members of regional, departmental, and municipal councils as well as mayors, and a sizable number have been serving as members of the European parliament. All these activities have cut deeply into the time available to the deputy (or senator) to devote himself to his parliamentary work, let alone oppose his government.

Such limitations on the power of the deputy have not served to improve his or her public image or, indeed, self-image. Still, there is no proof that individual legislators in France are substantially less powerful or less rewarded than their counterparts in Britain. In 1979 the gross annual salary of deputies was about $55,000 (roughly corresponding to that of higher civil servants and senior university professors), a sum that included base pay plus rental and other allowances. In addition, the typical deputy received about $16,000 a year for an administrative assistant, as well as travel allowances and tax concessions.

For many deputies, such compensation is insufficient to cover the cost of maintaining two apartments and traveling to and from their constituencies. Hence they may be forced to pursue as best they can their "normal" professions.

Most deputies are not rich; in fact, in terms of social background, age, and occupation they are reasonably representative of the population. Statistics reveal that the Assembly elected in 1978 included 27 graduates of the prestigious National School of Administration (ENA) and—at the opposite end of the spectrum—30 workers (among them 27 Communists). In terms of age, the Assembly was "average": 90 deputies were 40 years old or less, and 91 deputies were over 60. Only in terms of sex was there a noticeable imbalance: 18 of the 491 deputies (i.e., under 4 percent) were women. As for the composition of the Assembly elected in 1981, preliminary indications are that the number of farmers has been cut in half, the number of industrialists and shopkeepers drastically reduced, and the number of women doubled. A reflection of the predominance of Socialists in the new Assembly is the enlarged presence of government officials: 261, or 53 percent, of the 491 deputies (as compared to 40 percent in the Assembly elected in 1978, and 31.5 percent in 1973). One subcategory of "government officials" is particularly noteworthy—that of professional educators (see table 7.2 on page 106). Incidentally, 82 of the deputies are mayors (71 of them Socialists).

The Administrative State

One of the features of the French polity that has been subjected to relatively little change and that is not likely to alter drastically in the near future is the administrative system. Since the time of the Old Regime and Napoleon, it has been highly centralized; the various echelons below the national government—departments, districts (*arrondissements*), and communes—have remained administrative rather than decision-making entities, whose responsibilities can be defined, expanded, or contracted at will by the national government.

At the pinnacle of the system is the permanent civil service. Defined in its broadest sense, it is the corpus of about 3 million government employees and constitutes about 15 percent of France's total labor force. In addition to the ordinary national civil servants, it includes military officers; teachers from the public elementary schools through the university; em-

TABLE 7.2

Professional Background of Deputies Elected in 1981

Profession	Socialists	Communists	Gaullists	Giscardists	Unaffiliated	Total
Farmers	1	3	2	4	—	10
Employers, shopkeepers, artisans, business managers	1	—	9	2	—	12
Physicians	19	1	6	5	—	31
Veterinarians	1	—	2	2	1	6
Lawyers	15	—	4	6	—	25
Self-employed workers (e.g., insurance agents)	3	—	2	—	—	5
National government officials	30	1	19	13	3	66
Elementary education	19	6	1	—	1	27
Secondary education	77	7	2	2	4	92
Higher education	41	—	3	4	—	48
Local officials	3	1	1	—	—	5
Officials and employees of nationalized enterprises	14	5	3	—	—	22
Private sector: Workers	4	13	—	—	—	17
Other employees	28	4	17	13	1	63
Journalists	7	2	3	1	—	13

SOURCE: Based on "Les élections législatives de juin 1981," Le Monde: Dossiers et Documents, June 1981; and Le Monde, 8 August 1981, p. 6.

ployees of local bodies; and the staff employed by the railroads, civil aviation, electric power companies, and other nationalized sectors.

The civil service proper numbers about one million. It is subdivided into a number of categories ranging from the lowly custodial and manual workers to high administrative functionaries who are directly responsible to Cabinet ministers. The civil service is functionally divided into "sectoral" categories; the most prestigious of these are the General Inspectorate of Finances, the Court of Accounts, the Foreign Ministry, and the Council of State (the pinnacle of the national administrative court system) — collectively labeled the *grand corps:* they are the chief agents of the government on departmental and regional levels and are under the authority of the minister of the interior.

Since the time of Napoleon, recruitment to the higher civil service has been tied to the educational system. A variety of national schools, the likes of which are not found in other countries, train specialized civil servants. These schools, the *grandes écoles,* are maintained alongside the regular universities and have highly competitive entry and graduation requirements. The best known are the *Ecole Polytechnique,* for training civil engineers, and the *Ecole Nationale d'Administration* (ENA). The latter school, which opened its doors only in 1946, has trained the majority of higher administrative personnel for the grand and prefectoral corps. It numbers among its graduates many Cabinet ministers, as well as a President of the Republic (Giscard).

For many years, the French have criticized the important position of the higher civil service. They have argued that while it makes for stability, it has undermined democracy. This criticism has been based on the upper- and upper-middle-class origins of most of the higher functionaries, on the fact that they are subject to neither popular elections nor adequate controls, and that they have tended to serve not the citizen but an abstraction called "the state."

Nevertheless, the higher civil service has not been monolithic or dictatorial, nor has it been immune to internal conflicts and external pressures. Although the ENA has recruited only a minuscule portion of its student body from the working class and the peasantry, its graduates — the *Enarques* — have been as likely to be identified as progressives, or even leftists, as conservatives or reactionaries. There is sometimes a conflict between those civil servants who work for the ministries of finance and industry, who often have close personal and ideological ties with big-business managers, and those who work in the ministries of health and education, who tend to have affinities with their clientele and therefore to have a "social-reform" outlook. There is also a certain tension between the traditional bureaucrats who serve in the standard ministries and have a legalistic orientation and the technocrats who have been trained in economics, statistics, and management methods and are found in the National Economic Planning Commission.

Public Corporations

A component of the administrative system that is difficult to categorize, yet is of great importance, is the nationalized sector. In France, about 15 percent of the economy is in government hands: mass transport; gas; electricity; nuclear energy; postal service; civil aviation; the manufacture of cigarettes and matches; broadcasting; most of fuel distribution; and a large proportion of the insurance, banking, and automobile manufacturing sectors. The reasons behind nationalization need not detain us here — the influence of socialist ideology, the limits of the private capital market, the monopolistic nature of certain enterprises, and so on. Suffice it to say that the state's involvement in the management of economic matters has resulted in special administrative approaches to recruitment, classification, and political control. Sometimes positions of responsibility in nationalized enterprises are given to individuals coopted from the private sector or handed over as political "plums" to politicians who have proved their loyalty to the President. Because of the complexity of the management problems, nationalized enterprises are difficult to subject to parliamentary surveillance; at the same time, their very existence can be a useful weapon in the hands of a government interested in long-term economic planning, or at least in influencing the behavior of the private economic sector in its production and pricing policies.

Control and Redress

One of the institutions that has played a significant role as a watchdog over administrative activities is the Council of State (*Conseil d'Etat*). Originally created by Napoleon (in 1799) for resolving intrabureaucratic disputes, it has gradually assumed additional functions. It advises the government on the language of draft bills; it passes on the legality of decrees and regulations issuing from the executive; and most important, it acts as a court of appeal for suits brought by citizens against the administration. Such suits, involving charges of bureaucratic arbitrariness, illegalities, or abuse of power, are initiated in department (prefectoral) administrative tribunals. Unfortunately, several years may elapse before such cases are dealt with by the Council of State.

A recent innovation is the "mediator," the French equivalent of the ombudsman, or citizens' "complaint" commissioner. This official, appointed by the President for a six-year term on the recommendation of parliament, may take upon himself the examination of a variety of complaints: for example, involving social security agencies, prisons, nationalized industries, and administrative and judicial malfunctions. He may request from any public agency information he considers pertinent, initiate judicial proceedings against misbehaving bureaucrats, and suggest improvements in the laws to the government. Recourse to the mediator (which is free of charge) cannot be direct; it must be done via a deputy or senator.

Subnational Government and Administration

The extent to which national decisions can be, or should be, influenced or deflected on local levels has been a matter of debate in France for the past decade. There has been some question whether the existing subdivisions are of the proper size, whether they are adequately financed, and whether they provide a meaningful arena for the political participation of citizens.

Metropolitan France consists of 96 *départements,* which are the basic subnational administrative units into which the country was divided during the Revolution of 1789. Each department is both self-administering *and* an administrative subunit of the national government. Whatever autonomy the department possesses is reflected by its elected General Council, which votes a budget; decides on local taxes and loans; and passes laws on housing, roads, welfare services, cultural programs, educational services (supplementary to those made mandatory by the national government), and so on. The General Council also elects a president, or chairman. The latter, however, is not properly speaking the executive officer of the department. That role is filled by the prefect, an agent of the *national* government who administers the department in behalf of the ministry of the interior and other national ministries. Thus the prefect (together with the mayor of a town) may be involved in the maintenance of public order; but the (local) police is seen as an instrument of national administration and, as such, is under the authority of the minister of the interior in Paris.

The prefect is assisted by a cabinet composed of specialists in public works, agriculture, housing, and other services. On the next lower level, that of the *arrondissement,* the prefect is assisted by a subprefect. The *arrondissements,* of which there are 324, are the basic (single-member) constituencies for parliamentary elections. (Some heavily populated *arrondissements* are subdivided into two or more constituencies.) A further subdivision is the canton, which contains a number of services such as a unit of the national gendarmerie, tax offices, and highway agents. The canton serves also as a constituency for the election of General Councils.

The lowest, but most significant, administrative unit is the commune. Communes, of which there are more than 36,000, may range in size from villages of fewer than 100 inhabitants to the national capital. Some communes have become too small to maintain services realistically; these have either been administratively merged with neighboring communes or compelled to associate with them functionally: under provisions put into effect in the early 1970s, certain services may be performed jointly by several communes, such as water supply and fire protection. Conversely, some communes are so large that special regimes have been invented for them. For instance, Paris and Lyon are themselves subdivided into *arrondissements.*

Paris has always represented a special case. Between 1871 and 1977, Paris did not have a mayor but was ruled by two prefects directly on behalf of the national government: a prefect of the Seine (the former name of the department in which Paris is located) and a prefect of police. Each of the 20 *arrondissements* had its own mayor, whose functions were generally limited to the maintenance of civil registers, the performance of marriages, the changing of street names, and so on. Since the reinstitution of the mayor for all of Paris, the 20 district mayors have been replaced by "civil administrators." The two national prefects, however, remain in place.

The relationship between the national government and subnational units has been rendered confusing by the existence of functional units that overlap geographical boundaries. Thus the 96 departments are grouped into 22 "regions," each of which is served by a "superprefect" (in effect, the prefect of one of the component departments who coordinates the work of the others). In addition, there are 25 "academies" for the administration of educational programs from elementary through higher institutions; 16 social security regions; and six military districts. All of these have been, in the final analysis, administrative conveniences put in place by the national government, and have provided very little in the way of local decision-making authority.

There is a possibility that under President Mitterrand and the Socialist-controlled Assembly local decision-making powers may be expanded. The Socialist party platform called for the replacement of prefects by "high commissioners," who would be responsible to directly elected regional assemblies. These assemblies, as well as municipal councils, would be given greater power to collect taxes and decide on expenditures. A bill embodying these proposals (the Defferre Law) passed the parliament early in 1982, but its implementation will take some time.

At this time the major purpose of subnational units is to serve as arenas of citizen involvement in politics and the recruitment of politicians. This is particularly true of the communes: the outcome of municipal elections, which occur every three years and elect some 500,000 councilors, ultimately affects the composition of the Senate, since the councils are part of the electoral college that chooses senators. The municipal elections also enable the citizenry to express "mid-term" attitudes regarding the performance of the national government. As a result of the municipal elections of March 6 and 13, 1983, many Socialist and Communist councilors (and indirectly, mayors) were replaced by Gaullists or Giscardo-Centrist ones. The outcome could be viewed as an expression of voters' impatience with the record of the Mitterrand presidency after less than two years in office: the (possibly precipitious) nationalization of a number of industries; the continued economic recession, accompanied by an austerity program which kept wages too low; an enfeebled currency; and above all, the failure to solve the unemployment problem. If the results are interpreted as indicating the government is too unpopular, the Communists might become a less docile coalition partner, and even leave the Cabinet.

8

Who Has the Power and How Did They Get It?

France has a complex political party system, which many view as symptomatic of disorder and confusion. At any given time—especially during elections—it is possible to distinguish several dozen parties. Some of these can be traced back several generations and have been of national importance; others are of passing interest because of their ephemeral or purely local nature or weak organization; and still others are mere political clubs, composed of small clusters of intellectuals more anxious to have a forum for expressing their political ideas than to achieve power.

From the point of view of national politics, one may identify six major "ideological families" within which political parties can be arranged: Communists and Socialists, Catholics and Radicals, and Conservatives and Gaullists. These pairs may in turn be grouped, for the sake of analytic convenience, into the left, the center, and the right. Each of the "families" has tried to represent different social classes and different views regarding economic policy, executive-legislative relationships, and the role of religion in politics. Before looking at specific parties, one should be warned that their positions have not always been consistent; that the traditional ideologies often failed to be adjusted in terms of changing socioeconomic realities, including the structure of the electorate; that politicians elected under the label of one party have sometimes shifted to another; and that tactical considerations have often forced parliamentary deputies to vote on issues in such a way as to ignore their party platforms.

The Old Right

Historically, the political right was characterized by its support of the political and socioeconomic status quo. It had favored monarchism and hence had deplored the revolutions of 1789 and 1848. Inclined toward authoritarian rule, the right evolved from support of Bourbon kings to that of Napoleon and other "heroic" leaders, and still later, to a Gaullist position. It favored an elitist social structure; defined society in "organic" and hierarchical terms; had contempt for the masses—who were considered too irrational and selfish to be entrusted with political participation—and invested the "state" with an aura of sanctity. Originally, the support of the right was derived from the established classes: the aristocracy, the landed gentry, the clergy, and later, the military and big business.

The transformation of society and economy reduced the importance of the political right. By the beginning of the Fourth Republic, much of that ideological family had become discredited because many of its adherents had been collaborators of the Germans during the war, while the "respectable" right had become converted to republicanism. The main political expression of the postwar right was the National Center of Independents and Peasants (CNIP), a group of politicians sometimes also known as "moderates." It was, however, feebly represented in the Assembly, in part because it reflected two conflicting positions: a "liberal" one (i.e., a belief in laisser-faire economics) and a "conservative" one (i.e., a continued commitment to the values of elitism, religion, and family). Another reason for the weakness of the traditional right was that it had to compete with the "center" parties for voters. A third, and most important, reason was the rise of Gaullism, a political movement that drained off many of the right's old supporters, notably the authoritarian (or Bonapartist) elements.

Gaullism is a unique phenomenon. Many Frenchmen had shared General de Gaulle's dislike of the Fourth Republic. They objected to its central feature: a parliament that was, in theory, all-powerful but in practice was immobilized because it was faction-ridden. They favored a regime with a strong leader who would not be hampered by political parties and interest groups; these were considered particularistic, unnecessary, and destructive interpositions between the national leadership and the citizenry. Gaullists, above all, wanted France to reassert its global role and rediscover its grandeur. Many of their early supporters had been identified with the General as members of his Free French entourage in London or had been active in the Resistance. Others had worked with him when he headed the first provisional government after the Liberation; still others saw in him the embodiment of the "hero-savior." Gaullism can thus be described as Caesaristic and nationalist. But it never had a clear or consistent domestic policy program and, at least in the beginning, did not seem to show great interest in economic reform or social justice, and therefore failed to get significant support from the working-class electorate. Yet Gaullists would vehemently reject the label of "rightist" because, they argue, nationalism is not incompatible with social reform, and because the first Gaullist party, the *Rassemblement du Peuple Français* (RPF), established in 1947, was intended to be a movement that would appeal to all social classes. The RPF, however, was not to become a mass party until the collapse of the Fourth Republic.

The Old Left

Leftism and socialism have been particularly important in modern French political history because they have stood for progress, equality, rationalism, and democratic government. In response to the gradual democratization of the suffrage and the growing electoral importance of the working class, many parties appropriated the label "socialist." Socialist parties have been inspired by different traditions, some of them dating to the eighteenth century—utopian, revolutionary, and reformist—but these parties shared a preoccupation with the systematic explanation of social phenomena; an emphasis on the importance of the total society; and a belief that economic, political, and social structures were intimately related.

The major party of the left is the Socialist party (*Parti socialiste*). Originally formed in 1905 out of small and disparate leftist groups, and known until 1969 as the SFIO (*Section Française de l'Internationale Ouvrière*), it was inspired by revolutionary Marxism and appealed to the industrial working class. Increased parliamentary representation, participation in bourgeois governments, and the takeover of leadership positions by intellectuals and other middle-class elements caused the Socialist party to lose its revolutionary dynamism and commit itself to the idea of gradual, nonviolent reformism. The party came to attach as much value to the maintenance of democratic processes as to socioeconomic redistributive policies. In 1936 Léon Blum, the party leader, headed a government that (with the support of some of the other leftist parties) instituted far-reaching social reforms. When the party was reconstituted in the Fourth Republic, it continued to promote progressive legislation. But the Socialist party was hampered from growing by competition from the Communist party.

Established in 1920, the Communist party had taken much of the Socialists' working-class electorate from them. The two leftist parties collaborated on many bills in the legislature; but whereas the Communists wanted to bring down the Fourth Republic, the Socialists were committed to maintaining it. In 1958, most Socialists voted in favor of the investiture of de Gaulle; the Communists opposed it. In the 1960s the Socialists lost much of their membership, while the Communists were able to retain most of their hard-core adherents. Both leftist parties were consigned to an Opposition status from which they emerged only in 1981.

The Old Center

For at least a century there has been a political family that has represented the broad interests of the *petite bourgeoisie*—the shopkeepers, artisans, and certain farmers—as well as portions of the intellectual and free professional classes. It has occupied the "center" position in French politics insofar as it rejected both the elitism of the Conservatives and the loudly articulated egalitarianism of the left. It favored progress and selective social reforms but rejected collectivism. It was committed to republicanism and to a progressive democratization of political institutions, which meant, among other things, the extension of the suffrage and the increased power of parliament. The political center has always been difficult to pin down with precision, because many centrists pretended to adhere to a more fashionable "leftism" and provided themselves with misleading labels, and because the center has been fragmented. It is necessary to distinguish between two basic kinds of centrism: Catholic and Radical-Socialist.

The Radical-Socialist party is the oldest existing party in France. Officially established in 1901, its origins must be traced to the beginning of the Third Republic, and, as some would insist, to the French Revolution. The Radical-Socialist party backed a strongly centralized republic, but has been consistently led by local notables. It was "radical" in the sense that it favored—and helped achieve—the elimination of the role of the church in politics and the promotion of a secular school system. It viewed the state as the enemy, and hence argued strongly for civil rights (especially property rights). But this did not prevent the Radicals from asking the state to give protection to the part of their electorate that felt its livelihood to be threatened by economic consolidation at home and competition from abroad. Such attitudes were "leftist" enough as long as the *petite bourgeoisie* constituted the bulk of the politically underprivileged masses. With industrialization, a new class became important: factory workers. The ideology of Socialist parties—the belief in the class struggle and opposition to private property—that this new class embraced made the Radicals' leftism increasingly illusionary and pushed them into a defensive posture. Nevertheless, the tactical position of the Radical party often made it an indispensable partner in government coalitions and allowed it to play a dominant role in the Third and Fourth republics and provide both regimes with numerous Prime Ministers.

Another orientation that must be classified as centrist is that of Christian Democracy. Originally, Catholicism could not be equated easily either with republicanism or with social progress; the Popular party established toward the end of the Third Republic, which fully supported the parliamentary system, was relatively insignificant. But political Catholicism gained a new respectability during World War II; after Liberation, devout Catholics who had been active during the Resistance established the *Mouvement Républicain Populaire* (MRP), which, while communalist in orientation and clericalist, was committed to civil liberties and social reform in a republican context. In the beginning of the Fourth Republic the MRP's position was leftist enough, and its parliamentary representation strong enough, to make it a coalition partner with the Socialists and Communists. Moreover, it competed with the Radical party in its adaptability. Toward the end of the Fourth Republic the MRP was weakened for the same reason as the Radicals: some of the party's leftist adherents turned with interest to the Socialists, while its conservative ones—who were far more numerous—embraced Gaullism. In 1958 a large proportion of the MRP politicians joined the Gaullist bandwagon. (The pitiful remnant of the MRP disbanded in 1966.)

Elections and Political Parties Since the Advent of Gaullism

The return of de Gaulle to power produced a temporary eclipse of all political parties that the public mind associated with the discredited Fourth Republic. Under that republic, an electoral system based on proportional representation had made it possible for many parties to gain parliamentary seats. The "game of politics" had been such that most parties could easily turn rightward or leftward, or switch from support of the government to Opposition status. The system of Assembly elections instituted in 1958, however, forced parties to make the kind of clear choice they were often unprepared to make. The present system is based on the single-member district: a candidate for the Assembly is required to obtain an absolute majority of all votes cast in his constituency. If no candidate obtains such a majority, a second, or "runoff," ballot must be cast a week later, in which a candidate needs only a *plurality* of the votes. (Only those candidates who received at least 12.5 percent of the first-ballot votes may run on the second.) The system of presidential elections is quite similar: if an absolute majority is not obtained on the first ballot, a "faceoff" contest occurs two weeks later between the two candidates who received the largest number of first-ballot votes.

Frenchmen are fond of saying that "on the first ballot one votes, and on the second, one eliminates." Electoral realism has required that a political party, in order to maximize its chances, think in terms of combining forces with another party by means of preelectoral deals and second-ballot withdrawal, or mutual-support agreements. Such activities have produced polarizing tendencies: the reduction of the number of political parties and their rearrangement into two opposing camps, much in the manner of the United States and Great Britain (see tables 8.1 and 8.2).

The Gaullist party emerged as the major beneficiary of the new system. Relabeled as the *Union pour la Nouvelle République* (UNR, subsequently renamed as *Union Démocratique pour la République*—UDR) and obtaining a dominant position in the Assembly, it became relatively institutionalized; in many localities, Gaullist machines were established and many local notables, drawn by the magnet of power, associated with them. Most of the old centrist formations remained in the Opposition (though a large proportion of centrist *voters* had deserted to Gaullism). One of the collecting points of centrist anti-Gaullism was the Democratic Center, which included some of the old MRP politicians who distrusted or detested the General.

Both major parties of the left, the Communists and the Socialists, were reduced to impotence. The Communist party could count on the support of about 20 percent of the electorate, but could not win without allies. Clearly, the only possible ally was the Socialist party. The Socialists had, theoretically, two options: an alliance with either the Communists or the Opposition centrists. In the presidential elections of 1965, a "united left" tactic was preferred, but one that implied the cooptation of part of

TABLE 8.1. Parliamentary and Presidential Elections, 1958–81 (in percent of total votes cast)

		LEFT			CENTER		RIGHT		
Parlia-mentary	Presi-dential	Commu-nists	Social-ists	Radicals & Left-Radical	MRP	Democratic Center	Independents & Moderates	Gaullists	Others
1958 (1)		18.9	15.5	11.5	11.6		19.9	17.6	5.0
(2)		20.7	13.7	7.7	7.5		23.6	26.4	0.4
1962 (1)		21.7	12.6	7.5	8.9		4.4[f]	31.9	0.4
(2)		21.3	15.2	7.0	5.3		1.6[f]	40.5	1.3
	1965 (1)	←	32.2[a]	→		9.6		43.7	8.3
	(2)	←	45.5[a]	→		7.8		54.5	—
1967 (1)		22.5	18.8[b]	→		15.8	37.8	→	3.0
(2)		21.4	24.1[b]	→		17.9	42.6	→	1.1
1968 (1)		20.0	16.5[b]	→		10.8	43.7	→	9.5
(2)		20.1	21.3[b]	→		10.3	46.4	→	4.4
	1969 (1)	21.5	5.1			23.4[c]	43.9	→	6.1
	(2)					42.4[c]	57.6	→	—
1973 (1)		21.5	21.2	→		13.1[d]	36.4	→	7.8
(2)		20.6	25.1	→		6.1[d]	46.2	→	2.0
	1974 (1)	←	43.2[a]	→		32.6[e]		15.1	10.1
	(2)	←	49.2[a]	→		50.8[e]			—
1978 (1)		20.5	22.5	2.3[h]		23.9[g]		22.6	8.2
(2)		18.6	28.3	2.3[h]		24.8[g]		26.1	—
	1981 (1)	15.3[i]	25.8[a]	2.2[j]		28.3[e]		17.9[k]	10.3[l]
	(2)		51.8[a]			48.2[e]			
1981 (1)		16.2	37.5[m]	→		19.2[g]		20.8	6.3
(2)		6.9	49.3[m]	→		18.6[g]		22.4	2.7

LEGEND:
(1) First ballot
(2) Second ballot
→ extent of support
a Mitterrand
b Federation of Democratic and Socialist Left (FGDS)
c Alain Poher, Christian-Democratic Centrist
d "Reformers"
e Giscard d'Estaing
f Independent Republicans
g UDF and "presidential majority"
h Left Radicals (MRG)
i Georges Marchais
j Michel Crépeau, a Left Radical
k Jacques Chirac
l Including 3.9 for Brice Lalonde, the Environmentalist candidate
m Including Left Radicals

NOTE: Vertical broken lines indicate division between opposition parties and government coalition.

the center. Both major parties of the left agreed on a single presidential candidate, François Mitterrand. Mitterrand's hand in relation to the Communists had been considerably strengthened after he succeeded in establishing the Federation of the Democratic and Socialist Left (FGDS), which grouped around the Socialist party a variety of small leftist clubs as well as the Radical-Socialist party (which had begun its decline into insignificance). But after various electoral failures, and because of the continued disunity between Socialists and Communists, this alliance disintegrated, and in 1969 each of the two parties fielded its own presidential candidate.

The Socialists then decided to restructure their organization, rejuvenate their leadership, alter their platform, and project an image of dynamism. One of the ideas the Socialists were (later) to adopt was *autogestion,* a form of self-management of an industrial firm by workers. The party enrolled many members of the bourgeoisie: shopkeepers, artisans, white-collar employees, technicians, and even devout Catholics. This position of strength encouraged the Socialists to rebuild their electoral alliance with the Communists. In 1972 the two parties agreed to sign a joint platform (the "Common Program of the Left") and to support each other in subsequent national elections.

The centrists, meanwhile, remained weak. The election of Pompidou in 1969 had been the excuse for some of the Democratic Centrists, already starved for power, to join the majority; they reasoned, somewhat disingenuously, that the new President, while a Gaullist, was much more inclined to accommodate himself to centrist thinking than de Gaulle had been. Specifically, they hoped that he would support the policies most dear to them: European unification, more power for parliament, and meaningful decentralization within France. Those centrists (led by Jean Lecanuet) who were still disinclined to make peace with Gaullism embraced another option: an electoral alignment with the Radical-Socialists, known as the Reformers' Movement. The establishment of that movement marked a turning point in French politics because it implied that the Catholic-anticlerical discord had been reduced to insignificance. But the movement rested from the start on too narrow an electoral base. Moreover, the left wing of the Radical party was offended by this open collaboration with "clericalist" forces and wanted no part of the Reformers' experiment; instead, they reorganized into a distinct party, the Movement of Left Radicals (MRG), which became the third partner of the Common-Program alliance.

TABLE 8.2
Composition of the National Assembly Since 1956

Parliamentary Elections	Communists	Socialists & Allies	Radicals & Allies	MRP & Center	Conservatives, Moderates, Independents	Gaullists	Miscellaneous and Un-affiliated	Total Seats
1956	150	99	94	84	97	22	50	596
1958	10	47	40	56	129	206	64	552
1962	41	66	43	55	268[a]	—	9	482
1967	73	121[b]	—	41[c]	242[a]	—	10	487
1968	34	57[b]	—	34[c]	344[d]	—	18	487
1973	73	100[e]	34[f]	—	270[d]	—	13	490
1978	86	105[e]	10[g]	—	123[h] 9[i]	153	5	491
1981	44	286[e]	—	—	62[k]	88	11	491

LEGEND:
a Gaullists and Independent Republicans
b Socialist and Radical alliance
c Progress and Modern Democracy
d Gaullists, Independent Republicans, and progovernment Centrists
e Socialist and Left Radicals
f Reformers (Moderate Radicals and Opposition Centrists)
g Left Radicals (MRG)
h UDF and "presidential majority" (Giscardists)
i Independents and Peasants (CNIP)
j Identified only (and directly) with UDF rather than one of its components
k UDF (Republicans, CDS, and Moderate Radical-Socialists)

Bipolarization and Fragmentation

By the early 1970s the French party system appeared to have become permanently bipolarized into a right-wing majority and a left-wing opposition. But the presidential elections of May 1974, into which France was propelled by the sudden death of Pompidou, began as a three-way race. Mitterrand was again the candidate of a united left. The Gaullist party's candidate was Jacques Chaban-Delmas, whose background as a faithful adherent of the late General *and* as a former Radical-Socialist could appeal to a good portion of the (heretofore oppositionist) centrist electorate. Giscard d'Estaing's candidacy complicated the presidential race. Giscard had been a prominent politician from the beginning of the Fifth Republic, had supported de Gaulle's Presidency, and had served as minister of finance for several years while never, formally, joining any Gaullist party. He had been originally associated with the conservative CNIP, which had remained a component of the majority. But in the early 1960s he had formed his own political organization with the help of a number of other CNIP parliamentarians.

This group, the Independent Republicans, articulated a technocratic, problem-solving approach to a policy of industrial modernization and a more serious reorientation to free market economics, as distinct from the Gaullist emphasis on the directing hand of the state. Giscard had differed from the Gaullists also in taking a stronger position in favor of civil liberties and an increased role for parliament, political parties, and interest groups. Finally, he had opposed the Gaullist-sponsored referendum of 1969 for the restructuring of the Senate, and was instrumental in its defeat, and thus in bringing about the resignation of de Gaulle. In any case, Giscard's background, his youthful image — he was born in 1926 — his selective non-Gaullist policy positions, his promises of social reform, and his apparent sympathy for close intra-European collaboration — all these secured for him the support of most of the Democratic Centrists and most Radicals. They were persuaded that Giscard was essentially a centrist himself and that he would pursue policies that would be neither Gaullist nor collectivist.

Giscard's accession to the Presidency (with the support of the Gaullists on the second ballot) raised the question whether the old polarization of French politics was ending and whether France was in the process of becoming "post-Gaullist." A year before the parliamentary elections of 1978, it still appeared that bipolar confrontation would continue. The parties adhering to the Common Program of the Left pledged to support each other electorally, and so did the various components of what had come to be known as "the presidential majority": the Gaullists, the Independent Republicans (now known as the *Parti Républicain*), the Radicals, and the Democratic Center (restructured since 1976, and relabeled the *Centre des Démocrates Sociaux*—CDS).

Unfortunately, the internal cohesion in both camps was more apparent than real. Within the left, a bitter quarrel had broken out between the Communists and the Socialists over the meaning of the Common Program, particularly the extent of the nationalization of industries, the equalization of wages, and the distribution of Cabinet seats in the event of a victory of the left. The Communist party accused the Socialist party of not wanting a genuine restructuring of the economy and of merely trying to "use" the Communists in order to gain power. The Socialists, now the senior partner of the leftist alliance, in turn accused the Communists of not having "de-Stalinized" themselves sufficiently and of hoping to destroy democratic institutional patterns. In the end, the left failed, by a few percentage points, to gain a parliamentary majority, a result widely attributed to the refusal of the left-wing parties in many constituencies to support each other on the second ballot.

Within the majority there were similar problems. Upon assuming the Presidency, Giscard had, so it seemed, managed to coopt the Gaullists—who had no place else to go—by giving them a few Cabinet positions and by retaining the essentials of Gaullist foreign policy: hostility to NATO, the development of an independent nuclear strike force, and a show of independence vis-à-vis the United States. Giscard's first Prime Minister, Jacques Chirac, was a Gaullist, but he resigned in 1976 in the wake of disagreements with Giscard over economic policy issues and over the distribution of responsibilities between the President and the Prime Minister. After his resignation, Chirac became the leader of the Gaullist party—now renamed *Rassemblement du Peuple pour la République* (RPR)—as well as mayor of Paris, and he made no secret of his ambition to run for the Presidency in 1981. Giscard, who had every intention to run for a second term, still needed the support of the Gaullists, the largest party in the Assembly, but he wanted to reduce this dependence. Shortly before the 1978 elections, he encouraged the establishment of the *Union pour la Démocratie Française* (UDF), an electoral confederation of all non-Gaullist elements of the presidential majority: the Republicans, the CDS, the Radicals, and a few smaller groups. The UDF had decided to put up single first-ballot candidates in many districts, and to support Gaullist candidates only if necessary on the second ballot. One of the results of this tactic had been a realignment *within* the majority: an impressive expansion of the number of "Giscardist" deputies at the expense of the Gaullist parliamentary group.

The Elections of 1981

Early in 1981, as the presidential elections approached, the Common Program had been shelved, the unity of the left appeared to have collapsed, and the Socialist and Communist parties each ran its own presidential candidate, François Mitterrand and Georges Marchais, respectively. Before the first round of balloting in April, Marchais had been almost as critical of Mitterrand as of Giscard; but after obtaining only 15 percent of the

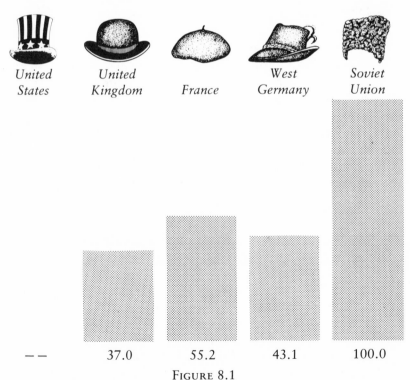

United States	United Kingdom	France	West Germany	Soviet Union
— —	37.0	55.2	43.1	100.0

FIGURE 8.1

Vote for Socialist and Communist parties (in percent)

popular vote (the lowest for the party since the end of World War II) as against over 26 percent obtained by Mitterrand, he endorsed Mitterrand on the second ballot without qualification — thereby permitting himself to claim the victory of the Socialist candidate as that of his own supporters. Similarly, the mutual-support agreement between Socialist and Communist candidates held for the second round of the parliamentary elections that followed in June in the wake of Mitterrand's election, and Socialist parliamentary candidates were the principal beneficiaries. After these elections it was clear that, while the Socialist party had emerged with an absolute majority of all Assembly seats (for the first time since 1936), the Communist party, with 44 seats, had been reduced to a marginal existence. Several reasons may be cited for this decline: the excessive Stalinism of its leadership; the deteriorated public image of its secretary general, Marchais; the party's refusal to condemn Soviet aggression in Afghanistan and elsewhere; a widespread attribution to the party of the blame for the defeat of the left in 1978; and the lack of internal democracy. In any case, the Communist party had been reduced to the status of a supplicant. In exchange for several unimportant Cabinet posts, the Communist party accepted the "conditions" imposed upon it by Mitterrand: a condemnation of Soviet actions in Afghanistan and Poland, a commitment to the Western alliance, a respect for public liberties, and adherence to a policy of transforming the economy (including selective nationalization) on the basis of gradual and democratic methods.

Within the camp of the Gaullist and centrist-conservative alliance there were far greater complications. On the first round of presidential balloting, both Giscard and Chirac were candidates, competing for the same (bourgeois and right-of-center) electorate. While continuing to be critical of each other's personalities and policy preferences, both candidates stressed the disastrous consequences for France in the event of a victory of the left. During the runoff between Giscard and Mitterrand, Chirac gave only a halfhearted endorsement of Giscard. Chirac's refusal to issue a clear call to his Gaullist supporters to vote for the incumbent was considered by the latter to have effectively "sabotaged" his reelection.

During the parliamentary elections, the erstwhile majority of Gaullists (RPR) and Giscardists (UDF) reestablished an uneasy electoral alliance known (optimistically) as the *Union pour la nouvelle majorité* (UNM), with the decision to support common first-round candidates in more than 300 constituencies, and the usual mutual-support agreements for the second round. The alliance was virtually buried by the Socialist landslide, which significantly altered the complexion of the parliament and, indeed, of the whole political system for the first time since the founding of the Fifth Republic.

There were a number of reasons for the defeat of the Gaullist-Giscardist forces. The first was the lack of unity: the incessant infighting between Giscard's friends and the "Chiraquists" had sapped the strength of both. Second, there were the growing inflation and unemployment and the widespread conviction that Giscard's policies were inadequate for dealing with these problems. Third, there were several scandals involving a number of ministers and, in fact, Giscard himself. The feeling that Giscard had been corrupted by power was exacerbated by his increasingly "monarchical" behavior: his contempt for parliament, his unsatisfactory press conferences (which, in terms of their stage-managed nature, came to resemble those of de Gaulle), the tightening of presidential control over the news media, and what many considered to be an unscrupulous use of presidential patronage—the appointment of many of Giscard's friends and relatives to important positions.

Many French voters had been uneasy over the prospect of having Giscard as President for fourteen years—a longer term than had ever been served by a President in France—and they thought that in a democracy there must be an occasional transfer of power from one group to another. But for many years the Gaullists and Giscardists had argued that a transfer of power to the left would be too dangerous, since the Socialists would be "hostages" to the Communists. Such an argument proved less convincing as the Socialist party strengthened its position vis-à-vis the Communists, and it lost most of its "scare value" after the first round of the presidential elections in which, as we have seen, the Socialists received nearly twice the support received by the Communists.

After the parliamentary elections, the now leaderless UDF was reduced to a demoralized vestige of some 60 deputies (i.e., about half of its previous strength). Some of the UDF politicians were hoping that, at some time in the future, Giscard would come out of his retirement, as de Gaulle had once done, and revive their party (and restore their own political fortunes). Several leaders of the CDS, the Christian-Democratic component of the UDF, were examining the possibility of autonomous behavior including, perhaps, a rapprochement with the new majority; the Radical party, however, had been so decimated that it seemed to have no credible options left (and not much of a future). Chirac now prepared to assume the leadership of the combined centrist-conservative (or Giscardist and

Gaullist) opposition forces. Thus Chirac appeared finally to have achieved his ambition of eclipsing Giscard—but it was a hollow victory, since the Gaullist contingent in the Assembly had itself been reduced from 153 to 83 deputies.

A note of caution is in order. The bipolarization of the party system and the now overwhelming dominance of the Socialist party apply to the Assembly but not to all other institutions in France. As table 8.3 indicates, quadripolarity (i.e., a four-party lineup) is still significant in the Senate, the General (regional) Councils, and the mayoralties of the larger cities.

TABLE 8.3

The Four Political Families in the Senate and Elsewhere, 1981

Political Party or "Family"	Senators[1]	Presidents of General Councils	Mayors of Cities with over 9,000 Inhabitants[2]
Communists	23	5	226
Socialists and Left Radicals	82	39	224
Giscardists (UDF and allies)	124	33	174
Gaullists (RPR)	41	13	70

Based on *Le Point,* 6-12 July 1981, pp. 38-39.

1. The remaining 35 senators belong to smaller conservative groups or are unaffiliated.
2. Note that this list represents fewer than 2 percent of the more than 36,000 communes. The mayors of most of the remaining small towns tend to be conservatives or centrists of one sort or another.

Interest Groups

A French citizen who becomes disillusioned with political parties, finding them confusing or doubting their effectiveness, has the opportunity to voice demands more directly through interest groups. Originally, political thinkers with "revolutionary" and centralizing perspectives were as suspicious of economic and professional associations as of political parties. Consequently, after the Revolution of 1789, organized groups were banned for nearly a century. Today, interest groups are freely organized and very numerous, and play a significant role in political life. There are groups representing, on a national level, every conceivable sector and interest: labor; business; agriculture; the free professions; teachers; and proponents of such diverse policies as laicism, Catholicism, elitism, racism, antiracism, birth control, women's rights, and environmental protection.

Interest groups in France participate in the political process in much the same way as they do in the United States. They lobby with legislators, help elect candidates to political office, engage in collective bargaining, and seek to influence the higher civil service and the leadership of political parties.

Two of the more important characteristics of French interest groups are their ideological fragmentation and their linkage to political parties. These characteristics can be clearly seen in the case of labor, which is represented by several competing organizations. The largest and oldest is the General Confederation of Labor (CGT). Essentially a federation of constituent unions (such as the automobile, chemical, and metallurgical workers' unions), it has had a revolutionary ideology, that is, the conviction that the interests of the working class can best be promoted through direct political action. In its belief in the class struggle and its opposition to the capitalist system, the CGT has shown a clear affinity to the Communist party. Many of the CGT's membership (said to number over 2 million) have in the past voted Communist, and a significant proportion of its leaders has been prominent in the Communist party hierarchy. In fact, the relationship between the CGT and the Communist party has sometimes been so close that the union has been described as the "transmission belt" of the party. The CGT has frequently engaged in strikes and other political action for the Communists' political purposes, such as opposition to NATO, to French policy in Algeria, and to German rearmament.

Another labor organization is the French Confederation of Democratic Labor (CFDT). Originally inspired by Catholicism, it split, in the mid-1960s, from the French Confederation of Christian Workers (CFTC —which continues to exist) and "deconfessionalized" itself. One of the most dynamic trade unions, it is closely related to, though not formally affiliated with, the Socialist party. An important idea of the CFDT, the promotion of self-management (*autogestion*), has been incorporated in the Socialist party program.

The Workers' Force (CGT-FO) and *Confédération Générale des Cadres* (CGC) are two other unions of some importance. The FO is an industrial workers' federation noted for its preference for union autonomy vis-à-vis political parties, for its emphasis on American-style collective bargaining, and for its staunch anticommunism. The CGC is not particularly ideological in orientation; it represents supervisory, middle-echelon technical, and other white-collar employees. This fragmentation, coupled with a relatively feeble extent of unionization—fewer than a third of French workers are unionized—has added to the predicament of organized labor. Until recently, unions had been at a disadvantage because their "patron" parties, notably the Communists and Socialists, were in the Opposition. In order to overcome their weakness, unions have learned to cooperate in practical matters. They often present common demands to employers and the government, and often join in demonstrations and strikes.

Organized business is much more unified than organized labor. The major business association is the National Council of French Employers (CNPF), the "roof" organization of more than 80 manufacturing, banking, and commercial associations that represent more than 800,000 firms. In its "lobbying" efforts, the CNPF has been fairly effective. Many of its leaders have old-school ties with the government's administrative elite; it is well-heeled financially; it provided ideas and other kinds of assistance to the Gaullist and Giscardist (notably the Republican) parties that ruled France from 1958 to 1981; and it has been an important partner of the government in the promotion of economic modernization.

Small and medium-sized manufacturing firms, shopkeepers, and artisans have their own organizations. These have lobbied separately in order to fight against economic consolidation policies that have been a threat to them, but their success has been mixed.

The greatest organizational complexity is found in agriculture, where associations reflect different kinds of farms, product specialization, ideology, and even relationships to the government. Thus there are associations of beetgrowers, wine producers, cattle raisers, young farmers, Catholic farmers, and so on. Most of these are, in turn, components of the National Federation of Farmers' Unions (FNSEA). In addition, there are separate cooperative and farm-credit associations, as well as a national organization of agricultural laborers.

Farmers' interests were in the past well represented by the centrist and conservative parties; the decline of these parties has been associated with the decline in the number of farmers and the reduced importance of agriculture in the total French economy. Still, the farmers cannot be totally neglected, if only for social reasons; and they often find a receptive ear in the government. In recent years, farmers' associations have collaborated with the government in the shaping of policies that encourage land consolidation, mechanization, the retraining of redundant farmers, and the promotion of farm exports, especially in the context of the European Common Market.

Patterns and Problems of Interest-Group Access

One of the important features of French interest-group politics is the fact that most groups have a fairly institutionalized relationship to government authorities. Several hundred advisory councils are attached to ministries; these councils, composed largely of representatives of interest groups, furnish data that may influence policy suggestions and regulations that emanate from ministries. Similar councils are attached to nationalized industries in which one finds spokesmen for consumers and trade unions. One of the most important entities is the Social and Economic Council, a body of 200 delegates of trade unions, business associations, civil servants, and other groups, which must be consulted on all pending socioeconomic legislation. There is, in addition, a network of regional economic development committees, composed in part of interest-group spokesmen, which provide input for the four-year economic plan. Similarly composed councils are attached to the highly differentiated national and regional social security organisms that administer statutory health care, unemployment insurance, pension schemes, and family subsidy programs. The implementation of pricing policies takes place with the participation of farmers' groups; the application of rules on apprenticeships involves employers' associations; and the adjudication of labor disputes takes place in specialized tribunals that include trade-union representatives. Interest-group delegates to these bodies and to regional professional, agricultural, and commercial chambers, factory councils, and similar institutions are elected by the groups' rank-and-file members without the mediation of political parties.

It is a matter of controversy whether the institutionalization of relations increases or reduces the power of groups. In the first place, not all interests are sufficiently important, or well enough organized, to benefit from reliable patterns of relationship with the government — for instance, foreign workers, ethnic minorities, domestics, and certain categories of small businessmen. Second, while a formalized network of involvement — sometimes labeled "neo-corporatism" — guarantees group access to public authorities, such access does not by itself guarantee that the viewpoint of a particular group will prevail. Furthermore, highly formalized relationships with the government may weaken the will of a group to bargain collectively or resort to more traditional means of pressure, such as strikes.

To many observers, the "events" of May-June 1968 suggested clearly that the access of interest groups to the authorities was either too underdeveloped or too insecure to influence political decisions. It is not necessary to recount the complexities of these events. Suffice it to recall that students and workers, in a rare display of unity, engaged in a massive general strike that, for two weeks, paralyzed the country and threatened to bring down the government and endanger the republic itself. These events had several causes: for the workers, dissatisfaction with de Gaulle over an economic and social policy that seemed to favor big business and permitted wages to lag woefully behind prices; for the students, disgruntlement over the failure to modernize, with sufficient speed and thoroughness, a university system whose curriculum was antiquated and not relevant to the labor market, whose physical facilities were cramped, and whose administration was (as noted earlier) too rigid. The general strike—as an example of *anomic* political behavior—achieved certain reforms that formalized interest-group relations with the government had failed to achieve: the partial democratization of university governance, enormous wage increases for workers, improved trade-union rights, and a loosening of relationships between social classes. In the process, however, General de Gaulle's leadership was discredited and his image severely tarnished.

The preceding discussion is incomplete because it has not dealt with a variety of noneconomic interests or sectors, such as women and environmentalists. France has several national women's associations. These may not be so large or so well organized as their American counterparts; still, they have succeeded in pressuring the government, since the middle and late 1960s, to foster the abolition of legal disabilities based on sex (e.g., inheritance, adoption, and property ownership rights), to legalize birth control and abortion, and to make the initiation of divorce easier for women. Environmental groups grew rapidly in the late 1960s; in fact, in the 1978 and 1981 parliamentary elections an environmentalist political party fielded its own candidates (with singular lack of success), and it had its own presidential candidate in 1981. The environmentalists' fight against the building of nuclear power reactors—a fight sometimes accompanied by violence, as in Brittany in 1980—had been unavailing under Giscard, in the face of a government determined to reduce their dependence on imported oil. But environmentalists' pressures did play a role in President Mitterrand's decision to shelve the Brittany project temporarily.

9

How Is Power Used?

The mere outline of the powers of the principal institutions—the executive, the legislature, and the civil service—as defined by the constitution and the laws cannot adequately convey how policies in France are decided and implemented. The distinction between what Frenchmen have called the "legal country" and the "real country" can be seen, first, in the tendency of Fifth Republic Presidents to interpret the constitution in such a way as to increase their power at the expense of that of the Prime Minister.

This has applied not only to Cabinet appointments, in which the President has given himself an almost free hand. Most important, it has also applied to the content of policy decisions. De Gaulle (who took little interest in economics) and Pompidou gave their Prime Ministers a great deal of discretion except, of course, in the areas of foreign and defense policy; but Giscard (a professional economist) took an active lead in almost all aspects of domestic policy, and even "meddled" in the drafting of the language of government bills.

In short, the President's domain, as distinct from that of the government, has been stretched almost at will. Under de Gaulle, presidential decisions included the blackballing of Britain's bid to enter the Common Market, the raising of the minimum wage of industrial workers, and the vetoing of an appointment to the prestigious *Académie Française;* under Pompidou, the devaluation of the franc, the lowering of value-added taxes on foodstuffs, and the modification of rules on the maximum height of buildings in Paris. Under Giscard, there were hundreds of "intrusions" in matters affecting taxes, wages, social security, and interest rates.

In promoting his policies, the President is helped by the Prime Minister and the Cabinet, and he "uses" his ministers to transform his ideas into concrete legislative proposals, to defend them in parliament, and to take the blame for them when they prove unpopular or unsuccessful. The distance the President thereby establishes in the public mind between himself and his ministers is a political convenience. To provide one example: Although the austerity policies adopted between 1976 and 1980 were largely of Giscard's inspiration, public opinion surveys showed that the President was less unpopular than Raymond Barre, his Prime Minister.

The President does not rely on the Cabinet alone. He appoints, and presides over, "restricted" committees composed of selected ministers, higher civil servants, and whatever additional personalities the President may coopt. Furthermore, there is a growing staff of presidential experts who, like the White House staff in the United States, often function as an unofficial and supplementary Cabinet.

Deputies and Decisions

In a formal sense, parliament has been weakened considerably by the constitution as well as by the legislature's own standing orders. Nevertheless, parliament is not *intrinsically* so weak as to be dismissed. Although in most cases — and certainly in all budget matters — the initiative belongs to the government, deputies have succeeded in significantly modifying government bills through amendments: for instance, on abortion, unemployment, farm credits, education, the structural reorganization of the public television network, and the reform of local fiscal administration.

Sometimes the government virtually abandons a legislative project to which it is ostensibly committed if it becomes apparent that there is insufficient support for the project among deputies belonging to the majority, as happened in 1976 with capital gains taxation. In still other cases, the government permits, or encourages, leaders of a parliamentary group belonging to the majority to introduce legislation. That is what occurred in 1980 with a Gaullist-sponsored bill on "participation" — the distribution of industrial shares to the workers in given firms. The government itself lacked enthusiasm for the policy but did not wish needlessly to antagonize the Gaullist party, whose support would be required for other matters.

If there are few evidences of an open conflict over policy between majority deputies and the government, that does not necessarily mean that deputies have resigned themselves to inaction from the start. Rather, it may indicate that the deputies have made their influence felt during the bill-drafting phase through informal "backstage" negotiation with ministers or higher civil servants. Frequently, too, a government bill reflects the pressures of interest groups. The watering down of tax bills, the softening of price controls, and the government's failure to institute genuine participation of workers in industrial decisions within firms — all these have been due largely to the successful lobbying of the National Council of French Employers. It must be understood that this is not lobbying American-style by means of appearances before legislative committees; rather, lobbying is done through frequent contacts between leaders of big business and higher civil servants. In this respect trade unions continue to be at a disadvantage, since the personal links of their leaders to the upper-echelon bureaucrats are weak. In the past, unions compensated for this weakness by threatening strikes and unrest, and succeeded in pushing the government into making periodic wage adjustments in their favor, particularly during election years. (Since the capture of control of the Assembly by the Socialists, the trade unions can look forward to fruitful access to that body.)

Parliamentarians who are unhappy with government bills have a juridical weapon at their disposal: they may try to block the passage of certain bills by resorting to the Constitutional Council. That body is not a "judicial review" organ in the sense of the American Supreme Court; it is not a court of appeals to which citizens' complaints of civil rights violations may be brought; and it has not been in the habit of nullifying laws (once passed). Its major legislative function is to examine "organic" bills (which also include the budget) *before* their parliamentary passage. In recent years, the council has widened its scope somewhat; for example, in 1971 it forced the government to withdraw a bill that would have given prefects the power to forbid or cancel public meetings. Here the council acted on the ground that the bill violated freedom of association. In 1977 the council nullified a bill that would have permitted the police, without a warrant, to search parked cars, because the bill violated a constitutional provision (Article 66) on judicial safeguards of individual liberties. In 1980 the council declared unconstitutional a bill aimed at special surveillance of foreign workers on the grounds that it violated the principle of equality before the law. Yet parliamentarians have resorted to the Constitutional Council infrequently, in part because it has continued to be heavily influenced by pro-executive considerations.

If contributions of parliament to the legislative process have amounted to relatively little, this has been in large part the fault of the deputies themselves. Parliamentarians have often lacked the expertise of the administrative professionals who draft government bills. Furthermore, the deputies' absenteeism has made it difficult for them to acquire mastery over a subject or participate in parliamentary debates with consistency. That absenteeism itself must, of course, be attributed to the "accumulation of mandates" that scatters deputies' responsibilities.

Even if such obstacles were overcome, deputies would still be unable to make their wills prevail as individuals. What about deputies as members of political parties? Under Gaullist and centrist-conservative Presidents, the deputies belonging to parties of the left lacked unity and voting strength; and the Gaullist, centrist, and conservative deputies were hesitant to confront the government in open parliamentary sessions, for they, too, were divided between enthusiastic and reluctant supporters of the government. Since the elections of 1981 the tables have been turned: the right-of-center Opposition parties are too small and fragmented to fight the executive, while the Socialist deputies can be expected on most occasions to be part of an obedient machine for endorsing presidential wishes.

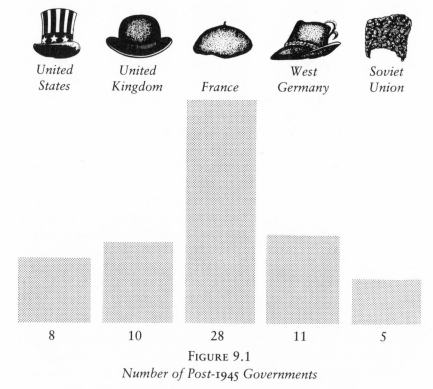

FIGURE 9.1
Number of Post-1945 Governments

NOTE: Includes changes of Prime Ministers as change in government even when no election was held; for USSR, indicates number of General Secretaries of Central Committee.

There is, first, the factor of party discipline, and second, the fact that individual majority deputies do not wish to endanger their prospects for political advancement (i.e., appointment to ministerial posts) or "pork-barrel" favors to their constituents.

Moreover, the lack of seriousness with which deputies view their own efforts—and worth—can be attributed in part to the realization that much of the work done in parliament does not necessarily have permanent value: the decisions that count are made elsewhere.

Bureaucratic Politics

In theory, civil servants do not make policy, but only do the research and prepare the groundwork for it and then implement it at various levels. But administrators have been in effect co-decision makers. During the Fourth Republic, the political executive had been subject to such frequent change, and hence had been so unstable and weak, that the permanent, professional civil service was depended on for decisional continuity and even initiative. In the Fifth Republic, the distinction between the political decision-making elite and the higher bureaucracy has been obscured by the tendency of Presidents to recruit a large proportion of the Cabinet from the administrative corps. In addition, civil servants have frequently dominated interministerial committees as well as the staffs of intimate collaborators appointed by each minister (the *cabinets ministériels*).

There are also the "study commissions" whose establishment is from time to time encouraged by the President, the Prime Minister, individual ministers, or the Commissioner of Economic Planning. These commissions (which are roughly comparable to the Royal Commissions in Britain) may include academics, managers of nationalized enterprises, and even parliamentarians; but civil servants have tended to dominate them. There have been many such commissions; for example, the Toutée Commission on wage negotiations in nationalized industries (1967); the Sudreau Commission on workers' participation in industrial management (1974); the Nora Commission on the impact of computer technology (1978); and the Giraudet Commission on the reduction of working hours (1980). The commissions' reports to the government, which reflect the input of interest-group leaders and miscellaneous experts, may be used by the government as a basis for legislative proposals; or, if the government does not agree with the reports' conclusions, they may be ignored.

Once the parliamentarians have passed a bill, it gains substance only when it is enforced. But governments (and higher civil servants) may demonstrate their reservations regarding a bill by failing to produce the necessary implementing regulations or ordinances. Thus the government has "denatured" acts of parliament by delaying, or omitting, follow-up regulations on bills dealing with educational reforms, birth control, and the financing of local government. Occasionally the administrative bureaucracy may, at the behest of a minister, produce regulations that contravene the intent of a law passed by parliament. For example, after parliament had passed a bill requiring equal treatment of immigrant workers, administrative regulations subjected them to special disabilities; similarly, an act of parliament forbidding discrimination on the basis of religion or race aimed at firms engaged in international trade was followed by a government regulation permitting discrimination. The Council of State may nullify such regulations after a legal challenge; however, litigation is selective and may take several years.

Parliament may intervene in the application of laws by setting up special investigation committees. But few committees have actually been established; the parliamentarians' timidity has been due less to government opposition to the appointment of such committees (which has slackened) than to an uncertainty whether they are of much use. One committee, appointed in the early 1970s to investigate the television and radio networks, proved to have little impact on government's management of the media.

The Delegation of Responsibility

In order to weaken the effects of long-established legislation, the executive and its administrators may resort to various forms of buck-passing. Thus, to avoid using public moneys to keep the governmentally controlled health insurance funds solvent, the funds were permitted to raise the social security contributions of the insured. Similarly, the autonomous public corporation that runs the Paris subway system contracted with private firms to obtain workers to clean the subway stations, instead of employing its own workers and having to pay them the minimum wages generally granted by legislation to public employees. Finally, although all subnational administrative activities are, theoretically, controlled or controllable by the national government, the latter has saved itself trouble and money by permitting considerable local variations in the implementation of elementary school curricula and vacation policies, public health standards, and social services for the aged.

Since the early days of the Fourth Republic, governments have been committed to a form of capitalist national planning. The four-year economic modernization plans were prepared through complex procedures involving the Cabinet (notably the Ministry of Finance), governmental statistical institutes, several hundred technocrats working in a National Planning Commission, and numerous interest-group spokesmen who were consulted regularly in the Social and Economic Council and the regional "modernization committees." This "concertation" of conflicting class interests was supposed to result in a fair plan that represented a fine balance between a "productivity" and a "social" orientation. Hence the plan was invested with a certain moral authority; it led the government and the parliament to process specific pieces of legislation that were consistent with the plan: for instance, bills on public-works investments, social welfare, wages, employment, housing, and so on. For both de Gaulle and Pompidou, the plan was an "ardent obligation"; under Giscard and his Prime Ministers, the planning institutions were retained, but planners did little more than prepare position papers and statistical forecasts, while many of their policy recommendations were ignored by the government.

There may, in fact, have been little alternative to ignoring the planners' recommendations because the projections on which they were based had increasingly acquired an air of unrealism in the face of external events (such as sudden increases in the price of oil, or the interruption of supplies of needed raw materials owing to *coups d'état*), which could not be predicted, much less controlled by the French government. Under Mitterrand national planning will undoubtedly be given new impetus with the appointment of a strong personality, Michel Rocard, as minister of planning and regional development. If the new planning conforms to recent Socialist party programs, it will be one in which as much attention will be focused on income redistribution and the provision of social goods as on growth and productivity; and in which parliament will be more active in balancing the "deals" made between administrative bureaucracy and big business.

Conflicts Within the System

It should not be inferred that governmental attitudes are monolithic. Occasionally, the national administration is hampered by internal conflicts as well as conflicts with politicians. For instance, the secretary of state for manual and immigrant workers has wanted to upgrade the condition of the unskilled labor force, largely by promoting higher wages. But the minister of finance has interfered with such a policy, in the interest of saving money both for the Treasury and for the influential business sector whose profits are maximized by cheap labor. While the minister of small business has been interested in protecting the livelihood of artisans and owners of small family firms, the Prime Minister, abetted by technocrats in the National Planning Commission, in the late 1970s promoted a policy of favoring (through subsidies and tax concessions) selected giant industrial sectors capable of competing in the international market. A conflict developed between the nationalized railroad network and the (equally nationalized) domestic airline; both of them practiced a policy of special rate reductions in order to attract customers and, thereby, capital for expansion.

Some of these conflicts are resolved in response to political (i.e., electoral) considerations rather than merely administrative ones. It is true that the Cabinet, the parliament, and other political institutions have been bureaucratized; it is also true that administrative institutions have remained politicized. Politicians serve on the boards of nationalized industries, in the *cabinets ministériels,* and in bodies involved in economic policy making. For example, the Delegation for Space Management and Regional Action (DATAR), which is concerned with regional economic expansion, is under the authority of the national government and is composed of professional bureaucrats; but it works closely, and competes with, the technocrats in the National Planning Commission as well as with the regional economic expansion committees, which include local politicians and parliamentarians. The deputy who chairs such a committee may be a trained technocrat or a former civil servant; he is at the same time (and perhaps primarily) a politician responsive to a local electorate.

The conflict between administration and politics is seen most clearly in the relationship between the mayor and the prefect. The prefect is legally responsible only to the national government; he has the power to nullify acts of a city council, to veto the budget adopted by the General (departmental) Council and even, under certain circumstances, to depose a mayor. He takes such action only rarely, for a mayor may be more powerful than a prefect, especially if the former is, simultaneously, a member of parliament or, better, a Cabinet minister. This would apply, for instance, to Jean Lecanuet, president of the UDF, former presidential candidate, ex-Cabinet minister, senator, and mayor of Rouen since 1968; or Jacques

Chaban-Delmas, former Gaullist presidential candidate, ex-Prime Minister, ex-Speaker of the Assembly, and mayor of Bordeaux since 1947. Mayors of big cities are particularly powerful because the national government cannot easily ignore their influence over a large electorate. Such mayors may bypass the prefect and have direct dealings with the finance and other ministries, and may secure funds for local industrial development projects.

Sometimes a mayor may be too political and *too* powerful to suit the taste of the national government. In 1978, Chirac, the mayor of Paris, was "punished" for his presidential ambitions and his unreliable support of the President and the Prime Minister: Chirac (probably at the President's instigation) failed to get a governmental financial supplement for the maintenance of the municipal police force—a development that forced the mayor to increase local tax assessments and threatened to reduce his popularity.

The preceding was not intended to dispel the notion that France has a hyper-presidential system. Still, the fact that the constitution has given the chief of state vast powers to make decisions and that he has added to these powers by one-sided interpretation does not mean that he always makes use of these powers. Under Giscard, for instance, the distinction between President and Prime Minister was made more obscure than before. Giscard did not, in reality, freely decide all policies. He sometimes avoided tough decisions for electoral reasons, contenting himself with making a good impression on television and otherwise "playing at being President."

A presidential decision may be "suggested" by collaborators or outsiders, may be unavoidable, or may simply be good politics. The decision to take a strong stand in farm price negotiations with the Common Market partners was not a freely chosen one, but was imposed upon Giscard by a well-organized agricultural sector. Similarly, his interest in promoting legislation to facilitate abortions was spurred by protest demonstrations. Conversely, demonstrations to protest against the building of a nuclear power station in Brittany were ignored under Giscard. At that time the President's adamant position was associated with little political risk because public opinion surveys had revealed considerable support for a nuclear construction program. Many decisions concerning wages, working conditions, and vacation policies officially promulgated by the President reflect collective agreements made between "social partners": trade unions and employers. In 1980, when negotiations over doctors' fees between medical associations and social security organisms were deadlocked the President and his ministers threatened to impose a solution, since the lack of agreement was widely interpreted as not in the public interest.

10

What Is the Future of French Politics?

Stability, Modernization, and Democracy

If institutional stability and economic progress are used as the principal criteria for judging a political system, the Fifth Republic must be considered a success. More than two decades after its inauguration, the regime has amply reflected the themes of "change within continuity" and "change without risks" articulated, respectively, by Presidents Pompidou and Giscard d'Estaing. A remarkable balance has been achieved between French traditionalism and the spirit of innovation; the old institutions have been kept, but their functional relationships have been rationalized. The executive has sufficient unity and power to make decisions, and it has used this power fairly effectively.

Political party conflicts have been simplified so that there is now a clearer distinction than in the previous republic between government and opposition. Subnational administration has been functionally adapted to respond to new realities, and local communities have been allowed to dispose of an increased budget. The voting age has been lowered to eighteen; great progress has been made in the direction of legal equality for women; and legislation regarding divorce, abortion, birth control, and the rights of illegitimate offspring has been liberalized. Institutions have been created to make the bureaucracy more accountable; prison conditions have been improved, and the rights of those detained for criminal investigation have been enlarged. Apart from occasional lapses, freedom of association, including the right of workers to organize in factories, has been made more secure. There has been continuing experimentation aimed at modernizing and democratizing the educational system and at adapting it to the requirements of the job market. Decolonization was achieved without undue bloodshed (except for Algeria) and without tearing French society apart, and the North African "repatriates" have been more or less successfully integrated. The French economy has adapted with remarkable success to the challenges of the European Common Market, and France has reached the status of the world's fifth largest industrial power and fourth largest exporter. The national and urban mass transport networks have been modernized, and are among the finest in existence. The social security system has responded fairly well to the needs of a majority. France has become a prosperous country oriented to mass consumption; its currency is relatively stable, and the living standard of its people corresponds to that of Americans. In international diplomacy, France has regained much of its earlier prestige and has constructed a privileged relationship with African and Arab countries. Its nuclear strike force has been sufficiently enlarged to convey the impression (or illusion) that France possesses the capacity to defend itself.

To be sure, some of these achievements have been based on groundwork laid during the Fourth Republic; others were emergency policy responses to the mass upheavals of May-June 1968 which involved millions of workers and students and nearly brought down the regime; and still others resulted from the dynamics of internal social changes and external economic pressures. But the Fifth Republic and its leaders have assumed most of the credit. The "legitimacy crises" that had beset earlier regimes seem to have been largely ended; the existing constitutional arrangement is now accepted by most political parties and by the bulk of public opinion.

Unresolved Institutional Problems

Nevertheless, there are institutional and policy problems that, if unresolved, might threaten the social and political order. While the present system is clearly presidential, the relationships between the President and the Prime Minister, and between the executive and parliament, are ambiguous enough to produce conflict. The President can exert his leadership best when there is no challenge to his decisions, the legitimacy of which derives from the fact that the President is the product of a democratic mandate (i.e., a popular election). The Assembly, which is also based on a democratic mandate, has so far not opposed the President effectively because of the lucky circumstance that the parliamentary majority, Gaullist, right-of-center, or Socialist, has more or less conformed to the political ideology of the four Presidents.

But what if an election produced a hostile Assembly majority, and the President still had several years left of his term of office? The new Assembly would attempt to impose its own choice of Prime Minister. If it succeeded, the Prime Minister would have a power base independent of the President; the government's policies would reflect the will of parliament, while the President's role might be reduced to that of co-decision maker or, worse, figurehead. If the President ignored the Assembly or resorted to dissolution, he would be guilty of contempt for the latest expression of popular choice; and if the newly elected Assembly were to have a majority equally hostile to the President, his prestige and authority would be impaired. Some political scientists have suggested that the problem of conflicting mandates be resolved by a reduction of the President's term of office from seven years to five. Giscard once favored such a solution, but abandoned the idea after his election to the Presidency. Before his election, Mitterrand also favored such a reform and the most recent Socialist party platform would go even further: either a five-year term renewable only once (as in the United States), or a single, nonrenewable, seven-year term. But power is often the graveyard of democratic intentions, and Mitterrand, once having gotten used to the Presidency, may not wish to undermine or limit it.

If it is true — as suggested earlier — that parliament's contributions to the legislative process have increased somewhat since Giscard, that has been less the result of an institutional upgrading than a matter of political convenience: the President's desire to share the burden for unpopular policies. Moreover, under Giscard, parliament's greater freedom of action was due to the inability of the President to control the majority within it as effectively as he would have liked. What is called the "presidential majority" is essentially an electoral majority; under de Gaulle, Pompidou, and Giscard it was invoked to elect the President and support him against challenges from the left. But it was not always a reliable "majority of action": during the Giscard Presidency, the various components of the UDF, the "Giscardist" alliance, often had conflicting legislative ideas, and the Gaullist parliamentary group, as the junior (and therefore disgruntled) constituent of the majority, went along reluctantly, if at all, with the President's legislative ideas. Under Mitterrand, a leftist "presidential majority" in parliament was sought (by dissolution) and a new election took place immediately after he had become President. The results enabled him to put into effect the policy changes expected by those who had voted for him and — incidentally — prevented a constitutional crisis.

In order to broaden the base of support for his policies, Giscard, before his election to the Presidency, had affirmed that he would be open to the ideas of the Opposition, notably the Socialists. But he did little to promote his long-promised "statute for the Opposition," under which Opposition deputies would be assured a number of committee chairmanships and a greater amount of time during legislative debates. If he followed the Socialist party platform and, indeed, his own frequently articulated positions, President Mitterrand would back legislation to enlarge the role of the Opposition in introducing bills and controlling the executive. But it is doubtful whether such measures would have much meaning in the near future, given the unimpressive parliamentary representation, the fragmentation, and the demoralization of the conservative Opposition parties — and, conversely, the size and discipline of the Socialist majority.

Political Parties and Their Persistent Weaknesses

While many Frenchmen concede that the President has too much power, it is doubtful whether they would consider political parties to be effective counterinstitutions. The French still vote massively — abstention rates in legislative and presidential elections are far lower than in the United States — but they are increasingly cynical with respect to political parties. There has been a growing "floating" vote, and electoral campaigns are often media contests revolving around personalities. Registered party memberships are lower than they were under the Fourth Republic, and the (usually exaggerated) statistics produced by individual parties concerning such membership include those who have ceased to pay dues. The weakness of political parties may be attributed to a variety of factors. Most parties are loosely structured national federations based on independent regional organizations, which in turn are often dominated by powerful local machines. Many parties are financially weak as well — a situation that has given rise to the as yet unmet demand for massive governmental subsidies. Party unity is variable: in the past it has ranged from highly disciplined voting in the Communist and to a somewhat lesser extent Socialist parties to the chronic fragmentation within the UDF.

The Socialist party has a growing membership and, in terms of its electoral appeal, has become the largest party in France. In the recent past it was beset with a fight for the leadership, and it is still riddled with factions based on ideologies, some of which correspond neither to the economic problems of the present day nor to the party's evolving electoral clientele. Despite François Mitterrand's continued commitment to the strategy of electoral unity — or at least collaboration — with the Communists (a strategy that helped to win the Presidency for him), this leader has often, with some justification, been accused of not being a genuine socialist. Early in 1980, his position as the national standard bearer for the Socialist party was challenged by Michel Rocard, a Socialist who had formerly been the leader of the *Parti Socialiste Unifié* (PSU). That party had been established in 1960 as a more "revolutionary" and more anti-Gaullist alternative to the SFIO; but, lacking a working-class electoral base, it was gradually reduced to insignificance. But Rocard's socialism, too, was suspect: in promoting his image as a prospective presidential candidate, he had come to sound more and more like a Gaullist.

With the election of its leader to the Presidency and its capture of control of the Assembly, the Socialist party has been given a new lease on life. The party's success has been due less to the intrinsic appeal of socialism than to the painstaking organizational work of Mitterrand and, equally, to disgruntlement and boredom with Giscardist and Gaullist leadership. In any case, the Socialists of France will, in the foreseeable future, be less inclined to use revolutionary rhetoric and will come to resemble the Social Democrats elsewhere in Western Europe.

The Gaullists still have a significant network of local machines, and an assertive leadership. But their main *raison d'être* and focus, the famous General, is gone; in 1974 they lost the Presidency, and now they have also lost the status of the largest party in the Assembly. Moreover, they have lost the distinctiveness of their orientation. The acceptance of the Fifth Republic's institutions is no longer a Gaullist monopoly; a part of their ultranationalistic rhetoric was long ago rejected as senseless, while some of their policies were appropriated by Giscard and his UDF and even — though more selectively — by the Socialists.

The UDF had been held together not by a common ideology but by presidential power and patronage. Now that Giscard has been replaced, the UDF's various component parties will find it difficult to resist the temptation to fragment again into grouplets of local and regional notables.

The Communist party is, in many ways, "not like other parties." It has a reliable and often devoted membership, a tight organization, a comprehensive and seemingly unambiguous ideology, and a healthy financial situation. It is the only party whose leadership contains significant elements of the working class, and it was consistently in the Opposition for over thirty years. The party is not likely to win national elections because many Frenchmen consider it—and its secretary-general, Georges Marchais—to be too closely identified with the Soviet Union. Until recently, the party's very existence, and the fact that it continued to garner a fifth of the popular vote, had cut into the power of the *democratic* left and reduced the prospects of a "right-left" alternation in national politics; but now the situation is quite different. With only about half the strength of its social democratic rival, and with no more than 15 percent support among the national electorate, the party must put the best face on an unpleasant situation; in exchange for the opportunity to participate in a government that would have solid parliamentary backing even without it, the Communist party must pretend to be constructive, pluralistic, and relatively moderate. Whether this implies a genuine conversion to "Eurocommunism" remains to be seen.

Administration and Justice: Developments and Reforms

To many of the French, especially Gaullists, the "administrative state" has been preferable to the "regime of parties" because civil servants have been viewed as more professional, less ideology-ridden, and less particularistic than party politicians. Being less influenced by electoral pressures, the administrative bureaucracy is supposed to be much better able to make long-term policy in the public interest.

It is true that most upper-echelon civil servants are highly cultivated and public-spirited; moreover, the social esteem and excellent pay they have received have made them, by and large, immune to corruption. But given their bourgeois or upper-class origins, they also tend to be elitist and paternalistic. They are often too far removed from the people, and their actions are not subjected to adequate parliamentary surveillance. The citizens' means of redress against bureaucratic misbehavior are unreliable, despite such institutions as the administrative courts and the French version of the "ombudsman."

The judicial system, too, whose essential features date to Napoleon's rule, is in need of liberalization. The network of courts is large; the appeals echelons are well distributed geographically; and most Western-type due-process criteria are accepted. Yet elements of class justice persist; preventive (pretrial) detention is often still too long, especially for suspects belonging to the working and peasant classes. Anglo-American style habeas corpus provisions are omitted in the constitution and are only gradually being introduced by means of ordinary legislation. The government's hesitancy with respect to the liberalization of the penal code can be attributed, to some extent, to continued fear (shared by large segments of the population) of disorder and violence. This fear had (until 1981) prevented the government from sponsoring legislation to abolish the death penalty; it has also explained the retention of the State Security Court, which deals with cases of sedition. This court had been established in 1963 in the wake of a series of violent acts by opponents of de Gaulle and his policies. Under Mitterrand, the State Security Court has been abolished.

In the spring of 1980, the government introduced (and the Assembly passed) a bill to reform the penal code. This bill, labeled "Security and Liberty," aimed at making the punishment for crimes of violence more

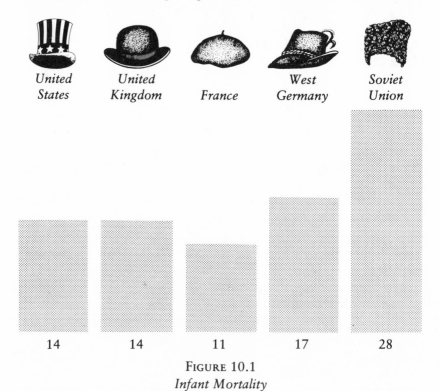

United States · United Kingdom · France · West Germany · Soviet Union

14 · 14 · 11 · 17 · 28

FIGURE 10.1
Infant Mortality

NOTE: Deaths in first year of life per 1,000 live births.

severe and at reducing the discretion of judges in the imposition of sentences. At the same time, the bill provided for a reduction of the maximum period of pretrial detention. Under the new President, the "Security and Liberty" legislation was largely rescinded, except for its liberal features.

In the past, the government has intervened in judicial matters, thus degrading political democracy. Such intervention was, on occasion, inspired by foreign policy considerations: for example, in 1977 the release, without trial, of an Arab suspected of criminal (terrorist) action in order to please the OPEC nations; and in 1980, physical interference by the (nationally controlled) Paris police in a peaceful protest demonstration in front of the Soviet embassy, in order to avoid antagonizing the Soviet Union. Given its long tradition, political interference in judicial matters may not be totally eliminated. Nevertheless, under Mitterrand one may expect a lessening of governmental constraints regarding the press and assembly and a drastic reduction in telephone buggings.

One of the most serious critiques of the government is that, after 1974, it was gradually restructured to serve the President personally—in short, that it was "Giscardized." The President appointed his political associates, his former collaborators in the Ministry of Finance, his personal friends, and even members of his and his wife's families to a variety of positions. These included directorships of ministries and nationalized industries and banks, prefectures, rectorates of academic regions, and posts of responsibility in the radio and television networks, which continued, as before, to emit one-sidedly progovernment, and therefore distorted, news programs. Before the 1981 elections, the Socialists had promised to make the media freer and more impartial. Now that Mitterrand is President, the networks will, in all likelihood, be equipped with new administrative structures that will render broadcasting more autonomous. In addition, the government has at last permitted the establishment of competing private radio stations.

In federal countries, the presidential spoils system is modified and balanced by provincial governments that may decide many of their own policies and make their own political appointments. While most French political leaders since the 1960s, including Giscard, have given lip service to "regionalization," they have done little more than invent new administrative coordinating bodies. Giscard, as President, argued that France could not afford the expense of new layers of government. In reality, he responded to the pressures of the Gaullists and many leaders of the left, whose "Jacobin" orientations predisposed them to argue that the creation of provincial governments would subvert national unity and lead to a dismantling of the French state. If the Socialist party program serves as a reliable guide, one may soon expect a more genuine effort at decentralization, beginning with the replacement of the prefect by a more regionally responsible official, and followed eventually by the devolution of significant decision-making powers to local and regional assemblies.

Since the mid-1970s, the minority cultures within France have articulated their demands for autonomy (in the case of the Bretons) or complete independence (in the case of some Corsican groups) with increasing frequency and occasional violence. But the French elite (of the right *and* the left) has tended to be intolerant toward such claims; it is convinced that a rational policy requires the dominance of a monolithic civilization, and it has, at best, recognized minorities as "folklore" groups and their speech as charming dialects in which songs may be sung. Mitterrand will probably not follow the practice of his predecessor in prosecuting for sedition the most articulate spokesmen of ethnic minorities, but it is doubtful that he will help promote genuine cultural pluralism.

The Economic Challenge: Welfare Statism and ''Neo-Liberalism''

More serious challenges have been economic in nature. Under Prime Minister Barre, the government decided to react to the petroleum crisis in a two-pronged fashion: an emphasis on nuclear energy and the adoption of "neo-liberalism."

The neo-liberal orientation had been reflected in a series of policy initiatives, known as "Barre plans," that combined austerity with an emphasis on the free market. In order to make France more competitive internationally and to encourage (or force) its industries to adopt more modern, productivity-oriented methods, the government began to abolish price controls. It reduced subsidies to the nationalized sector, which—accounting for about 15 percent of the economy—may be excessively large in comparison to other capitalist countries, and forced nationalized industries to be efficient and self-financing by raising charges to consumers. The government also helped selected large *private* industries (by means of credit and tax advantages) at the expense of smaller and more labor-intensive firms. But the government had appeared unwilling, or unable, to resolve the problem of growing unemployment that resulted from its market-oriented policies.

Another persistent problem has been income inequality, which is probably greater in France than in most other industrial democracies. It is true that the Giscard regime maintained the remarkable complex of redistributive policies inaugurated by previous governments (especially of the Fourth Republic). These included income supplements to families with several children; low- and moderate-rent housing construction; state-subsidized higher education; and (compared with the United States) generous retirement, unemployment, and medical benefits and paid vacations—financed in large part by employers. The system of semiautomatic wage increases, pegged to the cost-of-living index, was continued, and workers belonging to the lowest-income category even saw a slight increase in their purchasing power. The government also continued the policy of "participation" of workers in industry through the encouragement of stock purchasing. This policy had been inspired by Gaullists as a way of tying workers to management and weakening the impact of the class-struggle ideology. But little was done to reform the system of taxation, which remains relatively regressive and is subverted by widespread fraud. Such fraud is perhaps inevitable in a country in which there are still several hundred thousand small businessmen (including over 40,000 bakers) who are relied on to prepare their own annual income statements.

Barring unforeseen circumstances, the Socialist party platform and the pronouncements of Mitterrand and other prominent Socialist leaders suggest a certain number of policy changes that should make French society more egalitarian. The tax system will become more redistributive, with considerably higher taxes for upper-income brackets and a corresponding reduction for those with low incomes. Value-added taxes for luxury goods will be increased, while those for foodstuffs and other necessities will be reduced, if not abolished. There will be a nationalization program, but the number of firms to be nationalized will be limited, and the pace of such nationalization will be deliberate. The workweek will be reduced from the present 42 hours to 35; but this reduction will occur on a piecemeal basis, may take several years, and will probably be achieved by collective bargaining rather than government decree. Greater expenditures will be made for public investments, especially in the areas of low-cost housing, employment-creating public-works projects, social security benefits, and public—including vocational—education. The retirement age will be lowered somewhat; unemployment and retirement pension payments will be raised; and a fifth week of paid vacations, already in place in some industries, will become generalized. The minimum wage is likely to be raised to higher levels, and at a faster pace, than under the Giscard Presidency. Altogether, these economic policies will entail greater deficit spending than in the previous regime; however, price controls will not be reinstated (except perhaps selectively), and certain tax benefits will be accorded to those individuals and industries that save and invest.

In foreign policy, the Gaullist approach, which had been continued under Giscard with largely stylistic (as opposed to substantive) modifications, is not likely to be abandoned under Mitterrand. Pressures from the Gaullist party and the outlook of much of the intellectual elite had in the past predisposed France to a policy that was anti-NATO and nationalistic, and often had anti-American overtones. France's attitudes have in part been determined by fears of American economic domination and of what is referred to as "Anglo-Saxon" cultural hegemony; by doubts about the reliability of the American commitment to defend Europe in case of Soviet aggression; and, more recently, by doubts about the adequacy of American power. In order to demonstrate its freedom of action vis-à-vis the two superpowers, France has on occasion taken independent positions on Africa, the Communist bloc, and the Middle East. In effect, however, there has been a gap between aspiration to "grandeur" and the possession of real power. France's appeasement of the OPEC bloc—which is likely to be continued, though its tone may be less abject than under Pompidou and Giscard—has been determined by purely economic considerations: the desire to secure a steady supply of oil and a market for its industrial (including military) products, without which France's efforts to develop a streamlined economy would be frustrated.

Whether the Socialists' foreign and domestic policy alternatives will be radically different remains to be seen. But the mere fact that a government of the left could replace a government of the center-right after twenty-three years without cataclysmic international shocks or internal disorders is a testimony to the basic soundness of the French political system.

For Further Reading

ANDERSON, MALCOLM. *Conservative Politics in France.* London: Allen & Unwin, 1974.

ANDREWS, WILLIAM G., and HOFFMANN, STANLEY, eds. *The Fifth Republic at Twenty.* Albany, N.Y.: SUNY Press, 1980.

BERGER, SUZANNE. *Peasants Against Politics: Rural Organization in Brittany, 1911-1967.* Cambridge: Harvard University Press, 1972.

CHARLOT, JEAN. *The Gaullist Phenomenon.* New York: Praeger, 1971.

CODDING, GEORGE A., and SAFRAN, WILLIAM. *Ideology and Politics: The Socialist Party of France.* Boulder, Colo.: Westview Press, 1979.

CROZIER, MICHEL. *The Stalled Society.* New York: Viking, 1973.

FREARS, J.R. *Political Parties and Elections in the French Fifth Republic.* New York: St. Martin's, 1977.

GAULLE, CHARLES DE. *The Complete War Memoirs.* 3 vols. New York: Simon and Schuster, 1972.

GISCARD D'ESTAING, VALERY. *French Democracy.* Garden City, N.Y.: Doubleday, 1977.

HOFFMANN, STANLEY. *Decline or Renewal? France Since the 1930s.* New York: Viking, 1974.

KESSELMAN, MARK. *The Ambiguous Consensus: A Study of Local Government in France.* New York: Knopf, 1967.

KOLODZIEJ, EDWARD A. *French International Policy Under de Gaulle and Pompidou.* Ithaca: Cornell University Press, 1974.

LORD, GUY. *The French Budgetary Process.* Berkeley: University of California Press, 1973.

MITTERRAND, FRANCOIS. *The Wheat and the Chaff.* New York: Seaver Books, 1982.

PENNIMAN, HOWARD R., ed. *France at the Polls: The Presidential Election of 1974.* Washington: American Enterprise Institute, 1975.

SAFRAN, WILLIAM. *The French Polity.* New York: Longman, 1979.

SULEIMAN, EZRA. *Power and Bureaucracy in France: The Administrative Elite.* Princeton: Princeton University Press, 1974.

THOMSON, DAVID. *Democracy in France Since 1870.* 5th ed. New York: Oxford University Press, 1969.

TIERSKY, RONALD. *French Communism, 1920-1972.* New York: Columbia University Press, 1974.

VAUGHAN, MICHALINA, et al. *Social Change in France.* New York: St. Martin's, 1980.

WILLIAMS, PHILIP. *The French Parliament: Politics in the Fifth Republic.* New York: Praeger, 1968.

WILSON, FRANK L. *The French Democratic Left, 1963-1969.* Stanford: Stanford University Press, 1971.

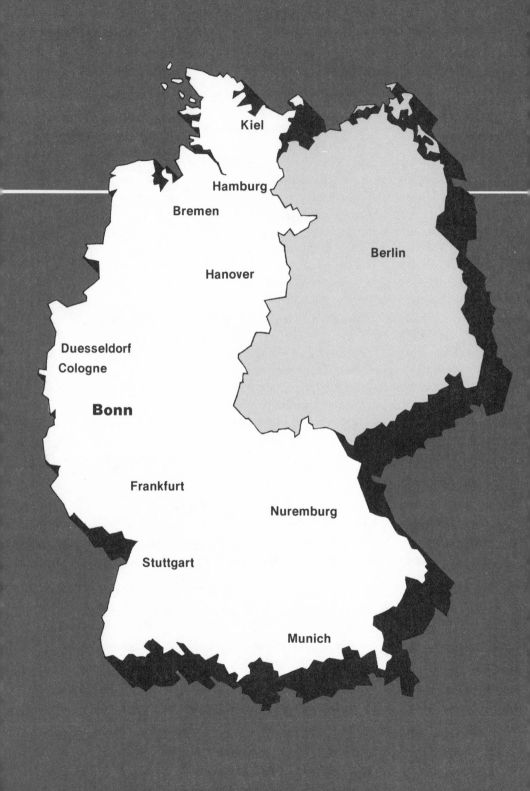

Kiel

Hamburg

Bremen

Hanover

Berlin

Duesseldorf
Cologne

Bonn

Frankfurt

Nuremburg

Stuttgart

Munich

Part Three

Germany

David P. Conradt

11

The Context of German Politics

Why study German politics? First, because Germany offers an exceptional opportunity to examine problems associated with political change and development. Few major countries have experienced such frequent and drastic changes in their political system as has Germany. In less than a century Germany has had an empire (1871-1918), a totalitarian dictatorship (1933-45), military occupation (1945-49), and since 1949 two German states: a federal republic and a communist state, the German Democratic Republic. Thus most of the major political and ideological movements in modern history can be examined through the German political experience. Second, the postwar development of West Germany illustrates the extent to which a country can largely overcome its political heritage and change its political culture. West Germany today is regarded by many as a model democracy. What social, economic, and political factors can explain this change? Finally, the Federal Republic is a very important country. It is the strongest nation in Western Europe. Together with the United States and Japan, West Germany has one of the most productive and prosperous economies in the noncommunist world. The Federal Republic is also a key ally of the United States and is assuming an increasingly important role in East-West relations.

Historical

Europe has known German-speaking people and German political units for almost a thousand years. Nevertheless, the Federal Republic of Germany, or West Germany, is one of Europe's and the world's newest states. In May 1979 it observed its thirtieth anniversary — a time span hardly comparable to that of most of its European neighbors. Although a relatively young state, the Federal Republic claims to be the legitimate successor to the Third Reich (1933-45) and the Bismarckian Second Reich (1871-1918). This claim also makes the Federal Republic the heir to the German political tradition, a tradition characterized by national division and frequent change. Before there were "Germans," Europe was populated by numerous germanic tribes: Saxons, Franks, Bavarians, Swabians, Silesians, and Thuringians, to name a few. German-speaking people are the most numerous in Central Europe, but no single German state has ever united all of Europe's ethnic Germans. The present postwar division between West Germany (the Federal Republic), East Germany (the German Democratic Republic), and the "Eastern territories," now under Polish and Russian control, is thus only one more variation on a constant theme in German and European history. The political division of the German nation has been the rule rather than the exception in European history.

The Empire (1871-1918)

Until 1871, Europe's German-speaking people were divided into many small principalities, a few moderate-sized kingdoms, and two large yet divided major powers: Austria in the southeast and Prussia in the north. The German Reich, or Empire, proclaimed in 1871, was a Prussian-dominated structure that did not include Austria. Nonetheless, it was by far the most successful unification effort in German history. This empire was largely the work of the Prussian Prime Minister and first Chancellor of the Empire, Otto von Bismarck, and was brought about through classical European power politics. Prussia, under Bismarck, fought successful wars against Denmark (1864), Austria (1866), and France (1870) to become the dominant power in northern and western Germany.

National unification did not, however, represent any success for German liberalism. Nationalism, which historically has been closely associated with liberalism in countries such as France and the United States, has been an illiberal force in the German political experience. The empire was established through the fabled "blood and iron" policies of Bismarck and not by Germany's parliamentary liberals. After 1871, they in fact deferred to the Iron Chancellor and became more national than liberal.

During the empire Germany became one of the world's great powers. Industrialization and urbanization proceeded at a very fast rate, as did the Reich's military power. Yet the industrialists and other members of the rapidly expanding middle class did not challenge the political authority of the traditional Prussian ruling elite: the military, the bureaucracy, and the landed nobility. Germany had become a modern society ruled by a premodern, traditional elite. The empire was an authoritarian political structure with some democratic features. While the Chancellor and his government were appointed by the Kaiser, a freely elected parliament held the power of appropriations and could exert some influence and control over the executive. The upper house, however, which could block most lower-house initiatives, was effectively dominated by Prussia. Elections in Prussia were still based on a voting system that gave a disproportionate influence to the upper-middle and upper classes. Military and foreign policy as well as internal security remained very much the province of the traditional Prussian elite. Parliament could not prevent, for example, Bismarck's campaigns of discrimination against Catholics and socialists.

None of Bismarck's successors could maintain the delicate foreign and domestic equilibrium that characterized the Reich from 1871 to 1890. In creating the Reich, Bismarck and the Prussians made many enemies in Europe, especially France, which lost the provinces of Alsace and Lorraine after the 1870 Franco-Prussian War. To the east Russia also feared German power. Bismarck was able to avoid a Franco-Russian alliance, but his successors were not. With a romantic nationalist, Kaiser Wilhelm, on the throne, Germany after Bismarck also sought to acquire overseas colonies and through the expansion of the fleet to challenge British naval superiority. By the turn of the century, post-Bismarckian foreign policy had managed to have Britain, France, and Russia allied against the Reich.

Internally, the paradox or contradiction of a rapidly modernizing society controlled by premodern political elites continued to produce socioeconomic and political tensions. The expanding working class provided a solid electoral base for the Social Democratic party, which, however, was unable to achieve political influence commensurate with its growing numerical strength. The middle-class parties that also grew throughout the empire were unable and probably unwilling to oppose the militarist and imperialist policies of the Kaiser and his Chancellor.

Indeed, in many cases Germany's middle-class parties deferred to the traditional Prussian elites and supported measures such as the naval arms race with Great Britain. Unlike their counterparts in Britain and France, the German middle classes did not exert a moderating influence on policy. Militant nationalism was one means by which the traditional elite could unify a divided society and maintain its power position.

The empire so carefully constructed by Bismarck did not survive World War I. As the war dragged on after the failure of the initial German offensive, the many tensions and contradictions in the socioeconomic and political structures of the empire became apparent. Socialists, liberals, and Catholics began to question a conflict that pitted Germany against countries such as Britain and the United States, whose democratic values and constitution they hoped someday to achieve in Germany. A victory on the battlefield would strengthen a regime they had opposed in peacetime.

Severe rationing caused by the Allied blockade, mounting casualty lists, and the pressures of wartime production began to take their toll on civilian morale, especially among factory workers. When the army's spring offensive in 1918 failed, the military, which in the final years of the war actually made most key economic and political decisions, advised the Kaiser to abdicate and the parliamentary leadership to proclaim a republic and negotiate a peace with the Western powers.

The Weimar Republic (1919-33)

In January 1919 Germans elected delegates to a constituent assembly that met in the city of Weimar to formulate a new constitution for the postwar republic. The delegates, many of whom were distinguished legal scholars, produced a model democratic constitution, one of the most advanced in the world. It contained an extensive catalogue of human rights and provided numerous opportunities for popular participation through referenda, petition, and the direct election of a strong President.

The republic began under unfavorable circumstances, however. Following the departure of the Kaiser, some German Marxists attempted to duplicate the Bolshevik success in Russia. Workers and soldiers councils were established in several cities, and in Bavaria a short-lived socialist republic was declared. A coalition of moderate social democrats, liberals, and conservative nationalists crushed these short-lived attempts at a communist revolution. But this attempt meant that the working class was to be divided throughout the Weimar Republic. It also established a pattern of political violence that was to continue throughout the period. In addition, the republic was identified from the beginning with defeat, national humiliation, and ineffectiveness.

The conservative nationalists, urged on by the military, propagated the myth that Germany had not really lost World War I but had been

"stabbed in the back" by the "November criminals," identified as socialists, communists, liberals, and Jews. Large segments of the bureaucracy
and the judiciary were also more attached to the authoritarian values of
the empire than to those of the republic, and they acted accordingly.

The republic's brief history was characterized by a steady polarization of politics between left and right. In the early elections of the 1920s
pro-Republican parties—Social Democrats, the Center (Catholic) party,
and the Democratic party (Liberals)—had a solid majority of seats. By the
early 1930s, the pro-Republican share of the vote had dropped from about
65 percent to only 30 percent. The Nazis on the right and the Communists
on the left together held over half of the parliamentary delegates. With
most voters supporting parties opposed to the republic, it became impossible to build a stable governing coalition. Policy making became increasingly the responsibility of the President, who made extensive use of his
power to issue executive decrees without regard to the wishes of the fragmented parliament.

The worldwide depression of 1929 dealt the republic a blow from
which it could not recover. By 1932 over a third of the work force was unemployed, and the Nazis became the largest party in the parliament. The
German public wanted an effective government that would "do something." The democratic parties and their leaders could not meet this need.

The Third Reich and World War II (1933-45)

The one party that thrived on this crisis was the Nazis—under its leader,
Adolf Hitler. The Nazis, or National Socialist German Workers party
(NSDAP), was one of many nationalist and *voelkisch* (racialist) movements that had emerged after World War I. It was Hitler's leadership ability that set it apart from the others. A powerful orator, Hitler was able to
appeal to a wide variety of voters and interests. He denounced the Ver-
sailles treaty, which had imposed harsh terms on Germany after World
War I, and the "criminals" who had signed it for Germany. To the unemployed he promised jobs in the rebuilding of the nation (rearmament and
public works). To business interests, he represented a bulwark against
communism. To farmers and small businessmen, caught between big labor and business, he promised a recognition of their proper position in
German society and protection against Marxist labor and "Jewish pluto-
crats."

In January 1933 Hitler was asked to form a government by President von Hindenburg. The conservatives around the President believed they could control and "handle" Hitler once he had responsibility. Two months later the Nazis pushed an "Enabling Act" through the parliament that essentially gave Hitler total power; the parliament, constitution, and civil liberties were "suspended." The will of the *Fuehrer* (leader) became the supreme law and authority. By 1934 almost all areas of German life had become "synchronized" to the Nazi pattern.

The Second World War in Europe was, in the words of the former Chancellor of the Federal Republic, Helmut Schmidt, "totally started, led and lost by Adolf Hitler acting in the name of the German people."[1] The world paid for this war with a total of 55 million dead including 8 million Jews and other political and racial victims murdered in concentration camps. The most ruthless and inhuman Nazi actions were directed against European Jewry. From the beginnings of the Nazi movement the Jews were regarded as the prime cause of all the misfortune, unhappiness, and disappointments endured by the German people. Hitler in his autobiography, *Mein Kampf,* written in the early 1920s, repeated in print his oft-spoken conviction that Jews were not humans, nor even subhumans, but rather "disease causing bacilli" in the body of the nation that must be exterminated. Unfortunately, at the time few took his rantings seriously, yet Hitler and the Nazis remained firm to this policy after they came to power. From 1933 on, first in Germany and then throughout the conquered lands of Europe, the Nazis systematically began a process that denied the Jews their dignity, economic livelihood, humanity, and finally, by the early 1940s, their right to physically exist. The "final solution" to the "Jewish problem" meant the deportation of millions of Jewish men, women, and children to extermination camps especially constructed for this purpose in isolated sections of Europe.

Only the total military defeat of the Third Reich by the United States, Britain, France, the Soviet Union, and forces from other allied nations in May 1945 prevented the Nazis from exterminating European Jewry. The remnant that remained amounted to less than 10 percent of the prewar Jewish population of Europe. The Federal Republic, unlike communist East Germany, has accepted legal and moral responsibility for the crimes committed by the Nazis in Germany's name. It is, of course, impossible for the Federal Republic to atone for the Holocaust. It has, however, since the early 1950s paid almost $50 billion in reparations to Jewish victims of Nazism and the state of Israel.

For many Germans, the real distress began after the war. During the war, the Nazis, mindful of the effects of Allied blockades during the First World War, had gone to extensive lengths to ensure a relatively well-fed, housed, and clothed population. That this meant the ruthless exploitation of regions conquered by the German armies was a matter of minor concern to the Nazi leadership. Military defeat ended this supply of foodstuffs, raw materials, and labor from the occupied territories. The Germans were put in the same position as the population in other European countries. In 1945 and 1946 the average caloric intake was set at only a third (800) of the daily requirement. In large cities such as Cologne and Duesseldorf 80 to 90 percent of all houses and apartments were uninhabitable; in Cologne, a city with a population of 750,000 before the war, only 40,000 people remained during the winter of 1945-46. Heating fuel was also in critically short supply. Before the war, the coal mines of the Ruhr had an average daily production of 400,000 tons; in 1945-46 this dropped to only 25,000 tons per day.

The end of World War II meant the end of Germany as a political entity. The victorious Allies returned some of the territory conquered by the Nazis to its prewar owners (Czechoslovakia, Austria, France), divided the remainder into zones of military occupation, and in 1949 created two new states from these zones: the Federal Republic of Germany, or West Germany (British, French, and American zones); and the German Democratic Republic, or East Germany (Russian zone).

During the past thirty years the Federal Republic has become a stable, effective, and legitimate political system. Unlike the Weimar Republic, the Bonn democracy has from the beginning been identified with economic prosperity and foreign and domestic policy successes. There is also considerable evidence that a consensus on democratic values and norms has developed during this period. The vast majority of the German people supports this system and believes in its fundamental norms: individual freedom, the rule of law, civil liberties, free political competition, and representative institutions. In this sense, Germany and the Germans have changed.

The Federal Republic

The history of the Federal Republic can be divided into three rather distinct phases. The first, from 1949 to 1961, was characterized by an empha-

sis on basic economic reconstruction and the stabilization of the new political system both internally and externally through German participation
in the European Community and the Atlantic Alliance (NATO). This stabilization occurred within the context of the intensive East-West confrontation. The construction of the Berlin Wall in 1961 marked the end of this
period. The cold-war foreign policy of "strength" had failed to reunify
Germany or "roll back" communism in Eastern Europe. The search for alternatives to confrontation had begun.

The second phase encompassed most of the 1960s and ended with the
election of 1969 when, for the first time in the Federal Republic's history,
the Christian Democratic Union (CDU) was put into the opposition and
was replaced by a government led by the Social Democrats (SPD). This
phase was marked by a search for new domestic and foreign policy directions. Many domestic areas such as education, urban development, economic planning, and social welfare programs, relatively neglected during
the hectic years of reconstruction, now moved up on the political agenda.
The 1960s also witnessed the beginning of the increase in mass political
participation that continued throughout the 1970s. The student protest
movement; the "extraparliamentary opposition," spawned by dissatisfaction with the 1966 "Grand Coalition" between the CDU/CSU and SPD;
and the beginnings of a grass-roots citizen action group movement (*Buergerinitiativen*) were all expressions of this growing politicization.

The third phase began with the socialist-liberal coalition of 1969. The
politics of "internal reform," criminal law reform, liberalized divorce and
abortion legislation, worker codetermination in industry, and the modernization of the republic's social security and welfare system were major
domestic developments in this period. The post-1973 energy crisis and
West Germany's relatively successful resolution of the economic difficulties associated with it was a further achievement of this phase. Although
Germany, like her Western neighbors, experienced a recession between
1974 and 1976, the levels of unemployment and inflation were well below
most other industrial societies. More important, the 1974-76 recession,
unlike the 1966-67 economic decline, did not produce any significant antisystem political movements. In foreign policy, reconciliation and normalization with Germany's Eastern neighbors were continued and extended
through treaties with the Soviet Union and Poland (1970), East Germany
(1972), Czechoslovakia (1973), and an additional agreement with Poland
(1976). New impetus was given to the European Community movement
through close cooperation between the Federal Republic and France.

TABLE 11.1

The Average German's Standard of Living, 1950-80

	Income and Expenditure Pattern for a Four-Person "Working-Class" Family	
Net Monthly Income	305 DM	2950 DM (after inflation: 1716 DM)
Food	46%	22%
Clothing	13	7
Housing (including utilities)	15	17
Discretionary income	26	54

SOURCE: For 1950: *Der Buerger im Staat* 29, no. 4 (December 1979): 217; for 1980: *Die Zeit*, no. 7 (19 February 1982): 18.

Common to all three phases was a relatively continuous pattern of increased economic growth and prosperity. While there were recessions in 1966-67 and 1974-76, both, and especially that of 1966-67, were "mild" by prewar German and international standards. The vast majority of West Germans were hardly touched by these economic declines. The emergence of a mass affluence in West Germany can be documented by a variety of measures: Car ownership, for example, increased from 1 percent (about 500,000 autos) of the population to 33 percent (25 million) by 1979. The data in table 11.1 show the income and expenditure pattern for a "typical" four-person family where the father is a worker or other "dependent" employee with a moderate income. The monthly net income of this group *after inflation* increased by over 550 percent between 1950 and 1980 (305 DM to 1716 DM). Significantly, the distribution of expenditures changed over this period with "discretionary" income increasing from 26 percent of net income in 1950 to 54 percent by 1980. The "bare necessities" of life became far less of a burden. In 1950 the average German family had to spend almost half (46 percent) of its income for food; by 1980, this proportion had dropped to less than a fourth (22 percent) of monthly net income. This economic growth and prosperity has been an almost constant feature of German life over the past thirty years and has had an impact on mass attitudes toward liberal democracy as practiced in the Federal Republic.

Federalism

West Germany, unlike Britain or France, is a federal state in which certain governmental functions are reserved to the constituent *Laender* (states). Each of the ten (with West Berlin the eleventh) has its own constitution and parliament. The states have fundamental responsibility for education, radio, television, and internal security and order (police power). In addition, most laws passed at the national level are administered by the bureaucracies of the *Laender*. As table 11.2 shows, German states vary widely in area, population, and socioeconomic character. The three "city-states" of Hamburg, West Berlin, and Bremen are largely Protestant and industrial-commercial in structure. They have generally been strongholds of the Social Democratic party throughout the postwar period. The two other northern Protestant states are Schleswig-Holstein, which is relatively rural and small-town, and Lower Saxony, which is more balanced between urban-industrial and rural-agrarian activity. Politically, Schleswig-Holstein's politics have been generally in the hands of the Christian Democrats, while Lower-Saxony has had a more competitive style of party politics with relatively frequent alternations between Socialist and Christian Democratic-led governments.

The most populous state is North Rhine-Westphalia, which contains almost 30 percent of the Federal Republic's 62 million inhabitants. A heavily industrialized and urbanized state, North Rhine-Westphalia has a relative balance between Catholics and Protestants. Its politics have been largely controlled by the Social Democrats and their liberal allies, the Free Democrats, especially during the past fifteen years. Another very industrialized, religiously balanced western *Land* is Hesse, which has known only governments controlled by the Social Democrats since 1946.

The remaining Western states—the Rhineland-Palatinate and the Saarland—are essentially Catholic in religious composition. The Rhineland is less industrialized than the much smaller Saarland, which has had an extensive but now declining steel industry. Both states have been largely dominated by the Christian Democrats.

The two "southern" German states—Baden-Wuerttemberg and Bavaria—are mainly Catholic with a balance between urban and rural occupational groups. They are also Christian Democratic strongholds. Bavaria, the only large German *Land* whose borders were restored intact following the war, is the most particularistic of the *Laender*. It terms itself a "free state" with its own strong historical traditions. Separatism in various forms has at times been a significant force in Bavaria's politics. When in 1979 the Bavarian sister party of the Christian Democrats, the Christian Social Union, threatened to pull out of the union and become a national

TABLE 11.2
The States (Laender) of the Federal Republic

State	Governing Party (1983)	1981 Population (millions)	Area (thousands of square km.)	Population Density (per square km.)	GROSS NATIONAL PRODUCT			POPULATION	
					Total (billions of dollars)	Proportion of Total	Per Capita (thousands of dollars)	Percent Foreign	Percent Roman Catholic
North Rhine Westphalia	SPD[1]	17.0	34.1	499	84.8	27	5.7	7.5	52
Bavaria	CSU[2]	10.9	70.5	154	51.2	17	5.2	3.8	70
Baden-Wuerttemberg	CDU[2]	9.3	35.8	257	46.0	15	5.4	9.3	47
Lower Saxony	CDU	7.3	47.4	154	30.4	10	4.5	3.6	20
Hesse	SPD	5.6	21.1	264	27.6	9	5.3	8.4	33
Rhineland Palatinate	CDU	3.6	19.8	183	17.2	6	4.8	4.1	56
Schleswig-Holstein	CDU	2.6	15.7	165	10.0	3	4.0	3.0	6
Hamburg	SPD	1.7	.7	2,215	14.4	5	8.4	6.2	8
Saar	CDU-FDP[3]	1.1	2.6	416	4.8	2	4.5	3.8	74
Bremen	SPD-FDP	.7	.4	1,723	5.2	2	6.7	6.2	10
West Berlin	CDU	2.1	.5	4,267	11.2	4	5.5	6.6	12

1. SPD = Social Democratic party.
2. CDU = Christian Democratic Union; CSU = Christian Social Union.
3. FDP = Free Democratic party.

political party unless its chairman was made the party's Chancellor candidate, it was placing itself in the Bavarian tradition of being "different" from the other German states.

Geographical

West Germany comprises about half of the pre-World War II territory of the German Reich. The remaining half is part of communist East Germany (the German Democratic Republic), Poland, or the Soviet Union. With a total area of about 96,000 square miles, the Federal Republic is about as large as Oregon. Its population of 61.5 million, however, makes West Germany one of Europe's largest and most densely populated states. Since 1945 the population has grown through the (1) influx of 14 million refugees and expellees from Germany's former eastern territories and East Germany between 1945 and 1961; and (2) the migration of foreign workers, which began in the late 1950s and reached a high point of about 3 million workers in 1973.

In recent years, however, the Federal Republic has had one of Europe's and the world's lowest birthrates. Indeed, deaths have outnumbered births since the late 1960s, and so whatever growth in population the Republic has experienced has been due to foreign workers and their much higher birthrates. While foreign workers and their families constitute less than 7 percent of the population, over 16 percent of all live births in recent years have been to foreigners. If these present trends continue and the number of "new" workers does not increase, the Federal Republic's population is predicted to fall to 59 million by 1990.

The effects of World War II are still noticeable in the age and sex distribution of the population. The low wartime birthrate and casualty losses have left the 25-35, 40-45, and 55-60 age groups underrepresented in the population relative to other groups. Because of the war, women are still in the majority (52 percent), and almost 60 percent of those between the ages of 55 and 75 are females.

Religion

Almost all (90 percent) Germans are "born" into one of two churches: the Roman Catholic or the Evangelical Protestant (Lutherans).[2] Since the

Reformation, Protestants and Catholics have divided along regional lines. The East and North are predominantly Protestant, while in the South and West adherents of Roman Catholicism are in the majority. Historically the respective secular rulers (princes) in these areas acted as "protectors" of the faith in their kingdoms, thus making the churches dependent on state authority for their survival. The close, dependent relationship with the state meant that both churches, but especially the Protestant, which has no international ties comparable to those of the Roman Catholics, were conservative, status-quo-oriented institutions. Thus, unlike the United States, the separation of church and state is alien to the German political tradition; both churches occupy a privileged position in German society and politics.

The church tax, a surcharge of about 10 percent on the individual income tax, is collected via withholding free of charge by the state. This tax ensures both churches a generous and inflation-proof source of income. An individual can escape the church tax only by formally leaving the church, a procedure that most West Germans have declined to follow. Religious instruction in public schools by teachers acceptable to the churches is also paid from public funds. The state also funds the salaries of some church officials.

Although formal affiliation with the established churches is automatic and hence high, most West Germans and especially Protestants are not very active. Only about 15 percent of Protestants and 45 percent of Catholics report a "regular" attendance at church services. Church activity is also strongly related to sex and age with older females being especially active.

In spite of this at best moderate level of religiosity in postwar Germany, the political position and influence of the churches is strong. The postwar occupation authorities viewed them as relatively untainted by Nazism and gave them preferential treatment in the early postwar years. In addition the Christian Democratic Union (CDU), the dominant political party from 1949 to 1969, was generally successful in projecting an image as a political movement that would govern with some regard to Christian principles. Cynics and political opponents strongly disputed this CDU claim to be more concerned with religion and morality than other parties, but the Union has definitely enjoyed the favor of especially the Catholic church. While in power the CDU reciprocated by being particularly sensitive to those issues, such as state support of church schools and strict divorce and abortion laws, stressed by the church. This close

CDU-Catholic church relationship also compelled the Social Democrats by the late 1950s to seek at least a normalized, nonconflictive relationship with the church.

Socioeconomic

The Federal Republic is an urban, industrial, and economically prosperous society. But it also has a stratified social structure with considerable degrees of inequality between different socioeconomic classes.

More Germans live in towns and cities with populations greater than 20,000, and about half of its 62 million inhabitants live on less than 10 percent of the land. There are seven major urban areas whose population exceeds one million: the Rhine-Ruhr region between the cities of Duesseldorf and Dortmund, the Rhine-Main or Frankfurt area, West Berlin, Stuttgart, Hamburg, Munich, and the Rhine-Neckar region.

West Germany is one of the world's major economic powers. Its per capita income, industrial production, and currency reserves are among the world's highest. It is the second (after the United States) largest trading nation in the world. The economic system is "mixed" with private proper-

TABLE 11.3
The Ten Largest Firms in the Federal Republic
(by gross sales)

Firm	Field
VEBA*	Energy/oil/chemicals
Siemens	Electronics
Volkswagen*	Automobiles
Daimler-Benz	Automobiles
Hoechst	Chemicals
Thyssen	Steel
Bayer	Chemicals
BASF	Chemicals
AEG*	Electronics
REW*	Energy/utilities

SOURCE: *Die Zeit,* 37 (9 July 1979): 34.
* Partially under state ownership.

ty and free enterprise coexisting with substantial state involvement. It is also a "social" market economy in which an elaborate social welfare system is supported by both management and labor as well as by all significant political parties.

Industrial production is the largest single contributor to the country's gross national product. A look at table 11.3 shows that the dominant industrial enterprises, after energy, are concentrated in the electronics, automobile, and chemical fields. Industrial workers are still the largest occupational group (45 percent of the work force in 1980); however, the fastest growing segment of the work force is composed of white-collar, technical, and service employees. Between 1950 and 1980 the proportion of the work force in these occupations increased from 23 percent to 43 percent. The remainder is composed of those in independent nonmanual occupations (small businessmen, shopkeepers), independent professionals (physicians, lawyers), and farmers.

As we discussed earlier, the fruits of the economic system have enabled the vast majority of Germans to achieve a high standard of living. In spite of inflation, the disposable income and buying power of all occupational groups, including industrial workers, has steadily risen during the past thirty years. Foreign vacations, automobiles, television sets, and modern appliances and gadgets are now commonplace in most German families.

Nonetheless, inequality is very much a characteristic of West German society. The same manual worker who is satiated with consumer goods is unlikely in his lifetime to own a home or apartment. His children in all likelihood will not receive a university education. This inequality is great-

TABLE 11.4

Income by Occupation, 1980

Average Net Monthly Income

Occupational Group

Independents (owners, directors of enterprises, free professionals, and farmers)	White-Collar, Civil Servant	Manual Worker
$4,500[1]	$1,800	$1,475

SOURCE: *Die Zeit*, no. 7 (19 February 1982): 18.
1. 2.00 DM = $1.00.

est in the areas of income and capital resources. Table 11.4 on page 169 presents the average monthly income in 1980 for independents (professionals, owners, and directors of enterprises), white-collar employees (including civil servants), and manual workers. Independents enjoyed an average net monthly income that was 160 percent greater than that received by white-collar employees and 205 percent more than the monthly income of manual workers. White-collar workers and civil servants had a 18 percent greater income than manual workers. When one examines the ownership of *capital resources* (land, stocks, bonds, securities, savings, life insurance) the differences are even greater (see table 11.5). Independents and farmers, comprising only 10 percent of all households, held over 44 percent of the nation's capital. On a per capita basis they had resources averaging about $190,000. For manual workers, the average amount of capital (mainly savings accounts and life insurance) was only about $4,600, and for white-collar employees about $8,500. Civil servants, although far below the level of independents, still held capital resources that were on the average worth over five times more than the capital of manual workers.

TABLE 11.5
Capital Resources,[1] by Occupation

Occupation	Percent of Total Households	Percent of Capital Resources	Per Capita Capital Resources (in $s)[2]
Independents (owners, directors of enterprises, free professionals) and farmers	10.2	44.1	190,000
Civil servants	6.3	4.4	25,500
White-collar employees	20.1	14.8	8,400
Manual workers	28.2	15.8	4,600
Nonemployed (retired, housewives, students, etc.)	35.2	20.9	3,900

SOURCE: Horst Mierheim and Lutz Wicke, *Die personelle Vermoegensverteilung in der Bundesrepublik Deutschland* (Tuebingen: J.C.B. Mohr Verlag, 1978), cited in M. Jungblut, "Die heimlichen Reichen," *Die Zeit,* no. 46 (10 November 1978): 25.
1. Land, stocks, bonds, securities, savings, life insurance.
2. 2.00 DM = $1.00.

These data show that beneath the surface prosperity of the Federal Republic there are large differences in personal wealth. This distribution of capital reflects in part the postwar decision of German and Allied occupation elites to take the free market route to economic recovery. West German political leaders have sought to create a favorable climate for investment capital through low tax rates on profits and dividends as well as subsidies and tax benefits for new plants and equipment. The currency reform of 1948, for example, clearly favored capital-holding groups. Germans with savings accounts or cash in old Reichsmarks received only about 1 new mark (DM) for every 14 old marks. Thus millions of lower- and lower-middle-class Germans saw their savings largely wiped out. Those with stocks, securities, and land lost nothing.

Education

The German educational system reflects and reinforces the socioeconomic inequality. Traditionally this system was designed to give a basic, general education to all and advanced academic training to only a few. Most German education is still structured along three tracks. At about the age of six all children enter a four-year primary school. But following the fourth year, with the children at age ten, the tracking process begins.

1. Most children will attend a general secondary school for an additional five years. After this, at about the age of fifteen, they will enter the work force, in most cases as apprentices, and attend vocational school part time until the age of eighteen.
2. A second group will attend an intermediate school (*Realschule*) for six years. The intermediate school combines academic and job-oriented training. Medium-level careers in business and administration usually require a middle-school educational background.
3. About 15 percent of each age group will pursue an academic or university-level educational program. Attendance at an academic high school (*Gymnasium*) for up to nine years culminates in the *Abitur* (a degree roughly comparable to an American junior college diploma) and the right to attend a university.

It is possible for children to change tracks, especially during the first two or three years, which are considered an orientation period. Most students, however, do not switch, and the decision made by their parents and teachers after the fourth grade is usually decisive for their educational and occupational future.

This entire system has a strong class bias. The *Gymnasium* and the university are still largely preserves of the middle and upper-middle classes, and the great majority of children in the general vocational track come from working-class backgrounds. But the trend in recent years has been toward a reduction of this bias. Between 1952 and 1980, for example, the proportion of children from working-class families enrolled at universities rose from 4 percent to 22 percent. This is in part the result of a large enrollment increase in the *Gymnasia*. Between 1966 and 1976 attendance in the university preparatory track almost doubled.

German education also has no lack of critics. There has been no more controversial policy area in the last fifteen years than education. Critics and reformers emphasize, in addition to the class bias, the system's inflexibility: the difficulty children have in changing tracks as their interests and values change. The key element in plans for reforming and restructuring German education is the merger of the three-tracked secondary system into a single comprehensive school (*Gesamtschule*). Instead of tracking after the fourth grade, all children would remain in the same school for an additional six years, or until about the age of sixteen. At that point the tracking process would begin. The purpose of the comprehensive school plan is to provide more equality of educational opportunity and social mobility. Since 1969, comprehensive schools have been introduced on an experimental basis in all states, but more extensively in those governed by socialist or liberal political parties. Conservatives have generally opposed comprehensive schools, citing their concerns about a decline in educational standards and their support for the traditional *Gymnasium*.

Attitudes

In 1949, few if any observers in Germany or elsewhere gave the Federal Republic much of a chance to survive, much less prosper. The decision to establish a West German state was made neither by German political leaders nor by the German electorate in any referendum; rather, it was the decision of the three victorious Western powers in World War II—the United States, Britain, and France. The Federal Republic was a product of the foreign policies of these countries that sought to counter what was perceived as a growing Soviet threat in Central and Western Europe. The Germans living in the American, British, and French occupation zones thus had a new political system, which they were to regard as their own, imposed on them by their conquerors. Moreover, the new state was to be a liberal, parliamentary democracy, a form of government that Germany had tried between 1918 and 1933 with disastrous consequences. Even the committed democrats in postwar Germany had few fond memories of that first democratic experience—the Weimar Republic. In addition, this establishment of a West German state was seen by some Germans as a move that would result in the permanent division of the country. Hence the regional and state leaders in the Western zones, who were requested to begin the process of drafting a constitution for the new state, were very reluctant to make the republic appear as a permanent entity. The constitution that was drafted was not even called such, but rather a Basic Law.

But while the Germans were not consulted about their new state, many of them in 1949 did not really care. The vast majority of the population had had enough of "politics," "parties," and "ideals." Following the mobilization of the Nazi years, the incessant propaganda, the endless calls for sacrifice, and the demands of total war, they wanted above all to put

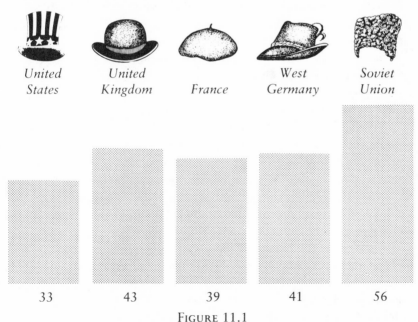

FIGURE 11.1

Public Expenditure as Percent of Total Gross Domestic Product

their private lives back together again. They had been badly burned by politics and were quite willing to let someone else, even foreigners, make political decisions for them as long as they were more or less left alone to pursue their private concerns—the family, making a living, catching up for all that was missed during the war years. This privatized character of postwar German attitudes meant that both Allied and German political elites had considerable freedom to develop and initiate policies. The Germans, in short, were willing to follow the orders of their occupiers that they now be citizens in a democracy, even though most inhabitants had little if any experience with a successful, functioning democratic political order. Thus the institutions of democracy preceded the development of an attitudinal consensus on democracy. The need to educate the postwar population and change their political attitudes was, however, strongly perceived by Western and especially American occupation authorities and by some Germans.

But one did not have to be an enthusiastic supporter of political democracy to oppose any sort of return to a Nazi-style dictatorship after 1945. Apart from any personal predilection for a one-party state, the *performance* of the Third Reich made it distinctly unattractive as an alternative to most Germans in the postwar period. While there has been a consistent relationship between a positive attitude toward the Third Reich and opposition to the key values of the Bonn Republic's institutions after 1945, it should not be overlooked that a sizable proportion of respondents with little sympathy for liberal democracy still rejected a return to some form of dictatorship. These non- or antidemocrats were nonetheless not willing to support a restoration. This was hardly a firm foundation on which to build a stable and effective political democracy, yet it did provide postwar elites and the consciously democratic segments of the larger population with a breathing space in which the republic was given an opportunity to perform and socialize postwar generations to its values and norms.

The early years of the republic were characterized by an ambivalence on the part of many Germans about political democracy. Surveys revealed that significant proportions of the population retained the traditional authoritarian if not antidemocratic attitudes acquired during earlier regimes. In the early 1950s, for example, about a fourth of the adult population still preferred a one-party state; almost half of the electorate in 1951 stated they would be "indifferent" to an attempt by a new Nazi party to take power; and one of every three adult Germans had positive attitudes toward a restoration of the monarchy. Moreover, although the turnout at elections was high, most voters went to the polls out of a sense of "duty" and not because they believed they were participating in the making of important political decisions. Only about a fourth of the population in the early 1950s expressed any interest in political questions, and most Germans reported that they rarely talked about politics with family or friends. Most Germans, in short, had largely withdrawn from political involvement beyond the simple act of going to the polls.

This pattern of mass political attitudes and behavior was not conducive to the long-run viability of the Bonn Republic should it have encountered a major economic or social crisis. Most Germans in the 1950s, even those with fascist or authoritarian dispositions, were quite willing to support political democracy as embodied in the Bonn Republic as long as it "worked," but they could not be counted on if the system encountered major problems. The Germans were "fair-weather" and not "rain or shine" democrats, but they were willing to give democracy a chance.

As the Bonn Republic enters its fourth decade of existence, this pattern of political attitudes has changed. There is now a solid consensus on the basic values, institutions, and processes of the Bonn democracy. Support for key values such as political competition, freedom of speech, civil liberties, and the rule of law ranges from a minimum of about 75 percent to over 95 percent for a principle such as political competition. Similar proportions of West German citizens by the 1980s had a positive orientation toward the parliament, the constitution itself, and the federal struc-

TABLE 11.6
Satisfaction with Democracy:
Germany, Britain, France, and Italy

Q. On the whole, are you very satisfied, fairly satisfied, not very satisfied or not at all satisfied with the way democracy works in (name of country)?

	Germany	Britain	France	Italy	European Community (10 States)
Satisfied	68%	60%	44%	21%	49%
Not satisfied	28	34	42	75	44
Undecided, no response	4	6	14	4	7

SOURCE: Commission of the European Communities, *Euro-Barometer* 17 (June 1982): 10.
NOTE: Satisfied = percentage "very" and "fairly" satisfied.
　　　Not satisfied = percentage "not very" and "not at all" satisfied.

ture of the state.[3] Consistent with this consensus on the present political system is the high level of satisfaction with the way democracy is "functioning" in West Germany. As table 11.6 on page 175 shows, Germans are the most satisfied of the major European countries in which this question was asked.

These data do not mean that the Federal Republic is a political system without problems or that it has become an ideal democracy. As we discuss later, West Germany is a society with many problems including discrimination against both political and social minorities as well as a myriad of economic and social problems—energy, inflation, unemployment—shared by all advanced industrial societies. It also does not mean that there are no West Germans calling for basic changes in the country's social, economic, and political structures. There is a significant segment of politically involved West Germans including numerous intellectuals who regard the Federal Republic as a reactionary capitalist society that is little better than the fascist system it replaced. Indeed, these critics treat the Federal Republic as a country in which the capitalist system, which they argue was directly responsible for Hitler and the Third Reich, was "restored." What the data do signify, however, is that these problems will be debated within a consensual political framework. In short, the question is no longer whether West Germany will remain a liberal democracy, but rather, what kind of and how much democracy Germany will have. This question is high on the country's political agenda, but it is also a problem facing other liberal democracies.

Notes

1. Helmut Schmidt, *"Erklaerung der Bundesregierung zur Lage der Nation vor dem deutschen Bundestag,"* 17 May 1979, printed in *Bulletin,* no. 64 (Bonn, 18 May 1979): 596.
2. About 30,000 Jews live in the Federal Republic. Seventy Jewish congregations receive state financial support. The largest (over 5,000 members) Jewish communities are in West Berlin and Frankfurt.
3. For an analysis of these changes, see David P. Conradt, "Changing German Political Culture," in *The Civic Culture Revisited,* ed. Gabriel Almond and Sidney Verba (Boston: Little, Brown, 1980), pp. 312-72.

12

Where Is the Power?

At the national level there are three major decision-making structures: (1) the lower house of parliament, the Bundestag (Federal Diet); (2) the upper house, the Bundesrat (Federal Council); and (3) the federal government or executive (the Chancellor and Cabinet). In addition the eleven states or *Laender* that constitute the Federal Republic play important roles, especially in the areas of education and internal security (police). These states also have a direct influence on national policy making through the Bundesrat, which is composed of delegates from each of the *Laender*. The Federal Constitutional Court, which has the power of judicial review, is also becoming an increasingly powerful institution. Finally, a federal President, indirectly elected and with little independent responsibility for policy, serves as the ceremonial head of state and is expected to be a unifying or integrating figure above the partisan political struggle.

Formal power is vested in these institutions, but their integration and effectiveness is also very much a function of the new party system that has emerged in the postwar period and the well-organized, concentrated system of interest groups.

Policy-Making Institutions

The Bundestag (Federal Diet)

Constitutionally, the center of the policy-making process is the Bundestag — a legislative assembly consisting of about 500 deputies who are elected at least every four years. They are the only political officials in the constitutional structure who are directly elected by the people. The constitution assigns to the Bundestag the primary responsibility for (1) legislation, (2) the election and control of the government, (3) the supervision of the bureaucracy and military, and (4) the selection of judges to the Federal Constitutional Court.

Parliamentary government has a weak tradition and a poor record of performance in German political history. During the empire (1871-1918), effective control over important areas such as defense and foreign affairs and the supervision of the civil service was in the hands of a Chancellor appointed by the monarch. In addition, Prussian control of the upper house meant that important legislative proposals of the parliament could be blocked at the will of the Prussian ruling elite. Parliament did have the power of the purse as a source of influence, but it could not initiate any major policy programs. Its position toward the executive, bureaucracy, and military was defensive and reactive. While parliament "debated," the government "acted."

Under the Weimar Constitution, the powers of parliament were expanded. The Chancellor and his Cabinet were directly responsible to it and could be removed by a vote of no confidence. But the framers of the constitution made a major error when they also provided for a strong, directly elected President independent of parliament, who could, in "emergency situations" (i.e., when the government lost its parliamentary majority), rule by decree. The Weimar parliament, especially in its later years, was also fragmented into many different, ideologically oriented parties, which made effective legislation difficult. The institution became immobile—there were frequent majorities *against* governments, but rarely majorities in favor of new governments. At the last elections most voters elected parties (Nazi, Nationalist, Communist) that were in one way or another committed to the abolition of the institution. The parliament became identified in the public mind as weak and ineffective. By approving the Nazi Enabling Act in 1933, the parliament ceased to function as a legislative institution.

In the first thirty years of the postwar parliament, this pattern of legislative immobilism has not been repeated. While important initiatives remain the province of the restructured Bonn executive, the parliament's status as an instrument of supervision and control has grown.

The Bundestag, similar to other parliaments, has the responsibility to elect and control the government. After each national election a new parliament is convened with its first order of business the election of the federal Chancellor. The control function is, of course, much more complex and occupies a larger share of the chamber's time. Through the procedure, adopted from English parliamentary practice, of the question hour, a member may make direct inquiries of the government either orally or in writing about a particular problem. A further control procedure is the parliament's right to investigate governmental activities and to demand the appearance of any Cabinet or state official.

The key organizational unit of the Bundestag is the *Fraktion,* the parliamentary caucus of each political party. Committee assignments, debating time, and even office space and clerical assistance are allocated to the *Fraktionen* and not directly to individual deputies. The leadership of these parliamentary parties effectively controls the work of the Bundestag. The freshman deputy soon discovers that a successful and influential parliamentary career is largely dependent on the support of the leadership of his or her parliamentary *Fraktion.*

The parliament has a committee system that is more important than those in Britain and France, yet less powerful than the committees in the American Congress. The nineteen standing committees, like their American counterparts, mirror the partisan composition of the whole parliament; but committee chairmanships are allotted proportionately according to party strength. Thus the minority opposition party or parties will chair several (in the 1976-80 Bundestag, seven) of the standing committees. These committees have become more significant in recent years due to the introduction of American-style "hearings" and the greater use of committee meetings as forums by the opposition. But German committees, like those in other unitary systems, are still reluctant to engage in the full-blown criticism of the executive associated with presidential systems. This is due to the generally higher level of party discipline and to the dependence of the government on a parliamentary majority. Committee criticism, if comprehensive enough, could be interpreted as an attempt to bring the Chancellor down. This is a major problem with strong committee systems in parliamentary governments.

There is also considerable specialization among committee members, and thus the day-to-day sessions tend to concentrate on details of proposed legislation and rarely do they produce any major news. German committees cannot pigeonhole bills; all must be reported out. About four of every five bills submitted by the government will be reported out with a favorable recommendation, albeit with a variety of suggested revisions and amendments. Outright rejections are rare. When the government discovers that a bill is in trouble, it is usually withdrawn for "further study" before a formal committee vote.

The Bundesrat (Federal Council)

The Bundesrat represents the interests of the states in the national policy-making process. It is composed of forty-one members drawn from the ten state governments. Each state, depending on its population, is entitled to three to five members. Most Bundesrat sessions are attended by delegates from the state governments and not the actual formal members, the Cabinet ministers from the state governments.

Throughout most of its history, the Bundesrat has concentrated on the administrative aspects of policy making and has rarely initiated legislative proposals. Since the states implement most national legislation, the Bundesrat has tended to examine proposed programs from the standpoint of how they can be best administered at the state level. The Bundesrat has thus not been an institution in the partisan political spotlight.

In recent years this has changed. While the Christian Democrats since 1969 have been the opposition party in the Bundestag, in 1972, as a result of a series of state election victories, they secured a majority of the Bundesrat's delegates. Since then, the frequency of Bundesrat objections to government legislation has increased to the point where SPD-FDP coalition leaders have accused it of becoming the "extended arm" of the parliamentary opposition. It was suggested that the CDU/CSU was seeking to obstruct the government's electoral majority by turning its majority in the upper chamber into a politicized counter-government. Thus the Bundesrat blocked or forced compromises on the government on issues such as divorce law reform, speed limits on autobahns, higher education reform, tax policy, the controversial "radicals" in public employment law, and the 1976 treaty with Poland.

To become a genuine second chamber, however, the Bundesrat's delegations, still controlled by state leaders, must also be willing to accept direction from the opposition party's national leadership in the lower house. Thus far, this has happened on only some issues. Generally the more remote the issue from the concerns of state leaders, the more likely they are to go along with the national leadership in the lower house and try to block the bill in the Bundesrat.

A Federal Council veto of a proposed bill by a majority of two-thirds or more can be overridden in the Bundestag only by a two-thirds majority of the *members present and voting*. This means that a party controlling twenty-eight or more delegates in the Bundesrat, which is in a minority in the Bundestag, can nonetheless bring the legislative process to a halt and force new elections. Such a development would run counter to the intentions of the framers of the Basic Law, who did not envision the Bundesrat as such a party-political body. Since the composition of the Bundesrat is determined by the respective state governments, political and electoral developments at the state level can have direct national political consequences. A victory by the CDU/CSU in the state of Hesse in October 1978 probably would have brought down the Schmidt government in Bonn. The 1966 victory of the Social Democrats in the state of North Rhine-Westphalia marked the beginning of the end of the Erhard government, which was replaced five months later by a national "Grand Coalition" (CDU/CSU-SPD).

The Chancellor and Cabinet

The chief executive in the Federal Republic is the Chancellor. The powers of this office place it somewhere between those of a strong President in the United States and the Prime Minister in the British parliamentary system. Constitutionally, the German Chancellor is less powerful than an American President, yet a Chancellor has more authority and is more difficult to remove than a Prime Minister on the British model.

The Weimar Constitution provided for a dual executive: a directly elected President and a Chancellor chosen by the parliament. The President was chief of state, commander in chief of the armed forces, and could in an emergency dismiss the Chancellor and his Cabinet and rule by decree. The President during the final years of the Weimar Republic, former Field Marshal von Hindenburg, misused especially this latter power and helped undermine public support for democratic institutions. The framers of the Basic Law sought to avoid a repetition of this problem by concentrating executive authority in the Chancellor. The President under the Bonn system no longer has any real political power.

The power of the Bonn Chancellor derives largely from the following sources: the constitution, the party system, and the precedent established by the first Chancellor, Konrad Adenauer. The constitution makes the Chancellor responsible for determining the "main guidelines" of the government's policies. This places him above his ministers, although they are in turn responsible for policy within their specific area. The Chancellor also essentially "hires and fires" Cabinet ministers. If the parliament wants the removal of a particular Cabinet member, it must vote no confidence in the whole government including the Chancellor. Bringing down the government via a vote of no confidence has, in turn, become more difficult in the Bonn system because of the *constructive vote of no confidence provision.* This means that a parliamentary majority against an incumbent Chancellor does not suffice to bring down the government; the opposition must also have a majority *in favor of a new Chancellor* before the Chancellor and Cabinet are dismissed. The provision was intended to protect the Chancellor from the shifting and unstable parliamentary majorities that brought down so many Weimar governments without, however, being able to agree on a replacement.

The constructive vote of no confidence has been tried only twice, in April 1972 when the CDU/CSU opposition attempted (unsuccessfully) to bring down the Brandt government and in October 1982 when Helmut Schmidt was replaced as Chancellor by Helmut Kohl. The rare use of this procedure reflects the strength of the new *party system.* A Bonn Chancellor, unlike his Weimar predecessors, can usually count on the firm support of a majority of the parliament throughout the four-year session. Since there are far fewer but larger parties in the Bonn Republic, the political ties between government and parliament are much stronger. The concentration of electoral support in two large, disciplined parties and a small third party has assured most Chancellors of firm parliamentary majorities.

The first Chancellor of the Federal Republic, Konrad Adenauer, set the standards by which future Chancellors would be evaluated. His performance in the office and the substance he gave to its constitutional provisions have influenced all his successors. Adenauer assumed the office at the remarkable age of seventy-three in 1949 and remained until 1963. Prior to the Third Reich he had been Lord Mayor of Cologne, but he had never held any national political office during the Weimar Republic. Shortly after the Nazi seizure of power in 1933, he was removed from office and was allowed to retire. Although he had some contact with anti-Nazi resistance groups and was arrested, imprisoned, and nearly executed in 1944, he essentially "sat out" the Third Reich.

His first government had a majority of only fourteen seats. From the beginning, his Chancellorship was characterized by a wide variety of domestic and foreign political successes: the "economic miracle," the integration of 10 million refugees from the eastern territories, membership in the European Community, and the alliance with the United States.

Adenauer used to the fullest extent the powers inherent in the Chancellor's office. In firm control of his party, he was "out front" on all major foreign and domestic policies and usually presented decisions to his Cabinet and the parliament as accomplished facts. Under Adenauer, there was no extensive consultation within either the Cabinet or the parliament before important decisions were made. The Chancellor *led;* he initiated policy proposals, made the decisions, and then submitted them to the Cabinet and parliament essentially for ratification. He did not always succeed in this approach, but on most major issues, such as rearmament, membership in NATO, and the Common Market, his views prevailed. During his tenure the office of the Chancellor became the center of the policy-making process. All his successors have benefited from the power Adenauer gave to the office. This presidential-like control over the Cabinet, bureaucracy, and even parliament soon became known as "Chancellor democracy"—a parliamentary system with a strong, quasi-presidential executive.

Adenauer was pessimistic about the capacities of the average German to measure up to the demands of democratic citizenship. Through his authoritarian-paternalistic style he encouraged Germans to go about the rebuilding of their private lives and leave the politics to the "old man," as he was often termed. Most Germans probably agreed with this approach, but it meant that his successors would encounter a host of unfinished business, particularly in the area of citizen involvement in public affairs. In retrospect, Adenauer's major contribution was to demonstrate to many Germans, who were indifferent if not ignorant of democratic institutions and values, that a liberal republic would be efficient and successful in Germany.

A look at table 12.1 on page 184 shows that, thus far, none of Adenauer's successors has come close to matching his thirteen-year tenure in office. His first two CDU/CSU successors, Ludwig Erhard and Kurt-Georg Kiesinger, assumed the office at the time when support for the CDU/CSU was on the decline. Erhard, a very successful economics minister, never had control of his party. As long as conditions remained favorable, he could attract voters and was thus tolerated by the Union. When the first real recession came in 1966-67, he was promptly dropped, with the CDU/CSU taking the lead in urging his departure. Kiesinger became Chancellor of the Grand Coalition government with the SPD, a novel arrangement that called for a person adept at compromise and mediation with a record of good relations with the Social Democrats. There was no one in Bonn who met these requirements, and Kiesinger came from Stuttgart where he had been the chief executive of Baden-Wuerttemberg. When the CDU/CSU failed to gain sufficient votes at the 1969 election to form another government, Kiesinger passed from the national scene.

TABLE 12.1
Chancellors and Governing Coalitions, 1949-83

Date	Governing Parties	Chancellor
1949-53	CDU/CSU[1]-FDP[2]-DP[3]	Adenauer
1953-57	CDU/CSU-FDP-DP-GB/BHE[4]	Adenauer
1957-61	CDU/CSU-DP	Adenauer
1961-63	CDU/CSU-FDP	Adenauer
1963-65	CDU/CSU-FDP	Erhard
1965-66	CDU/CSU-FDP	Erhard
1966-69	CDU/CSU-SPD[5]	Kiesinger
1969-72	SPD-FDP	Brandt
1972-74	SPD-FDP	Brandt
1974-76	SPD-FDP	Schmidt
1976-80	SPD-FDP	Schmidt
1980-82	SPD-FDP	Schmidt
1982-present	CDU/CSU-FDP	Kohl

1. CDU/CSU = Christian Democratic Union/Christian Social Union.
2. FDP = Free Democratic party.
3. DP = German party.
4. GB/BHE = Refugee party.
5. SPD = Social Democratic party.

The two Social Democratic Chancellors offer a contrast in personality, political style, and policy emphasis. Willy Brandt's two governments from 1969 to 1974 were characterized by the introduction of a new foreign policy of reconciliation with Germany's eastern neighbors and the acceptance of the permanence of postwar boundaries in Eastern Europe. This *Ostpolitik* (eastern policy) involved the negotiation and ratification of treaties with the Soviet Union (1970), Poland (1970), East Germany (1972), and Czechoslovakia (1973). This policy put West Germany at the forefront of the worldwide trend toward détente and made Brandt one of the world's most respected political leaders. For this policy of reconciliation he was awarded the Nobel Peace Prize in 1971, only the fourth German ever so honored. For many he personified the "other Germany," a man of peace and goodwill accepting moral responsibility for the acts committed in Germany's name by the Nazis. As the first Chancellor with an impeccable record of uncompromising opposition to Nazism, he contributed greatly to the republic's image abroad as a society that had finally overcome its totalitarian past. For many Germans, especially among the young, he became a symbol of a political system that was now liberal and democratic in content as well as form.

These foreign policy successes and great international prestige could not compensate for Brandt's ineffective leadership in most domestic political areas. During his first government (1969-72) his inability to institute a wide variety of promised domestic reforms (codetermination, profit sharing, tax and educational programs) could be attributed to the government's small (12-seat) majority. But after 1972 his second government held a comfortable majority of 50 mandates. Yet his domestic legislative program stalled again. Brandt had little interest in many internal policy areas and little knowledge of economics and finance. He was also unwilling to resolve the conflicts within the Cabinet and the SPD, which flared up after 1972. The very weak response of his government to the 1973 Arab oil embargo and the subsequent economic recession prompted suggestions even from within his own Cabinet that he step down. Finally, when an East German spy was discovered on his personal staff in April 1974, Brandt assumed full responsibility and resigned.

The fifth Chancellor, Helmut Schmidt, assumed the office with more successful national-level experience than any of his four predecessors. An academically trained economist, he had been the leader of the SPD's parliamentary party (1966-69), defense minister (1969-72), and finance minister (1972-74). In these posts Schmidt acquired the reputation as a very capable — some would say brilliant — political decision maker. He was also criticized for what some regarded as an overbearing, arrogant, "cold" personal style. He clearly lacked the emotional, "warm" image of Brandt, yet he is given higher marks for his concrete performance.

Schmidt became Chancellor in the midst of the worldwide economic recession that followed the 1973 Arab oil embargo and subsequent astronomical rise in oil prices. His expertise and experience in national and international economic affairs and his ability to take charge in crisis situations such as the 1977 terrorist hijacking and commando raid soon became apparent. Within two years, inflation was brought under control (i.e., less than 5 percent) and unemployment reduced from over 1 million to less than 700,000 (still well above pre-1973 figures). Moreover, the German international balance of payments remained in the black; by 1976, the Federal Republic's sale of manufactured goods to the Middle Eastern oil countries exceeded the value of its petroleum imports.

In addition, the Schmidt governments (1974-76, 1976-80, 1980-82) continued, albeit at a lower key, the *Ostpolitik* of their predecessors. A

1976 treaty with Poland extended the 1970 pact and provided for the resettlement of German nationals living in Poland but desiring to move to the Federal Republic. A variety of supplemental agreements with East Germany and the Soviet Union were also concluded. During the 1980 Afghanistan crisis, Schmidt consistently warned about losing the benefits achieved through détente. In June 1980 he traveled to the Soviet Union for talks, an expression of the Federal Republic's continued commitment to a relaxation of international tensions and Schmidt's independence vis-à-vis the United States and President Carter.

Unlike Brandt, Schmidt had little patience with the SPD's left. He was a strong supporter of the mixed economy and maintained a close relationship with the Federal Republic's economic and industrial elite. Indeed, he was seen even by many CDU voters as more capable than the Union's candidates. In mid-1980, for example, over half of the *CDU electorate* in the large state of North Rhine-Westphalia preferred Schmidt over the candidate of the CDU/CSU, Franz Josef Strauss, as Chancellor after the October 1980 election. His image as an achiever, "a man who gets things done," more than compensated in this case for his alleged "coldness" and arrogance.

However, Schmidt's electoral and policy successes were not matched by his performance as the leader of the SPD. Specifically, he was unable to overcome and integrate the opposition of the SPD left and especially the Young Socialists. He also overestimated the intensity of opposition within his own party and in the country as a whole to nuclear power as an energy source. Convinced that there is no alternative to nuclear reactors if the Federal Republic is to remain viable in the international market place, Schmidt sought allies outside the SPD in his struggle with party critics. While there was some closing of the ranks for the 1980 election, the Chancellor's relationship to his party was a problem that remained throughout his tenure in office.

In September 1982 Helmut Schmidt lost his parliamentary majority as the Free Democrats, the junior partner in the coalition with the SPD, left the government. Shortly thereafter, the leader of the CDU, Helmut Kohl, became the Republic's sixth Chancellor, heading a new coalition comprised of the Christian Democratic Union, its Bavarian sister party, the Christian Social Union, and the Free Democrats. At the March 1983 national election, the voters endorsed these parliamentary changes by giving Kohl and the CDU/CSU-FDP coalition a solid majority of 58 seats in the parliament.

Helmut Kohl has been a significant figure on the West German political scene since 1969 when he became chief-executive of the state of Rhineland-Palatinate (Rheinland-Pfalz). His successes at the state level coincided with the decline of his party, the CDU, in national politics. After CDU/CSU defeats in 1969 and 1972 Kohl moved out from his provincial power base and in 1973 assumed the leadership of a badly divided and weakened CDU. He is credited with initiating a thorough modernization and revitalization of the party's organization. In 1976 as the "Chancellor candidate" of the CDU/CSU he conducted a very well planned and executed campaign which almost toppled the SPD-FDP government.

Like Helmut Schmidt, Kohl is a political pragmatist. Unlike Schmidt, he does not have the reputation as a "crisis manager" or bold decision maker who can get things done in a hurry. He is also not an intellectual. In domestic politics he comes from a Catholic labor tradition which generally supports Germany's extensive social welfare state. In recent years, however, he has called for cutbacks in some social programs. The market economy is an article of faith as is anticommunism and firm support for the Atlantic Alliance. A Kohl-led government will probably take a harder line toward East Germany and the Soviet Union.

Formal Policy-Making Procedures

Legislation

Most legislation is drafted in the ministries of the national government and submitted to the parliament for action. Two additional but relatively minor sources of legislative proposals are the state governments and the parliament itself. State governments may submit national legislation via the Bundesrat (Federal Council), but at least six states (a majority) must support the bill. If at least 5 percent (about 25) of the parliamentary deputies support a bill, it also enters the legislative process.*

Before a draft bill is submitted to parliament, it is discussed and approved by the Cabinet (government). If the legislation affects several min-

---

*Administrative regulations and legal ordinances that deal largely with the technical, procedural aspects of existing programs are introduced and enacted by the government and do not require the consent of parliament. If regulations and ordinances affect the states, however, they must be approved by the Bundesrat. They can also be challenged in the courts. The President can in some cases refuse to sign the regulation or ordinance.

istries, the Chancellor's Office will coordinate the drafting process and attempt to resolve any interministerial conflicts. At the Cabinet level, the states through the Bundesrat will be asked to submit their reaction to the legislation. Since Cabinet approval is necessary for all draft legislation coming out of the ministries, a minister will usually have the legislation put on the Cabinet agenda only if approval is very likely. Indeed, since the Chancellor "quarterbacks" this entire process, most Cabinet meetings dealing with legislation already in draft tend to largely formalize decisions already taken informally between the Chancellor and the relevant ministers.

After governmental approval, the proposed bill is presented to the Bundesrat for its first reading. The Bundesrat usually assigns it to a committee, which issues a report and recommends the acceptance, rejection, or (in most cases) the amendment of the legislation. Since the Bundestag can override a Federal Council veto, it considers the bill regardless of Bundesrat action.

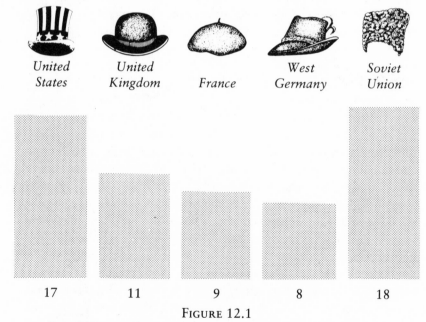

FIGURE 12.1

Defense Spending as Percent of Total Public Expenditure

NOTE: Many Soviet specialists consider it more appropriate to compare defense spending as a percent of GNP in which case the U.S. would be 6 percent and the USSR would be 12 percent.

In parliament the bill is given a first reading and assigned to the relevant committee. Since the government has a majority in each committee, a bill will rarely be returned to the floor with a negative report. The committee report before the whole chamber is the occasion for the second reading, at which time amendments to the proposed legislation can be considered. If after debate on the second reading the bill is approved without amendment, the third and final reading follows immediately.

After adoption by the Bundestag, the bill goes back to the Bundesrat for a second reading. If approved there without amendment, the bill goes directly to the President for his signature and promulgation. If the policy area requires Bundesrat approval and it vetoes the bill, it is dead. In some cases the Bundesrat proposes amendments to the lower-house version and the two houses form a conference committee to resolve the differences.

The Judiciary

West Germany is a law- and court-minded society. In addition to local, regional, and state courts for civil and criminal cases, corresponding court systems specialize in labor, administrative, tax, and social security cases. On a per capita basis, there are about nine times as many judges in the Federal Republic as in the United States. The German legal system, like that of most of its Western European neighbors, is based on code law rather than case, judge-made, or common law. These German legal codes, influenced by the original Roman codes and the French Napoleonic Code, were reorganized and in some cases rewritten after the founding of the empire in 1871. In recent years both the civil and the criminal code have been in the process of major revision.

In a codified legal system, the judge only administers and applies the codes, fitting the particular case to the existing body of law. A judge, in theory at least, may not set precedents and thus make law, but must be a neutral administrator of these codes. Counsel for the plaintiff and defendant assist the judge in this search for justice. The assumption behind this system, which is common to other Western European societies, is that a right and just answer exists for every case. The problem is to find it in the codes. The judge is expected to take an active role in this process and not be merely a disinterested referee or umpire of court proceedings. Court observers accustomed to the Anglo-American system would be surprised by the active, inquisitorial posture assumed by the judge. At times, both judge and prosecution seem to be working against the defendant. Unlike the Anglo-American system, the process is not one of *advocacy,* with both sides presenting their positions as forcefully and persuasively as possible and with the judge or jury making the final decision; it is more *inquisitorial* with all participants—defense, prosecution, and judge—expected to join together in a search for the "truth."

This approach to law has been termed "legal positivism" or "analytical jurisprudence." Some critics of the German legal system consider positivism as a basic cause for the scandalous behavior of German judges during the Third Reich when most judges disclaimed any responsibility for judging the contents of laws they were to administer.

The independence of judges, protected by law, is limited by their status as civil servants. All judges with the exception of those at the Federal Constitutional Court are under state or national ministries of justice. To move up the judicial hierarchy obviously requires that they perform their duties in a manner consistent with the standards set by their superiors. This bureaucratization of the judiciary, common to all Western European societies, puts limits on the extent of judicial independence.

Judges in Germany are also a tightly knit, upper-middle-class group. While hardly radicals, their attitudes and values (as determined in a number of studies) are quite conventional and conservative. Some critics have charged that most judges dispense "class justice" because they know little about the problems or life style of the working- and lower-middle class defendants who come to their courts.

Structure

The German court structure is extensive and specialized. There are five basic units:

1. The "ordinary" courts, which deal with most civil and criminal cases. These courts are organized at the local, regional, "higher" regional, and national levels. The first three levels can be courts of original jurisdiction and the latter three can function as appellate courts. At the local level, many cases are decided by a single judge, and in cases of major felonies, by a panel that may include a private or lay member. All cases at the upper three levels are presided over by a judicial panel.

2. The labor courts (local, regional, and national), which deal with labor-management disputes. In most of these cases counsel for workers will be provided by a labor union.
3. The administrative courts, which adjudicate conflicts between citizens and the state bureaucracy. They also have regional and appellate levels.
4. The social welfare courts, which deal with a wide range of problems associated with the social security and health systems.
5. The fiscal or tax courts, which handle the specific problems citizens and organizations have with the tax system.

The Federal Constitutional Court

The practice of judicial review—the right of courts to examine and strike down legislation emanating from popularly elected legislatures if it is considered contrary to the constitution—is alien to a codified legal system. Nonetheless, under the influence of especially American Occupation authorities and the tragic record of the courts during the Third Reich, the framers of the Bonn constitution created a Federal Constitutional Court and empowered it to consider any alleged violations of the constitution including legislative acts. Similar courts were also established at the state level.

This new court, located in Karlsruhe, has in its first thirty years built an impressive record of constitutional interpretation. In doing so it has also become an increasingly important political institution. Unlike other courts, it is independent of any justice ministry. Its members are selected by both houses of parliament, and its budget and other administrative matters are dealt with in direct negotiations with parliament's judiciary committees. It took several years for the Court to achieve this independence, but it was recognized as an indispensable prerequisite for the performance of its constitutional responsibilities.

In recent years the Court has rendered decisions on such controversial political cases as the *Ostpolitik* treaties, abortion reform, university governance, the powers of the Bundesrat, the employment of "radicals" in the civil service, and the 1976 Co-Determination Law. Like the U.S. Supreme Court, the Federal Constitutional Court has also been criticized for becoming "too political," for usurping the legislative and policy-making prerogatives of parliament and government, and for not exercising sufficient "judicial restraint." To students of judicial review this is a familiar charge, and reflects the extent to which the Court in the last thirty years has become a legitimate component of the political system. Most important, both winners and losers in these various cases have accepted and complied with the Court's decisions.

13

Who Has the Power and How Did They Get It?

Political Parties

One of the most striking changes in postwar Germany is the emergence of a system of political parties that has effectively organized and controlled the political process. Traditionally, parties were marginal factors in German political life. Their home was the legislature, but the executive and the bureaucracy dominated politics; the parties had little influence in these institutions. This pattern was also dominant during most of the Weimar Republic when the party system was fragmented and stable parliamentary majorities became impossible to form. By the late 1920s effective political power, in spite of the democratic structure of the state, had passed once again into the hands of the executive and the state bureaucracy.

This system of weak, unstable, and fragmented parties did not re-emerge after 1949. Indeed, democratic political parties began to assert themselves early in the Occupation period, and they assumed major leadership roles in the parliamentary council that drafted the Basic Law establishing the West German state. Never before in German history have democratic political parties been as important and powerful as they are in the Federal Republic today.

Related to the increased power of German political parties is the sharp decrease over the past thirty years in the number of parties seriously contending for power. During the Weimar Republic up to 100 parties contested elections, and as many as 25 gained parliamentary representation—with no single party able to secure a majority of seats. Coalition governments consisting of several parties were the rule. These were, for the most part, unstable; this meant governments had to expend their resources on surviving instead of planning and implementing policy programs. During the thirteen-year Weimar Republic there were twenty different governments.

In contrast, the Bonn party system has been characterized by a concentration of electoral support in two large parties—the Christian Democratic Union (in Bavaria the Christian Social Union)(CDU/CSU), and the Social Democratic party of Germany (SPD), together with a much smaller third party, the Free Democrats (FDP). At the 1983 federal election a new, small political party, the Environmentalists or Greens, also secured parliamentary representation. In 1949 seventeen different parties contested the first national election, and fourteen succeeded in entering the first parliament. By 1961 this had dropped to three parties. From 1961 to 1983 these parties at local, state, and national levels "carried" the Federal Republic. They dominated the selection and control of governmental personnel and had major influence in the setting of the policy agenda.

The postwar democratic parties had several advantages over their Weimar predecessors. First, their competitors in previous regimes—the state bureaucracy, the army, the landed nobility, and even big business—were discredited through their association with the Third Reich. Second, the parties from the outset enjoyed the support of the Occupation powers. This gave the parties numerous material and political benefits and put them in a strong starting position when the decision was made (by the Allies) in 1948 to launch a West German state. Third, the parties largely organized and controlled the proceedings of the parliamentary council. The constitution made the parties quasi-state institutions by assigning them fundamental responsibility for "shaping the political will of the people." This provision has also been used to justify the extensive public financing of the parties both for their normal day-to-day activities and during election campaigns. Fourth, these same parties, exploiting their strong constitutional and political position, ensured that the local, state, and national postwar bureaucracies were staffed, at least at the upper levels, by their supporters. In contrast to the Weimar bureaucracy, the Bonn civil service is not a center of antirepublican sentiment but is firmly integrated into the Republican consensus.

The Christian Democrats

The Christian Democratic Union (CDU) together with its Bavarian partner, the Christian Social Union (CSU), is a postwar political movement that only recently has attempted to become a political party. Like the Gaullists in France, the CDU/CSU developed largely as a vehicle to facilitate the election and reelection of a single political personality, Konrad Adenauer. The Union did not even have its first national convention until after it became the major governing party in 1949. From the outset in 1945, the CDU was a broadly based movement that sought to unite both Protestants and Catholics in a political organization that would apply the general principles and values of Christianity to politics. The religious division between Protestants and Catholics was regarded as one factor for the rise of Nazism. But the Union also stressed that it was open to all social classes and regions. The CDU/CSU became a prototype for the new "catchall" parties that emerged in postwar Europe: parties that sought through a pragmatic, nonideological image to attract as broad an electoral base as possible. The CDU wanted voters, not necessarily believers, and it refused to place itself in one of the traditional liberal, conservative, socialist, or communist ideological categories. To more traditionally minded politicians and some intellectuals, this was nothing more than opportunism. How could one have a party without a clearly articulated ideology and program? The CDU/CSU represented a new development in politics.

In the 1950s the remarkable success of Chancellor Adenauer in foreign policy and the free market policies of his economics minister, Ludwig Erhard, made the CDU/CSU Germany's dominant party. At the 1957 election it became the first democratic party in German history to secure an absolute majority of the popular vote. The CDU/CSU's program was very general: free market economic policies at home, alliance with the United States and other NATO countries, and a staunch anticommunism abroad; otherwise, "no experiments" (the party's main slogan at the 1957 election).

This approach worked well throughout the 1950s, but the Berlin Wall in 1961 and the 1966-67 economic recession showed the weaknesses in the CDU/CSU's policies. Anticommunism and a refusal to recognize the legitimacy of postwar boundaries in Eastern Europe had not brought Germany any closer to unification. Moreover, the weak American response to the Wall was for many a sign that the Federal Republic could not rely entirely on the United States to run its foreign policy. The 1966-67 recession, although mild in comparison with past economic declines and in comparison with those experienced by other industrial societies, indicated that the postwar boom was over and that the economy was in need of more management and planning. In addition, almost two decades of governing had taken their toll on the leadership of the CDU/CSU. Adenauer's successor, Ludwig Erhard, lacked the political skill of the "old man." Also the Social

Democrats, as we discuss below, had since the late 1950s begun to revamp their program, organization, and leadership. The collapse of the Erhard government in 1966 was followed by a Grand Coalition with the Union's chief adversary, the Social Democrats. The CDU/CSU, by sharing power with the SPD, enabled it to make inroads into the ranks of younger middle-class voters and made less tenable the long-time Union argument that the Socialists could not be entrusted with national political responsibility.

After the 1969 election, the SPD and FDP formed a coalition that ended twenty years of CDU/CSU government in Bonn. Lacking a programmatic focus, the party went through four different Chancellor candidates in search of a "winner" who could bring it back to power. In opposition it expended much of its time in internal conflicts revolving around this leadership question. The 1980 candidate of the party, Franz Josef Strauss, also failed to unseat the SPD-FDP coalition. Yet the CDU/CSU still regularly secures the support of at least 45 percent of the national electorate, remains in power in seven of Germany's eleven *Laender,* holds a majority in the Bundesrat, and is the strongest party in many small and medium-sized towns and several large cities.

After thirteen years in opposition the Christian Democrats in Bonn returned to power in October 1982. While the party did not receive any direct electoral mandate in 1982, both state elections and national public opinion polls showed that the CDU/CSU enjoyed a sizable advantage over the Social Democrats. This was confirmed at the March 1983 election when the Union secured 48.8 percent of the popular vote as compared to only 38.2 percent for the Social Democrats.

The new Christian Democratic government can be expected to favor a more "supply-side" approach to economic recovery: investment stimuli and tax incentives for business, already attempted by the previous regime, will be intensified. Efforts will also be made to contain the costs of social programs, especially in the pension and health areas, which have expanded rapidly in recent years. The Christian Democrats, however, by no means advocate a laisser faire approach to the relationship between the government and the economy. It was the CDU/CSU, for example, which in 1957 instituted the dynamic pension program, the foundation of the postwar welfare state, and supported its expansion in subsequent years. There is a Catholic labor wing in the party which has traditionally taken positions on social welfare issues similar to those held by the SPD and the trade unions. It is highly unlikely that a CDU-FDP government would attempt so drastic a turnaround in the government's socioeconomic role as that instituted by Prime Minister Thatcher in Great Britain or President Reagan in the United States. German political tradition and the social welfare teachings of political Catholicism both legitimate a major state presence.

The Social Democrats (SPD)

The SPD is Germany's oldest political party and the only one to emerge virtually intact following the collapse of the Third Reich. The heir to Germany's rich Marxist tradition, the SPD was outlawed and persecuted during the nineteenth century by Bismarck and the Kaiser, and by the Nazis in the twentieth century. In 1945 it appeared that the SPD's hour had finally come. Unlike other Weimar parties, its record of opposition to Nazism was uncompromising. In 1933 it was the only political party to vote against Hitler's Enabling Act. Its commitment to socialism had long been tempered by an even greater support for the principles and values of political democracy. Even during the Weimar Republic the party's interest in the class struggle and the realization of the revolutionary vision had given way to a policy of reformist gradualism designed to change the society and economy by peaceful, political means.

During the Third Reich the SPD retained a skeletal organization in exile and a small underground movement in Germany. While many Socialists did not survive the war and the concentration camps, the party was still able to regroup in a relatively short time after 1945 — its loyal members emerged literally from the ruins of Germany's cities to begin the task of reconstruction.

Yet the SPD at the first parliamentary election in 1949 did not become the largest party and found itself in opposition. After the landslide CDU/CSU victories of 1953 and 1957, it could claim the support of only about 30 percent of the electorate.

The SPD's first postwar leader, Kurt Schumacher, was unable to convert the party's unquestioned opposition to Nazism and its resultant moral authority into electoral success. While he made a substantial contribution to the Bonn democracy by preventing a fusion between the SPD and the German communists and shaping the SPD into a viable opposition party, his overall political strategy was incorrect. Specifically, Schumacher failed to recognize that the post-1948 success of free market (capitalist) economic policies left the bulk of the German electorate with little interest in socialism with its connotation of government ownership of the means of production, centralized economic planning, and the class struggle. He also overestimated the interests of the average German in an independent "nationalist" foreign policy designed to secure the reunification of the country. Most West Europeans at least by the early 1950s were willing to accept the division of the old Reich in exchange for the economic prosperity, individual freedom, and security they received from German integration into the American-led Atlantic Alliance. Finally, Schumacher's political style with its emphasis on conflict, polarization, and ideology simply reminded too many voters of the Weimar Republic. Postwar Germany and Western Europe had tired of this style of politics—this was the heyday of the "end of ideology," and most voters were supporting consensual, "middle of the road" parties and leaders.[1]

During the 1950s, however, an increasing number of SPD leaders in *Laender* such as Hamburg, Frankfurt, and Berlin began to advocate major changes in the party's program organization and leadership. Specifically, the reformers advocated that the party accept the pro-Western foreign policy course of Adenauer and abandon its opposition to the free market economic policies of the CDU/CSU. It was also proposed that the Social-

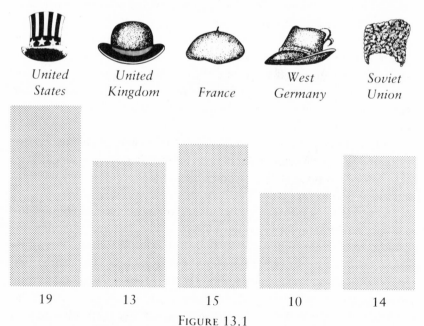

United States	United Kingdom	France	West Germany	Soviet Union
19	13	15	10	14

FIGURE 13.1

Spending on Education as a Percent of Total Public Expenditure

ists seek some sort of accommodation with the churches and especially Roman Catholicism.

This reform movement culminated in the party's 1959 program that was adopted at its convention in Bad Godesberg. In the Bad Godesberg program the SPD dropped its advocacy of the nationalization of the means of production and compulsory economic planning. It stressed its opposition to communism and its support of NATO and the Western alliance. Shortly thereafter the party sought to broaden its membership base to include more white-collar employees and even independent businessmen. It also made the young, politically attractive mayor of Berlin, Willy Brandt, its national chairman and 1961 candidate for Chancellor.

This new SPD quickly gained increased electoral support. Between 1957 and 1969 its share of the vote increased from 29 percent to 43 percent. In 1966 it entered a Grand Coalition with the CDU/CSU and acquired national political responsibility for the first time in the Federal Republic. Three years later it was able to form a coalition with the Free Democrats with Brandt as Chancellor, the first SPD Chancellor since 1930. Finally, in 1972, with 46 percent of the vote, it finally overtook the Christian Democrats and became the largest political party.

National political responsibility also brought new problems, especially from the SPD's "old" and "new" left. The "old" left, composed of socialists who had always opposed the Bad Godesberg reforms, and the new left, mainly in the party's youth organization (the Young Socialists, or "Jusos"), argued that the party had sold out its ideological and revolutionary heritage and its commitment to social and economic change for political power. It had become as opportunistic as the CDU/CSU and in reality a tool of the "ruling capitalist elite." While these critics remain a minority, their influence is still considerable because the Young Socialists tend to be among the most active party members. The maintenance of party unity remains a major problem for the SPD leadership

In October 1982, after sixteen years of governmental responsibility, the Social Democrats returned to the opposition. The party remains badly divided, with no clear programmatic direction, and an aging leadership. Former Chancellor Helmut Schmidt, the SPD's most effective campaigner, declined to lead the party at the 1983 election. His successor as Chancellor candidate, Hans-Jochen Vogel, was, in comparison, relatively unknown. At the 1983 election the SPD received only 38.2 percent of the popular vote; its lowest level in twenty-two years. Many SPD activists see the return to opposition as an opportunity to reunify and regenerate the party.

The Free Democrats

The Free Democratic party (FDP) is the only small party to survive the postwar emergence of a concentrated and simplified party system. Ideologically and programmatically it is somewhere between the two large parties: On economic issues it is still probably closer to the CDU/CSU than the SPD; but on matters such as education, civil liberties, foreign and defense policies, the FDP has had more in common with the Social Democrats.

The FDP owes its continued existence and relative success to the electoral system, which gives the party a proportionate share of the parliamentary mandates as long as it secures at least 5 percent of the vote. The FDP has held the balance of power in most national elections. Both major parties have tended to prefer coming to terms with the Free Democrats in a small coalition to forming a Grand Coalition with the other major party. Between 1949 and 1957, and again from 1961 to 1965, the Free Democrats were the junior coalition partner in CDU/CSU governments. From 1969 to 1982 it was in coalition with the Social Democrats. In 1982 the FDP changed partners once again and returned to the Christian Democrats. This last move sharply divided the party but it was still able to surmount the 5 percent barrier at the 1983 national election.

The "Greens"

In the late 1970s a variety of environmentalist groups with a common opposition to the government's plan for the expansion of nuclear energy plants banded together into a Federal League of Citizen Groups for the Protection of the Environment (BBU) (*Bundesverband Buergerinitiativen Umweltschutz*), or simply, the "Greens" or "Environmentalists." The Greens were a new face on the political scene. Their antiestablishment, grass-roots, idealistic image had an appeal that was especially strong among younger Germans. In October 1979 a Green party gained entrance into the parliament of the city-state of Bremen, and in March 1980 they surmounted the 5 percent hurdle in the relatively large state of Baden-Wuerttemberg. After a poor showing at the 1980 national election, the environmentalists, with the help of the "alternative" movement, rebounded by gaining representation in the state parliaments in Berlin, Lower Saxony, Hamburg, and Hesse.

The alternative groups, centered mainly in larger cities, trace their origins to struggles over inner-city housing (squatters), the arms race, and education. Many of their activists are former SPD members, veterans of the student protest movements and participants in various left-wing splinter groups. Generally, they are more experienced in organizing campaigns than their Green colleagues. In some areas the Greens are now termed simply GAL for "Green-Alternative List."

The Green-Alternative groups have a strong protest component in their image, and this has helped them skim votes from all the established parties, but especially the SPD and FDP. Nevertheless, they must overcome the charge of being simply a "single-issue" protest movement with no capability to assume or share in the responsibility for all the myriad tasks and problems of government. The established parties also stole some of their thunder by adding stronger environmental protection sections to their election programs. The Greens are divided internally; some of them are quite "red" and advocate measures such as German withdrawal from NATO, unilateral disarmament, and the nationalization of major industries and banks. One of their favorite slogans, "We are not left, we are not right—we are ahead!" does little to resolve the ideological differences within the party.

Their successes in state elections, their opposition to placing American middle-range missiles in West Germany, the continued stagnation of the economy, and increasing popular dissatisfaction with the major parties have given the Greens great visibility. At the 1983 election the Greens became the first party to break the twenty-two-year-old monopoly of the CDU/CSU, SPD, and FDP with 5.7 percent of the vote. They are also represented in six state parliaments and many local councils. The Greens, however, owe much of their success to their rejection of the political game as played by the established parties. They are therefore very reluctant to cooperate in coalition with any of these parties.

Other Parties. Since 1961, a variety of other parties have attempted to break the monopoly of the three system parties. Thus far, all of them have failed to surmount the 5 percent mark, but one of them came fairly close. In the mid-1960s the radical right (if not neo-Nazi) NPD won seats in several state parliaments and seemed to have a good chance to enter the national parliament at the 1969 election. The party secured only 4.5 percent and thus failed to win any seats. Following this near miss, the NPD faded quickly and by 1972 was no longer represented even at state levels.

Interest Groups

As in other advanced industrial societies, in the Federal Republic a wide variety of groups and associations play significant political roles. The major interest groups—business, labor, agriculture, the churches, and professional organizations—are well organized at local, state, and national levels and work closely with the political parties and state bureaucracy. The hierarchical organizational structure of the major German interest associations means that their top officials can speak authoritatively for the membership and ensures them access to state and party elites. Indeed, the rules of procedure in German ministries require officials to consult with the leading representatives of interest groups when drafting legislation that relates to the group's area of concern. Unlike the United States, where the terms "interest" or "pressure" groups and "lobbyist" have negative connotations, their German counterparts are treated as legitimate and necessary participants in the policy process. Each major interest-group alignment also maintains contact, although not to the same extent, with all major parties. Labor unions, for example, have closer ties to the Social Democratic party than to the Christian Democrats or the Free Democrats. Yet there is also a labor wing within the CDU; and the FDP, especially since its coalition with the SPD, also maintains contact with trade-union leaders. Business and industrial interests enjoy a warmer relationship with the center-right CDU/CSU than the SPD, but again there are supporters of the SPD among the ranks of Germany's business-industrial elite.

This pattern of strong government interest-group/political party integration even became somewhat institutionalized during the late 1960s when the top representatives of each area met in a Concerted Action, a regular conference at which general economic conditions were discussed and guidelines for wages, prices, and economic growth were set. At these meetings business, labor and the national government sought to reach a consensus on (1) what a "reasonable" wage increase would be for various industrial workers, (2) the "acceptable" level of price increases, and (3) the amount of government spending and taxation necessary to ensure stable economic conditions and moderate (i.e., noninflationary) economic growth. Although the Concerted Action disbanded in the late 1970s as labor interests became dissatisfied with what they felt were the unreasonable sacrifices they were called on to make, informal labor-business-government contacts continued. Concerted Action may well be revived in the near future.

Concerted Action and the other less formal interest-group/government contacts have prompted some observers to term Bonn a "neocorporatist" state.[2] Corporatism is an old term in social and political thought, and refers to the organization of interests into a limited number of compulsory, hierarchically structured associations recognized by the state and given a monopoly of representation within their respective areas. These associations become in effect quasi-governmental groups: training, licensing, and even exercising discipline over the members with state approval. The power of these associations is not determined by a group's numerical size alone but also by the importance of its function for the state and community.

Major Associations

Business and Industrial Interests. Three organizations speak for business and industry in the Federal Republic: the League of German Industry, which represents large industrial and business interests; the National Association of German Employers, which represents essentially small and medium-sized firms, and the German Industrial and Trade Chamber, composed of smaller, independent businesses (shopkeepers, artisans). Each association is organized at local, regional, state, and national levels.

The impressive accomplishments of the German economy and the importance of economic conditions for the political health of any government ensure these associations easy access to the political elite. Recently they have been most concerned with opposing plans for the expansion of codetermination, compulsory profit sharing, and labor's demand for the elimination of the lockout as a legitimate employer tactic during strikes. The proposal from the left wing of the SPD to institute a system of national economic planning with compulsory state control over investment and pricing decisions is also strongly opposed by these groups.

The ability of business interests to influence government policy even under the socialist-liberal coalition that governed from 1969 to 1982 is seen in the relatively weak Co-Determination Law passed in 1976, under which the representatives of capital and management still retained a majority on a firm's Supervisory Board; and the Apprentice Education Bill of 1976, which continued to assign fundamental responsibility for the training and control of young apprentices, who still account for over 60 percent of the 15-19-year-old age group, to employers and not the school or the state. Government efforts to institute a more progressive tax structure in the late 1970s were also, for the most part, successfully opposed by business interests.

Overall, the socialist-liberal years were good to business, and the government—and especially Chancellor Helmut Schmidt—enjoyed considerable popularity among many German businessmen and industrialists. Schmidt's image as a pragmatic, efficient man who got things done (*Macher*); and his cultivation of personal relationships with several key business leaders to an extent neutralized the inherent antipathy business has traditionally had for the "reds" (socialists). Nonetheless, at election time and especially for fund raising, the more conservative Christian Democrats can still count on the support of most business and industrial interests.

Labor. The German labor movement, like the German political parties, has changed extensively in the postwar period. During the Weimar Republic labor was divided along politico-ideological lines into socialist, communist, Catholic, and even liberal trade unions. These unions, especially the socialist and communist groups, were concerned with more than wages, hours, and working conditions. They sought to mobilize their members into supporting and implementing a comprehensive ideology of social, economic, cultural, and political change. Many of their resources were spent on developing and refining this ideology and the accompanying tactics that included confronting fellow workers in competing unions. The German labor movement was thus fragmented and relatively ineffectual in securing solid economic gains for its members or, of course, in preventing the Nazi seizure of power.

The postwar Western Occupation authorities and many prewar German trade-union leaders sought to restructure and reform the unions. The result of their work is the German Trade Union Federation, (*Deutsche Gewerkschaftsbund*—DGB), an organization composed of 16 different unions with a total membership of over 7 million.[3]

The DGB has become labor's chief political spokesman and has pursued essentially a policy of "business unionism" concentrating on wages and working conditions. Labor leaders as well as economic policy makers within the Social Democratic party advocate a pragmatic position toward the market economy best summed up by the adage "Do not kill the cow we want to milk." The DGB has also been more interested in policies of social and economic change than, for example, its American counterpart, and it has a left wing that espouses more radical policies such as compulsory economic planning and the nationalization of the means of production.

The trade-union movement has been successful in securing steady and solid economic gains for German workers. The unions are also very much a part of this prosperity. They have extensive interests in banking, retail food stores, and housing projects. One factor in the low strike rate is the economic strength of organized labor, which induces business to take union proposals seriously and seek compromises. Business knows that labor has the financial resources to sustain an extensive strike action. The unions' ties to all parties and especially the Social Democrats, who had national political power 1966-82, give them direct access to the government. This political power is an additional factor that produces close worker-management cooperation.

Nonetheless, the DGB's pragmatic, nonideological approach has drawn extensive criticism from Germany's new left. Specifically, the trade-union movement is charged with having done little or nothing to change the basic distribution of power in German society. In spite of widespread prosperity, there are few signs of any redistribution of economic wealth or of a democratization of economic decision making. While the German worker has a color television set, a comfortable apartment, an automobile, and a four-week vacation in Spain, he has little or no control over the economic decisions (investments, prices) that affect his life. Moreover, the working-class share of the nation's capital resources (land, securities, stocks, savings) has not risen significantly during the last twenty-five years. The economic gains of workers, critics charge, have come as a result of the "economic pie" becoming larger, not because of a bigger slice of that pie for manual workers. For many of Germany's young, critical intellectuals, the trade-union movement has simply "sold out" to the existing capitalist system. It is, in their view, conservative, status quo oriented, and incapable of leading any movement for real economic and social reform.[4] The increase in strike activity in the late 1970s and the increasing dissatisfaction with the leadership of the DBG on the part of some workers indicate that the debate over the direction of the labor movement will intensify in the years to come.

Agriculture. Few interest groups in the Federal Republic have been as successful in securing governmental policies beneficial to their members as have the various organizations representing German farmers. Farmers constitute less than 5 percent of the work force, and agriculture's contribution to the gross national product is less than 3 percent. Yet no occupational group is as protected and as well subsidized by the government. German farmers receive guaranteed prices for most of their products; they are given subsidies and tax benefits for new equipment, construction, and the modernization of their holdings. And the increase in the value of farmland has led some observers to term farmers Germany's "secret rich."[5] A 1973 survey found the per capita net worth of farmers to be almost a half million marks (about $250,000). While they may be "land rich" but "cash poor," it is difficult to consider them an impoverished or disadvantaged minority in West German society.

A succession of "green plans" has consolidated many small farms into larger, more efficient units, but German agriculture still could not compete with other Western societies were it not for the strong Common Market tariff system for farm products. These benefits to farmers have been estimated to have added an additional 10 to 15 percent to the food bill of German consumers; but all governments since 1949, regardless of their party configuration, have essentially continued these policies. Indeed, farmers never "had it so good" as they did under the socialist-liberal coalition.

The key to the success of agricultural groups is their cohesiveness and well-coordinated political activity. Almost all of the country's 2 million farmers are organized into three groups that constitute the "green front": the German Farmers League, the Association of Agricultural Chambers, and the Cooperative League. The latter group is also involved in retailing farm products and granting loans to farmers. These groups, unlike their American or French counterparts, do not pursue conflicting goals but work closely to secure desired policies. They can count on the steadfast support of about forty parliamentary deputies who sit on key agricultural committees.

Elections

Elections in the Federal Republic of Germany offer citizens their chief opportunity to influence the political process. Convinced that the German "common man" had been supportive of Hitler and the Nazi regime during most of the Third Reich, the Federal Republic's founding fathers essentially limited popular involvement at the national level to participation in periodic elections.[5] There are thus no provisions for the direct election of the President or the Chancellor, referenda, the recall of public officials, or direct primaries to ensure more popular involvement at the national level.[7]

As in other parliamentary systems, national elections do not directly determine the chief personnel of government. The Chancellor and Cabinet are elected by parliament after parliament has been elected by the voters. Elections must be held at least once very four years, but can take place more frequently if a government loses its majority and parliament is dissolved. The Federal Republic has automatic registration and universal adult suffrage for all citizens over eighteen years of age.

Electoral System

Generally there are two basic procedures in Western democracies for converting votes into legislative seats: a proportional system in which a party's share of legislative mandates is proportional to its popular vote and a plurality, or "winner take all" system, under which "losing" parties and candidates (and their voters) receive no representation. Proportional systems are usually favored by smaller parties because under "pure" proportionality, a party with even a fraction of a percent of the vote would receive parliamentary representation.

Conversely, plurality systems are usually favored by the large parties which have both the resources and candidates to secure pluralities in electoral districts. Some political scientists have hypothesized that there is a causal relationship between the electoral law and the number of political parties with a proportional law causing a multiparty pattern and a plurality system producing a concentration of electoral support in the two parties.

The German electoral law has elements of both plurality and proportionality, but is essentially a proportional system. One half of the delegates to parliament are elected on a plurality basis from 248 districts; the other half are chosen on the proportional principle from state *(Land)* lists. The voter thus receives two ballots — one for a district candidate, the other for a party. But the second ballot is by far the most important. The proportion of the vote a party receives on the second ballot determines ultimately how many seats it will have in parliament, because the district contests won by the party's candidates are deducted from the total due it on the basis of the second ballot vote.

TABLE 13.1
Seat Distribution in the 1980 Federal Election

Party	Percent First Ballot	Percent Second Ballot	Number of Seats Entitled to Under Proportional Representation	Number of District Contests Won (1st ballot)	Number of List Candidates Elected
CDU/CSU	46.0	44.5	226	121	105
SPD	44.5	42.9	217	127	91
FDP	7.2	10.6	53	0	53
Minor parties	2.3	2.0	0	0	0
TOTAL	100.0	100.0	496	248	249*

*The SPD received one extra deputy because it won an additonal district contest.

An example from the 1980 election should illustrate this procedure. In 1980 the SPD won 42.9 percent of the second ballot vote and was thus entitled to 218 mandates. Since it had already won 127 contests at the district level, however, these were deducted from the total due it on the basis of the second ballot vote. Thus its total of 218 was composed of 127 direct district victories plus 91 from the second ballot party lists. Similarly, the CDU/CSU with 121 district victories received an additional 105 from the second ballot to bring its total to 226. Note that the small FDP won no district victories, but did receive 10.6 percent of the second ballot vote. All of its 53 seats thus came from the party lists.

There are also two exceptions to pure proportionality: A party must receive at least 5 percent of the second ballot vote or win 3 district contests in order to share in the proportional distribution. In 1980 none of the small parties (see table 13.1 above) surmounted this barrier and the seats (about 10) they would have won under a pure proportional system went to the three parties that gained parliamentary representation. The other exception to proportionality involves the winning of more district contests than a party would be entitled to on the basis of the second ballot. Let us assume that in 1980 the CDU/CSU had won all 248 district elections, yet its second ballot percentage entitled it to only 105 seats. In this example, the CDU/CSU would keep its 248 seats and parliament would simply be enlarged to 601 deputies (496 plus the 105 excess mandates). An enlargement to this extent, however, has never taken place. The most excess mandates ever won by a party was 5, in 1961. The SPD, however, did win one excess mandate in the 1980 election.

This complicated electoral law, which most German voters do not fully understand, was intended to combine the best features of the plurality and proportional systems. The district contests were to introduce a "personalized" component into elections and give voters a means of identification with "their" parliamentary deputy; the party list allocations were meant to ensure that a programmatic or policy dimension to elections would be present. The 5 percent clause was designed to prevent small, antisystem splinter parties from gaining representation and making coalition building in parliament difficult. In spite of its basically proportional character, the German party system has become more concentrated during the last thirty years. Only one small party, the Free Democrats, has survived to benefit from proportionality. The FDP, of course, has opposed any changes in the law, such as a plurality system, which would mean its demise.

Candidate Selection

Candidates for the party lists are selected at state-level conventions held several months prior to the general election. The composition of a list involves considerable bargaining within the party and between it and its major interest clientele. Generally the very top positions are reserved for the party's notables in the state, followed by representatives of factions and interest groups. In some cases a candidate assigned a relatively weak district will be compensated by a promising list position. All participants in this procedure have a rough idea of how many list positions will be allotted to the party; that is, how many candidates will actually be elected. As the assumed cutoff point is approached, the intensity of the bargaining increases.

District candidates are nominated at local meetings of party organizations. These meetings are intended to provide an opportunity for all party members to screen prospective candidates. In fact, the district leadership of the party dominates the proceedings. Nonetheless, state and national party leaders have relatively little influence in the district-level nominating process, and there have been cases where prominent legislators have had difficulty because they had paid insufficient attention to the grass-roots membership.

Since most candidates are incumbents, the most obvious qualification for nomination to the Bundestag is previous experience in the job. A successful local- or state-level legislative background, long service in a local party organization, and close association with an interest group important to the party are other important qualifications. For a list nomination, expertise in a particular policy area can also be an important factor.

The German Voter, 1949-83

The results of the ten national elections held since 1949, presented in figure 13.2 on page 211, reveal several major trends in German elections:

1. A very high rate of turnout, which by the 1970s exceeded 90 percent, the highest proportion of any major Western democracy without legal penalties for nonvoting. This high turnout reflects the strong emphasis in the political culture placed on voting as a "duty," but it also indicates a growing tendency to perceive elections as a means of citizen influence in the policy-making process.
2. The increasing concentration of support in two parties and since 1983 two small but strategically important third parties, all of which support the basic democratic structure of the system.
3. The dominant position of the CDU/CSU between 1953 and 1969. During this period the Union was the largest political party and the major partner in all coalition governments.
4. The steady rise of the SPD between 1953 and 1972 from the "30 percent ghetto" to parity with the Christian Democrats.
5. The competitive character of voting since 1969. At each election, alternation of government and opposition was a real possibility.

In 1949 fourteen political parties secured parliamentary representation. Most of these were by 1957 absorbed into the Christian Democrats led by Konrad Adenauer. Extremist parties such as the Communist and several radical right-wing groups also disappeared by 1957, rejected by the electorate. Campaigns of the 1950s focused on the performance of Adenauer's governments. CDU gains during this period came largely from the ranks of the smaller parties. Most SPD gains between 1957 and 1972 were from CDU/CSU voters and new voters, not from those of the minor parties. The Free Democrats attempted to appeal to CDU/CSU and SPD vot-

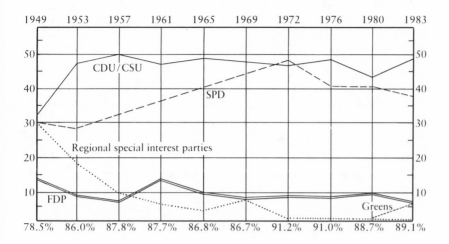

FIGURE 13.2
Voter Turnout and Results of Federal Elections, 1949-83

ers dissatisfied with their "normal" party. The FDP projects itself as a "liberal" corrective to the major parties: less conservative and clerical than the CDU/CSU, but not as "radical" or "socialist" as the SPD. In election campaigns the FDP must to an extent campaign against its coalition partner.

Like the CDU/CSU during the Adenauer years, the SPD in 1980 de-emphasized any new programs in its platform; rather, it told the electorate "it all depends on the Chancellor." The party's conventional electoral program made few promises and developed no clear-cut guidelines for the next four years. When new programs were mentioned (environmental protection, tax reform, male-female equality in the pension system, payments to housewives) they were made dependent on financial conditions.

Strauss and the CDU/CSU in 1980 attempted to portray the SPD, or at least its left wing, as steering the Federal Republic toward a neutralist position midway between the United States and the Soviet Union. While Chancellor Schmidt and most of his Cabinet were excluded from this charge, the Christian Democrats did focus on the SPD's national chairman, Willy Brandt; its parliamentary leader, Herbert Wehner; and the SPD general secretary, Egon Bahr, as leaders of a "Moscow faction." The Christian Democrats also emphasized the increasing influence of radical elements within the SPD and the danger of the Federal Republic's becoming a Marxist state and society. This tactic met with little electoral support.

At the 1983 election the voters solidly endorsed the CDU/CSU-FDP government of Helmut Kohl, which had governed since October 1982. The Christian Democrats with 48.8 percent of the vote achieved their best result since 1957. The CDU/CSU gains came largely at the expense of the Social Democrats and almost 2 million 1980 SPD voters switched to the Union. The major issues of the campaign were unemployment, the security of the pension system, the reduction of deficit spending, and price stability. In all of these areas the CDU/CSU was regarded as better qualified to deal with these problems than the SPD. The campaign of the SPD focused on the missile question, which was not nearly as important to the majority of the electorate as the bread-and-butter economic problems. The Social Democrats also failed in their attempt to attract the support of Green voters by moving toward the Green position on the missile and nuclear power questions. The Free Democrats with 6.9 percent of the vote were able to gain the support of those voters who did not want the controversial Franz Josef Strauss to join the Kohl government

Voting Behavior

The votes of most West Germans can be explained by: (1) demographic characteristics of voters, especially social class and religion; (2) voter attitudes toward major candidates; (3) the policies of the political parties; and (4) voter opinions about important policy issues confronting the country.

Demographics. Germany's manual workers still form the core of the Social Democratic electorate, while the Christian Democrats and the FDP do well in middle-class or nonmanual occupations. In 1980 manual workers preferred the SPD over the other parties by about a 2-1 margin. Among middle-class voters, Christian Democratic support is as high. The Free Democrats have done relatively well among the "new middle class": those voters in white-collar technical and administrative positions.

The religious factor also structures the party vote. Most German Catholics who regularly attend church are staunch supporters of the Christian Democrats. But the party preference of Catholics varies significantly by their attachment to the church (as measured by church attendance). Catholic voters who seldom or never go to church are far less likely to support the Christian Democrats than those who regularly attend services. For nominal Catholics, social class rather than religion is a more important determinant of voting. Both the SPD and the FDP receive disproportionate support from Protestants, especially those with a weak attachment to their church.

Until 1972 there were also significant differences in the party vote of men and women with the CDU receiving proportionately more support from females than the SPD or FDP. In recent elections, however, the male-female difference has greatly diminished. Another demographic factor influencing voting behavior is urbanization. The smaller or less urbanized the community in which the voter resides, the greater the tendency for him or her to support the Christian Democrats. The SPD and FDP vote conversely increases with the size of the voter's home community.

Attitudes Toward Candidates. Voters' perceptions of major candidates, especially party leaders and those slated for the Chancellorship or Cabinet membership, is an important influence on voting behavior. The incumbent Chancellor, for example, generally has an advantage, or "bonus," over the challenger. As in other Western societies, the chief executive can to an extent influence the news — announce new programs such as tax reductions, increased social programs, and subsidies to various groups — all timed to the election.

A major factor in the landslide CDU/CSU victories in 1953 and 1957 was the personal popularity of Adenauer. More voters liked Adenauer than actually supported his party, and the SPD's Chancellor candidates were less popular than their party. The 1980 victory of the SPD-FDP was aided by the popularity of Chancellor Schmidt and the negative image of his challenger, Franz Josef Strauss, who clearly hurt his party.

Party Policies. West German voters, in comparison to those in other Western societies, are very well informed. They are relatively quick to perceive changes in party policies and have on occasion acted accordingly. Most of the SPD gains between 1957 and 1972 came from middle-class voters responding in part to the party's change in policies. The SPD made a major effort to attract middle-class voters away from the CDU/CSU by abandoning more "radical" or Marxist components of its program.

The loss of support experienced by the Free Democrats after 1965 was also related to changes in its policies as it moved away from the CDU/CSU and more toward its future coalition partner, the SPD. Many old FDP supporters perceived a "drift to the left" and changed their vote.

Issues. In most elections the issues of prime concern to German voters revolve around the economy and social stability: inflation, law and order (terrorism), unemployment, and the viability of the social welfare system. "Security" is a word used often by all major parties in their electoral appeals; the bulk of the electorate does not want any major political or socioeconomic changes. Nonetheless, specific issues, while not of concern to a great majority of the electorate, can be important in effecting the small voting shifts that can be decisive in an election. In 1972, for example, the SPD-FDP coalition was clearly helped by the issue of *Ostpolitik* treaties. Some voters, normally CDU/CSU, supported the Brandt government because of this issue; they saw the treaties as a step toward a more lasting détente in Europe. In 1976 the "near miss" of the CDU/CSU was due in part to its position on the issue of "radicals" in public service. Some traditional SPD or FDP voters were troubled about the possibility of avowed communists inundating the school system or other areas of public service. Others believed that the government was not taking the threat of communist expansion seriously enough. In 1980 the issue of nuclear power plants probably cost the SPD and FDP some support, especially among younger voters, who either stayed home in protest or supported the "Green" parties.

Notes

1. For a discussion of this point, see Gordon Smith, *Democracy in Western Germany* (New York: Holmes and Meier, 1979), pp. 96ff.
2. Gerhard Lehmbruch, "Liberal Corporatism and Party Government," in *Trends Toward Corporatist Intermediation,* ed. Philippe Schmitter and Gerhard Lehmbruch (Beverly Hills: Sage, 1979), pp. 147-88.
3. There is a union for white-collar employees (*Angestellten*) with about a half million members that is not affiliated with the DGB. This is the only non-DGB union of any significant size in the private sector.
4. Andrei S. Markovits and Christopher S. Allen, "Power and Dissent: Trade Unions in the Federal Republic of Germany Re-Examined" (Washington, DC: Council of European Studies, March 1979).
5. Michael Jungblut, "Die heimlichen Reichen," *Die Zeit,* no. 46 (10 November 1978): 25.
6. K. Sontheimer, "Die Bundesrepublik und ihre Buerger," in *Nach dreissig Jahren,* ed. Walter Scheel (Stuttgart: Klett-Cotta, 1979), pp. 175-86.
7. Referenda are constitutionally possible in most states, and a little-known provision of the Basic Law allows local communities to be governed by citizen assemblies. Thus far, no locality has employed this form of governance.

14

How Is Power Used?

The Federal Republic is a complex political system characterized by the presence of several power centers. Although the national executive with its control over the civil service initiates the broad outlines of policy, it cannot secure the approval of its policy proposals or their implementation without at least the tacit prior approval of other actors in the political system: major interest groups, extraparliamentary organizations of the governing parties, "backbenchers" in the legislature, the states, and even the opposition party when it has a majority of the delegates in the Bundesrat. Strong opposition by any of these actors will hinder the efforts of the government and Chancellor to determine the "main guidelines" of policy.

Successful policy making must be accomplished within the framework of the politico-economic consensus that has emerged during the past thirty-five years. This means that the system resists any efforts at introducing major innovations within a relatively short time frame. Change tends to be gradual and incremental and rarely will it have a redistributive effect. The issue of codetermination, for example, has been a policy problem throughout most of the republic's history. Codetermination—the right of workers and other employees to share in a firm's decision-making process through equal representation on its supervisory board—was a key element in the SPD program in 1969 when it became the major partner in a coalition with the FDP and again in 1972 when this coalition secured a comfortable parliamentary majority. Yet in spite of these very favorable political conditions, the new Co-Determination Law, which finally went into effect in 1976, did not give a firm's workers' parity with capital and management. Attempts to change the tax system in the direction of more progressive rates have been stymied partly by the opposition of the small coalition partner but also through the efforts of well-organized interest groups that have extensive contacts with governmental ministries.

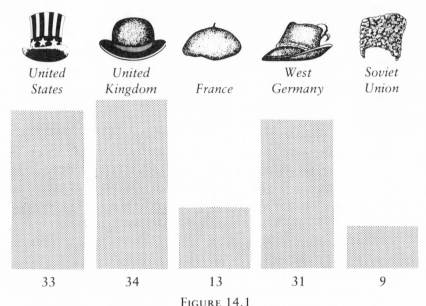

FIGURE 14.1
Percentage of Income Taxes in Total Revenue

The federal structure of the republic, which gives the states extensive responsibilities in implementing national legislation, represents a further dispersion of political power and is thus a further inhibiting factor on major policy innovation.[1] The importance of the constituent states in the policy process has increased as the scope of their veto power in the Bundesrat has expanded. At present, almost two-thirds of all legislation is subject to a Bundesrat veto. In addition, since 1972 the CDU/CSU has held a majority of delegates in the Bundesrat, which further reduced the chances of the national government to "use its power" without extensive bargaining with the states. Thus the 1976 treaty with Poland, although negotiated by the national government, was ratified only after a variety of changes and concessions were made at the insistence of the CDU/CSU majority in the Bundesrat. Planned changes in education policy and the liberalization of regulations governing the employment of "radicals" in the public service have also recently been thwarted by state (CDU/CSU) opposition. But even "friendly" states (those governed by the same coalition that governs in Bonn) can and have opposed national policy initiatives when they perceive a threat to state interests. Thus the national government has been unable to change significantly the distribution of taxes between the national and state government, or to expand its influence in higher education, urban planning, and environmental protection legislation. In these areas, all of the states have guarded their prerogatives.

The postwar German economic record—low inflation and unemployment, steady economic growth—is also the result of a consensus-oriented political leadership. Governmental budgets, regardless of the parties in power, have been relatively balanced in the postwar period. In a recent seven-nation study Germany ranked third in expenditures, but also third highest in taxes.[2] At the same time the social welfare system (pensions, health insurance) has helped maintain a high level of demand. Germany also ranked high in capital investment, which provided for an adequate number of new jobs.

In comparison with six other advanced industrial societies,

> Germany attained the best trade-off (the lowest inflation and jobless rates) because labor unions sought moderate wage increases, concentrated industries accepted the need for import-export competition, and the government enacted monetary and fiscal policies that stimulated moderately high aggregate demand—neither high enough to cause rapid price rises nor sufficiently low to produce high joblessness.[3]

The disastrous experience with inflation in the 1920s and the real economic gains in the postwar period have made all parties sensitive and responsive to inflationary problems.

The extensive welfare state is part of this consensus. The constitution, or Basic Law, states that the Federal Republic is a *sozialer* state, a state obligated to establish and maintain basic social welfare rights. Thus governmental policies designed to provide full employment, education, housing, child support payments, social security, and health care are, unlike in the United States, not matters of partisan conflict over the issue of whether the government should be involved in these areas; rather, the issue is the *extent* of government programs. All major political parties support the extensive welfare state; no group advocates the abolition of the national health insurance system, the pension program, or the *Kindergeld* (family allowance) payments. The partisan debates about these issues tend to revolve around problems of detail and administration. By 1980 the total expenditure for social programs by local, state, and national sources amounted to about one-third of the total gross national product.

A basic pattern of incrementalism, a problem-solving bargaining orientation to politics, continued unchanged under the socialist-liberal coalition that governed in Bonn until 1982. Indeed the socialists at least since 1959 have vowed not to change the "rules of the game" if they did achieve national political responsibility. Most of Germany's Social Democrats do not propose any basic changes in the structure of the economy or polity. In economic policy they have advocated only gradual changes in capitalism German-style. Capital and labor are viewed as "partners" rather than opponents with government mediating any major differences. This basic orientation means, of course, that governmental power will be used cautiously and above all in a manner that will not disrupt consensus. The thirteen years (sixteen including the 1966-69 Grand Coalition) of Social Democratic rule did not produce any basic changes in this pattern. What the socialists effected was a gradual shift in distributive policies in the direction of greater benefits for lower- and lower-middle status groups (tax, welfare, education policies) and the beginnings of a possible shift in the distribution of power and influence within the industrial enterprise (codetermination). The other major change associated with SPD rule since 1969 — *Ostpolitik,* the normalization of relations between Eastern Europe and the Soviet Union — did not in fact represent any major challenge to the consensus but drew on previous initiatives made during the mid- and late 1960s when the Christian Democrats were still the dominant party. Thus there was considerable support for this "new policy" within the parliamentary oppostion.

Conflicts between the two coalition partners were most frequent in socioeconomic policy and specifically over questions of the organization of the economy, the reform of vocational (apprenticeship) training, land-use laws, the inequality of capital resources (compulsory profit sharing), and tax reform. The Free Democrats generally are opposed to increased state intervention in the economy and the extension of worker participation in a firm's decision-making process at the expense of capital and management. The "leveling" implied in the profit-sharing plans supported by the socialists and their plans for increasingly progressive taxation were also opposed by the FDP. In short, when the issue involved the *redistribution* of economic resources and power, that is, increasing the resources of one group (workers) at the expense of another (the middle and upper classes), there was extensive conflict within the coalition. The FDP was usually able to force a compromise that benefited its largely upper- and middle-class clientele and potential clientele. The socialists in this area probably gave up more than their numerical strength required; also, the Free Democrats exerted more influence than their size would have entitled them to.[4]

The coalition was most harmonious when problems were largely regulative and distributive in character. There was essentially little difference between socialists and liberals in the areas of civil liberties, education, internal security, defense, and foreign policies. These latter problems dominated the legislative program of the first socialist-liberal government led by Willy Brandt (1969-72).

Policy Implementation

The process of implementing national legislation takes place largely through the administrative structures of the state *(Land)* governments. The national government is thus dependent, in many cases, on the states if legislation is to have its intended effect. At first glance this system would seem to allow the ten states, especially those governed by parties not in power in Bonn, to sabotage or undermine national legislation they oppose on ideological or partisan political grounds. In practice, this has not taken place.

German federalism has a number of unifying or centralizing characteristics that makes this implementation phase function remarkably well. First, as we have discussed, state governments and their bureaucracies have extensive input into the national level legislative process through their membership in the Bundesrat. They are well aware of what the legislation will entail in terms of administrative machinery and resources. Second, the laws and rules of procedures for state bureaucracies are unified. Unlike American federalism, constituent states do not have different laws for divorces, bankruptcy, or criminal offenses. Also, the rules by which the civil service operates are the same for all states and the national government. Third, the constitution, or Basic Law, requires that there be a "unity of living standards" throughout the Republic. In practice this has meant that richer states such as North Rhine-Westphalia or Hamburg must pay via grants and tax transfers to bring the poorer states up to their level of government services and standards. Thus the expenditures of poorer states for public works or welfare are not drastically different from those of more prosperous *Laender*. Differences between resources and expenditures are made up by this system of tax redistribution, or revenue sharing.

Differences between states do exist in policy areas where the *Laender* have sole or major responsibilities — mainly education (especially primary and secondary) and internal security (police and law enforcement). Educational reform, for example, has proceeded differently in the various states; although the CDU/CSU governs six of the ten *Laender,* only one of every ten comprehensive schools is in a CDU state. Procedures for the screening of candidates for public employment have also varied with CDU/CSU states taking a more hardline position on this issue. There have been cases of prospective schoolteachers whose applications were rejected in CDU/CSU governed states such as Bavaria or Baden-Wuerttemberg for alleged "radical" political activity securing positions in SPD states.

Notes

1. Although Bonn is the official political capital and the seat of parliament, not all major administrative units of the federal government have their central offices there. For example, none of the major federal courts are in Bonn; they are scattered about in Karlsruhe, Kassel, Berlin, and elsewhere. The federal railways and federal bank are in Frankfurt, the airline has its administrative center in Cologne, the national archive is in Koblenz, the Federal Criminal Office (the German version of the FBI) is in Wiesbaden. This dispersion of administrative office reflects the decentralized character of the Federal Republic and, perhaps more important, the fact that the states *(Laender)* preceded the federal government after 1945. Indeed many of these offices antedate the Federal Republic and were the product of the Occupation period.
2. Charles F. Andrain, *Politics and Economic Policy in Western Democracies* (North Scituate, Mass.: Duxbury, 1980), pp. 212-28.
3. Ibid., p. 167.
4. Manfred G. Schmidt, "The Politics of Domestic Reform in the Federal Republic of Germany," *Politics and Society* 8, no. 2 (1979): 165-200.

15

What Is the Future of German Politics?

As the Federal Republic begins its fourth decade, it is faced with a variety of domestic and foreign political problems, many of which are common to other advanced industrial democracies: unemployment, environmental protection, urban development, energy, the financing of the extensive social welfare system, economic growth, and East-West relations. But none of the republic's current tasks should obscure its fundamental accomplishment during the first thirty years: A consensus on liberal democracy has finally been achieved in a German political order. The Federal Republic has become a stable, effective, and legitimate democratic political system. Indeed, for some it has become a "model" of an advanced industrial society. Its critics — those who view it as a "republic in suspense," very vulnerable to a major economic crisis, and those who regard it as a neo-fascist "restoration" — are simply mistaken. That these clichés endure testifies to the power of stereotypes and not to any actual political developments in the last thirty years.

This process of consensus building and legitimation has taken most of the last thirty years to develop. As a result, many institutional and policy changes have been slower to emerge in the Federal Republic than in other Western democracies. Thus there is no lack of problems for the Federal Republic in the 1980s. Nevertheless, few modern industrial democracies have more resources to deal with these issues than West Germany.

Foreign Policy

The Federal Republic of Germany was originally a product of the cold war, and throughout its history, events in the international political arena have had an impact on the domestic political system. It is also the largest and most important Western state that borders the socialist bloc. With almost 300,000 American troops together with an additional 150,000 from Britain, France, and other NATO countries stationed on its territory, West Germany is affected by each shift or change in East-West relations. The Federal Republic is also unique among the members of the Atlantic alliance in that it remains a divided nation. The Bonn constitution, in its preamble, commits the new state to reunification "in peace and freedom" as its foremost policy goal. This, of course, has not been achieved, and reunification itself has been redefined in the context of postwar European and world politics. The majority of the West German public now accepts the existence of two German states and the loss of territories east of the present border between Poland and East Germany. What is now intended by West German leaders is a gradual integration between the Federal Republic and East Germany within the context of a general relaxation of tensions throughout Europe.

German political elites and the informed public know that few if any of Germany's neighbors in Western or Eastern Europe want a reunified Germany. Such a single German state would be more powerful than any major European country, although less powerful than the United States or the Soviet Union. It would probably become a direct or indirect source of tension in world politics. As long as both Germanys' neighbors are not indifferent to reunification (i.e., they still fear it), it would be politically impossible for any German government to bring a unified Germany about "in peace and freedom."

West German governments since the Grand Coalition in 1966 have thus sought to improve relations with East Germany through more extensive travel and communication programs, economic and trade arrangements, and joint projects such as new highway systems. An increase in the number of West Germans who visit East Germany or the number of letters and telephone calls between the two states is now viewed as in a way contributing to some sort of reunification in the distant future. Some Germans regard this approach as a "sellout" or betrayal of national interests, but to the great majority it is the only realistic policy consistent with the maintenance of world peace, which has always taken precedence over reunification.

The influence of East-West relations on the domestic politics of the Federal Republic is also illustrated by the emergence in 1980 of a nationwide "peace movement." In December 1979 the NATO countries, in response to the buildup of Soviet SS-20 missiles in Eastern Europe, agreed to begin the deployment of *Pershing-2* and *Cruise* missiles in West Germany, the Netherlands, Belgium, Britain, and Italy by late 1983. At the same time negotiations with the Soviet Union on reducing the number of these weapons on both sides were to be conducted. This so-called two-track decision became the focus of the peace movement organized shortly after the 1980 election by various left-wing splinter organizations, environmentalists, Protestant church groups, and intellectuals associated with peace research institutes at several universities. The Soviet invasion of Afghanistan, the collapse of the Salt II treaty, and the election of Ronald Reagan with his alleged hard-line approach to the Soviet Union were cited by the movement as evidence that the United States was not seriously interested in negotiations with the Soviet Union over the missile issue (the second track of the NATO decision). Moreover, the peace movement emphasized that the land-based deployment of the *Pershing* and *Cruise* weapons represented in effect an American attempt to contain a future nuclear conflict to Europe. The decision by the Reagan administration in August 1981 to proceed with the development of the neutron bomb further intensified the peace movement's opposition to the NATO decision.

Both the center-right Christian Democrats and the Free Democrats support the NATO decision. Most, but not all, of the SPD leadership support the missile deployment, but among the party's activists there is considerable opposition. During the fall of 1981 regional SPD membership meetings were held throughout the country in an attempt to confront and overcome opposition to the NATO plan. The peace movement, however, has also staged several massive demonstrations throughout the country.

Citizen Participation

A more pressing problem in the 1980s involves the growing demand for increased citizen participation in policy making and the weak response the established party system has made to this movement. As we discussed earlier, the framers of the Basic Law in 1948-49 had little confidence in the German common man and did little to encourage participation beyond periodic voting. But Germans in the 1980s are no longer in their democratic political infancy. Also, the political system has failed to adequately consider citizen input when dealing with a number of problems: nuclear reactor construction, protection of the environment, urban planning, housing development, education, and child-care and preschool programs.

Since the late 1960s, a wide variety of citizen action or initiative groups have emerged at the local and regional levels in response to the inability of the established state bureaucracy and party system to deal with these policy issues. The approximately 5,000 initiative groups are usually motivated by some specific local problem, such as inadequate playgrounds in housing projects, a planned *Autobahn* extension that would cut through a forest, a new train line affecting a recreational area, the need for better health care and educational facilities in rural areas, or urban transportation difficulties. About 60 percent of the groups are involved in one of three areas: nuclear power, urban problems, and education. By 1980 the total membership in all citizen initiative groups exceeded that of the three Bundestag parties. Clearly, the initiative groups were responding to needs and demands not being met by these established parties.

A national-level citizen initiative movement has developed only in one issue area: nuclear power. Although the number of nuclear plants installed in West Germany is still below the British or French level, the established parties have all been committed to a major expansion of nuclear energy. Antinuclear sentiment was not significantly represented at the leadership level of any system party. The consensus throughout the 1970s was that the continued growth and productivity of the economy and employment security depended on the development of nuclear energy. The response of government to protest demonstrations beginning in the mid-1970s in several states was very harsh: armed police, tear gas, mass arrests, and a general condemnation of antinuclear groups as "extremist" and "radical." But the ranks of the antinuclear forces grew. By 1978 several groups had banded together to form a national organization, state elections were contested by environmentalist or "Green" parties, and the antinuclear message began to be heard at the leadership level of major parties. In addition, at least two SPD state party organizations were against the Schmidt government's planned expansion of nuclear power plant construction, and antinuclear factions were identified in parliamentary delegations of the FDP and even the CDU/CSU. In spite of the inability of environmentalists to gain entrance into the national parliament at the 1980 election, the nuclear power debate and the related problem of citizen participation will continue to be significant issues in West German politics.

A variety of proposals have been made to increase citizen influence in the political process, many of them familiar to American students: the direct primary as a means of democratizing the political parties; the introduction of referenda so that issues of great concern, such as nuclear power, could receive direct popular input; more responsibility to local governments, especially in the education and urban planning fields; and the extension of citizens' rights to petition and recall public officials. For some critics of the present "limited middle-class" democracy, however, the question of citizenship participation in policy making can be resolved only if the *economy* and *society* are first *democratized.* Codetermination in industry is viewed by some as the beginning of such an economic democratization. The worker, according to this argument, cannot be expected to become an involved, active citizen if he has been taught through job and school experiences to be a subject, to follow orders and let the interests of those above him in the economic hierarchy determine when and how he should perform his job. Real political democracy is thus seen as dependent on economic and social democracy.

Thus far, there are few indications the existing Co-Determination Law has produced this new citizen. Nonetheless, the issue of participation and the related area of socioeconomic democratization will remain important. The SPD left and its allies, especially among younger intellectuals in large urban areas, are committed to overcoming what they see as the contradiction between the ideal of equality and the reality of stratification and inequality in the Federal Republic.

Minorities: Foreign Workers

The most difficult social problem confronting the Federal Republic is the condition of the almost 2 million foreign workers and their 2.6 million dependents living in West Germany. The economic miracle of the 1950s transformed Germany from an economy with a surplus of labor to one with an acute labor shortage. There were simply too many jobs available for the native work force, especially in menial, low-paying positions. To remedy this problem and maintain economic growth, the government, working closely with employers, recruited workers from Italy, Greece, Turkey, Spain, and other less developed countries. By 1973 there were almost 2.6 million foreign workers in the Federal Republic; the 1974-76 recession reduced this to the present 1.9 million. Guestworkers *(Gastarbeiter),* as they are euphemistically termed, usually occupy the lowest rung on the occupational ladder: unskilled manual positions, sanitary and sewage workers, custodial and janitorial staff. They tend to be concentrated in large cities: Berlin, for example, is the city with the third largest Turkish population in the world. They have been subjected to discrimination in housing and by private and public agencies. Apart from their jobs, most foreign workers have little or no social contact with the native German population. As one author put it, they "remain on the margins of the society, dispossessed and nearly invisible."[1]

The dependents of foreign workers, especially their children, make this a potentially explosive issue. Many of these children have spent most or all of their lives in Germany. Yet their parents cling to the goal of someday returning to their home country and thus want the children to retain its language and values. The result is that children grow up in a sort of twilight zone — they master neither their parents' language nor German. They invariably drop out of school and, urged on by the parents, attempt to secure employment to augment the family's finances and hasten its "return" to the homeland. But in recent years the tightened job market has made it difficult for young, half-literate, untrained foreign people to find employment. The result is a growing body of unemployed adolescents, especially in the large cities, involved in petty crime, and increasingly, the drug trade.

In spite of the stable number of foreign workers in recent years, their higher birthrates and the influx of family members has actually increased the total number of foreign residents to over 4.5 million. In some large cities such as Frankfurt, up to one-half of all newborn children are from foreign worker families, although *Gastarbeiter* constitute less than 10 percent of the total work force. There are now two and even three generations of foreign residents.

Discrimination, a lack of social mobility, and poor educational and job opportunities for their children are the result, in large part, of the guestworkers' lack of political influence. As non-Germans they cannot vote, and the acquisition of citizenship is a difficult process even for those foreign residents who want to be naturalized. The political system has simply not responded to the needs of an unorganized, politically powerless minority, and as long as foreign workers do not have the vote, it is difficult to envision any major changes. In fact, new restrictions on residency for foreign workers imposed by some local governments hinder their freedom of movement and hence decrease their prospects for upward social mobility.

The problem is compounded by the ambiguity of the foreign workers' future plans. Many still insist that their goal is to return to their home country. They are in Germany just to earn as much money in as short a period of time as they can and are thus not interested in becoming politically involved. For some, this "return to the homeland" has become a myth or illusion that enables them to endure the discrimination and deprivation they experience. By the second and third generation, however, it becomes less viable, and the frustration of their children increases. The potential for social unrest that exists in this situation should be obvious especially to American readers.

Several proposals have been made to improve the status of the guest-workers and their families. One involves giving the franchise to foreign workers for local elections. This would, it is argued, make local officials more responsive to their needs, especially in housing and education. Some students of the problem have advocated that all children of foreign workers, born in the Federal Republic, automatically become German citizens when they reach the age of eighteen. It would thus become simpler for the second and third generation to identify with the Federal Republic and reject the "return to the homeland" myth. Finally, it has been suggested that the naturalization laws be liberalized so that foreign workers could have a viable option to their present condition. Thus far, however, there is little significant support for any of these proposed changes. The SPD-FDP government established several advisory study commissions to investigate the problem, but did not submit any draft legislation. In a practical sense,

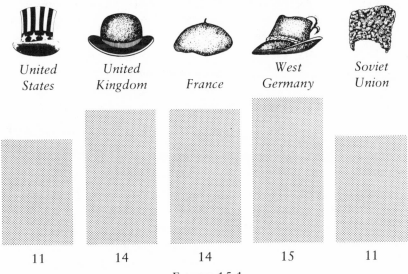

United States	United Kingdom	France	West Germany	Soviet Union
11	14	14	15	11

FIGURE 15.1

Population Aged 65 and Over (in percent)

German churches, labor unions (by requiring equal pay for equal work) and charitable organizations have in many cases done more to alleviate the problems than the government has. It may well take some "direct action" by foreign workers to eventually receive an adequate response from the political system.

Socioeconomic Redistribution

Policies of redistribution, which in essence involve taking goods and benefits from one group of individuals and giving them to others, are among the most controversial in any political system. Traditionally in European politics, redistribution has been associated with images of class struggle and even revolution. Thus far in the Federal Republic there have been few redistributive policies actually put into practice. The extensive social welfare system and the dynamic pension and health care programs are largely financed by employer and employee contributions and not from general government tax revenue. Bonn does not for the most part "take from the rich and give to the poor." Business or employer contributions to health and pension systems are viewed as business expenses and passed on to consumers via higher prices. When a proposed policy such as codetermination, or a more equitable distribution of capital resources *(Vermoegensbildung)*, or the reform of vocational education begins to assume a redistributive character, it encounters difficulty in the policy-making process.

The aversion of even Social Democratic leaders to redistributive policies thus far is in part the result of the continued expansion of the economy. As long as the pie continues to get larger, they see little reason to engage in the conflict necessary to pass redistributive legislation. There is also some evidence that most German voters will not support such measures.

One important means of redistribution is, of course, through the tax system. While the SPD has often discussed the institution of a more progressive tax system, that is, taxing higher incomes at a still higher rate than lower incomes, its proposals have always been modified or softened — either through the opposition of its coalition partners (the middle-class Free Democrats) or through the Christian Democrats by virtue of their position in the Bundesrat. It is thus not surprising that studies of the distribution of national wealth during the last thirty years have found little real redistribution.[2]

Since the early 1970s, most of the nations of Western Europe have experienced a slowdown or halt in their economic growth; the pie is not getting as big as fast anymore. West Germany has not escaped the higher inflation, increased unemployment, and decline in economic growth of its neighbors. By early 1982 unemployment approached the 2 million mark, the highest level in thirty years. Record deficit spending resulted in strong pressures to cut many social welfare programs in the 1982 budget. To the dismay of many SPD supporters, the Schmidt government did reduce spending for child allowance payments and pensions. Higher energy costs are responsible for much of this development, but the rising costs of the welfare state are also involved. Under conditions of increasing scarcity that will also characterize the Federal Republic, the frequency and intensity of demand for more redistributive policies will increase.

Civil Liberties

Since the early 1970s, a significant segment of German society has perceived a growing infringement of its civil liberties because of a "radicals decree" that was to set guidelines for conducting security checks of all applicants for public employment. In 1972 the national government and all state governments approved this decree, which essentially made membership or support of parties or groups opposed to the present constitution incompatible with becoming a public employee or remaining a civil servant. Since this applied to all employees, including teachers, its effects were far-reaching.

There were, however, numerous legal and administrative problems involved with its interpretation. Presumably the Communist party or the radical right National Democratic party were examples of such anticonstitutional forces mentioned in the decree. Yet neither these groups—nor others (Maoists, neofascists)—have been officially banned by the Federal Constitutional Court, the only institution with the legal right to make such a determination. In some cases applicants who were or had been members of these parties were denied employment on that basis. Moreover, the same rigid standards were applied to all applicants and employees regardless of the sensitivity of their job. Thus a locomotive engineer who was active in his local Communist party was fired, as was a cleaning woman in a public school. A young elementary school teacher, active in a small leftist group, was denied employment even though there was no evidence of any "anticonstitutional" activity. That her parents were Jews and communists and were persecuted by the Nazis made this case especially illustrative of the problems associated with the "radicals decree."

The extensive use of security and background checks has had an inhibiting effect on the political expression of young university students. Since the government is one of the largest employers, students have feared that participating in a demonstration or signing a petition could have a damaging effect on their careers. This issue also became linked in the mid-1970s with the problem of terrorism. Most Germans support a hard-line position on terrorism, such as that taken by CDU/CSU governed states and also by some SPD and FDP leaders.

By the late 1970s, however, opposition to the implementation of the "radicals decree" had led to major changes at the national level and in some states. Both the Chancellor in 1972, Willy Brandt, and Chancellor Helmut Schmidt repudiated the decree. Since 1979, the practice of automatically checking each application with security agencies *(Regelanfrage)* has been dropped for all national-level positions and in a number of states, including at least one, the Saar, that is governed by the CDU/CSU. Significant segments of leadership opinion in all parties now express concern and regret about the whole procedure. Clearly a combination of experience with the policy; the reaction of public opinion, especially among the younger, academically educated segment of the population; and foreign criticism of the Federal Republic had produced a trend away from the 1972 policy.[3]

Terrorism and the Computerized Police

A small remnant of the extraparliamentary opposition of the 1960s turned to political violence in the 1970s. Organized into a variety of "urban guerrilla" factions, the most notable being the Baader-Meinhof band, they committed bombings, kidnappings, and murders in the name of the revolution. Terrorist activity reached its zenith in 1977 when the chief federal prosecutor, the head of one of the largest banks, and a major industrialist were murdered. Links between German and Palestinian terrorist groups also became dramatically apparent in 1977 when a German commercial aircraft was hijacked by Arab terrorists who demanded the release of their German comrades. The dramatic rescue of the passengers at Mogadischu (Somalia) by special German commando units dealt a severe blow to the terrorist movement. Since 1977, there has been a decline in terrorist activity and several key figures have been captured or killed in clashes with police. Nonetheless, there is still a small, hard core of terrorists and several hundred sympathizers who constitute a threat to the republic's internal security and a challenge to its law-enforcement agencies.

In response to the terrorist problem, police and internal security agencies have established one of the most sophisticated systems of computerized and electronic eavesdropping in the world. Huge collections of personal and political data on hundreds of thousands of citizens, most of them with no connection to terrorists or the radical "scene," are stored in the computers of the Federal Criminal Office (BKA, the German version of the FBI). An increasing number of civil libertarians and some political leaders are greatly concerned about the possible abuse of these data by law-enforcement officials. Some cases of excessive police zeal have taken place. Given the memory of the Third Reich and its Gestapo, this issue has become one of the most sensitive on the current political agenda.

Notes

1. Ray C. Rist, *Guestworkers in Germany: The Prospects for Pluralism* (New York: Praeger, 1978), p. 57.
2. *Der Spiegel,* no. 23 (2 June 1980): 84ff.
3. The "radicals decree" was hardly successful in "uncovering" large numbers of radicals. In 1977, for example, only 115 candidates out of a total of over 210,000 new local, state, and national public sector employees were rejected because of doubts as to their loyalty to the constitution; at the national level, fewer than 10 applicants out of about 78,000 new employees were rejected. *Bundestagsdrucksache,* 8/2481 (22 January 1979): 43.

For Further Reading

BAKER, KENDALL L.; DALTON, RUSSELL; and HILDEBRANDT, KAI. *Germany Transformed*. Cambridge: Harvard University Press, 1981.

BECKER, JILLIAN. *Hitler's Children: The Story of the Baader-Meinhof Terrorist Gang*. Philadelphia and New York: Lippincott, 1977.

BRACHER, KARL DIETRICH. *The German Dictatorship*. New York: Praeger, 1970.

BRAUNTHAL, GERARD. *The West German Legislative Process*. Ithaca: Cornell University Press, 1972.

BROSZAT, MARTIN. *The Hitler State*. London: Longman, 1981.

CALLEO, DAVID. *The German Problem Reconsidered*. New York: Cambridge University Press, 1978.

CERNY, KARL, ed. *West Germany at the Polls*. Washington: American Enterprise Institute, 1978, 1982.

CONRADT, DAVID P. *The German Polity*. New York: Longman, 1982.

_____. *The West German Party System*. Beverly Hills: Sage, 1972.

CRAIG, GORDON. *Germany, 1866-1945*. New York: Oxford University Press, 1978.

DAHRENDORF, RALF. *Society and Democracy in Germany*. New York: Doubleday, 1969.

EDINGER, LEWIS J. *Kurt Schumacher: A Study in Personality and Political Behavior*. Stanford: Stanford University Press, 1965.

FEST, JOACHIM. *Hitler*. New York: Random House, 1975.

GATZKE, HANS W. *Germany and the United States*. Cambridge: Harvard University Press, 1980.

HAMILTON, RICHARD. *Who Voted for Hitler?* Princeton: Princeton University Press, 1982.

HEIDENHEIMER, ARNOLD J. *Adenauer and the CDU*. The Hague: Martinus Nijhoff, 1960.

JOHNSON, NEVIL. *Government in the Federal Republic of Germany: The Executive at Work*. London: Pergamon, 1973.

KOMMERS, DONALD P. *Judicial Politics in West Germany: A Study of the Federal Constitutional Court.* Beverly Hills: Sage, 1976.

LAQUEUR, WALTER. *Weimar, A Cultural History.* New York: Putnam's, 1974.

LOEWENBERG, GERHARD. *Parliament in the German Political System.* Ithaca: Cornell University Press, 1966.

MARKOVITS, ANDREI S., ed. *The Political Economy of West Germany.* New York: Praeger, 1982.

MAYNTZ, RENATE, and SCHARPF, FRITZ W. *Policy-Making in the German Federal Bureaucracy.* New York: Elsevier, 1975.

MERKL, PETER H. *The Origins of the West German Republic.* New York: Oxford University Press, 1965.

NELKIN, DOROTHY, and POLLAK, MICHAEL. *The Atom Besieged: Extraparliamentary Dissent in France and Germany.* Cambridge: MIT Press, 1981.

NOELLE-NEUMANN, ELISABETH, ed. *The Germans, 1967-80.* Westport, Conn.: Greenwood, 1981.

RIST, RAY C. *Guestworkers In Germany: The Prospects for Pluralism.* New York: Praeger, 1978.

ROMMEL-MUELLER, FERDINAND. "Ecology Parties in Western Europe." *West European Politics* 5, no. 1 (January 1982): 68-75.

SAFRAN, WILLIAM. *Veto-Group Politics: The Case of Health Insurance Reform in West Germany.* San Francisco: Chandler, 1967.

SCHOENBAUM, DAVID. *Hitler's Social Revolution.* New York: Doubleday, 1966.

SCHWEIGLER, GEBHARD. *National Consciousness in Divided Germany.* Beverly Hills: Sage, 1975.

SPOTTS, FREDERIC. *The Churches and Politics in Germany.* Middletown: Wesleyan University Press, 1973.

STERN, FRITZ. *The Failure of Illiberalism: Essays on the Political Culture of Modern Germany.* Chicago: University of Chicago Press, 1975.

STONE, DEBORAH A. *The Limits of Professional Power: National Health Care in the Federal Republic of Germany.* Chicago: University of Chicago Press, 1981.

TILFORD, ROGER. *The Ostpolitik and Political Change in Germany.* Lexington, Mass.: Heath, 1975.

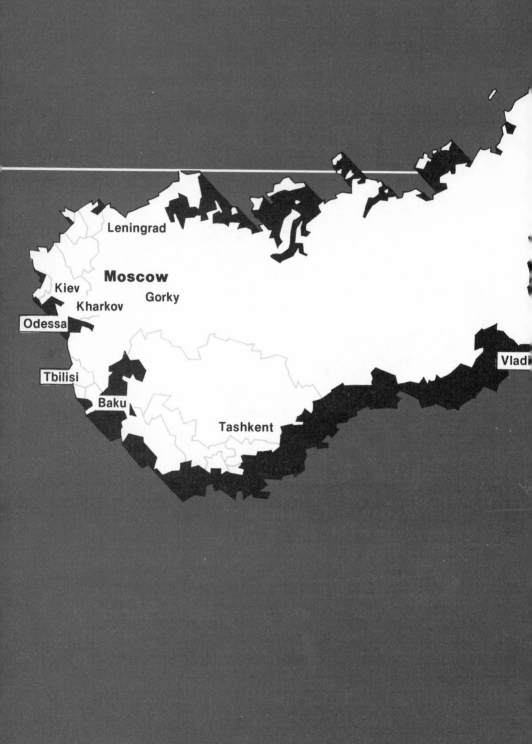

Leningrad

Moscow

Kiev

Gorky

Kharkov

Odessa

Vladi

Tbilisi

Baku

Tashkent

Part Four

The Soviet Union

Dan N. Jacobs

16

The Context of Soviet Politics

The three governments thus far presented in this volume, though differing greatly in the details of their experiences and systems, are nevertheless usually placed in the category "democratic." As such, they are fundamentally different from the government to which we now turn: that of the Union of Soviet Socialist Republics (USSR), the name by which Russia has been known since 1924.

Over the past four decades, but particularly in the early 1940s and '60s, there have been attempts to minimize the differences between the Soviet and Western systems, pointing out that because bureaucracy, policy making, problem solving, and so forth are involved in both East and West, the differences between the systems have been overstated. Or, if there had been large-scale differences, those differences have been persistently narrowed under the influences of industrialization and urbanization to which all modernizing states are subjected. The latter concept, that of the USSR and Western democracies coming closer together in their outlooks, problems, and methods used for problem solving, is known as "convergence."

In the late 1970s and early '80s, however, under the realization that the Soviet and Western systems remained far apart in outlook and evaluation (particularly in attitudes toward human rights) and that the distance between their positions was not lessening appreciably, a greater willingness developed among specialists to consider the Soviet Union as a "special case"—though perhaps not so special as earlier observers had made it out to be. How the Soviet Union is perceived makes a difference not only to specialists but to all of us, because how we perceive the USSR has a vital role in determining how we conduct relations with it.

Whether the Soviet Union is regarded as a "special case" or a variant on a more-or-less typical model is a matter of interpretation. Nevertheless, in one dimension the USSR undeniably differs from the United Kingdom, France, and Germany: its physical size.

Geography and Politics

The Soviet Union is the largest country in the world. Its 8,647,250 square miles make it nearly two and a half times as large as the United States and more than forty times the size of France. It covers one-seventh of the land surface of the world. From the Baltic Sea in the west to the Bering Straits in the Pacific, the USSR stretches for almost 7,000 miles. The train from Moscow to Vladivostok can take over three weeks, crossing eleven time zones. From beyond the Arctic Circle in the north to the Afghan border in the south, the country covers nearly 3,000 miles. It extends from frozen wastes (where the ground never defrosts more than six inches below the surface) to the semitropical Crimea. It is often overlooked that almost the entire Soviet Union is north of Minneapolis, Minnesota. Large parts of the country are climatically inhospitable and unhealthy—and almost all of it is terribly cold, with short growing seasons. All these facts place heavy burdens on the country's agricultural potential.

Another geographically important factor with political implications for Russia has been the absence of physical barriers. Soviet rivers are shallow and the mountains low, except on the southern borders. This has made it relatively easy for invaders to move across the country along its grassy plains, the steppes; and invaders have done this every century for over a thousand years. Scythians, Goths, Visigoths, Huns, Mongols, Swedes, French, and Germans are only some of the intruders who have left a variety of heritages in Russia, not least in the Russian psyche.

Though the attack by Hitler's Germany that began in 1941 is the invasion emphasized in contemporary Russia, because it is the most recent, the bloodiest, and the one successfully driven back by the system in power, it is probably not the most significant invasion. That distinction is attached to the Mongol invasion of the thirteenth century, led by Batu Khan, the grandson of the great Genghis Khan, the conqueror of China. The Mongols, though greatly reduced over the centuries in power and in the amount of land they controlled, continued to dominate parts of Russia until the end of the eighteenth century. The major impact of the Mongols —who galloped much farther into Europe but remained there for a much shorter time than in Russia and therefore had less of a lasting effect—was to isolate Russia from the West, particularly from two of the West's most formative developments, the Renaissance and the Reformation. The great liberating power of both, reviving as they did the mind and spirit of the West and opening new vistas, was largely kept out of Russia, with a resulting difference in Russian development that has continued to this day to influence the way that country and the West view one another.

Origins and Development of Tsarist Russia

It would be a mistake, however, to attribute the differences between developments in Russia and the West to the Mongols alone. The branch of Christianity to which the Russians adhered has played a substantial role as well. The traditional date for conversion is 988. Russia followed the Eastern Orthodox rite, which migrated north from Constantinople, and not the Roman church, which held sway in the West. In Russia, religious as well as political power came from the East, and the Russians continued to look in that direction for models and attitudes during the hundreds of years when Western society was being modernized and Eastern culture lay largely fallow.

Prior to the Mongol invasion, the Russian political entity had for hundreds of years centered on the steppe city of Kiev, along the Dnieper River, and accordingly has been called *Kievan Rus.* The Mongols destroyed Kievan Rus (according to the chronicles of the time, they used elephants to stamp its ruler to death). Many of Kiev's and the Ukraine's inhabitants fled to safer land beyond the steppes, into the forest region, which was less likely to attract invaders.

There were many forest settlements where the fugitives from Kievan Rus sought refuge. One of these, just beyond the steppes, was named *Moskva,* after the river along whose banks it stood. With the advantage of its location, safely inside the taiga but with ready access to the relatively easy communication offered by the steppes and the Moskva River, which flowed near the Dnieper and was only a short portage from the Volga, the village of Moskva flourished. It gradually overcame the physical domination, if not the influence, of the Mongols and by 1497 had ventured forth as the Grand Duchy of Moskva, or *Muscovy*—or *Moscow.*

During the half millennia since the establishment of the Grand Duchy the territories under Moscow's control have persistently and greatly increased. At times, such as the Time of Troubles in the seventeenth century and immediately following the 1917 Revolution, Moscow has lost some of its acquisitions. But always it has won them back—and moved beyond them. In the sixteenth century Muscovite control moved southward to the Caspian and eastward into Siberia; in the seventeenth century, when the Grand Duchy became Russia, it moved north and west toward Lithuania and south in the direction of the Ukraine. In the eighteenth century it established itself on the Baltic and in Belorussia, absorbed a major share of Poland, and extended its frontiers to the Caucasus and beyond. In the nineteenth and early twentieth centuries, it moved into Central Asia and furthered the empire in China and on the Pacific. In the years since World War II it has come to dominate Eastern Europe and has spread its influence to Cuba, Africa, the Middle East, and Southeast Asia.

As it expanded, particularly in the nineteenth century, Russia took huge numbers of "foreigners" under its wing. Sometimes those embraced were of ethnic groups closely akin to the "Great Russians," the original Muscovite stock. Included here were fellow Slavs, such as Belorussians and Ukrainians. But there were great numbers of non-Slavs as well: Lithuanians, Latvians, Estonians, Armenians, Georgians, Azerbaidzhanis, Tadzhiks, Ossetians, Uzbeks, Tatars, Uigurs, Germans, Jews—almost one hundred ethnic groups (some authorities say several times that many), speaking at least that number of languages and dialects. The prevailing relationship between the Great Russians and the minorities was that of superior and inferior. The minorities did not unbegrudgingly accept Russian domination, even on those rare occasions when it was applied with a light hand. But no matter how light or heavy the hand, minority groups in Russia maintained their own identification as an ever-present threat to the Great Russian determination to dominate.

Except for rare and brief moments in the past five hundred years, the only form of government the people of Russia have known has been authoritarian, one in which those at the center have controlled and those beneath them have been expected to follow orders unquestioningly. At times the control of the center has been weak because leadership has been weak or has been ineffective at distances far removed from the center, but the authoritarian model—known in tsarist times as *samoderzhavie,* autocracy—has remained the ideal. The Russian view is that some are created to lead and some are created to follow. It is the responsibility of each—justice demands it—to fulfill the assigned task. To attempt to do other is, by definition, to commit injustice. The goal—ordained by nature and expected by God—is order and obedience. Freedom, as it is understood in the

American context, is akin to anarchy and resolutely to be avoided. True freedom is in obeying. Such attitudes toward order, obedience, justice, and freedom have become traditional in Russia and have persisted across the centuries, no matter how the regime has described itself, tsarist or communist, or who the leaders have been. The persistence of these basic attitudes toward authority raises an important question for students of comparative politics: What accounts for the persistence of such ideas in the face of major social changes and constitutional reforms?

The values reflected in these attitudes are typical of feudal society, which developed in Russia during the sixteenth and seventeenth centuries, long after it had begun to decline in Western Europe. In Russian feudalism, the tsar, the anointed of God, reigned in God's name and served his Master. Below the tsar (or tsarina, for several queens were reigning monarchs in Russia), came the soldier-nobility, whose purpose was to protect, support, and serve the monarch. At the bottom were the peasants, who were to serve the nobility while the latter served the tsar. The tsar and the soldier-nobles profited from the arrangements of this "service" state; the peasants, who were at the base of the support pyramid, liked it less well and attempted to remove themselves from the structure. But the entire structure rested on their service. If they did not provide that "service" (hence, *serfs*), then the soldier-nobles could not serve the tsar and the tsar could not serve God. Accordingly, the loopholes whereby the peasants could escape were gradually closed; by the mid-seventeenth century it was virtually impossible for them to extricate themselves from serfdom. Advertisements offering to sell serfs, with or without their wives and children, that appeared in the St. Petersburg newspapers at the end of the eighteenth century attest to the great similarity between serfdom and slavery. The serfs were at the mercy of the lord of the manor; he could abuse them, sell them, or kill them with impunity.

By the early decades of the nineteenth century, it was apparent to all who could see the truth that serfdom was no longer economically (not to mention morally) feasible. Feudalism belonged to an earlier period of economic development. The world was entering a more efficient, industrial age, for which serfdom was not appropriate. Yet, the old soldier-nobles had grown used to the existing system. Over the years, their responsibility to the monarchy, the original justification for serfdom, had faded; but the institution remained. The serfs attended to every need of the aristocracy, provided them with food, sewed their clothing, minded their houses, cared for their children, and supported their sojourns in Paris and Rome.

Much consideration was given to the abolition of serfdom, but the nobility feared what would happen if the serfs were freed. The serfs constituted a large part of their capital. The nobles could not till the land by themselves. They lacked the funds to pay free peasants to till it for them. Nor could the nobles sell their land, because no one had the money to buy it. Owners of serfs understood that no matter what serfdom's shortcomings, its end would ruin them. As a consequence, serfdom continued in Russia until a disastrous war forced Tsar Alexander II to decree its elimination.

After the Russian defeat in the Crimean War at the hands of the British, French, and Turks, the tsar recognized that Russia had to enter the modern age. Emancipation was carried out in Russia in 1861, but it would have been difficult to have devised a more ruinous method for affecting it than the one adopted. The peasants were not freed outright but were "bonded" to the land. They could not leave the land until they had paid the nobles for it—which was to take forty-nine years. The peasants could pay off their bonded indebtedness in advance if they had the rubles, but where were they to get them? On the other hand, the nobility received no compensation until the peasants paid off their debt, although they could sell the bonds earlier on a prorated basis.

Many of the magnates did sell their bonds early, but this meant that they had little capital. They still owned the land not awarded to the serfs, but without capital and largely without know-how, how were they to farm it? The result of emancipation in 1861 was to ruin the aristocracy and not help the peasantry very much.

Road to Revolution

Opposition to the autocratic power of the tsar appeared soon after the Russian soldiers returned from the victory over Napoleon in 1815. They had conquered the French legions, but the culture, freedom, and excitement of France had captured many Russian soldiers, especially the officers.

How poorly Moscow contrasted with what Paris had to offer! Those who had seen Paris and were moved by what they thought Paris represented became the backbone of the Decembrist uprising (1825), which aimed at overthrowing the tsarist regime and replacing it with a more "contemporary" one. But there was little agreement among the Decembrists as to what they wanted, except the tsar's throne.

From the 1820s on, every decade of the nineteenth century had its revolutionary rhythm, opposed to the status quo, seeking alternatives and a successful revolutionary movement. The revolutionaries of the 1870s, called the *narodniki* (populists), were mostly the sons and daughters of the aristocracy and the middle class. They believed that the necessary changes in Russia could be brought about by going to the people (*v narod*), to the peasants who made up the overwhelming majority of Russians and in whom, as the *narodniki* saw it, resided all the virtues of simplicity and forthrightness that their own lives lacked. The *narodniki* proposed immersing themselves in the peasants' lives, using the opportunity to convince the latter of the need to bring about changes, and enlisting their support in forcing tsarist acquiescence. It soon became apparent that the peasants would not respond to *narodnik* overtures and that the government did not appreciate the efforts of the *narodniki*. The movement collapsed.

Some among the *narodniki* subsequently reasoned that it had been half a century since the Decembrist uprising and that in the interval, in spite of numerous efforts, the tsarist regime had not become more demo-

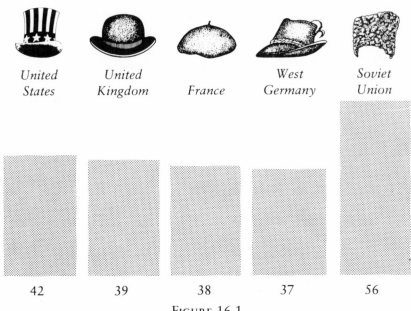

United States	United Kingdom	France	West Germany	Soviet Union
42	39	38	37	56

FIGURE 16.1
Female Participation in Workforce (in percent)

cratic, more liberal, more yielding, but had grown more despotic and oppressive. A few among the *narodniki* began to proclaim that only violence — terrorism — would disorganize the system and bring it to its knees. At the beginning of the 1880s, the new and small People's Will party besieged the Russian court. Generals, ministers, and members of the royal family were killed. The tsar was so in fear of his life that his entourage traveled on two trains, which followed close behind one another. The tsar would change from one train to the other at frequent stops so that potential assassins would have a difficult time determining which train to attack. Even such precautions did not save Tsar Alexander II; he fell before the People's Will on 1 March 1881.

Contrary to the expectations of its perpetrators, the assassination of Alexander did not topple the tsarist regime but strengthened its resolve to survive. Alexander's son and successor, Alexander III, destroyed the People's Will, greatly expanded the activities of the secret police (the *Okhrana*), and determined not to move even a step in the direction of liberalization. He believed that the chief result of concessions would be demands for more concessions.

Terror seemingly of little avail in modifying Russia, those interested in changing the country looked about for other methods. It was at this time, the early 1880s, that Marxism reached Russia through Georgi Plekhanov, who had originally been a leader of the *narodniki*. Throughout the 1880s, Plekhanov (subsequently known as the father of Russian Marxism) attempted to foster Marxism, which held that all countries had to undergo similar stages of economic development and that the revolution would break out in the country of the highest development of capitalism. This, Russia certainly was not. Marxism, which seemed to say that Russia would have to wait in line for a long time for its turn at revolution, was not received enthusiastically. At the beginning of the 1890s, Marxism in Russia was not a creditable movement and was of little concern to the Okhrana.

It was at this point that Vladimir Ilyich Ulyanov appeared on the scene. He would be known later as one of the most controversial figures among Russian revolutionaries, as the reason for the existence of the Bolshevik party, and as the founder of the USSR. Ulyanov had more than a hundred aliases, but his favorite was Lenin.

Lenin was the epitome of the determined revolutionary. He was relentless, single-minded, and unbending in pursuit of his goals: a revolution in Russia and power for himself. Lenin was not without a sense of humor, but his humor, like all else in which he was involved, centered on the revolutionary movement. He loved music but said he couldn't listen to it often because it took his mind off the class struggle. Being a revolutionary required complete and total concentration.

Experts on Lenin have difficulty agreeing on how Lenin came to have such singleness of purpose. Some observers attribute Lenin's devotion to revolution to the execution of his brother, Alexander, at tsarist hands. (Alexander had led a botched plot to assassinate the tsar in 1887.) They say Lenin became a revolutionary because he idolized his brother and wanted to emulate him, or because he wanted to prove that he was a better revolutionary than his brother, or because he hated his brother and felt great guilt when the latter was hung. Other commentators, playing down the brother aspect, find different reasons for Lenin's behavior: a family tradition, personal insults suffered, and so forth. Perhaps it is no more possible to pinpoint the source of Lenin's partiality to revolution than the motives of other revolutionaries of middle-class origin.

While in exile in Siberia at the turn of the twentieth century, Lenin, with time on his hands, worked out the principles on which he was to base his revolutionary movement. As he wrote in his famous pamphlet *What Is to Be Done?* he sought a small group of full-time revolutionaries, completely dedicated to revolution, with no familial or professional concerns beyond it. Such an organization, forged in the heat of confrontation and led by himself, he believed would succeed. Lenin was unwilling to bank on Marx's assurance that sooner or later the revolution would break out, no matter what any individual did to help or hinder it. Lenin wanted the revolution in Russia sooner, not later; he wanted it in his own time, and he wanted to lead it. To secure his objectives, he was prepared to use any means that would help.

Not everyone in the Russian Social Democratic Labor party (RSDLP), the Marxist movement in Russia, agreed with Lenin's ideas about the movement. Some preferred a mass party, one that would enroll large numbers of workers in its ranks. As a prelude to revolution they believed that the revolution would break out elsewhere, in a more highly developed country, not Russia. And they did not approve of Lenin's uncompromising tactics, his vituperation against comrades who disagreed with him, and his unyielding insistence that only he knew what was right for the revolution. As a result, at the first meeting of the RSDLP in 1903 (called the Second Congress; what was to be called the First was broken up by the police before it could accomplish much), there was a split that would permanently divide the RSDLP into two sections: the *Mensheviks* (or Minority-ites) and the *Bolsheviks* (or Majorityites).* Here, as on other occasions, Lenin preferred to divide rather than lose. Because of this predilection, he later came to be known, among revolutionary opponents, as the "splitter."

Prior to coming to power, Lenin's Bolsheviks were never the largest Russian socialist organization, but they became the most controversial. Lenin's positions on the revolutionary issues of the day became the point of departure for almost all socialists. Lenin would take a stand, and those in the opposition would respond. They would concentrate, not so much on establishing their own positions, as on reacting to Lenin's.

In 1905, largely as the result of another calamitous military defeat, this time at the hands of the Japanese, a revolution did break out in Russia. Almost all elements of the population—workers, peasants, middle class, intelligentsia, even some members of the aristocracy—united in opposition to the bungling, oppressive tsarist regime that had permitted the Japanese "dwarfs" to inflict such a humiliating debacle on the Russian people. But those opposed to the system could not unite on what they wanted in its place, and by a calculated maneuver that encouraged the opposition to back off by seeming to agree to many of its demands, the tsar managed to survive. Nevertheless, the revolution of 1905 demonstrated the vulnerability of tsarism. During the revolution, the revolutionaries—Bolsheviks and others—experienced the excitement and satisfaction of holding power through *soviets,* councils of workers, peasants, and soldiers. The revolutionaries, especially Lenin, determined the next time a revolutionary situation arose, they would gain power permanently.

The next time was a decade later, in the wake of more Russian military defeats, this time in World War I. During the years between 1905 and 1914, the tsarist regime had opportunities to change its policies, to modernize and popularize itself so as to mute the appeals of the revolutionaries. To some degree it did this, but it moved slowly to meet the needs of the masses. It maintained its traditional stance toward oppositionists, favoring oppression and violence to accommodation and reconciliation.

Nevertheless, when war broke out in August 1914, the Russian populace rallied around the flag. The Germans were a nearby enemy, not six thousand miles away, as the Japanese had been. Russians had been fight-

---

*Though there were far more Minorityites than Majorityites, the Bolsheviks reserved the name that stuck with them because, in one vote at the Second Congress, they had the majority.

ing Germans for six hundred years and more, since before the Teutonic Knights had moved eastward onto Russian soil. At first the war went well, for the Germans were preoccupied in tryng to overcome the French in the west. But early Russian victories gave way to losses. Time and again the Germans defeated the tsar's forces, exposing the Russian army's lack of preparedness and faulty leadership. Repeated defeats and growing shortages brought chaos to Russia. Out of that chaos came a new "revolutionary opportunity."

In restrospect, Lenin had felt that he had not made as much as he could have out of the 1905 opportunity. Perhaps he had remained too long in Switzerland, where he was in exile, before returning to Russia. The next time, he determined, he would return home as quickly as he could. In early March 1917, when news came that rioting mobs had forced the tsar to abdicate and that the old regime had been replaced by a provisional government, Lenin hastened to Russia.

Arriving a month later at Petrograd's* Finland Station, after having coaxed and cajoled passage through the German lines, he immediately insinuated himself into the situation, seeking to oust the Provisional government, which had succeeded the tsar, and replace it with his own.

Before Lenin could take over Russia, he had to take over his own party. The overthrow of the tsar had come suddenly and for many revolutionaries, Lenin included, unexpectedly. They had long forecast tsarism's demise, but they were nonetheless surprised when it came. The Bolsheviks, like revolutionaries in general, were not certain what they wanted. Should they wait to see how the Provisional government was doing? Should they wait until elections could be held so that the people might speak? Should they give the dust time to settle before they acted? Lenin knew what *he* wanted: to make another revolution, which would bring him and his party to power.

By early May Lenin convinced the Bolsheviks to follow his lead. By June he decided to use the soviets devised in 1905 as vehicles to engage the masses. The masses were to enroll in the soviets, which Lenin believed the

*As the capital of Russia was then known. In 1703 Peter the Great had founded a new "Western" capital to replace the "Oriental" Moscow and named it St. Petersburg for his patron saint. During World War I, it was decided that the German "burg" was not acceptable, and the name St. Petersburg was changed to Petrograd (Peter's city in Russian). Soon after the Bolsheviks took power, Lenin decided to move the capital away from the west and back to Moscow, to protect against Western attacks and influence. When Lenin died, the name of Petrograd was changed to Leningrad, the name it bears today.

Bolsheviks did or soon would control. Thereby, the Bolsheviks would control the masses. Lenin's slogan became "All power to the Soviets." The soviet tactic backfired, however, when the masses insisted on making a revolution for which they were not ready. Faced in July with the choice of abandoning the masses or going down to defeat with them, Lenin took the latter alternative. As a result, he was forced to go into hiding in Finland. He was replaced as the on-the-spot leader of the revolution in Petrograd by Lev Davidovich Trotsky, an extremely able independent socialist who had returned from America in May and made common cause with Lenin a month later.

TABLE 16.1

Revolutions in Russia in the Twentieth Century

Revolution	*Result*
1905 Revolution	Tsarism remains, but in weakened condition
February Revolution 1917	Tsarism falls; Provisional government in
October Revolution 1917	Provisional government falls; Bolsheviks in

Trotsky, at first operating out of prison, where he had been incarcerated following the July failure, convinced the Provisional government that the major threat to its continued existence came from the generals and other defenders of the deposed tsar on the right and not from the left, or Lenin. As a consequence, the Bolsheviks were permitted to openly develop their revolutionary strategy under the guise of preparing to defend the Provisional government. When the government proved itself incapable of solving Russia's problems and chaos was rampant, the Bolsheviks were ready — the trap was sprung. Meeting scarcely any resistance, the Bolsheviks quickly seized control in Petrograd and shortly thereafter in the rest of Russia. The date was 7 November 1917, known to history as the October Revolution,* or simply, the Revolution.

---

*In 1917 Russia still used the Julian calendar, which Britain and its colonies had discarded in 1752 and replaced by the Gregorian calendar. In the twentieth century the Julian calendar is thirteen days behind the Gregorian calendar. This means that while the date of the revolution in the West (and after 1918 in Russia) is November 7, in Russia the date was October 25. Therefore, the October Revolution. Similarly, the revolution that occurred in March 1917 is known as the February Revolution.

17

Where Is the Power?

The regime Lenin established was in many ways an adaptation of its predecessor. Lenin replaced the tsar; the Bolsheviks replaced the court circles that surrounded tsars; the people's commissariats replaced the ministries, with many of the latter's bureaucrats initially serving under the Bolsheviks. There were also many other changes. Under Lenin and Joseph Vissarionovich Stalin, the Georgian who succeeded Lenin when he died in 1924, the system gradually began to assume the institutional form it bears today.

The revolution Lenin sought throughout his life and achieved in 1917 was supposedly carried out by the people for the sake of the people. According to Marx, power after the revolution was to be in the hands of the people. But Lenin did not trust the people any more than his aristocratic predecessors had done. For Lenin, as for them, the masses were lazy and slothful. They had to be goaded into action and controlled, lest they act against what Lenin and the Bolsheviks considered the people's best interests. A professed Marxist could never admit to such little faith in the masses. He needed institutions that would display the primary role of the masses, provide mass participation, and give the appearance of mass control; but institutions that would at the same time preserve power for the leadership.

Formal Governmental Organizations

The primary popular institution devised to accomplish this, thus legitimizing the system, was the soviet. In 1980 over 2.2 million Soviet citizens were elected to more than 50,000 soviets, which operated at every level throughout the USSR. Everyone above the age of eighteen was expected to participate in elections to the soviets and, almost without exception, did. Over 99.9 percent of the population voted. In the 1981 elections to the supreme soviets of the republics, 176,447,621 voted for the list presented and 118,081 voted against it.

Supreme Soviet

Below the national level, the USSR is for the most part divided into republics, oblasts, raions, and localities. These are somewhat parallel to states, counties, and localities in the United States — plus one additional division because the USSR is so much larger than the United States. In the USSR there is a soviet at every one of these levels. At the top is the Supreme Soviet, which is divided into the Soviet of the Union and the Soviet of Nationalities. It is the only bicameral legislature in the USSR; one house is based on the total population of the country and the other on the major national groups that make up the USSR. The Soviet of Nationalities indicates the interest of the Soviet system in all its minority nationalities. But the Soviet of Nationalities, like the Soviet of the Union, is a largely ceremonial body. It meets several times a year, rarely for more than a week at a time, and usually limits itself to listening to speeches and ratifying actions taken elsewhere. Only a very small percentage of Soviet legislation originates here, and never at the instigation of rank-and-file members.

Nevertheless, it is an honor to be nominated to the Supreme Soviet. The most important political actors in the Soviet system are also members of the Supreme Soviet. Membership in either house is regarded as a reward from the system for having been of particular service. It provides tangible benefits in the form of heightened prestige; free trips to Moscow; and access to deluxe restaurants, hotels, and scarce consumer items.

Besides the Supreme Soviet, there are over 50,000 other soviets. The more local they are, the more often they are likely to meet; at no level do they exercise substantial power, although in the late 1970s there were some overtures toward increasing their role. Nevertheless, according to the Soviet table of organization, power is supposed to be in the soviets.

Sovmin

A second place where power is supposed to be is the Council of Ministers (*Sovmin*). The Sovmin does exercise *administrative* power. One of the "cabinets" of the Soviet system, it is far more extended than the presidential Cabinet in the United States, for in the USSR all economic activity is in the public sector. The Sovmin directs and oversees activities in what is the equivalent of both private and public sectors in Western economies. In the Sovmin there are not only ministries of Foreign Affairs and Defense, but also ministries of Machine Building, Industrial Construction, Timber and Woodworking Industry, Transport Construction, Coal, Culture, Fisheries, Education, and dozens of other operations blanketing public and private life.

The Supreme Soviet and the Sovmin (there is also a sovmin in each of the various republics within the USSR) are the leading governmental institutions in the USSR. But, as indicated, neither contains within it the chief decision-making apparatus of the system. Decisions are made in both bodies. In the Supreme Soviet those decisions are overwhelmingly confirmatory. Decisions made in the Sovmin have to do with carrying out the instructions that emanate from other sources. But these are not the most significant decisions in the Soviet system. Significant decisions are made, not in the formal governmental structure, but elsewhere, namely, in the *Communist Party of the Soviet Union* (CPSU).

True Locus of Political Power: The CPSU

This seeming contradiction—that the "government" is not in charge of the government's business—has been difficult for people outside the USSR to grasp, particularly because the Soviet constitution maintains that the Soviet government holds and exercises all power. The difference between appearance and reality has allowed the Soviet system—particularly during the first forty years of its existence when comprehension of how it operated was not widespread, but even today among groups with little familiarity with its mode of operation—to speak with two voices, appealing to different audiences. The Soviet government has been involved in regular relations with other governments, establishing embassies and signing treaties. At the same time, the party has been involved in encouraging and supporting forces that have as their goal the overthrow of those same governments. When the threatened governments have protested to the Soviet Ministry of Foreign Affairs that the USSR is menacing their continued existence, the ministry has replied, technically truthfully but all the same disingenuously, that the revolutionary efforts of "individuals" (i.e., members of the CPSU) have nothing to do with the Soviet government.

Lenin's criterion of a small professional organization directing the affairs of the communist movement has dominated the operation of the Communist party of the Soviet Union throughout its existence, in revolutionary as well as postrevolutionary periods. Nevertheless, the size of the party has grown far beyond the 250,000 members it had in late 1917. By 1927 it had 1,213,000 "full and candidate" members. After World War II, its numbers increased markedly, particularly under the leadership of Nikita Sergeyevich Khrushchev. At the Twenty-Sixth Party Congress in 1981 it had 17,480,000 members, over 15 percent of the total population.

In addition to the party there are party-inspired, mass-membership organizations such as the Young Communist League (*Komsomol*), the

TABLE 17.1

CPSU Membership, 1918-81

Year	*Full and Candidate*[1] *Members (in thousands)*	*Percent Change Since Previous Congress*
1918	390	
1919	350	− 9.8
1920	612	+ 74.9
1921	733	+ 19.8
1922	733	− 28.0
1923	499	− 5.5
1924	472	− 5.4
1925	802	+ 69.9
1927	1,213	+ 51.3
1930	1,678	+ 38.3
1934	2,701	+ 61.0
1939	2,307	− 14.6
1952	6,708	+ 190.8
1956	7,174	+ 6.9
1959	8.239	+ 14.8
1961	9,279	+ 12.6
1966	12,357	+ 33.2
1971	14,455	+ 17.0
1976	15,694	+ 8.6
1981	17,480	+ 11.4

1. No candidate members 1918-21.

Young Pioneers, and the Little Octobrists. In 1981 the Komsomol alone had 40 million members and the Young Pioneers almost 30 million.

The party, like the government, has a system or organization that ascends hierarchically. At the bottom are primary party organizations (PPOs), which, with occasional exceptions, have between fifteen and forty-nine members. At times and in countries where the party is not in power, the PPOs are called "cells." Every party member, even top Soviet leaders, belongs to a PPO. PPOs elect delegates to raion party conferences, which elect delegates to the oblast conference, which elects delegates to the republic congress, which elects delegates to the congress of the CPSU where, according to the party rules, all power in the party resides. The party congress, which has approximately 5,000 delegates—a number set by the seating capacity of the Palace of Congresses in the Kremlin where it meets—is required to convene only once every five years and remains in

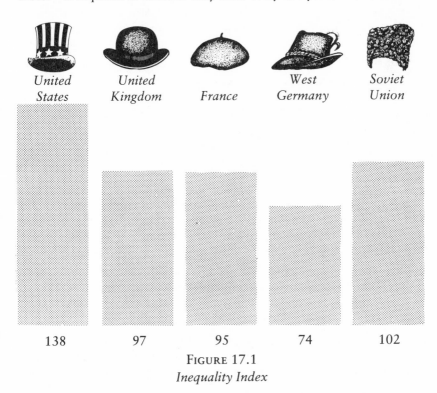

United States	United Kingdom	France	West Germany	Soviet Union
138	97	95	74	102

FIGURE 17.1
Inequality Index

SOURCE: Michael Don Ward, *The Political Economy of Distribution* (New York: Elsevier, 1978). A composite index based upon measures of individual income inequalities, sectoral inequalities, and social mobility.

session for two weeks or less. A congress with so many delegates, meeting so infrequently and for so short a time, can scarcely be the chief policy maker, the chief retainer of power, for an entire nation. The foundation of power in the USSR is to be found elsewhere.

The Central Committee

Again, according to the Party Rules, the congress is to elect the Central Committee (CC), which is the repository of authority between party congresses. The Central Committee (472 full and candidate members were elected to it at the Twenty-Sixth Party Congress in 1981) has among its numbers the most powerful figures in the Soviet establishment: party and government bureaucrats, editors, ideologists, marshals and generals, academicians, and so forth—the cream of the power elite. In their own right these individuals are strong power personalities, wielders of power levers within Soviet society. To a degree, their power is enhanced by being members of the Central Committee. Nevertheless, because the Central Committee meets only a few times per year (and then but for a few days at a time) and because its membership is so large (in Lenin's time it had fewer than 21 members, and only 133 as recently as 1960), its power, while greater than that of the party congress, is also limited.

The Politburo

The main source of power in the Soviet system is to be found in the *Politburo* (PB). This body, which is theoretically in control when the CC is not in session, in fact rules the USSR. Here, top decision making is carried out in the USSR. Until recently, the Politburo was not mentioned in the constitution, as those at the top sought to hide how few held power. But, in one form or other, it has existed since 1917 — and for most of that period it has been the perch from which the roost has been ruled. While Lenin was alive, the Politburo was incidental to his power. Most members were at the front or on assignment; Lenin held the fort in Moscow. But when Lenin died, the seven-man PB collectively constituted the top leadership of the country.

Bit by bit, beginning in 1922, Stalin forged his way to the top of the Politburo and became its master. He held life-and-death power over its members; in a large sense, he *was* the Politburo. Nevertheless, although he sometimes abused and murdered PB men, and turned the institution into a personal instrument, he did not disregard the Politburo because he required it not only for the exercise of power—it provided the scenario for his greatest triumphs—but also because he found it useful as an excuse. Whenever something unpleasant was required or an unpopular decision was handed down, Stalin could always blame it on the Politburo, allowing hints to be dropped that he really had been opposed but that the Politburo had "overruled" him.

The experience of Khruschchev, who was a member of Stalin's Politburo for over a decade, indicates the character of Stalin's domination of the PB. After Stalin's death, Khrushchev described how he managed to survive under the Soviet dictator by laughing when Stalin said *laugh* and dancing when Stalin said *dance*. One of the dozen top leaders of the Soviet Union during the last decade and a half of Stalin's life, Khrushchev played the clown in order to survive. The Politburo was the center of Soviet power; but while Stalin lived, it was under the control of a single individual: Stalin.

With Stalin's death, the Politburo became more or less an organ of collective leadership; however, in five years it again fell under the control of one individual—this time Stalin's court clown, Khrushchev. But because the times were different and the persons were different, Khrushchev never controlled the Politburo to the extent that Stalin had done. Khrushchev lacked Stalin's "life and death" powers, and consequently lacked Stalin's ability to force others to laugh and dance. Nevertheless, Khrushchev, once in power, was undoubtedly in command. He used the Politburo largely as he wished. He rarely called all its members together at the same time; he used their expertise, and that of other specialists, when and as he needed it. He was open to argument, at times even inviting it. He made decisions unilaterally, but his word did not necessarily still the opposition.

Khrushchev's successor, Leonid Ilyich Brezhnev, was even less able than his predecessor to wield total control over the Politburo. Brezhnev came to power, not as a dynamic leader with great drive and personal determination who had emerged victorious over his peers, as Stalin and Khrushchev had done, but as first among a number of equals. The equals had put together a coalition that ousted Khrushchev from office and insinuated themselves in his stead. At times in the late 1960s and early '70s, Brezhnev attempted to assert himself as the Great Leader in the tradition of Stalin and Khrushchev, but he was caught in the vise of his own situa-

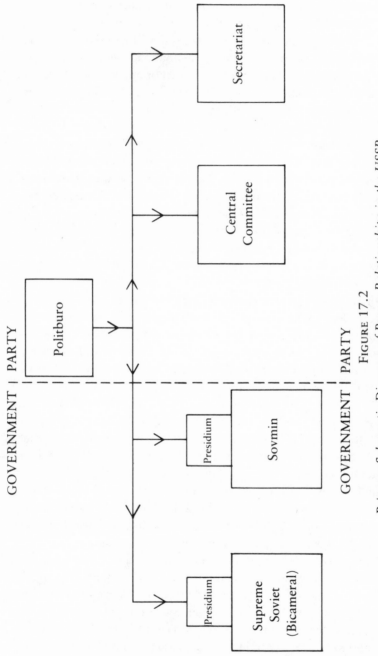

GOVERNMENT | PARTY

FIGURE 17.2

Primary-Schematic Diagram of Power Relationships in the USSR

tion and personality. He lacked the will of his predecessors to dominate —
and his contemporaries were not about to allow him to assume the role.
Brezhnev governed by reconciling varying interests. Under him, the Politburo met at least weekly and often more frequently and arrived at its decisions collectively. Some members of the Politburo were more important
than others, but none was all-important, as had previously been the case.

Whether the Politburo makes decisions collectively or an individual
makes them, PB members divide responsibility among themselves, to
some degree as members of the Sovmin do. Since there are fewer PB members than Sovmin people, however, and because the PB covers all Sovmin
concerns plus such additional ones as relations with Communist parties in
power and relations with Communist parties out of power, the domains
of each PB member are more extensive than those of Sovmin members.

In theory the Central Committee is the creature of the party congress,
and the Politburo is the creature of the CC; the fact is quite to the contrary. The Politburo determines who will belong to the CC and the party
congress, when and where they will meet, and to a great degree (though
not to the same extent as when Stalin was alive), what they will discuss.
Power in the Soviet Union flows from the top down, not from the bottom
up. The only important exception to this is when there is an interregnum:
when a Lenin or a Stalin is no longer in power and the succession has not
yet been determined. Under such circumstances, the Central Committee
may have greater independence. Politburo members, when they are jock-
eying for power and not of one mind, have been successfully overruled by
the CC.

When I state that that the Politburo is the chief decision-making body
in the USSR, this does not mean that it makes decisions unaided. The two
dozen or fewer men in the Politburo — there has only been one woman in
the PB — cannot perform the broad array of functions their positions require without proposals and information that emanate from outside
sources. The Politburo requires a full-time professional staff that extends
throughout the country. This role is performed by the *secretariat*.

The Secretariat

No figures on the size of the secretariat have been published in the USSR
since the 1930s, but it seems likely, based on various hints that have appeared from time to time, that there is one member of the secretariat for

every one hundred party members, or about 170,000 secretariat members.

The secretariat has its own leadership, which, confusingly, is also known as the Secretariat. The latter consists of less than a dozen officials, four or more of whom are also members of the Politburo. These members of the Secretariat meet weekly to discuss the activities of the secretariat staff, who are known as members of the party *apparat* (apparatus), or party *apparatchiki*.

The chief of the Secretariat is the Secretary General of the Central Committee of the Communist Party of the Soviet Union, a position Stalin made the most powerful one in the country and that remains so to this day. (From 1952 to 1968, it was known as "First Secretary.") The pre-Stalin secretariat was a small and comparatively inconsequential organ. None of the early Soviet leaders cared to be its "director." When in 1922 Stalin was appointed Secretary General of the CC, no one paid much attention. Neither the secretariat nor Stalin were highly regarded, particularly by the cognoscenti, who were increasingly concerned not with what they considered the boring details of party administration but with who was going to succeed the critically ill Lenin. Stalin was allowed to do with the secretariat pretty much what he wanted. What he wanted was to turn it into a power base for establishing himself as the new Lenin.

Under Stalin the secretariat developed sections *(otdely)* to select and supervise personnel, to issue and convey instructions to lower party echelons, to oversee the administration of those instructions, and to investigate their fulfillment and nonfulfillment. By the mid-1930s the secretariat had also taken up the task of providing information on which decisions could be made at upper levels. The secretariat became the eyes and ears of the Politburo, honeycombing the Soviet system and controlling it at every point. As Stalin became the Politburo, the secretariat became his eyes and ears and, to a large degree, his physical presence everywhere throughout the USSR — garnering information, making decisions and judgments, conveying them, supervising their administration, putting men and women in positions of power — and removing them. Under Stalin, the secretariat, like every other echelon of Soviet life, was subject to his almost every whim. But even then, as an assemblage of those who knew how the system worked and how to make it work for them, the secretariat developed a bureaucratic power of its own that increased significantly in the years following Stalin's death. Power resides in the Politburo, but the Politburo moves through the secretariat and depends heavily upon it.

18

Who Has the Power and How Did They Get It?

The Soviet Political Elite

Next to the Secretary General of the Communist party, the second most powerful person in the Soviet Union is usually the chairman of the Presidium of the Sovmin, who is also a member of the Politburo. When one person holds both jobs, as Stalin did for many years and as Khrushchev did from 1958 to 1964, that person dominates the system and is the manipulator of the Politburo, using it almost as a personal instrument. If the secretary generalship and the Sovmin Presidium chairmanship are held by different Politburo members, there is likely to be a competition between the two, with the Secretary General attempting from time to time to strengthen his position, looking toward taking over the Sovmin Presidium chairmanship, while the Presidium chair strives to prevent this from happening and to augment his own role.

Generally speaking, the third most important position in the Soviet system belongs to the chairman of the Presidium of the Supreme Soviet. This is true, not because the Supreme Soviet is so important, but because the man who has the job is usually an honored elder statesman of the Politburo and is given the Supreme Soviet job because he no longer wishes (or is able) to play a daily role in the PB but is not ready to retire. When it became clear to Brezhnev that he could not acquire the chairmanship of the Presidium of the Sovmin to go with his Secretary General post, he decided to seek the other Presidium chairmanship, that of the Supreme Soviet, which he succeeded in securing and holding until his death in November 1982. By holding it, he was not so powerful as Stalin or Khrushchev had been, but he was more than just Secretary General.

Beyond the foregoing, the relative importance of individuals in the Politburo depends on such factors as their personalities, personal relationships, the length of their tenure in the PB, and areas of expertise and responsibility. Generally speaking, a PB member who also is a member of the Secretariat holds greater power than a PB member who has Sovmin duties.

Below the Politburo, power resides in other members of the Central Committee. These include members of the Secretariat who are not PB or deputy PB members, other secretaries and party officials, ministers, and military leaders. There is also a smattering (less than 10 percent) of plant directors, workers, and trade-union leaders, kolkhoz chairmen, and academicians—most of whom are on the CC not as evidence of the power they hold but to bear witness to the accessibility of the CC to all echelons of the population.

Beyond the Politburo, the Secretariat, and the Central Committee, power is to be found among the other top echelons of the secretariat, the governmental bureaucracy, the military, and the intelligentsia. While every one of the 17 million people who belongs to the party cannot be said to be part of the power elite in the USSR, no one who does not belong to the party can be part of that elite.

What kind of people are the leaders of the Soviet system? In general, they are older men. At the end of 1982, the average age of a Politburo member was seventy-one; it was sixty-four in the CC, sixty-eight in the Secretariat, and sixty-seven in the Sovmin. They have held on to their positions for a long time. Some have moved up as their predecessors have been removed for cause, but the chief reason for advancement is the death or retirement of senior officials.

The top leaders were born, for the most part, between 1908 and 1918. They were too young to participate in the Revolution, but they experienced the hard times of the 1920s and came into their own under Stalin, during the 1930s, and in World War War II.

Few among them are like Khrushchev, who was born a decade earlier, was eighteen at the time of the Revolution, and when it broke out had not yet learned to read and write with ease. But, like him, today's leaders are mostly from proletarian/peasant backgrounds. They were eager to take advantage of the opportunities that opened up in Russia in the late 1920s. They attended the one- and two-year technological institutes established to provide the system with trained personnel. They came from a variety of work backgrounds: agricultural, industrial, technological. Generally they worked in their professional specialties for a number of years, sometimes decades, before turning to party work. They made the change

TABLE 18.1
Politburo, Full Members, 1983

Name	Office	Year of Birth	Nationality	In Party Since	In CC Since	In PB Since
ALIEV, G.A.	1st Deputy Chairman Sovmin	1923	Azerbaijani	1945	1971	1976
ANDROPOV, YU.V.	Secretary General, CC, CPSU	1914	Russian	1939	1961	1967
CHERNENKO, K.U.	Secretary, CC, CPSU	1911	Ukrainian	1931	1966	1977
GORBACHEV, M.S.	Secretary, CC, CPSU	1931	Russian	1952	1971	1979
GRISHIN, V.V.	Secretary, Moscow CP Comm	1914	Russian	1939	1952	1961
GROMYKO, A.A.	Sovmin, Foreign Minister	1909	Russian	1931	1956	1973
KUNAYEV, D.A.	1st Secretary, CC, CP Kazakhstan	1912	Kazakh	1939	1956	1966
PEL'SHE, A.YA.	Chairman, Party Control, CC, CPSU	1899	Latvian	1915	1961	1966
ROMANOV, G.V.	Secretary, Leningrad CP Comm	1923	Russian	1944	1961	1973
SHCHERBITSKY, V.V.	1st Secretary, CC CP Ukraine	1918	Ukrainian	1941	1961	1966
TIKHONOV, N.A.	Sovmin, Chairman	1905	Ukrainian	1940	1961	1978
USTINOV, D.F.	Sovmin, Minister of Defense	1908	Russian	1927	1952	1966

because they saw additional opportunities in such work or because higher-ups singled them out and coopted them. Usually their new party work included supervision in the occupational areas where they had their previous experience, but their party position changed their frame of reference: They were required to see things not as technicians attempting to do a job but as party *apparatchiki* making certain that others carried out their assigned tasks.

In many respects, the top leaders of the Soviet Union could be described as survivors. They survived a civil war, famine, purges, World War II, Hitler, and Stalin. Those experiences shaped their attitudes. The leading Soviet officials are tough; they have to be tough to stay alive and prevail. They have gone through severe trials in which their mettle has been tested and proved. They have grown up in the Soviet school of *kto kovo,* "who does what to whom." For decades under Stalin, even when they seemed to be in positions of power, they were the ones to whom it was done. Now they are the doers. They have the power. They act in accordance with what they think their status demands and as they believe they are entitled.

The experiences and successes of Soviet leadership have whetted their appetite for power. Having held power, they want more. They are constantly on the lookout to improve their own and Russia's positions. But success and age have also rendered them fearful. They could lose their power; it has happened to others. It will inevitably happen to them as a result of infirmity and death, if for no other reason. But they will hold on as long as they can. They will avoid retiring, if they possibly can. They do not want once again to become the *kovo* to whom it is done; they seek to remain the *kto* who does. This is a fundamental consideration. When the opportunity to increase power arises, they find it difficult to withstand the temptation to check it out. If their investigation indicates that the possibility is one that is risk free, or nearly so, they seize the opportunity.

Once embarked on full-time party work (indications are that for most of those on the top this has occurred in their late thirties), ability, luck, and determination will determine how far they will go. Certainly finding a "protector" who is himself upwardly mobile helps. Most of those who have occupied top spots in the Soviet system in later years, Brezhnev and Kosygin included, and more recently Tikhonov, achieved their positions because someone they previously worked under summoned them to Moscow after the latter had reached the top. The nearer to the top one gets, the fiercer the contest for power and position becomes. When the pinnacle is involved, the struggle has at times literally been one of life and death.

The Dilemma of Succession

There is no fixed order of PB succession in the Soviet system. The Party Rules state that the membership of the Central Committee shall be determined by the party congress and that the membership of the Politburo and the office of Secretary General shall be determined by the Central Committee. Technically that is the way it works, with changes most often announced — sometimes long after the fact — at party congresses. In fact, the Politburo in cooperation with the Secretariat determines the membership of the Central Committee and the party congress. Then who names the members of the Politburo, and in particular, the Secretary General? They name themselves. More precisely, a few top PB members name the rest. In Stalin's time, *he* named the rest.

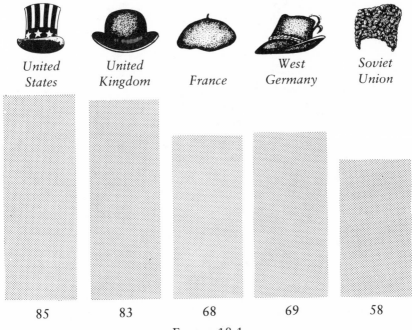

United States	United Kingdom	France	West Germany	Soviet Union
85	83	68	69	58

FIGURE 18.1
School Age Population in School (in percent)

When the figure to be replaced is "one of the crowd," not a top leader, he will be replaced at the discretion of the top leader or leaders of the Politburo. Who replaces a departed top leader when there is a collective leadership at the time of departure, as there was for many years under Brezhnev? There are a number of possibilities. What seems probable is that the remaining top leaders would, at least in the short run, attempt to close ranks and share the leadership among themselves in defense of the status quo. That might work for a while, but it seems likely to assume that a collective leadership, particularly an aged collective leadership, would be a do-nothing leadership. Given the preponderance of single-person dominance in Russian and Soviet history, sooner or later a single individual would probably attempt to gain control, opening a struggle for power perhaps no less intense than the struggles that preceded it in the Soviet period, unless the others at the top were too exhausted or weak to make a determined stand.

When Lenin died in 1924, there were five chief contestants for power, all Politburo members: L.D. Trotsky, N.I. Bukharin, L.B. Kamenev, G. E. Zinoviev, and J.V. Stalin. Of the five, Stalin was seen by most of his peers as the least likely successor, though Lenin, prior to his death, had considered Stalin seriously as his heir — and rejected him. To Trotsky, Kamenev, and Zinoviev, Stalin seemed intellectually and morally unworthy to succeed the great Lenin. It was widely agreed that Trotsky was the most likely successor. Accordingly, Stalin, Kamenev, and Zinoviev, who all wanted the job, united against Trotsky. Kamenev and Zinoviev, regarding themselves as Lenin's "chief disciples" and therefore the most deserving of being his successor, took the lead in attempting to destroy Trotsky's reputation. Stalin remained in the background. Trotsky, in turn, attacked Kamenev and Zinoviev. In the war of words (called the "literary debate") that ensued, Trotsky, Kamenev, and Zinoviev greatly weakened one another, only later realizing what was happening: They were destroying one another while Stalin was using the Secretary General's office, which none of the others had wanted, to increase his power.

Still not feeling strong enough to stand alone, Stalin next sided with Bukharin to attack Trotsky, Kamenev, and Zinoviev. Stalin was finally seen by them as the chief threat, and they determined to stop him. But it was too late. Stalin and Bukharin destroyed what remained of the power of the "opposition" — Trotsky, Kamenev, and Zinoviev. Then, having rid himself of those three contestants, Stalin turned against his erstwhile ally, Bukharin, and overcame him. Within five years of the death of Lenin, Stalin emerged as the new Soviet chief. Though he could not rest easy until all opposition was not only politically but physically destroyed, he nevertheless was in command in the USSR — and his power would be unequaled in his time, and arguably in the history of the world.

When Stalin died in 1953, he was succeeded by a single leader in a process that bore a remarkable similarity to that which had brought him to power three decades earlier. At Stalin's death, the likely successors included G.M. Malenkov, L.P. Beria, V.M. Molotov, and L.M. Kaganovich. There was also one other person, largely unknown to the outside world, and because of his coarse manners and loutishness, virtually discounted by his fellow Politburo members, in much the same way as Stalin had been: Nikita Sergeyevich Khrushchev.

Malenkov was generally thought of as the most likely successor. On Stalin's death he immediately assumed the two top positions of the system, becoming First Secretary of the party and chairman of the Presidium of the Sovmin. But his colleagues in the Politburo were unwilling to concede the struggle to him. They forced him to surrender the First Secretaryship, which was assigned to Khrushchev, who was to hold it as a kind of trustee because no one could take "Khrushchev the clown" seriously as successor to the great Lenin and the great Stalin. With Malenkov's wings clipped, the chief contender for power became Lavrentia Beria, head of Stalin's secret police, his biographer, and his chief hangman. Within a few months of Stalin's death, the other aspirants to power turned on Beria and arrested him at gunpoint. They later tried him for treason and executed him. About a year later, Khrushchev, Molotov, and Kaganovich turned on Malenkov, who resigned, giving as the reason that he lacked experience to fulfill the duties of chairman of the Presidium of the Sovmin. And then there were three: Khrushchev, Molotov, and Kaganovich.

In the fall of 1957 Molotov and Kaganovich tried to oust Khrushchev. But the latter, by successfully enlisting the Central Committee (see p. 255) — whose ranks he had used his position as First Secretary of the party to inflate with his own loyal supporters — turned the tables on Molotov and Kaganovich and removed them both from the Politburo. Thus, by 1958, five years after Stalin's death, the single leader had again been replaced by a single leader.

The resemblance between 1924-29 and 1953-58, while not complete, is impressive. In both instances the process took approximately five years. And in both instances a lightly considered candidate, possessing the Secretary General's prerogatives, united with other candidates against the front runners. Then, when the leading contenders had been knocked off, the former dark horse turned against the survivors, ousted them, and assumed the mantle of power himself.

There is yet another similarity between the two instances: While the purpose of the struggle was to determine the succession, it was not fought out in terms of whether Stalin or Trotsky (or Molotov or Khrushchev) was better for the job but in terms of the policies for future Soviet evolution that were put forward by each. The great issues of Soviet development—collectivization and industrialization in the earlier period, economic and political reform in the later one—were the vehicles through which the struggle for succession was contested. In this way, and for practically the only times in Soviet history, the great issues of Soviet policy were publicly debated.

The next succession situation that the USSR experienced occurred in 1964 when Khrushchev was forcibly removed from office. He was arrested on order of PB members as he alighted from a plane on his return from a vacation in the Caucasus. During his years at the top, Khrushchev had alienated most of the power groups in the Soviet Union by the style as well as the substance of his actions. In the freer atmosphere that followed Stalin's death, it had become possible for dissatisfaction to be communicated among PB members, something that could never have happened with impunity in Stalin's time. A less terrorized Politburo decided to get rid of Nikita Sergeyevich.

With Khruschchev removed, there was no reason why the struggle for power could not have developed as had happened when Lenin and Stalin died. It didn't. In part this can be attributed to the less dynamic characters and fairly advanced ages of the survivors. In part it was the result of the circumstances under which they came to power. Khrushchev had been a boat-rocker. Brezhnev, Kosygin, and company, who put together the coalition that displaced Khrushchev, wanted quieter times. They knew this required not setting one group against another, as a power struggle would certainly do, but reconciling differences. But perhaps the most important reason why a power struggle did not develop after Khrushchev's ouster was because now, as had probably not been the case in 1953-58, the potential participants in the struggle were aware of the dynamics of 1924-29 and 1953-58 and were loathe to embark on a similar confrontation.

There were instances in the late 1960s and '70s when Brezhnev seemed to be receiving significantly increased attention in the Soviet press, as though the groundwork was being laid for his elevation to the position of

Secretary General-chairman of Sovmin Presidium status. Whenever that occurred, however, Kosygin, the chairman of the Presidium of the Sovmin, would begin to receive increased attention and appreciation, and the previous balance of forces would be restored. It seems certain that Brezhnev's failure to be named chairman of the Presidium of the Sovmin and his having to settle for the chairmanship of the Presidium of the Supreme Soviet can be attributed to the determination of active power participants to limit his authority—and his inability to muster the support to overcome that determination.

In the Politburo at the end of 1982, when Brezhnev died, the rules governing the succession of CPSU secretary generals remained the same: There were *none*. The Lenin and Stalin successions were remarkably similar, leading some observers to conclude that they indicated a pattern. The Khrushchev succession was considerably different. Whether the post-Brezhnev succession would be like the first two instances or like the third, or whether it would develop along still different lines, depended on circumstances and individuals. In the first weeks after Brezhnev's death, it seemed there was a very smooth transition of power to Yuri Vladimirovich Andropov, former head of the KGB who became the new Secretary General. Undoubtedly, in late 1982 there was a general understanding among Soviet leaders that the first two post-revolutionary successions had been dysfunctional. They had resulted in the removal from power, in many cases the death, of leading party cadres, had absorbed tremendous amounts of energy, and in general interfered with the smooth progress of Soviet development. But the recognition of the undesirability of succession crises was no guarantee they would not occur. If one or more contestants were willing to risk all and could gather significant followings in the upper echelons of the Soviet power apparatus, the battle to determine the new Lenin, the new Stalin, would be joined, dysfunctional or not.

The foregoing discussion of power in the Soviet system has emphasized the position of the Secretary General and the Politburo. Correctly so. The final word is his and theirs. Alone or with others whom they permit to participate in individual decisions, they determine the major policies to be pursued and actions taken. There is no independent Congress as in the United States with the power to block or impeach. There is no Supreme Court to declare acts of the Politburo unconstitutional. Yet the power of the Kremlin leadership is not unlimited. The men in the PB are constrained by an assortment of forces that, in the post-Stalin years, have become varied and stronger.

Stalin, even in his despotic prime, could not do everything he wished. He could kill, he could force acquiescence and compliance, but he could not force others to believe in their minds that he was always right and that he deserved, by dint of his superiority, to be *vozhd,* the "boss." And he was convinced that those he suspected of not agreeing with him 100 percent were plotting against him. Stalin ruled by fear and coercion, but he recognized that he could not rule alone. A system in which only one person had power was an impossibility. Others had to express authority as surrogates. The problem was to prevent those surrogates from uniting against him. This Stalin did successfully by sheer terror but also by setting various participants in the system against one another. In this way he manipulated the party bureaucracy, the governmental bureaucracy, the Red Army, the secret police, and the intelligentsia. As with potential successors, Stalin let them experience his favor until he felt that their increased strength, which came largely as a result of his favor, might cause them to become a threat to him, at which point he withdrew his favor and bestowed it on another. In this way the various power centers were kept out of phase and dependent on him—and he was able to maintain his "absolute" authority.

Khrushchev grew up in the Stalin school. Undoubtedly, in the early 1950s Stalin was his role model of what a proper Secretary General should be. But Khrushchev could not attain the total control exercised by the "man of steel." (*Stalin* comes from the word "steel.") Though he believed in "acting like Stalin"—that is, with determination, self-assuredness and, if need be, ruthlessness—he was not as paranoiac as Stalin had been, not as prepared to suspect everyone for almost any reason. Moreover, he lacked an essential ingredient that had sustained Stalin: a secret police force he could use as he wished with no questions asked. The secret police still existed, but Politburo members had determined among themselves not to use it as Stalin had done. Thus the imprisonment and execution of colleagues who disagreed with Khrushchev was not acceptable. Without such threats in his arsenal, Khrushchev could not inspire the overwhelming fear that his predecessor had used.

Unable to control through terror, Khrushchev tried to maintain his position through reliance on other supports. As time went on, however, he seemed increasingly incapable of holding the allegiance of the groups he needed. He persistently alienated those around him. To the Soviet elite, as to the average Soviet citizen, Khrushchev seemed to be a clumsy oaf— by no means the paragon of strength and dignity that Stalin had been.

They remembered Khrushchev falling down drunk in front of the Yugoslav parliament building, publicly Indian-wrestling with Mikoyan and offering to take on all comers, humiliating party and government officials by
shouting denunciations at them at meetings, and, perhaps most embarrassing, removing his shoe and striking the rostrum of the United Nations
with it to give emphasis to his remarks. He offended government old-
timers by suggesting new methods that threatened their positions; he offended the party by splitting the secretaries' jobs in two, thus reducing the
power of the existing leaders; and he offended the military by indicating
that the Tank Corps, which played the leading role in the Red Army, was
obsolete. By 1964 almost everyone except his family had turned against
Nikita Sergeyevich, and other Politburo leaders were able to displace him
and institute themselves as his successor.

Brezhnev and company recognized that Khrushchev had fallen because he alienated everyone. They were determined not to make the same
mistake. Instead of alienating people, pushing "hare-brained schemes" to
modernize the Soviet economy, as Khrushchev was accused of having
done, Brezhnev pursued policies of conciliation. He sought to satisfy the
demands of as many power sources as he could. If industrialists wanted to
keep on emphasizing heavy industry, who was he to say no? If the party
elite wanted to strengthen their sinecures and further aggrandize themselves and their families, why not? And if the military sought additional
funds for development and production of nuclear and conventional weapons, whatever you want! Such an attitude would not and did not bring the
Soviet leadership to grips with its growing economic and social problems,
but it did win support for the Brezhnev corps — and kept it in power.

Many disdained Leonid Ilyich's "sweet reasonableness," and what
they interpreted as his and his regime's permissiveness and lack of assert-
iveness. They lamented that foreign visitors with "corrupting" ideas and
habits were allowed into the country in large numbers; that Russians were
permitted to travel abroad and bring back alien ideas and bad habits; that
hundreds of thousands of Russians had shortwave radios and listened almost nightly to the BBC and the Voice of America — and the next day discussed among themselves the un-Soviet and anti-Soviet news they heard.
People at all levels seem to be pursuing their *own* selfish, acquisitive,
sometimes questioning goals, not those goals dictated by the needs of socialism. Many leaders have lamented that things are not as they were
when Stalin was around. Then, Stalin gave the orders; the others obeyed.
Clearly, in contemporary Russia there are doubts about the easing of con-

trols that have occurred in the post-Stalin period. There is a longing expressed by some at all levels of society to return to the "Stalin way," a longing to which in the late 1970s the Brezhnev regime at times acceded. What effect such cravings will have on the attainment and maintenance of power by successor administrations only time can tell. But it is impossible to re-create the past—and it is highly unlikely that those who long for the Stalin days recall, or are aware of, the suffering and misery that accompanied them.

19

How Is Power Used?

The Locus of Policy Making

Since 1917, the essential policy-making machinery of the Soviet system has resided in the hands of the Secretary General, the Politburo, or occasionally the Central Committee. The power these bodies and individuals have wielded is awesome and extensive, but even in the heyday of Stalin's one-man rule, it was not unlimited. Although Stalin arbitrarily arrested tens of millions of people and was responsible for the deaths of millions, he could not do everything he wanted, or obtain whatever he desired. But if Stalin could not get his way in everything, how much less so could Khrushchev, Brezhnev, or Andropov.

Still, to say that the Secretary General could not do whatever he wanted by no means signifies that the rest of the population was, or is, free to pursue its desires. Generally speaking, the Soviet system regards the masses as Stalin regarded a piece of paper — it will put up with anything put on it. To a far less degree than in Western countries does the regime feel it has to be concerned with public opinion. Controlling all the means of communication, it has the power to shape public opinion to its liking. When it fails to do that, it has the power to coerce. Not many are so courageous or masochistic as to oppose the power of the Soviet system.

In spite of the regime's confidence that it controls the masses, there is the lingering fear a situation will arise that it will not be able to control, one in which the masses will be ignited, become frenzied, and run roughshod over everything in their way, including the party and the system. Care must be taken not to drive the masses too far. On the other hand, it is necessary to knock heads together from time to time so that it will be clear the party is not losing its resolve. So, while keeping the terror option alive, the regime is aware that a continual reliance on terror is dysfunctional.

There is a realization in ruling circles that if the goal is to modernize the USSR and further augment its productive strength and international reputation, what is required is not domination over the masses but the securing of their active cooperation, particularly that of the intelligentsia. It is possible to force compliance with rules; it is much more difficult to force innovation, enterprise, and creativity, all of which are required to achieve the goals the USSR seeks. To obtain these goals, the regime must let up on the stick and offer the carrot. This it does hesitatingly because it is used to the stick, and it always maintains the option of withdrawing the carrot.

Within the limits indicated above, the Politburo can make any decision it wishes. Does this mean that the PB makes all decisions in the system? Technically speaking, all decisions are made subject to its approval, but it is obvious that the tens of thousands of decisions necessary to keep the Soviet Union operating cannot all be made by the Politburo. The day-to-day operations of the system, the carrying out of policies made elsewhere, and the establishing of policies by which orders from above are administered reside in the Sovmin and its subordinate institutions.

Who decides what the important decisions are? Who determines what the Politburo must discuss and make decisions about? In part, the agenda of the Politburo is determined by events, by crises. The threat of an impending invasion, news of a breakdown in oil production, apprehension over a possible uprising in a client state — these are things that the PB inevitably is going to discuss. They are matters of great moment that literally bring themselves to the PB's attention.

Items that do not rise to the top so spontaneously come before the Politburo in a number of ways. They may be brought there by the secretariat that prepares the PB agenda, in which case it is likely that the matter of concern has been passed up the line on a number of occasions and has been repeatedly emphasized by lower secretariat levels. Or the discussion may be instigated by a PB member, especially a prominent one, as a matter of particular concern. In the latter instance, it is unlikely that the concern has arisen in the PB member's mind *sui generis*. It is there because someone or something put it there. It may be that on an inspection tour a Politburo member has observed a problem firsthand, or a plant manager has suggested a particular solution to a long-festering problem. Or the PB member may have been the recipient of letters from factory managers he met on his way up; or scholars from the university may write him urging a particular technological solution; or he may have read an article in the press suggesting a certain course of action. In short, problems and solutions may come to the agenda of the PB because they have impressed themselves on a particular PB member as serious and worthy of discussion.

In the Soviet system, if one is not in the Politburo and still wishes to achieve a particular result, the above indicates how to proceed. It is not possible in the USSR for interests to unite in a formal, institutionalized sense. All groups in the USSR must be system generated, or they are not tolerated. Even parent-teacher groups are formed at state instigation. Any group not formed by the system is automatically suspected of being a real or potential counterforce to the state. Therefore, an interest group cannot organize without the system's doing the organizing, and it is usually not the system's style to abet such undertakings.

Still, those at the top require information and require solutions, particularly from those involved in the day-to-day operation of factories and farms, for they are the people who know what is going on and what is required. The observations, insights, and proposals of such people are then brought to the attention of those capable of affecting the PB agenda in the ways suggested above: by incidental suggestion, by letter or telephone call, by journal or newspaper article, and through personal contacts at meetings or on social occasions.

Such expressions are always limited to areas where a PB member is prepared to accept discussion and suggestion. And the article-letter writer-contactor must be on be on guard against going "too far" and offending the PB member's sense of what is acceptable, or achieving the reputation of being a troublemaker. But experienced bureaucrats have a sixth sense of what is acceptable. They are not likely to get caught on that score.

It is in this way, mostly through informal channels, that interests are translated into political action. Thus, even though formal interest organization is not possible, interests in the Soviet system are expressed; but there is no way in which interests can successfully approach a Politburo member unless he is willing to be approached. There is no right of access, and the possibilities for orchestrating the promotion of interests are far more limited than in the United States.

The same mechanisms prevail for any figure lower in the Soviet pecking order seeking to influence a superior. In all systems, a wide circle of acquaintances is of great assistance in achieving influence, but in the Soviet system it is particularly important because other channels of bringing matters to someone's attention are not available. In the USSR contacts are likely to cluster around World War II experiences or the old school tie (the technological institute or university attended) as well as previously held posts.

Entering a concern on the PB agenda obviously is only part of the battle. It is also necessary to have the clout to achieve acceptance of the position advocated. Here it is virtually indispensable to have the support of the Secretary General. In fact, at those times when his power is predominant, it is usually he alone who needs to be influenced. If the Politburo is in a more collegial phase, then it is necessary to convince a majority. Accordingly, even though a "sponsor" has been found on the PB, it is necessary for "interests" to continue to inspire articles, write letters, and make contacts in order to influence a greater PB audience.

The more sensitive the issue (e.g., any proposal that involves a possible diminution of Politburo control is very sensitive) and/or the more radical the solution proposed, the more likely that the PB will move slowly. Since the 1930s, the overwhelming propensity of Soviet leadership has been to avoid change. Only when the argument has been marshaled that change is unavoidable has the Politburo moved, and then reluctantly. With such disinclination to innovate, the PB usually seeks as much advice as it can get—from the secretariat, from ministries, from specialists and scholars. Rather than introduce change on a wide front, it may encourage experiments in a single factory or farm or ministry. Then, if the experiment is successful and an acceptable model results, the PB may decide to implement the innovation more broadly. If it decides the innovation is dangerous or "untimely," it can quietly drop it.

What the foregoing indicates is a broad participation in policy making. Workers, peasants, journalists, scholars, factory directors, kolkhoz managers may and do play a role in affecting policy. Through the writing of letters and articles or through personal contact policies are encouraged, modified, and opposed by individuals at many levels of Soviet society. Nevertheless, the efficacy of the procedure depends to a great degree on party, and particularly Politburo, tolerance. The PB can proscribe topics, it can proscribe solutions. If changes are made, they come only as a result of the active participation of the Politburo, or in some circumstances, by virtue of its passive acceptance. But, at any point, if it is willing to accept the consequences of its acts, the PB can successfully interfere to make change or stop change. Though not unlimited in its powers—indeed, those powers have become increasingly circumscribed in post-Stalin times —the Politburo remains highly unfettered compared with analogous institutions in the West.

Studies in Policy Making:
Collectivization and Industrialization

The decision-making apparatus of the Soviet system has been in place for the better part of six decades, but only at two points during those years has it experienced periods of innovative decision making. Both occasions followed the death of a leader and a subsequent struggle for power.

In the first years after the revolution, Lenin's main efforts were directed toward keeping his Bolsheviks in command. The disintegration that resulted from the tsar's fall did not come to an end; with the outbreak of civil war, it became even more widespread. As Red and White forces struggled for advantage, the country was devastated. Kiev, for example, was taken and retaken by opposing forces eight times within a brief period. Industrial and agricultural production virtually ceased. Terror, hunger, and inflation stalked the country.

In the midst of chaos, Lenin tried to establish order by fiat. Workers who failed to maintain production goals were put in uniform and ordered to remain at the workbench on possible penalty of death. Workers who thought they had fought the revolution to free themselves from the iron fist of capitalism begrudgingly accepted this "War Communism"; but in the second half of 1920, when Bolshevik forces under Trotsky seemed to have put down the White opposition, workers began to resist. Is this what we fought the Revolution for, they asked—to be chained to our workbenches? In the countryside, peasants who had seen their seed grain taken from them in confiscatory raids by Red Army detachments were sometimes even more dissatisfied than the workers. Anger and frustration were widespread and were communicated to Red military units with the result that in March 1921 a mutiny broke out among the 14,000 soldiers and sailors stationed at the Kronstadt fortress near Petrograd. The Kronstadt rebels sent out messages trying to rally the erstwhile revolutionaries of Russia to their support. They demanded "communism without Bolsheviks," indicating that they were not against the revolution but opposed what Lenin's party had done to it.

In mid-March 1921, in a driving snowstorm, Trotsky led the Red Army against the mutineers and overcame them. But Lenin, having sensed the gathering working-class and peasant recalcitrance even earlier, counseled an end to War Communism and the introduction of the New Economic Policy (NEP). The NEP called for a partial reinstitution of capitalism in Russia. It promised the peasants there would be no further forced extractions of grain. They would receive better prices for the product of their efforts, and there would be goods available on which they could spend their money. For the workers there were promises of relaxed discipline and greater availability of goods. Small businesses and services such as tailors, watch repairmen, and stationers were allowed to operate independently. Many of Lenin's colleagues could not abide such a resurrection of capitalism, but Lenin justified it on the basis of "two steps forward, one step back." It is sometimes necessary to retreat in order to consolidate and advance farther at a later date. Lenin very much feared that if he did not retreat, it might not be possible to survive, let alone advance at some future date.

The NEP proved an effective solution to Russia's immediate economic problems. The economy recovered so that by the mid-1920s Russian production was approximately at the levels of 1913, the last normal year before war, revolution, and civil war. This was no small achievement considering the disintegration of urban and rural production in Russia—but compared with the tremendous advances in productivity being made in the West at that time, particularly in the United States, Russia was falling farther and farther behind the capitalist world. Whereas in 1913 it took eight Russians to do the job of one American, by 1923 it took ten Russians to do that job. What was the solution? Modernization, industrialization. But the creation of modern industrialized economy required the accretion of capital.

Among the upper echelons of Soviet leadership there was widespread agreement that Russia required industrialization and that for industrialization it required capital. But about how to obtain that capital there was disagreement. Both sides agreed that Russian agriculture, in which four out of five Russians were engaged, had to be the major source of capital formation. But they disagreed over how best to extract the capital from the land. The right-wing position argued that the peasant should be encouraged to produce still more than under the NEP by extending still greater incentives. Higher prices for grain and more and better-quality yet inexpensive consumer products should be offered the peasantry to spur them on to greater activity. The left-wing position, which was advocated by Trotsky, held that this would never succeed in producing sufficient capital to raise Soviet production to Western levels. This was so because individual farming on comparatively small plots precluded the use of heavy equipment, which would make farming more efficient. Moreover, if the effort to spur the peasant on to greater productivity required emphasizing consumer production in order to satisfy peasant demands, one of the major requirements for the modernization of the Soviet economy — concentration on the development of *heavy* industrial facilities (coal and iron mines, steel mills) — would not be given the emphasis it required.

What the left, led by the economist-politician E. A. Preobrazhensky and Trotsky, advocated was the collectivization of agriculture. They argued that the small Russian farm operated by individual families and using techniques employed for hundreds of years was basically inefficient. What was needed were huge farms that could effectively utilize the latest mechanical devices for agricultural production: tractors, trucks, mechanical plows, reapers, threshers. The independent peasant in Russia could never justify the utilization of such devices. But the collectivized peasant could. The peasant established on the collective was to be worked as hard as possible and given as little back from the system as possible (as few consumer goods and as little food as possible). The remainder of production would be used to build the industry of Russia on a planned basis as rapidly as possible.

This was the idea for the collectivization and industrialization of Russia that Stalin at first opposed — because it came from Trotsky and probably also because originally Stalin was not convinced of its advantages. But Stalin later adopted collectivization and industrialization, and when the time seemed right, he brought them forth as *his* plan, arguing that what is most significant is not who thinks of an idea first but who determines that moment when the idea's time has arrived. In 1928 Stalin decided that the time had come for collectivization and industrialization.

The twin concepts of collectivization and industrialization — the former as support for the latter — furnish the economic basis of the Soviet system as it has developed in Russia and been exported abroad over the past half century and more. It is a system for modernizing the economies of backward countries. As such, be it noted, collectivization and industrialization have nothing to do with Marxism. Karl Marx was primarily interested in and wrote about industrial economies that were fully developed, not those that had scarcely emerged from feudalism. Though the Soviets have labeled collectivization and industrialization "Marxist," they are not Marxist — and considering the manner in which they were realized in Russia and elsewhere, Karl Marx, had he been present, would certainly have disowned them.

But Marx was not around. Stalin was — and he considered collectivization-industrialization to be the best bet for bringing Russia up to the level of the United States, one of his primary objectives. Accordingly, in 1928 Stalin began the collectivization of Russian agriculture. It was to become a bloody affair.

Collectivization

Stalin first tried to win the peasants over to the idea of collectivization. It would be more scientific, production would grow, the peasants would benefit. The peasants did not see it that way. They were being called on to turn over their houses, their animals, their equipment, and most important, *their land,* to the collective — in return for what? The right to labor for a salary on what had once been their own land? Conceivably, peasants who had become landholders for the first time in 1917 were not so attached to their farm, but those — particularly in the Ukraine — whose families had owned the land for centuries, had fled central Russia and the tsar's regime in order to obtain that land, and had tended it and fought for it for hundreds of years, were not about to hand it over simply because Stalin encouraged them to do so. They resisted.

As the Red Army approached to force them to hand over their homes and equipment and animals, they set fire to their homes, smashed equipment, and slaughtered animals. In retribution, army detachments rounded up the peasants, machine-gunned thousands, and sent tens of thousands to labor camps. The famed White Sea Ship Canal, which enabled seagoing vessels to enter Lake Ladoga, was built between 1931 and 1934, almost entirely by peasant slave laborers who resisted collectivization.

Despite the resistance, Stalin did not let up on collectivization but pushed it faster and harder. By 1931 it was 50 percent completed, and by 1936, 90 percent completed. But not before Russian agriculture had been devastated and a famine induced in which millions perished. According to figures given by Stalin himself at the Seventeenth Party Congress in 1934, over 30 million head of cattle and 100 million sheep and goats were slaughtered by "saboteurs," and the horse population of the country was lowered from 34 million to 16 million. It would be forty years before Soviet animal husbandry would recover.

The organizational arrangement Stalin sought in the countryside was one in which the peasant would farm the land as the worker labored at his bench. The raw materials, the seed, would be provided by the state, as would the land and the equipment. The worker would provide only his labor, and would be paid for that at a fixed amount. It soon became apparent to Stalin that agriculture would not produce under such circumstances, if only because the peasant would not work at it. The peasant would put in time, but if the land was not his, the attention necessary to bring forth an abundant harvest was not forthcoming. And so Stalin retreated and established the *kolkhoz* (collective farm) as the agricultural form for the great majority of Russia's peasantry.

The kolkhoz is a mixture of private and communal farming. Most of the land is farmed in common, but the peasant receives a small allotment to cultivate on a personal basis. The peasant was expected to put in at least half his time working on the collective. He received a unit of credit known as the *trudoden* (labor day) for each day put in. The more skilled the peasant, the greater number of *trudodni* he received for each day worked, up to five *trudodni* for a tractor driver, the highest category. At the end of the year, the profit earned by the kolkhoz was divided by the total number of labor days worked by all those on the kolkhoz. The quotient was the number of rubles to which the worker was entitled for each day worked. The system required the keeping of extended records. It is often observed that the most important person on a kolkhoz is the bookkeeper.

The per diem amount was usually rather small, except for skilled workers such as mechanics and tractor drivers, whose efforts were credited at a high rate. Others, particularly ordinary peasants without special skills, concentrated their efforts on the small amount of land, much less than an acre, allotted to each family. The peasants farmed these personal plots intensively, tending them carefully, applying fertilizer and protecting the young plants against the cold. They made much more by working on "their" own acreage than by cultivating the collective. Thus, as a consequence, the land of the collective tended to be neglected, while lavish care made private plots flourish. In 1979, 42 percent of the fruit and berries, 40 percent of the pork, and 60 percent of the potatoes in the Soviet Union came from private plots. During the 1970s, using a variety of devices including special "factories" for the raising of chickens and mechanization for potatoes and other crops, Soviet agriculture for a time was able to reduce reliance on the private sector somewhat. But the best fruits and vegetables, poultry, and dairy products in the USSR still originated on private acreage.

In the post-Stalin period, the Soviet leadership has tried to turn the peasant away from the kolkhoz, but not by coercion. While Stalin was alive, Khrushchev recommended the establishment of *agrogorodi* (agricultural cities) where peasants would enjoy the advantages of living in town and be transported to the countryside daily. There they would put in their eight-hour shift, be paid on an hourly basis, then return home in the evening to their apartments—analogous to the pattern of the industrial worker. The idea never got off the ground. No such comprehensive concept appeared, although the regime did from time to time indicate that the *sovkhoz* (state farm), where the peasant is a salaried, full-time employee but still lives in the village, was the desired pattern. Early in the Brezhnev era, the *trudoden* was supposedly replaced by a kolkhoz minimum wage. However, the surplus, the distributable income above the minimum, apparently continued to be allocated according to the *trudoden* system. Through the use of economic and other incentives, some peasants were induced to leave the kolkhoz, although they remained in agriculture, working on huge poultry and beef-producing complexes, for example. Then, in 1979, a surprising development began, which picked up momentum in the years immediately following. The system, desperate for increased agricultural production, encouraged the kolkhoz peasant to utilize his private acreage more intensively; offered him improved seed and livestock to pursue that goal; and contemplated the manufacture of farm implements for use on small plots. Moreover, it encouraged *sovkhoz* peasants, who did not have or had neglected their private plots, to begin intensive "personal" farming.

Soviet agriculture is generally regarded in the West as a failure. In most years it cannot provide adequate food for its populace and must purchase substantial amounts of grain from the United States, Canada, and Argentina. To a significant degree, the shortcomings of Soviet agriculture can be attributed to the cold Russian climate. Winter temperatures are extreme, early falls and late springs are common, and growing seasons are comparatively short. Moreover, in areas where much of the richest soil is to be found, rainfall is sparse, only one-third of that found in similar areas in the United States. During most years, optimal conditions for producing large crops do not exist in the Soviet Union. Nevertheless, it must be pointed out, Russia has some of the richest farmland in the world and at the beginning of the twentieth century it was the breadbasket of Europe, exporting large amounts of grain.

The primary reason for the disappointing performance of Soviet agriculture is the failure of the regime to enlist the wholehearted support of the peasantry. Though peasants have long since ceased overt resistance to collectivization, they have not embraced it. Their attitude is reflected in the sentiment that if this is what the system wants, it can have it—but don't expect us to be wildly supportive.

For decades the system did little to alter such feelings. It consistently gave the countryside the lowest investment priority. While social security was the pride of the Soviet system, it existed only for urban workers, not for the peasant. Any young peasant with ambition left the farm as soon as he or she could. Khrushchev and Brezhnev tried at times to make country life more appealing, less poverty-stricken and boring, but they generally failed in their efforts because they were unwilling or unable to make sufficient changes to alter these conditions. As a consequence, the Soviet Union has an agricultural system that, in spite of the large numbers of workers—it is the principal occupation of almost 40 percent of the population, versus 2.7 percent of the U.S. population involved in farming—produces at an unsatisfactory rate.

The continued success of and renewed emphasis on the private plots suggest that a return to rural capitalism would increase Soviet agricultural production. It is highly unlikely that any Soviet leadership in the near future will consider such a proposal, however. Collectivization is a corner-

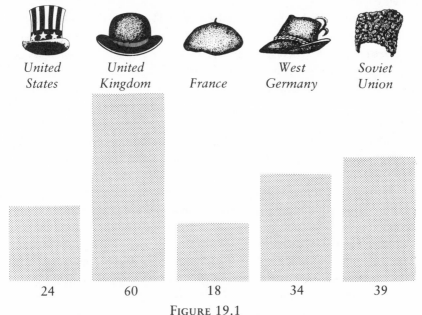

United States	United Kingdom	France	West Germany	Soviet Union
24	60	18	34	39

FIGURE 19.1
Urban Population (in percent): Cities over 100,000

stone of Soviet ideology. Even though it might be argued that it has served its purpose — or failed to serve its purpose — the system seems irretrievably wedded to it. To abandon it would be regarded as tantamount to abandoning Marx, although the latter had nothing to do with collectivization as such.

Industrialization

The concept that Stalin began to operationalize in the late 1920s was that of relying on the capital provided by collectivization in order to rapidly industrialize the country. Whatever profits accrued — to be maximized by pushing the workers to work as hard as possible and paying them as little as possible — would be plowed back into the planned buildup of the system. Heavy industry and communications would be emphasized and the added capacity resulting from the new industry would be utilized to build a still greater capacity. Only when the "commanding heights" of industry, as the Bolsheviks called their iron mines, steel mills, and railroads, were well established would it be possible to turn the nation's attention to consumer goods.

In 1928 the USSR embarked upon its first Five-Year Plan (FYP) to industrialize the country. The overall supervision of the industrialization effort was the Politburo's responsibility, but defining specific objectives was the work of Gosplan, the state planning agency. Gosplan had (and still has) the goal of stating the precise tasks for each sector of Soviet industry: how much it was to have for investment, and what results were expected from it.

An early decision was that industrialization had to rely at the outset on imported technology. The menu of foreign technology from which the USSR selected was, in most instances, exceedingly long. An early requirement, therefore, was to determine which categories would receive initial attention, and within those categories, which specific items. Hundreds of makes of trucks, railroad locomotives, telephones, and the like were manufactured abroad. Which ones should the USSR select as models? The criteria were not only which represented the "highest" technology but which best fitted the existing capacities and geographic needs of the USSR.

The industrialization of Russia in the 1920s thus began with some of the best available Western technology — and it moved forward quickly. Huge hydroelectric dams were constructed in the Ukraine. New mines were opened there and in the Urals. The huge new steel mills of Magnito-gorsk were developed. The biggest truck factory in the world was built under Ford supervision in Gorky. The Trans-Siberian railroad was completed and the tracks for the Turk-Sib, connecting the Urals with Central Asia, were laid. Production boomed. It increased 100 percent, 300 percent, 1000 percent, seemingly overnight.

The growth of Russian industry in the 1930s was a heady potion to many of those who participated in it. Suddenly, huge new opportunities were available. Planners were needed: factory managers, scientists, technologists, supervisors, and foremen. Anyone who had a proletarian background and was willing to learn was eligible. Training was specific and brief, and promotion was rapid. Rewards in status and material advantages seemed tremendous, particularly for those with peasant backgrounds, whose expectations had been to gain little more than what their parents had achieved. Upward mobility was the order of the day.

The Soviet industrialization drive imparted a great sense of achievement and purpose, even optimism, to the lives of those involved in it. The impression of accomplishment was reinforced by contrasting the rapid development in Russia to the Great Depression and deepening malaise in the West. In Russia, in spite of resistance and famine in the countryside, and in spite of the purges, there was a sense of change, growth, and opportunity. Purges even enhanced the opportunities as hundreds of thousands of those at the top were removed from the employment pool. Among the industrious youth of Russia there was enthusiasm for the future.

There can be little doubt that industrialization in the 1930s helped the Soviet Union withstand the German assault in the 1940s. Without it, Russia would have succumbed to Hitler. And the experiences of the 1930s provided a large cadre of skilled technicians and managers, which grew during the war, in spite of heavy losses of manpower. At war's end, large areas of the USSR were in ruins; but the system had the know-how and vitality to rebuild. By 1948 production levels had been restored approximately to what they had been prior to the outbreak of the war. Granted that some of the refurbishing of the Soviet industrial plants was achieved by moving to the USSR the surviving factory equipment, rolling stock and bridges of the Eastern European countries taken over by the Red Army, the primary credit for the rapid recovery of the Russian economy can be attributed to the resiliency and complacency of the Russian people, the sizable body of skilled manpower available, and the determined party leadership.

At the same time that the Soviet industry was recovering from the war, it was becoming increasingly evident that there were self-limiting factors in the Soviet system. Soviet leadership, although obviously gratified by the leading role Russia played on the international scene in the postwar period, aspired to greater heights. It wanted to be Number One. But Soviet production remained far behind that of the United States—a situation that had to be altered if the ideological and nationalistic objectives of the leadership were to be realized. By the late 1940s it was apparent to some that unless the Soviet system was modified, it would have great difficulty in meeting those goals.

What were the problems? One was centralization. Lenin had insisted on centralization; it was the foundation of his organizational concept. In industrialization, centralization worked well in getting Soviet modernization off the ground. It enabled the comparatively limited number of decisions and actions that were involved in starting up Soviet industry to be made with maximum efficiency and dispatch by a small coterie of individuals at the center. But as the industrial machinery grew, it became increasingly complex. The most efficient and effective decisions could no longer always be made by those at the center. Those on the scene, at district and local levels, knew best what a particular situation required. But for the central leadership to allow those at lower levels to decide what models to produce and how to produce them, or what materials and designs to use, or even what minor modifications of the Moscow-determined model to adopt, awakened the basic Russian and Bolshevik fear of anarchy.

Soviet leadership is deeply convinced that it is necessary to control very tightly—or everything will fall apart. It will not do for Ivan to make one decision and Misha another and Sonya a third. Who knows whether each will make the correct decision?

In the early 1950s Stalin recognized the problem but consciously left it for his successors to handle. Khrushchev indicated an awareness of the problem, and in the late 1950s there was a great deal of discussion about it. Some experimentation with local decision making was carried out, and some modifications were introduced. But with Khrushchev's demise, and particularly after the decision to suppress Czech attempts at economic reform in 1968, a conscious bias against change prevailed among the old-timers who dominated the PB. Inevitably, modern technology required some concessions, but they were to be minimal. The objective was to maintain as much central control as possible and to give way only when compromise was unavoidable.

This requirement of preserving strong central control has limited the system's flexibility and hobbled initiative within it. Ideally, initiative has had a high priority in the ordering of Bolshevik values. For more than half a century, Soviet slogans have urged it as a characteristic to which the Soviet people should aspire. But, in practice, centralized control has had a much higher priority. Adhering strictly to the established way of doing things has been much safer. Using "initiative" has gotten managers and workers into trouble when it was not successful, or when it was seen by those in command as threatening their authority. Better proceed along the proven path. Follow the leader.

This need for change but fear of its consequences has been exhibited in other areas important to Soviet production. The system has believed not only in centralized control but also in the necessity of constantly driving the working force. The view that the Russian masses are slovenly, lackadaisical, and disposed to seek every opportunity to do nothing unless constantly prodded is deeply imbedded in Bolshevik attitudes. Out of such sentiments has come the concept of "campaign strategy," the conviction that it is necessary constantly to be involved in campaigns: a campaign to fulfill the monthly production quota by the fifteenth; a campaign to fulfill production quotas for the first six months by the May 1 holiday; a campaign to celebrate International Women's Day by overfulfilling the weekly quota; a campaign to fulfill the annual production quota by November 7.

This seemingly unremitting pursuit of goals has created a constant tension; those living under the system have found it oppressive and have sought to lessen it. One obvious way of satisfying the demands of goal fulfillment while keeping tensions at a tolerable level has been to set the goals very low. Thus they have been easy to fulfill and overfulfill. In the Soviet Union individual goals have been kept low so that great successes have seemed to be achieved, though the reality has often been different.

Even when goals were attainable, a pattern developed wherein Soviet workers, assigned monthly goals, took the first ten days of the month easy, picked up activity the second ten days, and then pushed so hard the last ten days that they exhausted themselves, or thought they had. As a consequence, the period immediately after goal fulfillment was again one of slight effort, or as some have described it, total collapse.

It became apparent to Soviet specialists and leaders that spending the last ten days of the month in feverish activity, followed by ten days of minimal activity, and then ten days of average activity as the work force geared up to spend the last ten days in hectic pursuit of the quota, was not very efficient. It made a great deal more sense to work at an even pace throughout the month. Certainly it was far more efficient to have a steady stream of products coming off the assembly line than to have a huge periodic volume requiring either storage facilities or a greater number of railroad cars, most of which sat idly by until the next great outpouring from the plant.

Thus, in the 1960s and '70s the system raised quotas to a level that more accurately reflected the ability to produce. It reduced expectations for early fulfillment and demands for overfulfillment. But it could not give up the campaign habit. It distrusted the willingness of workers to produce without campaigns. Workers must be pushed, or else they will tarry. No doubt the Russian worker, brought up on campaigns, now expects them. They are part of the system—indistinguishable from it—but they are not very efficient.

Another problem in the Soviet industrialization model developed under Stalin was that of enlisting the active support of leading scientific and other innovative intellects. The Soviet Union, in striving for international leadership, required advanced technology. It had the trained personnel to provide such technology, but they needed the appropriate cultivation in order to fulfill their potential. For example, they needed contacts with foreign centers and scholars working in related fields. Soviet science was not going to be maximally productive if it relied only on itself. It needed to be aware of what was happening among scholars studying similar problems in the United States, West Germany, and Australia.

Contact with foreigners is something the regime does not easily accept. It fears that contact between Russians and citizens of capitalist countries will infect the Russians. They will succumb to the lures and license of the West and be lost to the USSR. The system does not generally permit its citizens to correspond freely with foreigners; it does not permit the average Russian to travel abroad to meetings and conferences. Why, then, should it so permit its scientists? Why can't scientists be treated the same as everyone else? The people are told to produce—and they produce. Why not scientists?

Stalin believed that scientists could be forced to produce for the system. In the 1940s he established special prison facilities for recalcitrant scientists. The prisons were among the most advanced research facilities in the USSR. Some positive results were achieved under prison conditions, but Stalin's successors recognized that they generally were not conducive to producing major scientific breakthroughs. Since the mid-1950s the USSR has eased the way for Soviet scientists to have freer interaction with the scientific community outside Russia. But only some scientists — those the system believes it can trust. By and large, this does not include those in the social sciences, and close surveillance is maintained over those who are in contact with foreign nationals.

Soviet industrialization has not produced the expected achievements. It has slowed down. Except in defense industries, it has consistently failed to meet objectives. For example, in 1979 the overall growth rate was 3.4 percent, compared with the planned rate of 5.7 percent. Production in oil, coal, steel, machine tools, mineral fertilizers, trucks, paper, cement, shoes, knitted goods, and other products was below plan. "There were serious failings in the transportation section, along all of the railroads, as well as in other communication sectors." Labor productivity, a key factor in the labor-intensive Soviet industry, rose only 2.4 percent, far below what was planned; productivity actually fell in some vital sectors.

Soviet leadership is keenly aware of these shortcomings; from time to time, it openly admits to them. But in the Brezhnev era the old men in the Politburo were unwilling, perhaps unable, to remove existing restrictions and take the steps necessary to increase productivity. They tinkered with the established model. They made a few changes here, they allowed a bit more leeway there. Overall, they did not make significant alterations. They feared losing control and preferred to tolerate lackluster performance rather than establish the conditions necessary for better results. In the post-Brezhnev period, the new leadership emphasized its determination to improve industrial and agricultural performance. But it was unclear, even with the best and wisest intentions at the top and the strongest will, that the system itself would be willing and able to overcome inertia and resistance and adopt the proposed reforms.

Before leaving the subject of Soviet collectivization-industrialization, there is a not insignificant academic question that requires consideration. If there had been no Stalin-dominated collectivization-industrialization of the Soviet Union, would Russia be as advanced as it is? Who knows what might have been. But it is arguable that without Stalin's brutally enforced collectivization, there would not have been the loss of animals and farm equipment during the 1930s; there would not have been the great famine; there would not be an agricultural system that seems to discourage production, a system that turned a country that was once a grain exporter into one of the world's largest importers of grain. The Soviets argue that collectivization was necessary to support industrialization. But some modern Western studies indicate that the damage done by collectivization was so great that it is more accurate to say that industrialization was carried out, not on the basis of collectivization, but in spite of it.

It can also be argued that had there not been the chaos imposed on Russia by the Bolsheviks—the revolution, the civil war, collectivization, the purges, World War II (would Hitler have arisen if there had not been a "Bolshevik menace"?)—the nation would be far more advanced than it is. After all, Russia is a very wealthy country. Prior to 1917, it was on the way to becoming a modern industrial state. Industrialization has been accomplished in many countries without Bolshevik leadership. Did the Russians need Lenin and Stalin to become modern? Is it not more likely that, if there had been a stable leadership in Russia, one that would not by its very nature have caused and elicited such violence, Russia would be far more modernized than it is today?

Although it is interesting to make conjectures about possibilities, the majority of experts would probably say that if the primary objective is modernization and there is less concern for the upset caused in the lives of individuals, the Soviet system has advantages for achieving the speedy modernization of an economy *in the early stages of development.* Moreover, as indicated previously, given the Bolshevik seizure of power in 1917, if it had not been for the industrialization of the 1930s, skillfully and brutally carried out by Stalin, Russia could not have successfully thrown back Hitler in World War II.

20

What Is the Future of Soviet Politics?

The preceding chapters on the Soviet Union have indicated major problems: in succession, in agriculture, in industry. But these do not exhaust the list. A significant problem area, for today and tomorrow's Soviet leaders (as for their predecessors) is that of *opposition* to the regime.

Opposition under Lenin and Stalin

The standard Soviet position on opposition is indicated in an interview Stalin granted Roy Howard, publisher of the Scripps-Howard chain, in 1936. Howard asked the Soviet leader if it were true that there was only a single political party in the USSR. Stalin replied that it was true, that there was only one party because there was only one class. If other parties existed, they would represent other classes — opposition — and there is no place for that in Soviet society. The only proper position of the party toward opposition is to suppress it.

At the time of the Revolution some colleagues convinced Lenin that, at least in the beginning, the Bolsheviks were too weak to govern alone. Lenin did not want to make common cause with other groups, but he allowed himself to be convinced and established an alliance with the "left" SRs (Social Revolutionaries). When it quickly became apparent to Lenin that he did not need them, he proceeded to get rid of them.

One by one, and sometimes more than one at a time, the Bolsheviks took on all the opposing forces in postrevolutionary Russia — Social Revolutionaries, Mensheviks, anarchists, Whites, nationalists — and overcame them all. But Lenin found, as Stalin was later to discover, that the making of policy in itself created opposition: the more radical the policy, the more violent the opposition. This problem Lenin was able to handle during the comparatively short time he was in power by ousting the opposition from any positions of influence or exiling them from the country. Stalin had difficulty tolerating the continued physical existence of any opponent, no matter how impotent and far removed.

Stalin was determined that everyone should agree with him; if they didn't, something had to be done about it. He could understand that those who had grown up under the old regime might harbor *perezhitki*—the remnants of the past. But he could not fathom how those who had been nurtured by the party from their youth, who had been fed, clothed, and educated by the party, could disagree with him. He could attribute their disagreement only to disloyalty—and disloyalty, even though it might be unknown to those who harbored it, had to be ruthlessly extirpated lest it spread throughout the system. He was a firm believer in the great-oaks-from-little-acorns principle. Any act with the implications of resistance, opposition, or hostility—no matter how seemingly innocuous—was dangerous because it carried within it the potential for growth. The masses—amorphous, indolent, accepting—were under control; but, any moment they might explode. They were a potential tinderbox.

In Russia, both under Stalin and today, all groups must be organized by the state (see page 273). According to Marx, economics determines everything; but in the Soviet Union, politics determines everything. Any organization is a potential threat to the state because it may become a center of dissent. Accordingly, organizations exist only at the behest and under the direction of the state. Any organization that is not so founded or controlled, whatever its stated purpose, is illegal and subversive.

Stalin ruthlessly suppressed any opposition he could detect and much that he only paranoically suspected. He established slave-labor camps—the famed "gulag archipelago"—throughout the desolate reaches of Russia, particularly in the frozen hinterlands of Siberia, and populated them with "enemies of the people." No one knows for certain how many Soviet citizens died in the Soviet *lagerya* (camps) but a frequently given figure is 30 million. The actual numbers may be much greater.

In the 1930s when the large-scale deportation of Soviet citizens began, most Russians who heard about the purges, but were not touched by them personally, convinced themselves that the people who were transported to Siberia deserved what they got. The newspapers were filled with stories of former high officials of the Soviet regime—Trotsky, Kamenev, Zinoviev, Bukharin, and others—who had performed nefarious and traitorous deeds against the Soviet homeland. No statements defending them were permitted to circulate. Even if the average Russian had doubts as to the guilt of some specific deportee, it was too threatening to believe that these men and women had been arbitrarily or falsely accused. To mention doubts was to risk identification with the miscreants; to harbor doubts was the prior step to mentioning them. It was much more comforting, much safer, to believe that the accused were guilty and that the same fate could not possibly befall you because you were innocent.

As the purges continued during World War II and into the postwar period, undoubtedly more and more Russians knew what was happening, but they did nothing about it. They continued to adjust to terror by denying it, hoping against hope that it wouldn't touch them. The years from 1948 to 1953, after the notable victory against the Germans, which should have caused Stalin to trust the Russian masses, were in many ways the most difficult for the average Soviet citizen. It was then that the characterization of Russia as "gray" and of the average citizen as trying just to "hold on" was most accurate.

Since Stalin's death, the slave-labor network has been greatly reduced, though it still exists on a limited and standby basis. During the more liberal Khrushchev period, leading Soviet figures, whose families had suffered from Stalin's purges and the camps, demanded "justice," which meant the rehabilitation of the reputations of those who had perished in the camps and the freeing and exoneration of those still alive. The camps were largely emptied. But Khrushchev, and Brezhnev and Kosygin to a greater degree, did not know how else to deal with those who continued to take political exception to the regime. They continued to use the camps and relied heavily on another device used by Stalin, the psychiatric hospital. Those who disagreed with the system were by definition mentally ill and in need of rehabilitation and "retraining," which was available in state asylums. It is interesting to note that in Russia, the majority of psychiatric facilities are under the control of the KGB, the secret police.

The continuation of such centers notwithstanding, the worst excesses of the Stalin era have been muted. Today the system seeks to avoid sending political offenders to their deaths, particularly if they are well known and their deaths will bring international recriminations against the USSR.

Intellectual Opposition

In recent years, despite the continuing threat of long-term incarceration in camps, prisons, and psychiatric wards, a few people have been prepared to take on the system. Some are survivors of the camps who feel that the system has already done its worst to them. Others are children of victims of the camps. Still others are ordinary citizens determined not to be silenced by the authorities. They *will* and *do* speak out against what they see as injustice and stupidity. Such men are Alexander Solzhenitsyn, Andrei Sakharov, the Medvedev brothers, Anton Antonov-Ovseyenko, and dozens of others. In the total population of Russia, their numbers are few. But almost as soon as they are arrested or forcibly exiled from Russia, others come forward to replace them.

These men and women, mostly intellectuals, represent one kind of opposition in Russia, one aspect of the so-called dissident movement. It consists largely of intellectuals: authors and scientists, many of whom have achieved international standing in their chosen professions, they are aware of the conditions in the outside world and of the inferior status of freedom in Russia compared with freedom in the West (see page 286). They know that something is wrong in Russia, and they want to right it. But it must be observed as an indication of their weakness that they cannot agree among themselves as to the direction they want Russia to take. Some would send Russia on the Western democratic path; others think that the present communist system would be acceptable if only less evil men were directing it; still others feel that the only salvation for Russia is to abrogate the present system and return to the traditional Russia of the tsars.

The Soviet regime resents the dissidents, who receive a great deal of notice in the international press, but it does not fear them nearly so much as it does other real and potential opponents.

Ethno-National Opposition

Probably the potentially most threatening opposition to the regime comes from ethnic groups. How many separate ethnic groups there are in Soviet Russia depends upon who is doing the counting. The urbanization and general assimilation of the past century have removed the distinctiveness of some elements in the population. Nevertheless, in its 1979 census the Soviet regime recognized over ninety ethnic groups. Almost all of them, in varying degrees, resent the leading role played in the USSR by the "Russians," by Russian culture and Russian interests.

The "Russians"—demographers refer to them as the "Great Russians" —make up just over 50 percent of the Soviet population. All the Slavs, including the Ukrainians, the Belorussians, and the Great Russians, make up 72 percent of the country's population. The balance of the population is largely made up of Baltic people, Transcaucasians, and Central Asians. In addition, there are dozens of smaller groups, among them Moldavians, Jews, Chechens, Ossetians, Buriats, Mordvinians, and many others.

The rate of population growth has slowed markedly among the Slavs in recent decades but has continued at a high level among some other groups, particularly those in Central Asia. The population of the Great Russians increased 6.5 percent from 1969 to 1979; the population of the Turkmen, Uzbek, Kazakh, Kirghiz, and Tadzhik groups increased by 24 to 36 percent. Moreover, as is indicated in table 20.2, the Central Asian ethnic groups make up an increasingly large proportion in their republics, their numbers growing more rapidly than those of other elements in the population or outsiders moving in. Such demographic developments are of no small moment to the Russians, who are paranoiac about being dominated by Central Asians whom they regard collectively as descendants of the Mongol hordes that swept across Russia in the thirteenth century.

TABLE 20.1
Soviet Republics and Their Population
(Most recent decennial census, 1979)

Union of Soviet Socialist Republics	262,442,000
Russian Federated SSR	137,552,000
Ukraine SSR	49,757,000
Uzbek SSR	15,391,000
Kazakh SSR	14,685,000
Belorussian SSR	9,559,000
Azerbaidzhan SSR	6,028,000
Georgian SSR	5,016,000
Moldavian SSR	3,948,000
Tadzhik SSR	3,801,000
Kirghiz SSR	3,529,000
Lithuanian SSR	3,399,000
Armenian SSR	3,031,000
Turkmen SSR	2,759,000
Latvian SSR	2,521,000
Estonian SSR	1,466,000

TABLE 20.2

*Percentage of Indigenous Population in the Soviet Republic**

	1959	1979
Russian Federated SSR	83.3	82.6
Ukraine SSR	76.8	73.6
Uzbek SSR	61.1	68.7
Kazakh SSR	29.8	36.0
Belorussian SSR	81.1	79.4
Azerbaidzhan SSR	67.5	78.1
Georgian SSR	64.3	68.8
Moldavian SSR	65.4	63.9
Tadzhik SSR	53.1	58.8
Kirghiz SSR	40.5	47.9
Lithuanian SSR	79.3	80.0
Armenian SSR	88.0	89.7
Turkmen SSR	60.9	68.4
Latvian SSR	62.0	53.7
Estonian SSR	74.6	64.7

SOURCE: Adapted from S. I. Bruk, *Isotria SSSR,* September/October 1980, pp. 24-27, as reported in *Current Digest of the Soviet Press* 32, no. 50 (1980): 10.
* Great Russians in RSFSR, Ukrainians in Ukraine, etc.

But the Russians, not the Central Asians, were the conquerors. Whatever their reaction to being absorbed into "Russia" in earlier centuries, with the rise of nationalism in the nineteenth century, they resented being the subjects of the Great Russians. In addition, Lithuanians, Latvians, Estonians, Ukrainians, Belorussians, Armenians, Azerbaidzhans, Georgians, and others wanted their own countries.

Karl Marx considered nationalism a "trick" of the capitalists, who used it to deflect the attention of the working class away from its real enemy, capitalism. According to Marx, if capitalists could get French workers and German workers to hate one another, then the proletarians would be too preoccupied to hate their capitalist masters. Nationalism, held Marx, was a snare and a delusion—and Lenin agreed with him.

Nevertheless, in time it became clear to Lenin that in Russia appeals to nationalism were one way to recruit opponents to the tsar. Ukrainians, Latvians, and Georgians were inclined to revolution not because they were advocates of the working-class movement but because they wanted to establish their own countries. If Lenin spoke against nationalism, he stood in danger of losing badly needed revolutionary support. So, until the revolution was victorious, he made his peace with the nationalism of some Russian minorities, holding out the promise of independence.

Once the revolution was successful, Lenin opposed nationalism and used the Red Army where he could to defeat independence movements. In the Ukraine, Belorussia, and the Caucasus he succeeded; in the Baltic region, independent countries were set up in Lithuania, Latvia, and Estonia. An independent Finland was established; and Poland, which had been divided by Russia, Prussia, and the Austro-Hungarian Empire at the end of the eighteenth century, reemerged as an independent country.

While most of Russia was put back together again after the civil war (1918-21), and the nationalists were shot or exiled, nationalism remained a fact of life with which the Bolsheviks had to deal. They were certain that in the long run, nationalism, which Marx called a relic of the capitalist past, would disappear. They sought to blunt nationalistic impulses in the USSR by giving minority groups institutions that superficially satisfied their nationalist yearnings but that were, in fact, dominated by the Russians or their agents. The Soviet leaders divided the USSR into a number of union republics. Today there are fifteen: the Russian Soviet Federated Socialist Republic plus fourteen others, each representing a national group.

In addition, there are autonomous republics and autonomous regions and national areas each representing a different ethnic group. Generally speaking, whether a designated group has a union republic, an autonomous republic, an autonomous region, or a national area depends on the number of constituents. Some groups, like the Bashkirs and Tatars, though large enough numerically to have their own union republics, only have autonomous republics because they are within the RSFSR. Other large groups, such as Jews and the Volga Germans (Germans who settled in the Volga region mostly in the eighteenth century) have no national units partly because they are scattered throughout European Russia and partly because they are distrusted.

According to the Soviet Constitution, union republics are "sovereign" states. In fact, they are completely subordinated to the decision makers in the Kremlin. To guarantee the dependency of union republics and other ethnic groups, Moscow has followed the policy that while there will be Uzbek, Armenian, and Ukrainian nationals in the top echelons of republic power, there will also be Russians there, if not in the number-one position in a ministry, or department, or military unit, then in the number-two position, to ensure that Russian national objectives are realized.

TABLE 20.3
Federal Territorial Structure of the USSR

15 Union Republics
20 Autonomous Republics
 8 Autonomous Provinces
10 National Districts

Russian Federated Soviet Socialist Republic
    Bashkir Autonomous Soviet Socialist Republic
    Buryat Autonomous Soviet Socialist Republic
    Daghestan Autonomous Soviet Socialist Republic
    Kabardinian-Balkar Autonomous Socialist Republic
    Kalmyk Autonomous Soviet Socialist Republic
    Karelian Autonomous Soviet Socialist Republic
    Komi Autonomous Soviet Socialist Republic
    Mari Autonomous Soviet Socialist Republic
    Mordovian Autonomous Soviet Socialist Republic
    North Ossetian Autonomous Soviet Socialist Republic
    Tatar Autonomous Soviet Socialist Republic
    Tuva Autonomous Soviet Socialist Republic
    Udmurt Autonomous Soviet Socialist Republic
    Chechen-Ingush Autonomous Soviet Socialist Republic
    Chuvash Autonomous Soviet Socialist Republic
    Yakut Autonomous Soviet Socialist Republic

    Adygei Autonomous Province
    Gorno-Altai Autonomous Province
    Jewish Autonomous Province
    Karachayevo-Cherkess Autonomous Province
    Khakass Autonomous Province

    Aginsk National District
    Evenki National District
    Komi-Permyak National District
    Koryak National District
    Nenets National District
    Taimyr National District
    Ust-Orda National District
    Khanty-Mansi National District
    Chukotsk National District
    Yamal-Nenets National District

    Ukraine Soviet Socialist Republic

TABLE 20.3 *(continued)*

Byelorussian Soviet Socialist Republic
Uzbek Soviet Socialist Republic
    Kara-Kalpak Autonomous Soviet Socialist Republic
Kazakh Soviet Socialist Republic
Georgian Soviet Socialist Republic
    Abkhazian Soviet Socialist Republic
    Adzhar Soviet Socialist Republic

    South Ossetian Autnomous Province

Azerbaidzhan Soviet Socialist Republic
    Nakhichevan Autonomous Soviet Socialist Republic
    Nagorno-Karabakh Autonomous Province

Lithuanian Soviet Socialist Republic
Moldavian Soviet Socialist Republic
Latvian Soviet Socialist Republic
Kirghiz Soviet Socialist Republic
Tadzhik Soviet Socialist Republic
    Gorno-Badakhshan Autonomous Province

Armenian Soviet Socialist Republic
Turkmen Soviet Socialist Republic
Estonian Soviet Socialist Republic

In the realm of culture, Russian communism also has recognized the nationalistic impulses of non-Russian ethnics. All works of art may be "nationalist in form," but they must also be "socialist in content." In practice, while the performers may be dressed in Uigur costumes and speak in Uigur, the words they utter, even if the play's actions takes place in the thirteenth century, must express contemporary Russian socialist values such as the evils of capitalism, the saintliness of the working class, and the eternal vigiliance of Russians for the interests of minority nationalities.

Thus the Russians have allowed minorities to continue to maintain many of the old forms—though far from all of them—but they have consistently looked toward the day when form and content will be uniform throughout the USSR, though in recent years perhaps with less insistence than in the Stalin period.

In areas where a non-Russian populace predominates, parents may send their children to schools conducted either in the local language or in Russian. If children attend schools in the local language, they must also learn Russian. Generally speaking, the reverse is not the case. In Stalin's time, all university classes were conducted in Russian. Today some classes in a few republics are conducted in the local language. But *all* university courses in subjects such as math and science are taught in Russian, no matter what the republic. Obviously, all business between headquarters in Moscow and local headquarters is conducted in Russian. Anyone who aspires to success in the Soviet system outside his own republic, and generally inside it as well, must speak Russian fluently.

It has often been pointed out, in defense of the opportunities for minority groups in the USSR, that many minority leaders have risen to political prominence. Stalin was a Georgian, Mikoyan an Armenian, Gromyko a Belorussian, Aliev an Azerbaijani, Kunayev a Kazakh, and so on. The important point is that none of these leaders could have maintained a strong identity as a Georgian, Armenian, Belorussian, and the like and have attained success. In order to achieve the top political rank, they had to doff their nationality and don the cloak of socialism, which, in the Soviet context, has come to mean Russian national interest. In Russia, to be successful, one has to be an advocate of Great Russian interests.

This putting of Russian national interests ahead of the interests of other national groups antagonizes non-Great Russians whenever they come in contact with Russians. Outside Russia, such Great Russian chauvinism has been resented in the postwar world by Yugoslavia, Poland, Hungary, and Czechoslovakia. Inside Russia, it has been resented in the Lithuanian, Latvian, and Estonian republics, which were independent countries between the world wars; in Belorussia, the Ukraine, and the Caucasus; and particularly in Central Asia, where national differences between Russians and the local population are heightened by racial and religious differences.

There can be little doubt that many national groups would establish their independence from Russia if they could. But most members of minority groups recognize that they cannot escape Russian domination, and so they adjust. Some form dissident groups, which exist in every republic in European Russia. In general, these groups are even less effective than the groups formed by dissidents among the intelligentsia, if only because they usually lack the intelligentsia's contacts with circles outside Russia.

Though the pressure for conformity is great in Russia, large numbers of ethnics retain their identity and on rare occasions strongly defend it. In April 1978, when the Soviet government sought to promulgate a new constitution in Georgia that dropped Georgian as the national language, thousands of people demonstrated in the streets of Tiblisi against the decision — and they won. Similarly, attempts in the Armenian SSR to drop Armenian were successfully resisted. Of course, the central government could have suppressed the opposition, but it judged that the circumstances did not warrant the upset that would result.

Examples of Soviet masses protesting what they conceive of as threats to their national identity are few. But those few instances reflect the pent-up hostility to what national minorities see as the oppressive power of their Moscow masters, whom they dislike not only because they are masters, perhaps because they are communists, but more than anything else because they are Russians. While dissident movements among minority nationalists remain small, they have a great potential for growth because each member of the minority nationalities that make up almost half the population of the USSR has an almost inborn resentment and is a possible opposition recruit. Or so the regime fears.

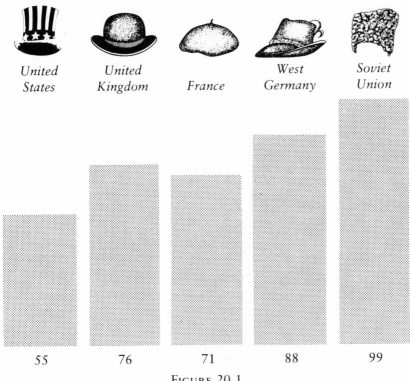

United States	United Kingdom	France	West Germany	Soviet Union
55	76	71	88	99

FIGURE 20.1
Voter Turnout in Most Recent Election (in percent)

While national differences have the potential to set one Soviet citizen against another, they also have potential for solidifying the Great Russian population, which still constitutes the majority of Soviet citizens. The Great Russians, who are themselves fiercely nationalistic, may well react to hostility from the other nationalities as they have in the past—by rallying in support of their own national identity. But among these everyday Great Russians, as among others, there are also reasons for dissatisfaction with the regime. One of the chief problems is the communist attitude toward religion.

Religious Opposition

The oft-repeated Marxist attitude toward religion is that it is the "opiate" of the masses. It soothes the masses, makes them endure their lot, convinces them that it is divine providence that has decreed their poverty (whereas, in truth, it is the economic system). As Lenin saw it, the Russian Orthodox church, the state church of Russia, was in the employ of the tsars. After the Revolution, Lenin regarded the church as a negative influence. It turned the people against the new system and served as a nucleus around which opposition could form. It was a group that the system did not originate or control. Therefore, the church and the product it was selling had to be discouraged and ultimately eliminated.

But in the 1930s Stalin, witnessing the rise of Hitler to power and fearing that Germans would soon be marching against the Soviet Union, decided to strengthen the church. Stalin was aware that the Bolsheviks in power had alienated a very substantial portion of the population, whose support he now required. He decided to use the church for the purpose of serving and abetting the state.

Stalin attempted to make peace with tractable church leaders. He did not give the church sufficient support to flourish as it had in earlier days, but he provided it with funds to sustain itself and in some instances even to rehabilitate some of the edifices and institutions that had fallen into disrepair.

Being seen in church attending a christening or a wedding or a funeral was still dangerous for a party member or one with professional aspirations, but it was tolerated for old people and women. Under Stalin in the 1930s, the Orthodox church made a limited comeback. Although he disapproved of it, he still used it.

The same use was not made of other religions in Russia: Moslems, Catholics, Jews, and scores of Christian sects that had been at odds with the Orthodox church since the seventeenth century. Stalin made no attempt to coopt them as state churches, though he did infiltrate their clergies. He regarded non-Orthodox religions as more dangerous than the Orthodox church because they had large numbers of coreligionists outside Russia. They were potential vipers in the Soviet midst. Everyone who belonged to an outside-connected religion was a suspected "enemy of the people," and for Stalin, as has been observed earlier, there was little difference between potential and actual enemies.

In post-Stalin Russia, there has been a somewhat greater tendency toward religious tolerance. Even middling-high party officials have been seen attending weddings in small Orthodox churches in the country, fifty or a hundred miles from Moscow. (It still would not be politic to be present at a big-city observance.) And christenings for the children or grandchildren of party members have been observed. Nevertheless, regular church attendance and high party standing remained incompatible—and at the end of the Brezhnev era even the thin aura of tolerance seemed to be growing ever more fragile.

Those who belong to non-Orthdox churches are freer than in Stalinist times to practice their religion if they can find a mosque, church, synagogue, or even a room to use for worship. However, the state continues to regard non-Orthodox religions as dupes of foreign governments (Israel, the Vatican, the United States, and so forth). Party members of Moslem, Catholic, Jewish, or non-Orthodox Christian background seldom dare to be seen at a service of the faith with which they have earlier been identified. It would indicate that they may be partial to some other interest than that of the USSR.

Religious instruction in the Soviet Union is outlawed. Youngsters do not receive religious education unless it is within the family. As for the training of ministers, there are seminaries for the preparation of Orthodox priests, but not nearly enough to serve the needs of the community. Even fewer Catholic priests are trained and, to all intents and purposes, no rabbis or mullahs are prepared. However, many Russian sects do not use clergymen and therefore have had centuries-long experience in maintaining themselves without seminary-trained leadership.

One reason that the Soviet regime regularly gives for refusing to permit the training of religious instructors and leaders is that there is no demand—and there is a certain amount of truth in this allegation. As is demonstrated by Russian Jews who have recently migrated from the USSR, there is relatively little interest in formal religion among the great majority of urbanized Russians. They have had no instruction in religion; they feel no need for it; they identify it with backwardness. In short, they have accepted the value judgment of the regime that religion is the opiate of the masses.

Yet it is also true that millions of people in the Soviet Union of all religious backgrounds have not acceded to the system's position. They feel the absence of God and religion in their lives, and they are determined to have both. Some people are obviously more determined than others. For some, their interest in religion is part of the nostalgia for the "old days" when life was uncomplicated by the demands of city and industrial life. But for others, "belief" in God is a strong affirmation of inner faith. To the extent that the regime opposes this belief, pooh-poohs it, and attempts to repress it, those who hold to it oppose the state — and compose an element of often fearless determination to counter the evils of the state, regardless of the consequences to themselves. Such people can be coerced only so far. They will not give in, even at the threat of death, to the demands of the state, which is to them the apotheosis of the anti-God, against which their faith requires them to battle.

Opposition in the Communist Camp

Formation of the Soviet Bloc

The Soviet leadership has confidence in its ability to control the various competing forces, dissidents, and opponents within the system. They see the system as strong and developing, fulfilling the Marxist prophecy of the world triumph of socialism. Yet, there is in the background the fear that Russia could ignite at any moment. Even though the men in the Kremlin are not so paranoiac as Stalin, they still regard themselves as surrounded by potential enemies. These potential enemies exist within the Soviet Union — among intellectual, religious, and national dissidents, and among the people in general — and they exist outside the USSR. In the early days after the Revolution, Lenin feared that it was only a matter of time before the stronger capitalist countries, apprehensive that communism would spread to their domains, would move against the new Soviet state and destroy it. That this did not happen scarcely reduced the fear that it would. One of the rallying cries of the Stalin period was "capitalist encirclement." The Russian people had to be constantly on guard against enemies and had to endure seemingly permanent sacrifices so that those enemies might be overcome. And in the 1980s, even though the Soviet Union has developed its military strength until it challenges, and in some aspects surpasses, that of the United States, Soviet leaders maintain the deepseated feeling that Russians and communism are despised by the other nations of the world. They hold on to a nightmare vision of the powers of the world—the United States, Western Europe, Japan, Islam, even China —uniting and turning against communism, and finding support among the Soviet people.

Most particularly, Soviet leaders suspect that the people of those nations supposedly closest to them—the other communist countries of Eastern Europe—hold them in contempt and enmity and would gladly separate from them if only they had the opportunity. For over three decades, beginning in the 1940s, the Soviet Union regularly and repeatedly declared the existence of "unbreakable" ties of friendship with the people of Poland, East Germany, Hungary, Czechoslovakia, Rumania, and Bulgaria. But it failed to convince itself of the permanence of these ties, and it failed to convince most Poles, East Germans, Hungarians, Czechs, Rumanians, and Bulgarians.

Marx's thesis was that the revolution would spread from one country to another in the wake of the inevitable breakdown of the capitalist system. To this, Lenin and his successors added the concept of other nations embracing communism. It would prove so inviting that the nations of the world would rush to adopt it. In practice, communism came to power outside Russia, not because of the inevitability of the iron laws of economics or the attractiveness of the communist system, but because of the superiority of communist arms. Prior to World War II, there was only one communist country other than the USSR: Outer Mongolia, which had been captured by the Red Army in 1921 and was reconstituted as the People's Republic of Mongolia. Out of World War II came the other communist states of Eastern Europe, established by the Red Army after it had rolled across Europe in pursuit of Hitler's fleeing legions. The governments established in the countries of Eastern Europe, with the exception of the government of Yugoslavia, were headed by nationals who had spent the war years in Russia and followed the Red Army to power at home. In Yugoslavia, a strong guerrilla movement had warred against the Germans for years. It was led by the communist Josip Broz (Tito), who became a national hero and subsequently the head of the postwar government. The people of the Eastern European states were, for the most part, attracted to neither Russia nor communism. They regarded those who rode Soviet coattails to power as Russian puppets, as agents of a foreign country sent to coerce them in the same way that the Nazi *gauleiters* had done. As time went on, the leaders installed by Moscow often gave the people ample reason to feel that way.

The Soviet attitude toward the countries of Eastern Europe, regardless of whether they had supported Hitler during the war or opposed him, was the same. They must all participate in an all-out effort to rehabilitate the war-ravaged USSR as quickly as possible, stripping themselves to do so. Particularly after the cold war began in 1946, Moscow argued that the welfare of the Soviet state had to take precedence over all other considerations. The West was once again threatening to encircle and destroy the USSR, the "fatherland" of world socialism. Those dedicated to socialism had to devote their resources to rebuilding the Soviet Union as quickly as possible, before the United States and its minions could strike. Decades earlier, Lenin had indicated his belief that what was good for the Soviet Union was, by definition, good for international communism. Stalin's decision that all efforts had to be expended to rebuild the Soviet Union *first* was an extension of Lenin's preferences to the contemporary period.

Stalin ordered that what remained of Eastern European industrial development—factories, mining equipment, smelting furnaces, railroad rolling stock, bridges—should be uprooted, dismantled, and shipped to the USSR. Stalin also ordered that the newly reestablished armies of the Eastern European countries should be outfitted in Soviet uniforms, equipped with Soviet arms, and trained in accordance with Soviet manuals. Soviet texts, translated into local languages, were to be used in schools. All children were to learn Russian in addition to their own language. If the number-one person in a Polish, Hungarian, or Bulgarian ministry was a Pole, Hungarian, or Bulgar, then the number-two person had to be Russian. The Russians were determined to dominate in Eastern Europe.

Eastern Europeans did not appreciate taking second place to Russian interests. The Yugoslavs, who had fought against the Germans even longer than the Russians had in World War II and whose own forces had been highly instrumental in liberating their homeland, particularly resented the treatment they received from the Soviet Union. They did not take kindly to being plundered for the sake of Soviet industry; they saw no reason why Soviet citizens should be strategically placed throughout their military and civilian bureaucracy in order to guarantee loyalty to the USSR. Were Yugoslavs not to be trusted? When the Yugoslav communists stood up to Stalin, the Soviet leader responded by kicking them out of the communist sphere and threatening their political existence.

At the same time that turmoil was brewing in Soviet-Yugoslav relations, another situation developed that, despite the surface appearance of strengthening international communism, actually further aggravated Stalin: the establishment of the People's Republic of China (PRC). Stalin feared a strong China, particularly one headed by an independent-minded Mao Zedong. Stalin was concerned about Chinese competition for the leadership of the communist world, and he sought to postpone the founding of the PRC.

The close juxtaposition of the assertion of Yugoslav independence and the successful establishment of the PRC filled Stalin with foreboding about the future. He feared that the examples of Yugoslavia and China would infect his Eastern European domain. In the late 1940s he embarked on a campaign to eliminate all "bourgeois cosmopolitan" elements in Eastern Europe — by which he meant anyone he did not trust. In a series of purges he liquidated many Eastern European leaders who had followed the Red Army back into their own countries only four or five years previously. Now Stalin saw them as actually or potentially more sympathetic to their own people than to the USSR.

Strains Within the Soviet Bloc

While Stalin lived, he was able to maintain the appearances of a monolithic Eastern Europe (with the exception of Yugoslavia) completely under Moscow's domination, with all the wires, down to the most minute detail in the most remote village, pulled from the Kremlin. But with Stalin's death in 1953 it became clear that the Eastern European bloc was no paradise of contented agreement under Soviet suzerainty. There was an uprising in East Germany in 1953. Escapees from Poland and Hungary spread stories of Soviet oppression. Without Stalin in control, the empire began to unravel. After Khrushchev's "secret" speech of February 1956 at the Twentieth Party Congress, revealing Stalin not as the great genial leader he had always depicted himself but as a paranoiac, blood-stained despot, the disintegration accelerated. Tens of thousand of members of the Polish communist movement tore up their party cards as a sign of their shock and dismay and in October 1956 Khrushchev was barely able to avoid an armed uprising in Poland. A few weeks later, the Hungarian people, under communist leadership, took to the streets in open revolt against the USSR and were suppressed only after the intervention of the Red Army.

The last part of 1956 and early 1957 saw the communist movement throughout the world in danger of dissolution. Who could believe in a system in which the leader, for decades presented as one of humanity's finest specimens, was shown to have been a bungler and a predatory despot? Hundreds of thousands had joined communist parties throughout the world because they believed those parties would lead the way to a better tomorrow. Now they were seen to be instruments of coercion and deception. Erstwhile members dropped out of the party in disgust and horror.

At this point the Chinese Communist party, its authority strong after its recent triumphs in establishing the People's Republic of China, intervened to play a major role in holding the communist world together. As a part of the price for preventing the disintegration of the international movement, Khrushchev had to reiterate that there were now "many paths" to socialism, not only the Russian path. The Chinese demanded even more for their role in holding the movement together. They sought co-leadership, or at least a junior partnership in directing the world communist destiny. This Khrushchev refused to grant; the Chinese broke with him, and the movement has never since been reunited, though it is not for want of trying on the part of the Soviet party leadership.

Repeatedly in the 1960s and '70s, the Kremlin chiefs attempted to bring "unity" to the movement once again, even if it was "unity" without China. But other communist countries and parties frustrated the Soviet efforts. They had lingering memories of what the movement was like when it was under Stalinist domination: When orders from Stalin were not carried out immediately—whether in Poland or France or Mexico—he used assassins to enforce his will. Communists in other countries bristled at the constant Russian pressure to conform to the Soviet model of how things should be done. They remained devoted to socialism, but they preferred to pursue their own paths in securing it.

Polycentrism and Eurocommunism

Particularly among Eastern European communist parties there was the realization that a multicentered communist world provided more room to

TABLE 20.4

Communist Countries and Their Relationships to the USSR

Country	Relationship to USSR
Afghanistan	Close
Albania	Negative
Bulgaria	Close
China	Negative
Cuba	Close
Czechoslovakia	Close
East Germany	Close
Hungary	Close
Kampuchea	Close
Laos	Close
Mongolia	Close
North Korea	Independent
Poland	Close
Romania	Close
Vietnam	Close
Yugoslavia	Independent

maneuver. With strong independent communist parties in China, Yugoslavia, Italy, and France, the Soviets could not coerce a communist country so easily. A march on Warsaw or Budapest or Bucharest could not occur without heated and prolonged protests from other communist countries, and while expectations of such protests might not stop the Soviet Union from moving if it felt threatened, they would cause it to hesitate and perhaps tread more lightly. Eastern European countries, principally as the result of the invasions of Hungary in 1956 and Czechoslovakia in 1968, became aware that certain actions, inexactly defined as the local communist party "losing control," would bring an invasion of the Red Army. But if the local party were careful not to "lose control," there were numerous ways in which it could act independently of Moscow and could pursue its own path to socialism. If Moscow had complete control of the movement, such latitude would not be permitted.

Moreover, in the 1970s, communist parties not in power but aspiring to power in countries such as Italy, France, and Spain came to realize that one of their chief handicaps was identification with the Soviet Union. Such parties, operating within democratic societies, needed to increase their strength among the electorate, which, disenchanted though it may have been with conventional political parties, was fearful that a vote for the communist party would be a vote for the end of democracy, for the elimination of political parties other than the communist one, and for the despotism and slavery they identified with Moscow and communism.

Western Europe's aspiring communists, asserted that they represented the new "Eurocommunism," which denounced such facets of the Soviet and Marxist models as the class struggle and the takeover by a disciplined minority, and even the idea of revolution. While such denunciations did not bring them to power, and they sometimes halfheartedly and out of habit returned to the old ideas, they still avoided the embrace of the USSR. They had a warm spot for it because it was where the Revolution had first occurred, because the Russians had endured much, and because communist ideals offered a contrast to the inadequacies of their own governments. But those with Western-oriented values found it increasingly difficult to blind themselves to the fact that the USSR was a politically bleak and inhospitable place whose system had caused the imprisonment and death of tens of millions of Russians and others. And they came to realize that in spite of all its promises, and in spite of the tremendous efforts and suffering of the people of Russia, the country's economy was sluggish and its standard of living far behind that of many non-Soviet countries.

It was no model.

Thus, while in the years after World War II the Soviet empire expanded and communism spread to many parts of the world, the Soviet model, which the leadership of the Russian party thought would become the model for the world, was cast into doubt. The model proved successful in rapidly modernizing societies, but only at the cost of deprivation of freedom. It proved unsuccessful in accomplishing the continued economic development of societies once they had advanced to more sophisticated levels.

Prospects

There is nothing on the horizon that indicates that the current crop of Soviet leaders will be able and/or willing to make changes in the system that will enable it to pick up economic momentum or to change the image of the USSR as a land that frustrates freedom. This does not mean that the Soviet system is doomed. Over the years it has become inextricably linked with Russian nationalism. Any attack on the system is seen by the masses as an attack on Russia, for which so many millions have given their lives.

Today's Russians, too, will fight for their country—and that includes fighting for the system, bad as it may be, for to turn against the system has been made to seem identical with turning against the country. Communism may not work but it is *theirs,* and they will defend it to the death.

This does not mean that there is great affection for the system, other than in a defensive way. Overwhelmingly it is tolerated, put up with, adjusted to. Its officials, their self-seeking privileges and nepotistic indulgences, are widely resented. But Russians have few traditions of asserting human rights against the will of governing authorities. This is reinforced by the unmistakable determination of the regime to suppress any expression of popular dissatisfaction. In Russia, among the masses, there is little evidence of widespread discontent with the system, let alone the will to do anything about it.

As traditional as arbitrary governmental action and contempt for human rights have been in Russia, just as traditional have been society-wide outbreaks of violence against the regime when pent-up exasperation has been suddenly released as the result of unforeseen developments, usually involving the particularly callous use of force by the government. Such occasions are characterized by what seems to be an almost spontaneous and cascading outburst throughout the country. The oppression, frustration, and humiliation of the past well up. An accounting is demanded from the authorities. The regime tries to contain the explosion in the only way it knows, through force. Usually it succeeds, sometimes it fails. If it fails, the regime falls.

This has been the Russian past—as the men in the Politburo are well aware. How often do they fear it could be the Russian future as well?

For Further Reading

ANTONOV-OVSEYENKO, ANTON. *The Time of Stalin: Portrait of a Tyrant.* New York: Harper and Row, 1982.

ARMSTRONG, JOHN A. *Ukrainian Nationalism.* 2nd ed. New York: Columbia University Press, 1963.

BIALER, SEWERYN. *Stalin's Successors.* Cambridge: Cambridge University Press, 1980.

BILLINGTON, JAMES H. *The Icon and the Axe.* New York: Knopf, 1966.

BRESLAUER, GEORGE W. *Khrushchev and Brezhnev as Leaders.* London: Allen & Unwin, 1982.

BRZEZINSKI, ZBIGNIEW, and HUNTINGTON, SAMUEL P. *Political Power: USA/USSR.* New York: Viking, 1964.

CAMPBELL, ROBERT W. *Soviet-Type Economies: Performance and Evolution.* 3rd ed. Boston: Houghton Mifflin, 1974.

DANIELS, ROBERT V. *The Conscience of the Revolution.* Cambridge: Harvard University Press, 1960.

DEUTSCHER, ISAAC. *The Prophet Unarmed: Trotsky, 1921-1929.* London: Oxford University Press, 1959.

ERLICH, ALEXANDER. *The Soviet Nationalization Debate, 1924-1928.* Cambridge: Harvard University Press, 1960.

FAINSOD, MERLE. *Smolensk Under Soviet Rule.* Cambridge: Harvard University Press, 1958.

HAZARD, JOHN N. *The Soviet System of Government.* 5th ed. Chicago: University of Chicago Press, 1980.

HOUGH, JERRY F. *The Soviet Prefects.* Cambridge: Harvard University Press, 1969.

———, and FAINSOD, MERLE. *How the Soviet System Is Governed.* Cambridge: Harvard University Press, 1979.

JACOBS, DAN N. *Borodin.* Cambridge: Harvard University Press, 1981.

KATAEV, VALENTIN. *Time Forward.* Bloomington: Indiana University Press, 1976.

KENNAN, GEORGE F. *Russia and the West Under Lenin and Stalin.* Boston: Little, Brown, 1961.

KOESTLER, ARTHUR. *Darkness at Noon.* New York: Macmillan, 1941.

LANE, DAVID. *Politics and Society in the USSR.* 2nd ed. New York: New York University Press, 1978.

_____. *Leninism.* Cambridge: Cambridge University Press, 1981.

LEITES, NATHAN C. *The Operational Code of the Politburo.* New York: McGraw-Hill, 1951.

LERNER, WARREN. *Karl Radek: The Last Internationalist.* Stanford: Stanford University Press, 1970.

MEDVEDEV, ROY A. *Let History Judge.* New York: Knopf, 1971.

MEYER, ALFRED G. *Communism.* 3rd ed. New York: Random House, 1967.

PIPES, RICHARD. *The Formation of the Soviet Union: Communism and Nationalism, 1917-1923.* Rev. ed. Cambridge: Harvard University Press, 1964.

POND, ELIZABETH. *From the Yaroslavsky Station: Russia Perceived.* New York: Universe, 1981.

RABINOWITCH, ALEXANDER. *The Bolsheviks Come to Power.* New York: Norton, 1978.

RIGBY, T.G. *Communist Party Membership in the USSR: 1917-1967.* Princeton: Princeton University Press, 1968.

SALISBURY, HARRISON. *Black Night, White Snow.* New York: Doubleday, 1978.

SHARLET, ROBERT. *The New Soviet Constitution of 1977.* Brunswick, Ohio: King's Court, 1978.

SMITH, HEDRICK. *The Russians.* New York: Quadrangle, 1976.

SOLZHENITSYN, A. *The First Circle.* New York: Harper & Row, 1968.

_____. *One Day in the Life of Ivan Denisovich.* New York: Praeger, 1963.

TUCKER, ROBERT C. *The Soviet Political Mind.* New York: Norton, 1972.

_____. *Stalin as Revolutionary.* New York: Norton, 1973.

ULAM, ADAM. *Stalin.* New York: Viking, 1973.

_____. *Dangerous Relations: The Soviet Union in World Politics, 1970-1982.* New York: Oxford University Press, 1983.

WILSON, EDMUND. *To the Finland Station.* New York: Doubleday, 1940.

WOLFE, B.D. *Three Who Made a Revolution.* New York: Dial, 1948.

YANOV, ALEXANDER. *The Russian New Right.* Berkeley: Institute of International Studies, 1978.

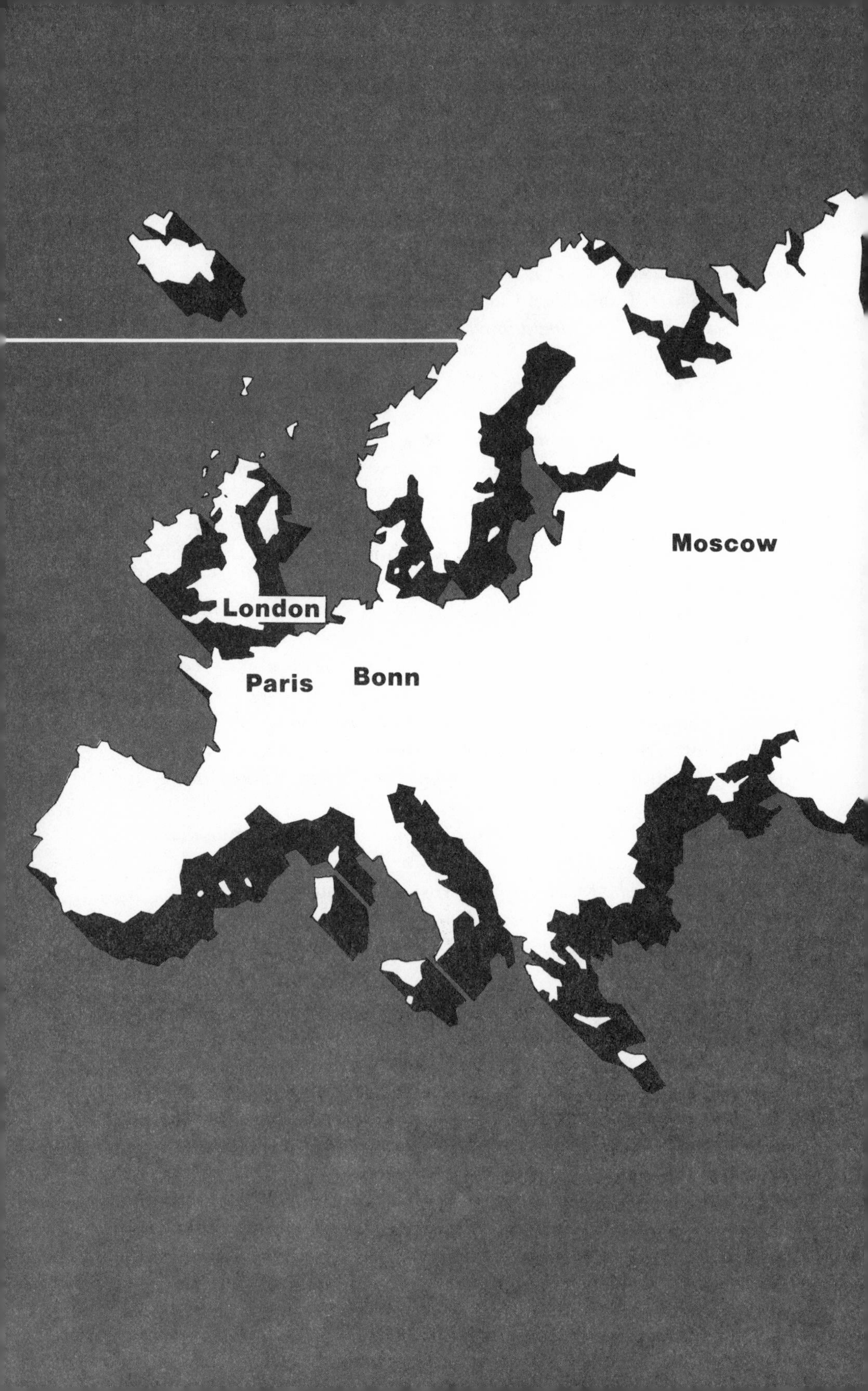
London
Paris
Bonn
Moscow

Part Five

Comparative Political Analyses

21

Political Ideologies and Belief Systems

David P. Conradt

At various times in their histories all the countries examined in this book
have been governed by regimes that have based their policies and popular
support on a specific set of ideas and beliefs or ideology. Although it is difficult to establish that ideologies cause certain actions and policies of political leaders and their followers, they have been frequently claimed as the
source for such behavior. Political ideologies—sets of interrelated propo-
sitions about politics—are probably a universal political phenomenon,
yet differ in their complexity, coherence, and above all, impact. The ideologies that have had the most influence in the political experience of the
countries examined in this book are conservatism, liberalism, socialism,
fascism, and communism. These five "isms" are also frequently cited as
"classical" ideologies; they are all relatively complex with numerous variations and extensive intellectual histories. In recent years a "new left" ideology and movement has also developed in many modern societies.

Ideologies have also influenced the character of political beliefs and
values held by the mass of the population. The term *political culture* is
usually used to refer to the structure of these popular beliefs, attitudes,
and values. This chapter examines the major political ideologies in Europe
and discusses various patterns of political culture found in these societies.

Political Ideologies

Conservatism

Classic conservative ideology is largely identified with the writings of the

British political philosopher Edmund Burke. The alleged excesses of the French Revolution provided the impetus for his most important statement of conservative thought, *Reflections on the French Revolution* (1790). Later in the nineteenth century, conservatives in France and Germany adopted and expanded his basic themes.

Conservatism, as a political philosophy, is distinguished by several basic assumptions about the nature of society, the individual, and political authority.

1. Conservatives view society as a natural, organic product of slow historical growth. Established social and political institutions embody "wisdom of the ages." Change, according to conservatives, can be successful only if it is evolutionary rather than accomplished by revolution.
2. Man is seen as a creature of habit and instinct as well as reason. The community, or society as a whole, is considered by conservatives as superior to its individual parts. Some parts are more important than others, and some interests or groups must be subordinate to others. Hierarchy or inequality is thus inevitable in society. Nevertheless, the relationship between classes or groups must be harmonious if society is to function effectively.
3. Leadership in the conservative view is a quality given to only a few "natural leaders" born and bred to rule. To elect leaders in mass elections by no means ensures that the most able people will be chosen. There is thus a strong element of elitism in the conservative position. Since society is a community, conservatives generally have little problem with the welfare state. In this community the less fortunate, the sick, and the otherwise disadvantaged must be cared for by the community as a whole. There is also a paternalistic component to this conception of authority. The natural leaders have a responsibility to protect and care for the weaker members of the community.

The elements of classical conservatism can still be found in some of the programs and style of the European parties such as the British Conservative party as well as some of the small right-wing groups located in Italy and Spain. But most competitive center-right political parties have adapted their programs to the demands of mass politics and representative government.

Liberalism

Liberalism as a political ideology is closely associated with the Enlightenment, the emergence of a modern secular society, and the "free market" economy. Major philosophers of political and economic liberalism were Adam Smith, Jeremy Bentham, John Locke, Jean Jacques Rousseau, and John Stuart Mill. The core liberal value is individualism. A liberal political order attempts to create and maintain an environment that will facilitate individual self-development and fulfillment. Political liberalism is composed of three fundamental principles:

1. *Human freedom.* The primary function of the state is to limit all unreasonable external restraints on individual freedom, thus allowing the maximum opportunity for self-development.
2. *Constitutionalism.* The primary vehicle for creating this environment of maximum individual freedom is a written constitution that explicitly limits government and makes it responsible to the governed. In addition, the constitution should contain specific guarantees of basic civil liberties such as speech, press, and assembly.
3. *Popular sovereignty.* All political power, in the liberal view, ultimately resides in the people, individually and collectively. Government is imposed by the people on themselves. Each citizen is also regarded as politically equal with the same rights and opportunities to share in their governance.

Where political liberalism was the dominant force, such as in nineteenth-century Britain, free market capitalism flourished. The market economic system, however, produced considerable economic and social inequality. By the end of the nineteenth century, the extremes of wealth, status, and power associated with capitalism made the liberal claim of political equality seem hollow to many. A more radical or democratic variant of liberalism, one that accepted state intervention in the economy in the form of social welfare programs (unemployment, pensions, health) and government regulations (monopolies, safety, pricing) developed in many Western societies. The state was to lessen the harshness of the economic cycle and ensure minimum levels of welfare for all citizens. Political liberalism without this socioeconomic component was also not an attractive political alternative to many voters in most Western societies. Today the "pure" liberal parties in Europe are relatively small, but the elements of classical liberalism are an important component of all major political parties.

Socialism

The core value of socialism is economic, social, and political equality. The chief means for its realization are the communal ownership and control of the means of production and the equal distribution of the goods and services that flow from the production process. Although these ideas are as old as any other philosophy, they were first developed into a viable political ideology by the German philosopher Karl Marx. Marx formulated his version of socialism in response to the great social and economic inequities that accompanied the development of the liberal, free market economy. This inequality, Marx contended, was inevitable in the capitalist system, which would eventually be replaced by a socialist order. This change was to take place by means of a revolution when the exploited proletariat or working class reached a point where its size, extent of exploitation, and degree of organization were superior to that of the ruling capitalist class. The socialist revolution would thus inherit the developed capitalist economy, but without the capitalists. Freed of the restrictive effect of private ownership, the economy would then be developed to higher quantitative and qualitative levels until a veritable Utopia of material abundance would be reached.

Democratic Socialism

By the last quarter of the nineteenth century it became apparent to many socialists that, contrary to Marx's prediction, the capitalist system was not about to collapse, nor was the capitalist class of property owners and entrepreneurs becoming smaller. Indeed, the growth of Western market economies was creating whole new occupational groups of managers, technicians, engineers, and other salaried employees who did not own the means of production but were directly involved in their control. The new class was thus neither a proletariat nor a classic property-owning middle class; rather, a new class sold their labor and expertise but were not exploited in the Marxian sense; their wages and salaries were not kept to a minimum, but increased steadily. Moreover, the economic condition of the manual working class (the proletariat) was not deteriorating but gradually improving.

In response to these developments a revisionist movement within the socialist camp emerged. Its chief ideologist was the German Social Democrat Eduard Bernstein. The revisionists suggested that the expansion of civil rights such as the suffrage to workers would eventually enable socialist parties to come to power through the ballot box and not by revolution. Once in power with majority support the socialists would be able to nationalize the means of production and build a socialist society. Thus democratic socialism became identified with working-class parties operating within the liberal framework of civil rights, the rule of law, and representative government to acquire political power in order to effect economic and social change.

Democratic socialists are committed to the democratic political system: Human freedom, the rule of law, majority rule, and minority rights are fundamental principles. Unlike communism or even capitalism, democratic socialism does not view the state as a negative force but regards it as a major instrument in the achievement and maintenance of economic and social justice. The "class struggle," as envisioned by democratic socialists, takes place in the voting booth. Measures such as the nationalization of the means of production and compulsory economic planning must receive majority support and be consistent with constitutional guarantees protecting individual property rights if they are to be implemented by any democratic socialist government. Articles 14 and 15 of the West German constitution, for example, allow the nationalization of land, natural resources, and the means of production—but only by laws, which also provide for just compensation to those affected.

Democratic socialism, as practiced in Britain, France, Germany, and elsewhere in Western Europe, has become the dominant political force on the left of the ideological spectrum. Democratic socialist parties, however, such as the Socialists in France, the Social Democrats in West Germany, and the British Labour party, owe a great deal of their electoral and political successes in the postwar period to their efforts to become more broadly based center-left parties of reform. They emphasize that not only the traditional working class but also the rapidly growing new-middle-class segment of the electorate—the technicians, managers, and administrative personnel—can find a political home in democratic socialism. Attracting the support of these groups has usually been crucial to the attainment of governmental power.

Soviet Communism

While Western European Marxists reacted to the resilience of capitalism in the late nineteenth century by adapting to the demands of mass democratic politics, Lenin drew a different conclusion. The proletariat, he argued, was unable to develop the proper revolutionary consciousness because of its "mental enslavement" by the bourgeoisie. The working class thus could not spontaneously develop the proper revolutionary consciousness but must be properly led to it. This leadership, according to Lenin, could be provided only by the Communist party, which was conceived by him as a revolutionary elite or vanguard that would in effect do for the proletariat what it could not do for itself: Seize power. Liberal parliamentary democracy, which the revisionists had embraced, was just another name for capitalism. Led by the party, the workers would undertake an armed uprising against the bourgeoisie state and establish a dictatorship of the proletariat until all counterrevolutionary capitalist remnants were eliminated. Then the establishment of the socialist and later communist society could begin.

Marxism-Leninism, as interpreted by the Communist party elite, is the official ideology of the Soviet Union. It emphasizes a militant commitment to the party as the leading institution in state and society, the rejection of all political values not contained within the ideology, and the necessity for strict discipline by the nonelites to the party's decisions and commands. The political culture enunciated by the party elite is also utopian. After a long and difficult struggle, the goal of an egalitarian, affluent, stateless, and humane society is promised. The official political culture assigns to the mass of the Soviet populace only the role of "subject participant." The Soviet "common man" is to participate enthusiastically in the fulfillment of the policies and goals formulated by the party elite, but he is to have no direct and binding influence on their development. Public opinion is extensively studied in the Soviet system, but only as an aid to the elite, not as a determinant of elite composition or decision making.

The New Left

The New Left is a general movement of protest and discontent that began in the 1960s among university students and younger intellectuals in several advanced industrial societies. New Leftists are sharply critical of the political, economic, social, and cultural forms that characterize modern societies whether they are capitalist, socialist, or communist. All of these societies are considered repressive, impersonal, and authoritarian. The individual is dehumanized; people become pressed into common computerized molds. The production process reigns supreme as it lays waste to the environment and through the use of nuclear power ultimately threatens the physical survival of the entire population. The New Left began and for the most part remains centered in the more prosperous industrialized societies: the United States, Japan, West Germany, France, and Holland. The young activists of the New Left are generally the sons and daughters of the middle and upper classes. Beginning at universities, the New Left protested the impersonality and bureaucratic atmosphere of mass higher education. In the United States this form of student protest began in California in the early 1960s and received added impetus through the growing opposition to the Vietnam war. In France student unrest in 1968 spread to workers, farmers, and white-collar employees as strikes and demonstrations brought the country to a standstill.

The New Left sees modern man as alienated, that is, estranged from society. Modernization has uprooted individuals from their primary groups (family and community) and the "uncomplicated life" associated with traditional societies. Industrialization with its intense division of labor has mechanized human relationships and reduced people to productive factors in the name of rationality. The productive process—whether capitalist or communist—is seen as separating workers from any control or identification with what they produce. Work is no longer creative; it offers no sense of self-fulfillment or personal satisfaction.

Much of the intensity of New Left activity derives from the frustration experienced by its activists as they confront the generalized consensus that has characterized political and economic life in most Western societies in the postwar period. The New Left is especially upset at modern liberals and democratic socialists who, they contend, have sold out their progressive principles for political power; together with the conservatives, business, media, universities, or churches, they also preach the message of "consumption for consumption's sake" and practice what German New Leftists call *Volksverdummung,* literally the process of making people stupid, through the manipulation of the socialization process. Faced by massive consensus, the New Left sees revolution, or the explosion of society, as the only recourse.

What is the New Left's vision of modern society after the revolution? Most analysts of New Left ideology have identified three dominant elements in its "new society": anarchism, participation, and the quality of life.[1]

1. *Anarchism.* The New Left distrusts all "hierarchies" or institutional rule-making structures, which, they maintain, repress individual and group initiative. Like classical anarchists of the nineteenth century, the New Left seeks the reduction and eventual elimination of the state bureaucracy, the courts, police, and the military. Replacing these structures would be a communal-like sense of "collective responsibility."

2. *Participation.* The active, involved individual can hardly be alienated from his community. Widespread popular participation in political, social, and economic decision making is a key element in New Left ideology. Workers must participate in the industrial enterprise, not only in matters involving the conditions of work, but also in the firm's investment, employment, and pricing policies. In this way individuals will become real citizens, in control of their own destinies.

3. *Quality of Life.* No concern of the New Left has attracted as much interest and support as its critique of modern life and specifically the damage done to the environment by the industrial system. The huge flow of material goods produced by this system is seen as the consequence of policies that encourage "wasteful consumption." People are taught to accumulate and consume vast quantities of goods with little or no regard for their effect on the quality of life. Automobiles, high-rise architecture, unrestrained urban growth, and, of course, nuclear power are considered major sources of environmental damage.

Fascism

Fascism became a significant political force between World Wars I and II in several European political systems. Fascist political parties emerged as the carriers of this ideology, and in Italy and Germany they succeeded in assuming control over the state. Initially fascism was more of a political style or technique than an ideology. Its early supporters were returning

World War I veterans. The war, they believed, had been lost not by the superior power or courage of the victors but by the decadence of the liberal or bourgeoisie systems in their own countries. Labor unions or socialist parties at home also contributed to this internal weakness by their involvement in the international "Marxist-Bolshevik" conspiracy. Fascist groups in Italy and then Germany, with the support of some business and military interests and the tacit consent of parts of the judiciary and police, transferred the techniques of military combat to the domestic political arena. Political rallies were turned into street fights with opponents. Terror, intimidation, and extortion were regarded as legitimate means of political conflict.

As an ideology fascism was distinguished more by its negative or protest components than by its positive vision of the future. Fascists were both antiliberal and antidemocratic. Liberalism with its emphasis on individualism and competition was rejected as a divisive philosophy that fragmented the national community. Fascism, especially its German variant, emphasized both the importance of the racial community and the inequality or hierarchy within it. The fascists also supported an all-embracing or totalitarian conception of the state. The state was the supreme social unit, the political embodiment of the national community.

The German National Socialist variant of fascism addressed, more specifically than did Italian fascism, the question of the proletariat or manual working class and its integration into the national community. The German workers, it was emphasized, should seek to improve their socioeconomic condition by cooperation with their German employers and the German state, rather than through involvement in international movements.

Fascism also stressed that "will" or "feelings" could at times be superior to reason as a guide to action. They often explained their successes by referring to the triumph of the will over objective reality. Possessing and expressing the right feelings were in many cases a more important requisite for a responsible position in the fascist state than objective competence.

Related to this irrationalism was the fascist attachment to instincts and myths of racial supremacy and purity that were in many cases regarded as superior to logic. When reminded of the damage to scientific research caused by the forced emigration of so many scientists and scholars, German fascists responded by citing the superiority of the "racial community's feelings" to any findings of scientific research.

Political Culture and Beliefs

The development and explicit use of these and other political ideologies have been largely associated with political elites and the more politically involved strata of the population. Modern social science research has shown that mass publics, at least in Western societies, have little knowledge of these "isms." But they do have political beliefs and values, albeit less structured and sophisticated, which to varying degrees affect their political behavior, especially at the polling booth and in their expression of political opinions. These beliefs and values of mass populations are frequently referred to as a "political culture." Some scholars have contended that specific countries or national communities have developed a unique mass political culture that does influence the actions of government.

Political culture has, for example, been used to explain why countries with very similar levels of socioeconomic development still have different policy priorities. Compare the American commitment to free or low-cost public education from kindergarten to graduate school with the more restrictive educational systems of America's European "cousins," such as France, Germany, Italy, or Britain. The latter countries, on the other hand, allocate more of their public resources to ensure every citizen, regardless of income or socioeconomic status, easy access to health care. While it may be relatively easy to acquire a low-cost college education in the United States, this does not apply to the financing of health care for a major illness. Conversely, British children have a variety of obstacles to obtaining a university education, but they have no problems with paying for health care—it is free to all.

A similar difference in policies that can be related to differences in political culture can be seen in the pattern of property or home ownership in the United States and Western Europe. The policies of American governments from the Homestead Act through the VA and FHA programs have encouraged the creation of a large class of small property owners through subsidies and tax concessions. These programs are consistent with the liberalism articulated earlier by Jefferson and others, and are now part of American political culture. In most Western European societies home ownership has been far more restricted than in the United States. Most manual workers and even many white-collar employees, even in contemporary Europe, will never own their own homes.

The attitudes that are usually identified as central to the determination of a country's political culture include those dealing with governmental structures, others in the political system, and one's own political activity.[2]

Governmental Structures

What do citizens know about their basic state and governmental institutions, symbols, and officials? How do they feel about them? Are they supportive? Indifferent? Do they regard governmental directives as right and proper? In short, is the system regarded as legitimate by its citizens, and why? Legitimacy can have numerous sources. In traditional societies the ruler's adherence to religious customs and rituals may be crucial for legitimacy. The legitimacy of political officials in modern democracies is usually based on their selection in competitive elections or according to formal, legal procedures. The Soviet Union presents a case where legitimacy is based, in part, on the ideology of Marxism-Leninism. How do citizens feel and respond toward demands for public policy (inputs) and the actual policy decisions made by government (outputs)?

Others in the Political System

Do citizens strongly identify with the nation as a whole or with a particular region, community, or group? Political continuity is difficult if not impossible if most citizens do not share a common sense of national identity. The persistent problem of Northern Ireland in British and Irish politics illustrates the importance of this component of political culture. Among the countries examined in this book, a sense of national identity is probably strongest in France, followed by Britain, the Soviet Union, and West Germany. In France and the United Kingdom, however, regionalist movements challenge the central, national government. In the Soviet Union a variety of national minorities are a latent source of political discontent. The postwar division of the German nation and the creation of two new German states meant that a sense of national identity had to be redeveloped and redefined in both East and West Germany.

Are citizens trustful, tolerant, and cooperative in working with others, or does a general atmosphere of distrust and suspicion characterize interpersonal relationships? Are attitudes favorable to social cooperation (teamwork) or social isolation? The capacity of political institutions to develop and implement policy programs is in part dependent on the degree of trust or confidence citizens have in these institutions and their personnel. Citizen compliance with governmental programs is also related to this feeling of trust. There is, for example, a strong relationship between citizen trust in government and a country's tax system: the higher the level of trust, the greater the reliance on direct taxation (income tax, property tax) for governmental revenue; conversely, lower levels of citizen trust (like that found in countries such as Italy) relate to a greater use of indirect taxes (sales tax, value-added tax). The decline in trust found in the United States during the past twenty-five years appears related to the trend toward more indirect taxation. Historically, trust in government has been strong in Great Britain and the United States in comparison to the more unstable regimes of Western Europe: Italy, France, and Germany.

One's Own Political Activity

What is the extent of political interest and participation in the community? What are the levels of voting turnout, the extent of "talking politics," attending political meetings, joining political parties, contacting public officials, working in election campaigns? How do citizens feel about their participation? In Britain, France, and West Germany voting turnout at national elections is usually above 80 percent. Generally, political participation increases with a citizen's socioeconomic status. As these societies have modernized in the postwar period, the proportion of their citizens with the socioeconomic resources to participate has risen. Nevertheless, the sense that participation has little effect on governmental decision makers is also a significant characteristic of attitudes toward participation in modern societies.

Patterns of Political Culture

In those countries where information on the major components of political culture is available, analysts have been able to discern a number of distinctive patterns or configurations. First, some countries have essentially fragmented political cultures. The population "lacks broad agreement upon the way in which political life should be conducted."[3] Society is divided or fragmented into a number of subcultures whose values and behavior are incompatible with one another. These groups are usually isolated, distrustful, and suspicious toward government and public officials. Their conceptions of how political life should be organized and what policies government should pursue are far apart.

Contemporary Italy is often cited as a prime example of a fragmented political culture. Research has found high levels of social alienation and mistrust in Italian society. Italians, perhaps with good reason, are cynical about the effects of their political participation on their country's political institutions and processes. The party system is also fragmented into a variety of left, center, and right parties, some of whom are fundamentally opposed to the existing political, economic, and social order. These parties have managed to bring down Italian governments at the rate of once every nine months over the past thirty-six years. Finally, during the last decade political violence and terrorist groups have also been significant features of Italian political life. Fragmented political cultures have also been attributed to France, Germany (at least until the mid-1960s), contemporary India, and Tanzania.

The integrated political culture is characterized by reasonably strong and durable regime and national loyalties, diffuse political trust among social groups, low levels of political violence, the dominance of formal or legal procedures for conflict management, and strong identifications with established interest groups and political parties. Great Britain and the United States are usually cited as the best "real world" examples of an integrated political culture. Recently West Germany and Japan have been given a similar classification.

A country's political culture is not a static phenomenon. A new analysis of British political culture, for example, shows a significant decline in the kinds of loyalties and trust in government considered essential for cultural integration.[4] In the United States the levels of trust in government have declined steadily over the past twenty-five years.[5] During the same time period West Germany's political culture, as we have seen, has undergone fundamental changes in the direction of greater integration as well as social and political trust. These changes seem related to the quality and quantity of governmental performance. Whereas Great Britain, for example, has a strong tradition of positive and diffuse regime loyalties and trust, the poor record of British institutions in the postwar period, especially in the economic area, is taking its toll on the "reservoir of goodwill" the British system has enjoyed. The Vietnam war, the Watergate scandals, urban unrest, chronic inflation, and unemployment have also had an impact on the American political culture. In the final analysis, neither ideologies nor the political culture that draw from them can remain unaffected by system performance.

Notes

1. Roy Macridis, *Contemporary Political Ideologies* (Cambridge, Mass.: Winthrop, 1980), pp. 258 ff.
2. Walter A. Rosenbaum, *Political Culture* (New York: Praeger, 1975), pp. 6-7.
3. Ibid., p. 37.
4. Dennis Kavanagh, "Political Culture in Great Britain: The Decline of the Civic Culture," in *The Civic Culture Revisited,* ed. Gabriel A. Almond and Sidney Verba (Boston: Little, Brown, 1980), pp. 124-76.
5. Norman Nie, Sidney Verba, and John Petrocik, *The Changing American Voter* (2nd ed.; Cambridge: Harvard University Press, 1978), pp. 278-79.

22

Political Leadership and Elites

William Safran

Gaetano Mosca, an Italian scholar, wrote in *The Ruling Class,* "In all societies, from the most primitive to the most advanced, there are two classes: one which rules, and one which is ruled." The character of a political system is largely determined by the size, origin, and complexity of its ruling class, the legitimacy of its rule, and the power that it exercises over those who are ruled.

In earlier times the ruler derived his political power from his military prowess, which enabled him to conquer his opponents; from his large landed estate, the chief source of economic wealth; or from his ability to convince others that he had been divinely ordained for leadership. During the age of absolutism, kingship was hereditary; descent from a noble family provided sufficient legitimation for membership in the political elite. The ideal advanced political system today has a political leadership based on more modern and more democratic criteria. It is nonhereditary, competitive, legitimated by popular choice or endorsement, and subject to controls and periodic replacement.

All four countries studied in this book conform to some extent to the modern democratic model. Their elites are complex, recruited from an enlarged pool of aspirants, and selected on the basis of criteria other than wealth or family (e.g., those of knowledge, responsiveness to the masses, or party affiliation). In all these countries, the elite is chosen in an institutionalized, and therefore predictable, fashion.

Each country has a single figure who represents national sovereignty, in whose name political decisions are made, and who is the focus of the national orientations of the masses. In all four countries there exists a functional division of leadership, that is, a distinction between the chief of state (a survival of royal absolutism) and the chief of government. The constitutional theories of each country define the roles and relationships of executives differently, but their actual positions do not always conform to those theories. In Britain, official decisions are made by the "Queen-in-Parliament," and no act of Parliament or decision of the Cabinet is legitimate without the Queen's signature. Nevertheless, no English Queen or King has exercised the veto since 1710, and no monarch is expected to exercise it in the future, so the monarch's role is purely symbolic. West Germany is much like Britain in this respect: a clear distinction is made between the President, who cannot make independent political decisions, and the Chancellor, who is the effective leader of government. In the USSR, the constitution, and more important, the theory of the Communist party, provides for collective leadership, to be exercised by the Politburo as a body. Since the days of Stalin, however, actual leadership has tended to devolve upon the First Secretary of the party, who has simultaneously assumed the position of prime minister or (under Brezhnev) president of the Soviet Union. In France, the President's role, as envisaged by the Fifth Republic constitution, is that of moral stewardship and "arbitership" implied by the chief-of-state function, while the government is headed by a Prime Minister. In fact, this formal distinction has not excluded active policy leadership by the President, a leadership that has undercut the power of the Prime Minister and diluted the idea of the "dual executive."

The Bases of Authority

The authority of the leader may depend on the extent to which he or she is the focus of the affective attitudes of the citizens. In Britain the masses genuinely admired George V (who died in 1936) and, to a lesser extent, his royal successors; but in recent times Britons have rarely admired a Prime Minister (except possibly Churchill during World War II), whose authority is based essentially on the fact that he leads, and is supported by, the dominant party in the House of Commons. In France de Gaulle was the object of hero worship when he was President; his successors—despite being the products of direct popular election—have hardly shared this honor. In Nazi Germany Hitler captivated the masses and made them blind followers; in contrast, the chiefs of state in the Bonn Republic have been relatively colorless and unambitious individuals who, like Presidents in the French Third and Fourth republics, have often been chosen for their lack of epic qualities. Chancellors have occasionally derived some of their authority from their personal charisma (e.g., Konrad Adenauer and Willy Brandt); but typically their position is legitimated by their leadership of a political party, their support in parliament and, increasingly, a widespread recognition of their technocratic competence. (Much of the authority of the former German Chancellor Helmut Schmidt was based on his reputation as an economist.) Of course, position and peer support often depend on leadership style. A forceful personality may stretch the role assigned to him; conversely, a weak or reticent politician may underutilize the powers granted to the office. Chancellor Adenauer presided over the Cabinet so autocratically that the government came to be called a "democratorship," whereas his successor, Ludwig Erhard (the "Rubber Lion"), barely held the Cabinet together. Prime Minister Margaret Thatcher (the "Iron Lady") tends to run the Cabinet in an authoritarian fashion, whereas Clement Attlee preferred to chair it and be a "first among equals." As for the French Fifth Republic, it is difficult to imagine a President whose role is reduced by a combination of his own lack of forcefulness and a strong and ambitious Prime Minister—unless the latter had overwhelming parliamentary support.

In the Soviet Union, Marxist doctrine has eschewed heroic leadership; nevertheless, Lenin is (in retrospect) considered a true hero, in part because he was the principal founder of the Soviet system and in part because the system still needs a heroic historical figure around which to build mass loyalty.

Leadership and Social Classes

To the extent that a regime is democratic, the exercise of leadership must ultimately be approved by institutionalized popular support, expressed periodically through elections. In the classical parliamentary regime, such support is accorded in the first place to the legislature, which is the repository of the people's will.

In Britain the pinnacle of the decision-making elite is the House of Commons. Since this body is renewed at least once every five years on the basis of free, competitive elections, and since the Prime Minister and the Cabinet are accountable to it, one may speak of the democratic responsiveness of British leadership. In fact, there is little rotation; a large proportion of the membership of the House of Commons is almost automatically reelected, and relatively few members of Parliament are new faces. The membership tends to have a middle- and upper-middle-class bias, which is particularly pronounced in the Conservative party. In 1970, for example, more than half of the Conservative MPs were graduates of elite "public schools" *and* of Oxford or Cambridge. About one-third were businessmen, while only two (out of 330) were workers. Of the MPs belonging to the Labour party, which has claimed to represent the working class, fewer than 25 percent were workers—and most of these were union officials. In the House of Lords, the upper-class social bias is much more pronounced in both parties.

In France in 1971, the majority of Assembly deputies were identified as well-to-do professionals (with industrialists, higher civil servants, university professors, and physicians each constituting about 10 percent of the total, while workers and farmers provided only about 5 percent each).

In the West German Bundestag, too, there was in the 1970s a heavy preponderance of free professionals, businessmen, and career civil servants. Although a large proportion of the Social Democratic deputies were classified as trade unionists, most of them had long ceased to be active industrial workers and had become, in effect, professional politicians.

In the Supreme Soviet, about half of the membership is said to belong to the category of workers and peasants—a proportion that is similar to that found among the delegates to the All-Union party congresses. But that is largely a matter of official classification of social origins. Many of those described as workers have for years been employed as party officials.

It could be argued that the imperfect "representativeness" of parliaments tells us little about the democratic nature of the political leadership; for in all four countries, parliaments are weak institutions compared to the executive. In France, the role of deputies has been reduced both by constitutional provisions and by the "accumulation of mandates," under which most deputies must allocate their working hours among the national, regional, and local assemblies to which they belong simultaneously. In Britain and West Germany, deputies are subject to party discipline and have little scope for legislative initiative. In the USSR, the Supreme Soviet, which meets fewer than four weeks every year, functions as a device for applauding and ratifying decisions made elsewhere.

The farther one ascends in the pyramid of power, the more apparent the social selectivity of its echelons. British and West German Cabinets include few if any representatives of the poorer classes. Even Labour or Social-Democratic Cabinets have been dominated by academics, career politicians, high union officials, and other members of the middle class. In France, fewer than 3 percent of the members of Cabinets constituted since 1969 have been workers or farmers by profession. The Politburo of the Soviet Communist party in 1976 was composed entirely of members of the intelligentsia—higher party officials, academics, and technologists—industrial or collective farm workers having not even token representation. The large Soviet cabinet reflects similar selectivity.

It is possible to point to certain individuals who reached high political office despite early poverty: Khrushchev, who remained semiliterate into early adulthood; and Willy Brandt, the illegitimate son of a housemaid. Here unusual ambition, intelligence, and political accident (the replacement of a regime, and adherence to the right political party) combined to overcome the handicaps of a disprivileged social condition. But these are exceptions. It remains true that a person born into wealth and privilege is more likely to reach the top politically than one who grew up in an impoverished household. High birth alone does not guarantee success in climbing the ladder to political leadership. Valéry Giscard d'Estaing made his way to the Presidency because a good education combined with intelligence and abundant ambition; conversely, many an English nobleman, lacking such qualifications, has "made it" only to the House of Lords, an institution without much power.

Professionalism and Specialization

The complexity of political decisions is such that, increasingly, special qualifications are required of people who make them. One of the characteristics of modern political systems is the expansion of the bureaucratic establishment, composed of people who have made a career of government and whose background and outlook differ from those of mere "politicians." While deputies are legitimated by electoral majorities, civil servants are qualified by special training for what Max Weber, the celebrated German social theorist, called "the vocation of government." Deputies are, theoretically, birds of passage; civil servants have long tenure. This tenure makes them much more impervious to public pressures.

In theory, it is thus possible to distinguish between the administrative elite and the political elite; and to suggest that while ministers and parliaments *make* political decisions, higher civil servants only prepare groundwork for, and subsequently *implement,* these decisions. In practice, such a functional distinction is difficult to make. The expertise of higher civil servants may be so great, or so widely acknowledged, that their administrative "suggestions" may serve as the basis of political decisions; moreover, in France, and to a lesser extent in West Germany, higher civil servants are often directly recruited into the Cabinet and, as we have seen, are heavily represented in parliaments.

In earlier times, professional civil services hardly existed; tax collectors, police officers, and other agents of the national government secured their jobs on an "ascriptive" basis through inheritance, nepotism, or the spoils system. Today, special educational attainments are required. In West Germany, which conforms in this respect to the traditional continental model, most entrants to the higher civil service have graduated from a law school, though an increasing number have recently come also from certain social science faculties and technical institutes. Many federal civil servants had begun their bureaucratic careers at the provincial (*Land*) level.

More than two-thirds of the entrants to the administrative class of the British higher civil service had studied — more often than not at "Oxbridge" — the arts and humanities, and only a quarter had studied the social sciences. Specialized training of the young entrant was, until recently, frowned on; he was expected to become a specialist on the job. Instead, the emphasis was placed on the characteristics of the "gentleman": good background in the classics, fine speech, and refined comportment. Although since the mid-1950s recruitment has opened more widely to graduates of less renowned universities, including technical institutes, the old recruitment patterns have continued to prevail, with the result that the administrative elite in Britain still largely reflects its social elite.

France and the USSR show the most extensive pattern of training specialization. In the Soviet Union, most higher civil servants are graduates of one of the numerous specialized technical institutes (e.g., for engineering, metallurgy, foreign trade, transportation, mining, or chemicals). In France the *grandes écoles,* some of them established by Napoleon, have had a virtual monopoly on the training for the higher bureaucracy. One of the most prestigious of the national "postgraduate" schools is the Ecole Nationale d'Administration (ENA); it has provided the vast majority of recruits for the uppermost echelons of the civil service: the inspectorate of finances, the prefectoral corps, the directorships of ministries and, since 1958, the Cabinet as well. It must be understood that these higher civil servants are not mere technocrats. The graduates of Soviet technical schools are also recipients of Marxist-Leninist ideological training and are, at least overtly, loyal communists; the ENA graduates are distinguished from one another in that some are Gaullists while others are Socialists or liberals, although most of them are committed to notions of the supremacy of the state and the ideals of "expertocracy."

The civil service is not the only source of recruits for political leadership positions. In France as in the United States and to a lesser extent West Germany, members of the national political elite often got their start in local politics, usually by way of capturing control over local party machines and securing a local or regional elective office. In Britain, however, a Cabinet minister has often begun his apprenticeship on the national level, rising from the position of lowly House of Commons backbencher and passing through junior ministerial appointments. In the USSR the typical member of the Politburo, who may simultaneously be a member of the Council of Ministers (and incidentally also of the Supreme Soviet), has gradually passed through the ranks of local or regional party apparatus, and often has held positions of responsibility in economic management.

Peculiarities and Preferences in Leadership Selection

In each country there are "background preferences" for recruitment to leadership positions—whether in Cabinet, parliament, or civil service. Such preferences are heavily influenced by the value system, or the political culture, peculiar to that country. In the United States a President frequently appoints leaders of big business to Cabinet positions, reflecting the tendency of Americans in general, and Republicans in particular, to consider market relationships and business management approaches as models for the political process. In France intellectuals—teachers, professors, and writers—are found in large numbers in parliament and in the Cabinet, largely because of the importance Frenchmen have attached to abstract ideas, to rhetoric, and to the government's concern with culture and the arts. In the Soviet Union there is a continued insistence that recruits to political leadership positions show proof of adequate ideological indoctrination, given the overriding importance of the communist belief system as a unifying element. For many years, West Germans heavily preferred lawyers because of a desire to return to pre-Hitler definitions of the *Rechtsstaat* (i.e., a state based on the rule of law); while the British still often look to upper classes for political leadership because of the traditional (largely Tory) idea that certain classes are more "naturally" equipped to rule than others and therefore deserve a deferential regard by the masses.

Conversely, for the sake of safeguarding the democratic ethos or image of its political leadership, each country has developed its own system of exclusions; that is, it has tried to avoid recruiting from certain social or political categories. In Britain Cabinet appointments are almost never made from the higher civil service, in order that the (theoretical) distinction may be preserved between the "political" ministers and the "nonpartisan" bureaucracy. In the United States professional academics (sometimes referred to as "eggheads") have only in rare instances been considered presidential caliber. In the USSR people with bourgeois backgrounds were, at least until the late 1930s, excluded from Communist party membership and were seldom given responsible administrative positions. Today such exclusion is no longer practiced because (officially) the bourgeoisie no longer exists and all entrants, therefore, come from the working class. However, Jews and members of certain other non-Russian national groups cannot seriously aspire to national leadership positions.

In Britain, France, and West Germany — the latter two countries for reasons of recent history — the military officer corps is no longer looked on as a pool of recruits for political decision-making positions. In post-Liberation France the prefectoral corps, the judiciary, the parliament, and other political institutions were purged of persons who had collaborated with the Germans during the war. In West Germany attempts were made in the late 1940s and early 1950s to exclude from positions of political responsibility those who had compromised their credentials by membership in the Nazi party. Such a policy had been inspired by a genuine desire to democratize the decision-making establishment as well as by the need to improve West Germany's international image. The attempt was only partly successful; by the early 1960s, a large proportion of the higher civil service and the judiciary consisted of former Nazis. Furthermore, in 1966, a former Nazi became Chancellor; and in 1979 an ex-Nazi was chosen President of the Republic. This does not mean that ex-Nazis in leadership positions will pursue undemocratic policies. For it is clear that the behavior of political leaders is to a large extent determined by the overall political context, by evolving public attitudes, and by the outside pressures and the role expectations to which they are subject.

Political decision makers, responsive to electoral pressures, tend to be more ideologically inclined, more dynamic, and more sensitive to social problems; higher civil servants, their tenure assured, tend to be more conservative and more technicist. However, upper-class higher civil servants are constrained on the one hand by the instructions they receive from their political superiors, and on the other hand by the nature of certain technical problems that require largely technical solutions (e.g., defense, environmental pollution, unemployment, inflation). In the Soviet Union, while all members of the Politburo are inspired by Marxist-Leninist ideology, the fact that most of them have technological training is bound to introduce technicist criteria into their decisions.

Contemporary Aspects of Leadership

Since many political problems are economic in nature, all individuals involved prominently in economic affairs belong to the decision-making elite. In a country in which political and economic systems are intertwined, political and economic elites cannot be separated. This is clearly the case in the Soviet Union, where virtually all economic decisions are made by the government. Thus, many Politburo members have had experience as managers of metallurgical industries, electric power stations, or construction enterprises; and the directors of economic enterprises are themselves members of the civil service. Conversely, economic directorships are sometimes given as political "plums" to well-connected *apparatchiki* of the Communist party.

In capitalist countries the linkage between the official (governmental) elite and the private, or functional (business or labor-union), elite is much more complex. In Britain, West Germany, and France, many parliamentary deputies, particularly those elected under the labels of more conservative parties, have come from the business establishment and continue to maintain ties with it. In these countries, moreover, managers of nationalized industries are sometimes drawn from private business. In France (as in the United States) there is more often a reverse "lateral" movement: many higher civil servants, after several years' work in the government, may "slip" into directorships of large private firms. Furthermore, in all three countries leaders of organized business, agriculture, and labor are so often consulted that a system of "elite management" or, as some have called it, "consultative administration," has developed. There is no reliable way of measuring the impact of private economic leaders on political leaders—in other words, of analyzing the effect of the participation of business or labor leaders on political decisions. Nevertheless, the process of consultation is now so institutionalized—that is, formalized, legalized, and even overt—that the distinction between governmental and private economic leadership has become somewhat obscured. Some consider this interconnection of elites as leading to a "privatization" of governmental decisions and to a subversion of the government's capacity to act in the public interest. Others, on the contrary, see it as a means of coopting the elites of the private sector for public purposes and as a way of rendering the political decision-making process more realistic, more broadly based, and more "polyarchic." For still others, the cooptation of the leaders of the private economic sector is a phantom; rather than provide genuine participation to these leaders (and hence to the public they represent), co-optation has the effect of "imprisoning" private interests while permitting the government to pretend that decision making is broadly shared and therefore democratically legitimated.

The courts and the press may be the handmaidens of the decision makers. In totalitarian regimes (e.g., the Soviet Union) they are indispensable for helping to engineer consent, if not obedience, by rationalizing the actions of the political leadership, even if these actions are not legal. In Western democracies, in which one finds independent judiciaries and freedom of expression, the courts and the press may be viewed in a different light. The courts may nullify legislation, as they have been doing in the United States, West Germany, and to a lesser extent France. Widely read journals (e.g., the *Spiegel* in West Germany, the *Canard Enchaîné* in France, and the *New York Times* in the United States) may embarrass governments and influence decisions. Clearly judges and journalists (sometimes called, respectively, "willful men" and "irresponsible rabble-rousers"), while not official decision makers, must be considered as belonging to an "external" or parallel political elite.

The foregoing discussion suggests that the more developed and complex a society, the more political leadership tends to be diffused among a variety of actors or elites. This phenomenon implies, alternatively, inter-elite collaboration and conflict, and often makes it difficult for a political scientist to pinpoint *the* decision maker with regard to a specific issue.

A more serious problem is the fact that "modern democratic leadership" is an ideal type, to which no country has completely conformed. In the Soviet Union leadership rotation is imperfectly institutionalized, often unpredictable, and sometimes associated with illegality if not violence. In all four countries there are pathologies of elite recruitment: for instance, the appointment and promotion of individuals to leadership positions on the basis of nepotism, the "old boy network," and other ascriptive criteria. There is the related problem of "gray eminences," "kitchen cabinets," or "powers behind the throne" that may decisively influence the political actions of Presidents or Prime Ministers.

Furthermore, there is the question whether leadership and democracy are not contradictions in terms. Democracy implies more or less popular or egalitarian recruitment, if not rule directly by the people. But if the people rule, there is, by definition, no political elite. The distinction between leadership and the mass is based on position and power, which are in turn based increasingly on a professionalism and an expertise not possessed in equal measure by the people. To the extent that professionalism implies continuity of service, it is not surprising that many organizations that do not rely on frequent elections but that are clearly involved in the decision-making process — bureaucracies, political party machines, and interest groups — show even greater tendencies to self-perpetuating oligarchism than do parliaments. The great problem confronting modern states that aspire both to rational decision making and to democracy is to assure a relationship between the leadership and the led that will represent a proper combination of both values.

23

Revolutions

Dan N. Jacobs

The twentieth century, particularly since World War I, has witnessed a worldwide explosion of revolutions. This proliferation has turned scholars to the study of revolutions. How has the concept of revolution developed? What brings revolutions about? What happens to revolutionary leaders once revolutions have succeeded? This chapter touches on some of the more significant conclusions reached by researchers on revolution.

There have been violent political upheavals—changes in the leading governmental personnel through the use of force—as long as there have been politics. But political *revolution,* in the contemporary sense of eliminating the existing elite root and branch and establishing a new "system" that will permanently affect the nature and relationships of power is, for the most part, a phenomenon of the past two centuries.

Until the French Revolution of 1789, most theories of revolution had aimed at restoring the status quo ante. They had been, in that way, counterrevolutionary, implying that things were once better, had deteriorated, and must be restored to their former, more acceptable state. Such "theories" of revolution were in keeping with the attitude toward historical development that prevailed throughout most of human existence, namely, that the path of history was circular or cyclical. History either went around and around or up and down, with things sometimes better, sometimes worse, but without any lasting or qualitative improvement. There are two French expressions that capture the prevailing attitude of humankind toward the historical experience throughout its existence until the most recent times: *déjà vu,* it has been seen before; and, *plus ça change, plus c'est la même chose,* the more things change, the more they are the same.

With the spread of the ideas of the Renaissance, which sent abroad a spirit of secular enlightenment, and the Reformation, which held that people could be saved through their own efforts, and with the advent of capitalism, the Industrial Revolution, and particularly the Age of Invention, a new concept began to develop. This new concept, Progress, held that humanity is not trapped forever within a wheel that is getting nowhere but that it has the capacity to break away and build more magnificent cities, compose more sublime symphonies, devise more wondrous creations than ever before existed. A major problem with achieving the *new* is that for it to flourish, the *old* has to give way. As time went on, it became apparent that the existing institutions and the elites that controlled them would not step aside voluntarily. They were determined to hold on as long as they could, and would not leave the scene without a struggle.

During the late eighteenth and early nineteenth centuries, many advocates of the forcible elimination of established institutions and wielders of power appeared. They maintained that the great masses of humankind were oppressed, prevented from the enjoyment of life by ogres of the *ancien régime* who stubbornly held on to what did not belong to them, wealth which they had not produced. Freedom, equality, and prosperity were possible for all, maintained the advocates of the new. The question was how to gain them. In some circles, the answer was *through revolution.*

The great purveyor of revolution as the eradicator of humanity's enslavement, the philosopher with whom the concept of modern revolution is most closely identified, was the nineteenth-century German Karl Marx. Marx advocated the destruction of all existing political institutions and power elites and their replacement by a new leadership that would permit society to develop along the lines of his principles of universal justice.

At the time Marx was promulgating his revolution, recent history had already seen two great "revolutions," the American and the French, both of which had marked impacts on their own time and have continued to shape political ideals and visions. The American Revolution—carried out in the name of freedom *of* the individual and *from* a great imperial power—provided an ideal for those oppressed by their own or foreign governments. Similarly, the powerful slogan of the French Revolution—Liberty, Equality, Fraternity—the strains of the *Marseillaise,* and the French tricolor encapsulated the yearning for the abolition of tyranny and the triumph of the will to be free.

Marx's reaction to both these revolutions was that while they may have signaled new freedoms, they did so, even in their own countries, only for part of society. The American Revolution — with which Marx was less familiar or concerned — and the French Revolution represented the victory of the middle class, of the bourgeoisie. They did little for the worker, the proletarian, who remained enslaved in the economic system. Freedom in bourgeois society, held Marx, was not for everyone but only for those who were rich enough to take advantage of the opportunities such societies provided. Did the poor have enough education to know how the law might protect the individual? Could they afford to hire a lawyer to defend themselves? Did it make any difference that there was freedom of speech if they couldn't make enough money to feed their families? The revolution Marx preached became the goal of many (though not all) working-class movements in Europe in the latter part of the nineteenth century.

By the end of that century, there were three major revolutions upon which the thoughts of those dissatisfied with the status quo fastened. Two of these revolutions — the American and the French — had already been achieved; the third — the Marxist — was still in the offing. Among the discontented of the world, each revolution had its adherents. Among those who were primarily interested in freeing their countries from colonialism, in driving out foreign occupiers and establishing independence, the American revolution was the primary model. Among those whose dominating consideration was the elimination of tyrants, it was the French revolution. Among those who were concerned most about redressing the economic imbalance of society, it was the Marxist revolution.

Such was the condition of revolutionary models when in November 1917 there occurred in Russia what came to be known as the first successful Marxist revolution. It was not really a Marxist revolution. Marx had said that the revolution would break out in the country of the highest development of capitalism. Overproduction in a fully developed capitalist economy was to be a major reason for the revolution. Russia was an underdeveloped country, only a few years removed from feudalism and scarcely embarked on capitalism. But there was a successful revolution in Russia — more properly a *coup d'état*. Its number-one man, V.I. Lenin, who gained great authority by his successful seizure of power, called it a Marxist revolution. It came to be accepted as such by the world, and became a third realized revolutionary model.

Earlier it was indicated that each revolutionary model had its own adherents. However, the advocates of the French and American models were not primarily concerned about the spread of their model. America was interested in America; France, as ever, was interested in France. It would be nice, thought the Americans and French, if the world would be more like the United States and France, respectively. But the success of the American and French revolutions, as their advocates saw it, did not depend on there being similar revolutions in other countries. It was not so with the Russian Marxist revolution.

Marx had held that each country would undergo capitalist development, and each country would have its own revolution. The verification of his theory required a repetition of the revolutionary experience in country after country. For Russians, the repetition of the revolutionary experience elsewhere was made even more fundamental. Because the revolution did not break out in the country of the highest development of capitalism but in a country of lesser development, there was the great fear that the more highly industrialized and powerful European countries would interfere to smash the Russian revolution unless the revolution could strike in those countries first and bring them into the ranks of communism.

The spread of the revolution became a matter of great concern to Lenin in the years immediately after 1917. But by 1920 he had reached the conclusion that the revolution was not going to spread to Western Europe. Fearing that continued, useless agitation would provoke the European countries to unite against the weak regime he had established in Russia, he called a temporary halt to openly pushing revolution in the West. But not for one moment did Lenin give up on advancing the revolution everywhere. He refocused his attention away from the great developed countries of Western Europe and in the direction of the colonial world. Here were scores of countries under foreign domination, victims of imperialist exploitation with strong motivation to break away from the occupying country and become independent. Lenin grasped the potential of the situation and advocated Russian support of what came to be known as "wars of national liberation." He offered backing to native movements, whether communist dominated or not, that sought the ousting of the resident colonial power. In a statement current at the time, the leadership of the Russian communist movement held that the "shortest distance to Paris was through Peking," meaning that the best way to speed the destruction of capitalism was to deprive it of the colonial bases of its prosperity. After 1917, if you were a nationalist leader in Indonesia or South Africa, seeking to oust the controlling colonial power, or if you were a working-class leader in France, Italy, or Germany determined to overthrow the capitalist bosses, Moscow, the capital of world revolution, came to be regarded as the source of external support for your revolutionary movement.

In 1949, after the Chinese People's Republic was established (in 1961 it split with the USSR), it too announced its support for revolution. It claimed that its more recent revolutionary experiences in a country of lower economic development than Russia made it a more suitable model for areas still under or recently liberated from colonial exploitation. But Chinese resources were fewer than those of the USSR, and Chinese efforts to dominate the world of revolution were puny by Soviet standards. There were also the Cubans and Vietnamese; they, too, sought to spread communist revolution.

Whether Russian or Chinese or Cuban or Vietnamese, communism had the reputation of being the premier revolutionary force in the world, a reputation augmented by changed circumstances in the United States and France, homelands of the other two "great" revolutions, and by their altered attitudes toward revolution. France, by creating a great colonial empire during the last four decades of the nineteenth century and then maintaining it until the 1950s, was seen by colonial countries seeking liberation as forfeiting any claim to revolutionary support. The United States was not identified with colonialism to the same degree as France. When it *was* judged to have embarked on colonial adventures, it sometimes received credit for granting independence to the Philippines and for its treatment of Puerto Rico. Nevertheless, after World War II, by which time the United States had become the leading nation in the world, its interests seemed almost without exception to be involved in preserving the status quo.

The United States supported conservative and even reactionary regimes because it was convinced that to favor the opposition forces was to turn the country in question over to the "communists" — as may well have been true in many cases because nationalists were also communists seeking not only to oust colonial regimes but to institute a socialist economic system. To fail to support the "revolution" and continue to support the existing power was a clear indication to those interested in "national liberation" that the United States was no ally. They could expect no help from that source. Moreover, in both France and the United States, as the concept of revolution was increasingly coopted by communists and others dissatisfied with the *domestic* state of affairs, interest was lost in homegrown revolutionary traditions that had been a glorious part of both of these countries' past. The idea of revolution came to be identified with beards, long hair, and the political left. It was anathema to the majority, who were satisfied with things as they were and only wanted more of the same. Among leaders and led alike, there was in the West little interest in fundamental changes explicit in revolutions, political and/or economic, such as those sought by the native inhabitants of colonies.

Thus the concept of revolution, which was capable of engendering great hopes among the disgruntled of the world, became, for better or worse, the almost exclusive possession of communism. In the great rush for change that followed World War II and resulted in the creation of scores of new countries (a process that continues today), communism, of whatever brand, came to be seen in many circles as the only faith for serious revolutionaries.

Whether it is communist revolutions or the American Revolution or the French Revolution that is under consideration, contemporary analysts of revolution see all revolutions as subject to analysis by the application of certain categories.

In the matter of causation, revolutions are regarded as having distant, immediate, and incepting causes. For example, a *distant* cause of the Russian Revolution of 1917 was the reactionary, feudal-favoring policy of the tsars. An *immediate* cause was the disastrous World War I, which made the inadequacies of the regime stand out for all to observe. An *incepting* cause was the failure of the cossacks, who had been the last bastion of the tsar's defense, to continue to protect his interests.

Distant causes can be subdivided into economic, psychological (deprivation), political (foreign occupation, governmental intransigence), and social (class antagonisms) categories. *Immediate causes,* which are also sometimes subdivided into the aforementioned categories, include war (the biggest cause of revolution in the twentieth century), economic crisis (particularly when the prosperity that has caused the public to expect much is followed by a sharp, persisting depression), and governmental inefficiency (crisis mismanagement). *Incepting causes* allude to the spark, in itself often comparatively trivial, that sets off the revolution. The student who fell into the orchestra pit in Bavaria in 1830 and the explosion of the arsenal at Hankow in 1911 are two examples of incepting causes frequently given. The spark is often accidental, as in the incidents above. There can also be a *planned* incepting cause, such as the conscious decision to attempt the seizure of power.

What is suggested is that the revolutionary scenario includes longstanding reasons for revolution, which are exacerbated by current circumstances and set on fire by a single incident. Not all these stages need to be highly developed. The most instrumental in creating the "revolutionary situation" is the immediate cause, where recent circumstances have created a situation that is extremely difficult for the masses to tolerate. Nonetheless, the revolution usually does not occur when the situation is blackest, but when it has already begun to improve.

Successful revolutions go through several stages. Stage 1 is the preparatory period when consciousness of intolerable circumstances dawns and begins to be cultivated. Stage 2 is the revolution; this is followed by stage 3, in which the revolution is consolidated, a new regime is established, and new policies are introduced. Some commentators divide stage 3 into a moderate introductory period, during which the new regime moves slowly and softly, seeking support, and a more radical later period when it determines to realize its revolutionary goals almost regardless of consequences.

A revolution may fail at any point along the line, arguably even after power has successfully been consolidated, if the revolution does not effect the changes that it has promised.

It is obvious that each stage of a revolution requires different leadership qualities. Though charisma will help at any stage, it is probably most valuable during the revolution itself. Stages 1 and 3 call for persistence. Stage 2 seeks a fiery, fearless, undoubting leader capable of galvanizing his forces and leading them into action. He need not be wise, but he must be sure of himself and able to convince others that he knows what he is doing. In stage 3 the need is for a tough and skillful strategist with the primary ability not to stir the masses but to quiet them and enlist their cooperation in the day-to-day affairs of the new system.

It is highly unlikely for one leader to prove equally adept at all stages. In the American Revolution Sam Adams and Tom Paine were of greatest importance in stage 1, but virtually disappeared in stages 2 and 3. On the other hand, George Washington was barely visible in stage 1, became highly involved in stage 2, and played a major role in setting up the constitutional system that still prevails in the United States. V.I. Lenin was very strong in stages 1 and 3, but when it came to the actual revolution, a far more important role was played by L.D. Trotsky, who was not as effective at other times. Tito and Castro are examples of leaders who functioned at high levels in all three stages, but they each demonstrated greater abilities in some stages than in others.

Numerous statistical and psychological studies completed on those who have made revolutions indicate that at the time of the revolution, most revolutionaries have been in their thirties and forties and have spent most of their adult lives working toward the revolution. They are overwhelmingly of middle-class origin and better educated than the average citizen. Most, though there are numerous exceptions, come from urban backgrounds.

Beginning in the 1930s, there have been numerous attempts to grasp the specific psychological motivations of particular revolutionary heroes. These studies have sought to trace revolutionary-proneness to traumatic experiences, displaced hatred of fathers, and so on. Such studies have proved interesting and even provocative, but they have not succeeded in answering the question why some people become revolutionaries and others do not. For example, that question is not answered by asserting (as some writers do) that Lenin became a revolutionary because the tsarist regime executed his brother. The regime executed many others, and not even a significant percentage of brothers of victims became revolutionaries. In a similar vein, it has been said that Marx became a revolutionary because he heard a local police chief castigate his father. Yet if every child who witnessed his father being berated by a policeman became a revolutionary, the revolutionary ranks would be swollen far beyond their historical numbers. Psychological explanations as to why people become revolutionaries are sometimes helpful in explaining conduct, but they are not full explanations. What this seems to indicate is that national oppression and unfulfilled expectations are prime general reasons for revolutionary activities and because revolutionary leaders come primarily from the middle class, social causation is more important than economic causation.

What are the requirements of a successful revolution? Leadership, organization, and ideology are three prime components, each of which is dependent on the other. Effective *leadership,* meaning different things at different times, is incumbent. No matter how potent the reasons for revolution, it will not develop unless someone assumes the lead.

The leader must be able to *organize* the forces necessary to effect the revolution. Generally speaking, the revolutionary corps the leader puts together will be an elitist group made up of full-time professional revolutionaries prepared to lead a spartan existence for as long as is necessary to achieve revolutionary goals. There have been no successful revolutions without prior organization.

Ideology is understood here as an emotion-laden system of ideas, myths, and values that challenges the existing regime and binds the revolutionaries. Ideology includes a denunciation of the present as untenable, a description of a better future, and the outlining of a plan for attaining that future. The purpose of the ideology is to gain the support of as broad a mass as possible. Because the public is so varied, it is incumbent that the ideology, while appearing to be steadfast and immutable, actually be capable of extensive flexibility so that it may appeal to a wide audience.

Even if the revolutionary movement has excellent leadership, is well organized, and has an effective ideology, it may still fail. The timing of the revolutionary effort may be off; or the leadership may adopt a misguided "revolutionary strategy"; or leaders may be killed; or the opposition may be strong, determined, and able to resist. Even if the revolution succeeds in establishing a regime, its troubles are far from over. Its policies may succeed not in enticing the masses but in angering them. Those who were earlier neutral or even supported the revolution may turn against it and become counterrevolutionaries. While, generally speaking, counterrevolutionaries have not succeeded in restoring the status quo ante, they have often caused the new regime to ameliorate its policies.

When revolutions break out in one country, it is likely that "revolutionary situations" will develop elsewhere as well. This happened in 1848 in Central Europe, after World War I, and again after World War II. In the even more recent past, the "Islamic Revolution" spread throughout the Middle East. The Soviet Union full well recognizes the tendency of revolutions and counterrevolutions to spread. In 1956 in Hungary, again in 1968 in Czechoslovakia, and in 1979 in Afghanistan, the USSR forcibly intervened in large part in order to short-circuit such a possibility.

All revolutions do not succeed; in fact, historically speaking, far more revolutions have failed than have succeeded—if success implies holding power for more than a brief interval. National revolutions, those that drive out the occupying colonial power, have had a much higher rate of success than social revolutions. Witness to this is the growth in the number of independent countries from around 50 in the early 1940s to the present number of more than 150.

In the preceding paragraph, a "successful" revolution is implied to be one in which power is seized and held for more than a few days or months. In the Marxist-Leninist view any revolution heralding values advocated by the movement, regardless of whether the revolution gains power or not, is regarded as a success because each failed revolution supposedly denotes the rising revolutionary consciousness of the working class and brings the successful revolution closer.

There is another sense in which revolutions can be judged to be successful: Do they bring about lasting change that is to the benefit of the majority of society? The reply depends upon who is answering the quesiton. Certainly nationalists whose revolutions have succeeded in the liberation of their country would reply almost without exception that the triumph has been worth the price. Marxist-Leninists assert that any revolution that drives out capitalism is a triumph, regardless of the subsequent suffering of the population. While the remnants of domestic enemies and old habits and encirclement by hostile powers may prevent the full flowering of the potential boons of the revolution, sooner or later the impeding forces will be overcome to the eternal benefit of the masses.

Increasingly in recent years, however, there has been serious questioning of the Marxist-Leninist assertion of the beneficial effect of revolutions. The purges that have killed millions and imprisoned tens of millions as communist regimes have moved to cement their power, the absence of civil rights, the low standard of living, the ill-functioning and malfunctioning of industry and agriculture and the economic system in general — all have led earnest observers to ask whether the Russian people would not be much further advanced technologically, have a higher standard of living and more individual freedom, and have endured far less personal suffering if there had been no revolution. Educational and economic advances made by the tsarist regime in the first part of the twentieth century are pointed to as an indication of Russia's ability to create a rapidly expanding industrial base, even under the tsars. It is further argued that any country with the material resources of Russia could not have escaped large-scale industrial development in this century. While the old regime had a horrible human rights record, it was probably a paragon compared to the Soviet regime. Certainly, many of the millions who died in the slave labor camps of the gulag archipelago would be alive today if the revolution had failed. Even if it is agreed that the Russian Revolution has resulted in commendable changes in some respects, hasn't the cost been too great?

Counterargument states that the Revolution of 1917 was one of the greatest events in the history of man, that it liberated the masses from the tyranny of the capitalistic bosses forever and established the most important right — freedom from want. Moreover, if it had not been for the new Soviet system, Russia would have succumbed to Hitler, and the world would be a far more dreadful place today.

Counterargument to this states — and on and on. The point is not whether there is a yes or no answer to the question of whether revolutions bring about lasting changes that are to the benefit of society, but to point out that increasingly in the last quarter of the twentieth century, people who are concerned about such things as revolutions have begun to raise questions as to their effectiveness as a means to secure lasting, desirable change. Specifically they are pointing to what is widely regarded as the greatest of the revolutions, that in Russia in 1917, and asking: Has it really made men and women happier? If the answer is no at this time, does it seem likely that it will be yes in the future?

Which brings us to our last point: the future of revolutions. Certainly there has been a great increase in the number of revolutions, particularly in the former colonial world, during the second half of the twentieth century. Most colonial countries have now been "liberated." The national revolutions have been successful. Yet it is unlikely that such countries are going to settle down — for a wide variety of reasons: because they were not countries before the colonial period but were artificially created by the imperial powers, often by pushing tribes that had been enemies for centuries together into a single territorial entity, and now one tribe can take out after another again; because they lack traditions of stability and the knowledge of the requirements of effective governmental operation; because independence has not brought the development and wealth anticipated; because some parts of the population want to move immediately beyond national revolution to a social revolution. While all the changes in regimes in the Third World can hardly be accurately called revolutions, there is no doubt that unrest and some revolution in a fundamental social sense can be expected to occur there.

In the developed world the situation is different. Certainly in recent years in France and Italy, two countries with large communist movements, sentiment has moved away from revolution. There, as well as in the United States, where "revolution" became a bad word, the lessons seemingly taught by the Russian experience seem to have made a deep impression. Revolutions do not make people happy; they bring bloodshed, inefficiency, and poverty. Change may be needed, but revolution is not the way. It needs to be pointed out, however, that such attitudes have developed under conditions of prosperity, particularly during the 1960s and '70s when everyone in Western capitalist society seemed able to envision a new car, a new home, or a new boat. In times of economic crisis, will recent Western attitudes toward revolution prevail, or will capitalism be blamed for the evil days and respite be sought in revolution? Will expectations unfulfilled in a developed society seemingly capable of producing enough to satisfy the needs of its people, but incapable of getting that production into their hands, lead to revolution? Karl Marx said it would. The Soviets think it will. Only time will tell if they are right.

24

Comparative Public Policy

B. Guy Peters

One means of assessing the performance of a government is its survival and its ability to exercise political authority within its boundaries. Another means is to examine the policy choices made by that government and the extent to which these choices contribute to the quality of life of its citizens. This latter criterion inevitably involves a number of value judgments, as reasonable people may well disagree on what constitutes a high quality of life. Some might argue that when governments become involved in making economic or social policy decisions, the quality of life is automatically reduced whereas those governing the Soviet Union would argue that a high quality of life was unattainable as long as private ownership of the means of production was allowed to continue. In this all-too-brief look at comparative public policies, we will assume that healthier, wealthier, better educated, and more secure societies have higher qualities of life than do poorer, sicker, ignorant, and less secure societies.

Governments do not operate in a vacuum. The ability of a government to produce the outputs it desires depends in part on the willingness of its society to comply with its wishes, as well as on social and economic conditions that support the desired ends. For example, if government is trying to improve the health of its citizens, then it is more than helpful for citizens to be able to afford an adequate diet, to eat that proper diet, to desire to exercise, and to use preventive medicine.

In addition to the effects of social and economic conditions on policies, the instruments chosen by governments to carry out their ends are far from uniform across countries, even when the ends chosen are the same. For example, in the countries we have been studying, the common response of government to an economic problem has been to nationalize the industries affected, whereas the most frequent response in the United States has been to regulate the industry.[1] All governments to some degree will use all available policy instruments, but they also have tendencies to choose one as opposed to others when compared with other governments.

In general, we can think of five broad kinds of mechanisms by which governments influence their societies and economies. The first is *money,* and the ability of governments to transfer money from one citizen to another through taxes and expenditures. Social security, national health insurance, industrial subsidies, and foreign aid are all examples of government using money to try to achieve its ends.

Second, governments can directly supply certain *goods and services* to citizens. In providing health care to citizens, governments have the option of providing transfers through health insurance (Germany and France) or through hiring doctors and nurses, building hospitals, and directly delivering the medical care (the United Kingdom and the USSR). In general, directly providing a service gives government greater control over the quantity and quality of the service provided. Also, governments can directly provide employment and industrial development, as when industries are nationalized, or at the extreme in the Soviet Union where virtually all jobs are provided by government.

Third, governments have at their disposal *laws and regulations.* These may be the most efficient means of achieving a desired end, for most of the costs of implementation are borne by citizens directly and do not require the expenditure of public money. For example, the costs of regulation in the United States in 1979 were over $121 billion, with a very small share of this expense reflected in the public budget. The remainder was reflected in compliance costs for the industries and in higher prices for goods (e.g., the increased costs of automobiles resulting from safety and pollution equipment).[2] Unfortunately, there are no comparable data for European countries for the costs of regulation. Regulation is a method that is generally available but some countries choose to use it more frequently. Economic planning, when backed by force of law, is another important regulatory device, especially when practiced for an entire economy as in the USSR.

Fourth, governments can use *incentives* to control the use of the resources in society. The majority of incentives are implemented through the tax code. For example, even though the United Kingdom spends a very large amount on its council housing programs, it also provides citizens with incentives to buy their own houses by allowing them to deduct the interest on their mortagages. In 1976 the tax relief on owner-occupied dwellings amounted to £2.33 billion compared with £4.83 spent for council housing.[3] This is a powerful incentive for individuals to purchase homes if they can at all afford to do so, for other taxpayers are in essence paying a substantial share of the total price. Also, indicative planning as practiced in France or the United Kingdom depends upon manipulating incentives rather than on actual control of resources. As with regulation, incentives are rather efficient mechanisms for implementing a policy because they generally involve the individual citizen's making the decision and doing the necessary work to receive the benefit of the incentive.

Finally, governments can attempt to influence their societies through *moral suasion.* That is, they can simply ask, demand, or plead that citizens do what government wants. This may be especially effective during times of national crisis and when the government is widely trusted and the policy choices in question appear to accord with the basic value structure of the society. Or this may be a response of a government that lacks more effective means of dealing with a difficult situation (e.g., economic management in an era of stagflation).

As noted, all governments use all these mechanisms, but to varying degrees. They may choose to use different instruments for different policy areas. For example, in almost every country the standard response to problems of the elderly is the use of money in some form of public pension program, although there are many direct provisions of benefits through public extended-care facilities, meals on wheels, and the like. In like manner, in almost all countries, education is generally directly provided.

Table 24.1 on page 354 presents information on the choices of policy instruments in five countries—the four discussed in the preceding chapters plus the United States—in a number of policy areas. The descriptions for each country for each area are generalities, pointing to a particularly great use of one of the instruments relative to other policies or other countries. In some policy areas—for example, defense and the environment—all countries tend to use the same instruments. Defense is always provided directly by government. So, too, is education, although the United States provides some tax incentives for education and has undertaken a number of experiments with vouchers. Environmental policy is dealt with primarily through regulatory means in each of the five countries, although a number of other instruments—such as moral suasion and the use of grants to industries to clean up their pollution in France and Germany—are also employed. Income maintenance is dealt with primarily with monetary grants, although in the Soviet Union problems such as unemployment or

TABLE 24.1

Types of Policy Instruments

	United States	United Kingdom	France	West Germany	Soviet Union
Health	M/Sr/Inc	Sr	M	M	Sr
Education	Sr/Inc	Sr	Sr	Sr	Sr
Income main- tenance	M	M	M	M	Sr/M
Defense	Sr	Sr	Sr	Sr	Sr
Industrial policy	R/Inc	Sr/M	Sr/M	Inc/Sr	Sr
Housing	Inc/Sr	Sr/Inc	Inc/Sr	Inc/Sr	Sr
Environment	R/S	R/M	R/S/M	R/M	R
Agriculture	M/R/Inc	M	R/M	M/R	R/Sr
Economic man- agement	M/S	M/R/S	M/R	M/R	R/Sr

M = Money; Sr = Service; Inc = Incentives; R = Regulation; S = Suasion.

dependent children are dealt with more directly by requiring that all adults have a job and providing nurseries for mothers who work.

Several policy areas—for example, health and housing—have two patterns of policy instruments. Two countries support health care through publicly supported and regulated health insurance programs, while two others directly provide medical care to its citizens. The United States is the exception to both patterns; it has some grants of money (Medicare and Medicaid), some direct provision of medical care (e.g., municipal hospitals, state mental hospitals), but relies primarily on incentives to individuals through the tax system to purchase health insurance. In housing, the two principal options are the direct provision of housing (e.g., council housing in the United Kingdom or publicly built housing in the Soviet Union) and incentives for individuals or communal organizations to build or purchase housing.

Support for industry and support for agriculture are both policies directed at promoting certain sectors of economic activity. Governments tend to approach these problems with different instruments. This is true not only when one policy area is compared to the other but also when national patterns of behavior are compared. One important pattern of dealing with industrial policies is to purchase industries outright and run them as public enterprises. This is clearly the dominant option exercised in the Soviet Union and has been the option selected for a number of industries in France and the United Kingdom. Another option is to regulate the way in which industries conduct their business, both to protect the consumer (rate setting and antitrust) and to protect the industries (assigned routes, assured profits from public utilities). Governments may also provide incentives for industrial development, as when West Germany does not collect taxes from profits of a capital asset held for six months or more, thereby encouraging private investment.

Agriculture and its particular policy problems are dealt with primarily through grants of money to farmers, generally in the form of guaranteed prices for agricultural products, as well as through regulation of entry of certain potential farmers. Both France and Germany still have large numbers of small agriculturalists, and the governments of these countries try to reduce the influx of "agribusiness" into the countries. Agriculture may also be dealt with as a problem for publicly provided goods and services, as on the collective farms of the USSR or through tax incentives and special treatment of agricultural land and products in the United States.

Finally, macroeconomic policy is dealt with primarily as a problem of the use of money — through the control of demand by the deficit on the public budget, or through the control of the money supply, or through regulatory instruments such as economic planning. Again, in the Soviet Union this policy area, as all others, is more subject to direct government intervention than would be true in Western countries. Also, economic management is frequently the subject of moral suasion, especially when there is a need to "bite the bullet" and make difficult economic choices that will harm some segments of the society. Of the five countries in question, the United States and the United Kingdom experienced the most economic difficulties in the 1970s. We place special emphasis on their use of suasion in economic management (e.g., the "social contract" and WIN).

When we compare countries rather than policy areas, the Soviet Union stands out as the policy-making system that relies most heavily on direct government intervention to solve social and economic problems. In almost all policy areas there was a direct government intervention into the area to provide the service, as might be expected when few private organizations are available to carry out the services through grants or incentives. At the other end of the spectrum the United States tends to use more indirect means of providing services than other countries do. There is more reliance on incentives and on regulatory mechanisms rather than monetary grants or the direct involvement of government to produce the service. The remaining three European countries are rather similar in how they choose to influence their societies. This is not to say that the content of the policy instruments will necessarily be the same, or that each country has the same priorities, but only that they try to affect policy problems through the same instruments.

Taxing and Spending

It is difficult to quantify and measure the overall impact of government on its economy and society, although we can identify the instruments employed. It is consequently difficult to gain an idea of the priorities given to different problems by different governments. The discussion of the availability of a number of policy instruments should point out that public expenditures by no means measure the sum of public activities. On the other hand, they are a useful measure of the priorities of government. This is especially true for policy areas such as defense, education, and environmental protection where the technology and the means of providing the service tend to be relatively uniform. Even in other policy areas (e.g., health), the total costs of providing the service may be about the same whether it is provided directly or paid for indirectly through insurance.

A first question that arises is what priority is attached to government activity compared with private consumption. In other words, just how big is big government? Table 24.2 gives some information about the size of total public revenue as a percentage of gross domestic product (a standard measure of the total goods and services produced in the economy). Of the five countries, the Soviet Union has by far the largest public sector, although it is difficult to measure much of public activity in this form of government. A great deal of Soviet government income does not come from taxes or fees for service but from the equivalent of profits from state-owned enterprises. With a narrower definition of the government budget, the Soviet government is not a great deal larger than that in many Western European nations. At the other end of the spectrum is the United States, which has a much smaller public sector than other Western countries. This does not include the significant effects of regulatory policies and incentives on the economy of the United States; but in terms of money actually extracted from the economy, the U.S. public sector is rather small. Also, the relatively small size of the public sector does not prevent more objections being raised about government taxing and spending than is true in countries with a larger government share of the gross national product.

TABLE 24.2

Patterns of Expenditure and Revenue

Expenditures[a]

	United States	United Kingdom	France	West Germany	Soviet Union
Total (as percent of GDP)	33	43	39	41	56
Defense	17	11	10	8	18
Health	5	11	14	14	9
Income maintenance	25	21	29	27	16
Education	19	13	15	10	14
Debt service	6	9	6	3	?
Housing	1	9	7	6	8
Revenue[b]					
Personal income	33	34	13	31	9
Corporate taxation	12	7	6	5	34
Taxes on goods and services	17	26	32	26	31
Social security	25	19	42	34	6

a. As a percentage of total expenditures.
b. As a percentage of total taxation.

Revenue Collection

How revenue is raised may affect citizen reaction to the size of the public sector. It also influences the ease with which government can raise revenue. In general, visible taxes such as the income tax arouse public ire but also respond effectively and almost automatically to inflation. The United States has the highest dependence on the income tax, with the United Kingdom also very dependent on this tax for its revenue. France, perhaps as a result of historical patterns of tax evasion, collects relatively little revenue from the income tax, although not so little as the Soviet Union. Both France and the Soviet Union have a relatively high reliance on taxes on goods and services (e.g., the value-added tax in France and the turnover tax in the Soviet Union). Both these taxes are analogous to national sales taxes, although they are levied at each stage of production rather than only at the point of sales. France also relies very heavily on social security taxes, whereas the United Kingdom and the United States finance relatively little of their public expenditure from these contributions.

Despite differences among types of taxes in individual countries, they collectively account for almost 90 percent of all tax revenue in each country. This also illustrates that if government wishes to collect large sums of revenue, as governments in any industrialized country will, they have the options of taxing incomes (income *and* social security taxes) or expenditures (value-added taxes, sales taxes, and so on).

Public Expenditures

Governments spend money for a variety of purposes ranging from national defense to industrial subsidies to care for the handicapped. All these expenditures are important, or those who must mobilize a political coalition to pass legislation would probably not have been able to muster the support for the spending program. Each country also has certain priorities, which are indicated through the relative amount of spending for different programs. The figures in table 24.2 indicate the designated function as a percentage of total expenditure.

One of the traditional functions of government is national defense. Although each of these countries is to some degree engaged in providing for its own defense, the levels of expenditure vary greatly. The United States and the Soviet Union spend the most for defense, both in absolute terms and relative to their total expenditures. In the United States, even after the "antidefense shift" in the post-Vietnam era, almost one dollar in five spent in the public sector is spent on defense. This is much higher than the defense spending of the three European countries discussed, although arguably their expenditures would be higher were it not for NATO and their reliance on the United States for a significant amount of their defense. The United Kingdom continues to spend a relatively large share of its public expenditure on defense, in part because of its continuing obligations to the Commonwealth and its few remaining colonies.

Income-maintenance expenditures generally constitute the largest single item of expenditure in the budgets of these industrialized countries, with the Soviet Union an exception to this generalization. Actually income maintenance is not a single item but an amalgam of a number of programs designed to spread the total income of a country more evenly among its citizens than would be true without the activities of government. As much of the financing of these programs is through social insurance, these programs to a great extent involve smoothing out the flow of income for citizens, taking money when people are working and paying out the money when they are disabled, unemployed, or retired.

The largest single income-maintenance expenditure is pensions for the elderly. It accounts for approximately 15 percent of government expenditures in the United States and 20 percent in the United Kingdom. Another item included in income-maintenance expenditures is the family allowance, or the support given each family in the four countries (other than the United States) with respect to the number of children in the family. These payments are intended to supplement the income of the family and provide a better standard of living for the children, although there is nothing to ensure that the money actually will be spent to benefit the children. Also included in income-maintenance expenditures are unemployment benefits, sickness benefits, and social assistance (what would be called "welfare" in the United States). Of total income-maintenance expenditures, pensions and family allowances typically account for 75 percent of the total. It should also be noted that income-maintenance expenditures account for a rather small share of total expenditures in the Soviet Union, in part because some of the benefits paid in Western nations are paid for conditions said not to exist in the Soviet Union (e.g., unemployment or the need for direct social assistance).[4]

As a proportion of total expenditures, education expenditures are highest in the United States and the Soviet Union. The United Kingdom also spends a rather large share of its total expenditures on education; France and the Federal Republic of Germany trail far behind. France spends less than half as much as a proportion of total public spending on education as do the United States and the Soviet Union. These figures imply a very high priority attached to education by the two superpowers, although perhaps for different reasons. It has been argued that education is used in the United States as a substitute for the lack of development in other aspects of the welfare state.[5] Education is used to try to provide an equality of opportunity at the beginning of the economic and social race, whereas more direct intervention in the economy is used by European countries to try to equalize outcomes. In the Soviet Union, education is seen perhaps more as a mechanism for the economic development of a country that is still rather poor when compared with many other industrialized countries.

Health expenditures constitute another large proportion of total public expenditure. As noted, these expenditures are sometimes for direct payments to doctors, nurses, orderlies, pharmaceutical companies, and the like, with medical care provided by government to citizens at little or no cost. Another option is to pay for health care indirectly through insurance payments. In the United States there is a mixed system in which there is some direct provision, some public insurance, and a great degree of subsidization of individuals for purchasing their own health insurance. In terms of a percentage of total public expenditure, the Soviet Union spends the most, and the United States spends by far the least. Interestingly, the amount of money does not appear to be particularly related to the quality of health as measured by standard indicators such as the rate of infant mortality or life expectancy. The Soviet Union actually has the highest rate of infant mortality of the five countries; France has the lowest. The United States, with its rather small public spending on health (albeit massive private expenditure) has the longest life expectancy at birth for females. Health care is clearly an area of expenditure where the size of the public interacts with a number of other aspects of the environment to produce a result.

Housing would be one expenditure that might interact with health expenditures. Here again the United States is the "welfare state laggard," spending by far the least for housing compared with the other four countries. The United Kingdom and the Soviet Union spend the most. Housing, however, is a policy area subject to influence by many of the indirect mechanisms previously discussed, and the public sector is capable of affecting the availability and real price of the commodity without direct intervention. Thus the size of the public expenditure for housing in the United States may seriously underestimate the total contribution of the public sector to housing. Nevertheless, clearly both the Soviet Union and the United Kingdom are more involved in the direct public provision of housing and as a consequence have significantly greater control over housing than the other three countries.

This brief examination of patterns of public expenditures should give some idea of the priorities and policies of these five nations. What is perhaps most remarkable is the similarity of the expenditure patterns rather than their differences. There seem to be some policy areas that must be performed by government directly and that are inherently expensive. Of the five countries, the United States and the Soviet Union have the most distinctive patterns of expenditure. This is in part a function of their status as superpowers and in part because of other national policy choices. In particular, there is the choice of the United States not to become involved in a comprehensive program of public health insurance and the relatively poor provision of income-maintenance benefits in the Soviet Union. Of the European countries, the United Kingdom is perhaps most notable for its heavy expenditure on housing and its relatively low expenditure on income-maintenance benefits.

Conclusions

Nations must make choices about what they want governments to do and how they want government to reach national goals. There are a variety of instruments through which governments can attempt to influence their economy and society—and perhaps other governments—and there is a virtual infinity of possible goals for governments to pursue through public action. This brief discussion of the policy choices made by five countries should point out that differences among the countries are based on factors such as wealth, political structures, and ideologies. There are also many similarities, implying that some functions (e.g., defense) must be performed by any government and some policies are best delivered in certain ways. We have been able only to scratch the surface of the differences and similarities, and we would urge students to pursue not only the differences of policy between the countries but also the variety of causes for those similarities and differences.

Notes

1. See Anthony King, "Ideas, Institutions and the Policies of Government: A Comparative Analysis," *British Journal of Political Science* 3 (1973): 293-313, 409-23.
2. Murray L. Weidenbaum, "The High Cost of Government Regulation," *Challenge* 22 (1979): 32-39.
3. J.R.M. Willis and P.J.W. Hardwick, *Tax Expenditures in the United Kingdom* (London: Heinemann, 1978), pp. 91-94.
4. Robert J. Osborn, *Soviet Social Policies* (Homewood, Ill.: Dorsey, 1970).
5. Henry J. Perkinson, *The Imperfect Panacea: American Faith in Education, 1865-1965* (New York: Random House, 1968).

For Further Reading

ALMOND, GABRIEL, and VERBA, SIDNEY. *The Civic Culture.* Princeton: Princeton University Press, 1963.

_____, eds. *The Civic Culture Revisited.* Boston: Little, Brown, 1980.

ARENDT, HANNAH. *On Revolution.* New York: Viking, 1963.

ARMSTRONG, JOHN A. *The European Administrative Elite.* Princeton: Princeton University Press, 1973.

ASHFORD, DOUGLAS E. *Policy and Politics in Britain.* Philadelphia: Temple University Press, 1981.

_____. *Policy and Politics in France.* Philadelphia: Temple University Press, 1982.

BELL, DANIEL. *The Cultural Contradictions of Capitalism.* New York: Basic Books, 1976.

BENVENISTE, GUY. *The Politics of Expertise.* Berkeley: University of California Press, 1972.

BONHAM-CARTER, VIOLET. *The Impact of Personality in Politics.* Oxford: Clarendon Press, 1963.

CREWE, IVOR. *Elites in Western Democracy.* New York: Wiley, 1974.

DOGAN, MATTEI, ed. *The Mandarins of Western Europe: The Political Role of Top Civil Servants.* New York: Wiley, 1975.

DUNN, JOHN. *Modern Revolutions.* Cambridge: Cambridge University Press, 1972.

EDINGER, LEWIS, ed. *Political Leadership in Industrialized Societies.* New York: Wiley, 1967.

FLORA, PETER, and HEIDENHEIMER, ARNOLD J. *The Development of Welfare States in Europe and America.* New Brunswick, N.J.: Transaction, 1981.

GURR, TED ROBERT. *Why Men Rebel.* Princeton: Princeton University Press, 1970.

HARTZ, LOUIS. *The Liberal Tradition in America.* New York: Harcourt, Brace, 1962.

HEIDENHEIMER, ARNOLD J.; HECLO, HUGH; and ADAMS, CAROLYN T. *Comparative Public Policy: Politics of Public Choice in Europe and America.* 2nd ed. New York: St. Martin's, 1983.

HUNTINGTON, SAMUEL P. *Political Order in Changing Societies.* New Haven: Yale University Press, 1968.

JOHNSON, CHALMERS. *Revolutionary Change.* Boston: Little-Brown, 1966.

KAPLAN, MORTON A. *The Many Faces of Communism.* New York: Free Press, 1978.

MACRIDIS, ROY C. *Contemporary Political Ideologies.* Cambridge: Winthrop, 1980.

MICHELS, ROBERT. *Political Parties.* Glencoe, Ill.: Free Press, 1949.

MILIBAND, RALPH. *Marxism and Politics.* New York: Oxford University Press, 1977.

MOSCA, GAETANO. *The Ruling Class.* Edited by A. Livingston. New York: McGraw-Hill, 1939.

NOLTE, ERNEST. *Three Faces of Fascism.* New York: Holt, Rinehart, and Winston, 1966.

PATERSON, WILLIAM E., and CAMPBELL, IAN. *Social Democracy in Post-War Europe.* New York: St. Martin's, 1974.

PRESTHUS, ROBERT V. *Elites in the Policy Process.* New York: Cambridge University Press, 1974.

PRYOR, FREDERICK C. *Public Expenditures in Capitalist and Communist Nations.* Homewood, Ill.: Irwin, 1968.

PUTNAM, ROBERT D. *The Comparative Study of Political Elites.* Englewood Cliffs, N.J.: Prentice-Hall, 1976.

RAWLS, JOHN. *A Theory of Justice.* Cambridge: Harvard University Press, 1971.

REJAI, MOSTAFA. *The Comparative Study of Revolutionary Strategy.* New York: McKay, 1977.

SIEGEL, RICHARD L., and WEINBERG, LEONARD B. *Comparing Public Policies: United States, Soviet Union, and Europe.* Homewood, Ill.: Dorsey, 1977.

SKOCPOL, THEDA. *States and Social Revolution.* Cambridge: Cambridge University Press, 1979.

SULEIMAN, EZRA N. *Elites in French Society.* Princeton: Princeton University Press, 1978.

WILDAVSKY, AARON. *Budgeting: A Comparative Theory of Budgetary Processes.* Boston: Little-Brown, 1975.

Index